LOST
KINGDOM

LOST KINGDOM

The Quest for Empire and the Making of the Russian Nation

From 1470 to the Present

SERHII PLOKHY

BASIC BOOKS

NEW YORK

Basic Books
Hachette Book Group
1290 Avenue of the Americas, New York, NY 10104
www.basicbooks.com

Printed in the United States of America
First Edition: October 2017
Published by Basic Books, an imprint of Perseus Books, LLC, a subsidiary of Hachette Book Group, Inc.

The Hachette Speakers Bureau provides a wide range of authors for speaking events. To find out more, go to www.hachettespeakersbureau.com or call (866) 376-6591.
The publisher is not responsible for websites (or their content) that are not owned by the publisher.

PRINT BOOK INTERIOR DESIGN BY LINDA MARK.

Library of Congress Cataloging-in-Publication Data
Names: Plokhy, Serhii, 1957– author.
Title: Lost kingdom : the quest for empire and the making of the Russian
nation, from 1470 to the present / Serhii Plokhy.
Description: New York : Basic Books, 2017. | Includes bibliographical references and index.
Identifiers: LCCN 2017021215 (print) | LCCN 2017021309 (ebook) | ISBN 9780465097395 (ebook) | ISBN 9780465098491 (hardback)
Subjects: LCSH: Nationalism—Russia. | Nationalism—Soviet Union. | Russia—History. | Russia—Territorial expansion. | Soviet Union—History. | Soviet Union—Territorial expansion. | Ukraine—History. | Belarus—History. | Imperialism—History. | BISAC: HISTORY / Europe / Eastern. | HISTORY / Europe / Russia & the Former Soviet Union.
Classification: LCC DK43 (ebook) | LCC DK43 .P56 2917 (print) | DDC 947—dc23
LC record available at https://lccn.loc.gov/2017021215

LSC-C

10 9 8 7 6 5 4 3 2 1

CONTENTS

INTRODUCTION

I N THE VERY HEART OF MOSCOW, ACROSS THE SQUARE FROM THE
Borovitsky Gate of the Kremlin, stands one of the tallest monuments
in the Russian capital. The statue of a man in medieval garb, with a cross
in one hand and a saber in the other, is eighteen meters high. The man is
Prince Vladimir, as he is known today to the citizens of Russia, or Volod-
imer, as he was called by medieval chroniclers. He ruled from 980 to 1015
in the city of Kyiv (Kiev), where he is known today as Volodymyr, and
left a lasting legacy by accepting the Christian religion for himself and his
realm—the medieval state of Kyivan Rus', which included vast territories
extending from the Carpathian Mountains in the west to the Volga River
in the east.

Many in Moscow believe that the impulse to erect the monument—
whose height and central location make it more prominent than the one to
Prince Yurii Dolgoruky, who is alleged to have founded Moscow in 1147—
was based on a desire to glorify none other than St. Volodymyr's namesake,
the president of Russia, Vladimir Putin. After all, it was Archimandrite
Tikhon, rumored to be Putin's confessor, who headed the committee that

chose the winner of the hastily organized competition. Moreover, the site chosen for the monument was in a historical zone protected by UNESCO and thus required a special permit from the Moscow City Council, which could be obtained only with the blessing of the Russian president.

But the real or imagined connection between Prince Volodymyr and President Vladimir Putin offers only part of the explanation for the importance of the monument and the reasons for its erection in the heart of Moscow. More than anything else the monument symbolizes the Russian claim for Kyivan heritage and underlines the importance of Kyivan Rus' for the historical identity of contemporary Russia. Otherwise, what would a monument to a prince of Kyiv, the capital of the neighboring state of Ukraine, be doing in such a coveted space in the heart of the Russian capital? The timing and circumstances of the monument's construction further stress the importance of Ukrainian themes in Russian history and politics. The first stone in its foundation was laid in 2015, soon after the Russian annexation of the Crimea, and was taken from that peninsula in the middle of the Russo-Ukrainian war. It was brought to the Russian capital from the site of the Byzantine city of Chersonesus, the legendary place of the baptism of Prince Volodymyr in 988.

The monument was officially unveiled on November 4, 2016—the Day of National Unity, a statutory holiday in Russia—by Vladimir Putin himself. The Russian president delivered a speech in the presence of the head of the Russian government, Dmitrii Medvedev, Patriarch Kirill of the Russian Orthodox Church, and the widow of Russia's most celebrated national writer, Aleksandr Solzhenitsyn. Vladimir Putin praised Prince Volodymyr as a "gatherer and protector of the Russian lands and a prescient statesman who laid the foundations of a strong, united, centralized state, resulting in the union of one great family of equal peoples, languages, cultures, and religions." Putin pointed out that the prince's choice of Christianity "became the joint spiritual source for the peoples of Russia, Belarus, and Ukraine, laying the foundations of the morals and values that define our life even to the present day."

DESPITE WHAT ONE READS IN TEXTBOOKS AND HEARS IN OFFICIAL pronouncements, Russia, especially by European standards, is a relatively young state. Its history as an independent polity officially begins less than six hundred years ago, in the 1470s, when Ivan III, the first ruler of the Grand Duchy of Muscovy to call himself tsar, challenged the suzerainty of the Mongol khans. At stake was not only the independent status of the rulers of Muscovy—the principality centered on the city of Moscow—but also their control over other Rus' lands, in particular Novgorod, whose independence from Moscow the Mongol khans sought to maintain. It was then that the Kyivan roots of the Muscovite dynasty and church helped form a powerful myth of origin that distinguished Muscovy from its immediate Mongol past and nourished its self-image as heir to Byzantium.

Most of Russia's wars were fought in its immediate East Slavic neighborhood, motivated and justified by its claim to be the legitimate political, cultural, and religious successor to the medieval state of Kyivan Rus' and its Byzantine heritage. Even the extension of the Soviet borders westward in the course of World War II was often justified with references to the Rus' princes and their military exploits. Despite Russia's long history of imperial conquest, its vision of "gathering the Rus' lands," initiated during the reign of Ivan III, was fulfilled only during the brief period from 1945 to 1991—less than half a century. In those years of superpower status, Moscow was able to extend its rule to the westernmost regions of the old Kyivan state, settled predominantly by Eastern Slavs—Ukrainian Galicia, Bukovyna, and Transcarpathia.

The Russian elites' claim for the Kyivan inheritance developed from a largely dynastic and religious concept into an ethnonational one with the start of the modern era. As the Russian Empire embraced the idea of nationality in the course of the eighteenth century, it created a particular model of Russian nationhood that included today's Russians, Ukrainians, and Belarusians along with imperial elites of non-Slavic origins that were Russified in political and cultural terms. The Russian Revolution began the process of untying this imperial knot of Russian national identity by assigning the status of separate nationalities to the Russians, Ukrainians, and Belarusians. Nevertheless, the Soviet project was anything but consistent in terms of its nationality policies. The communist government centralized the decision-making process in Moscow, used the Russian language across the whole expanse of the Union of Soviet Socialist Republics (USSR), promoted the cultural Russification of non-Russians, and in doing that created conditions for the development of post-Soviet Russian imperialism after the collapse of the Soviet Union in 1991. The emancipation of Russian national identity from this neo-imperialism is the main challenge besetting the country's current search for a new identity.

Russia today has enormous difficulty in reconciling the mental maps of Russian ethnicity, culture, and identity with the political map of the Russian Federation. In other words, it has a major problem in responding to the key demand of modern nationalism, famously defined by Ernest Gellner as "a political principle which holds that the political and the national unit should be congruent." Do Russia's present-day political borders coincide with the borders of the Russian nation? The answer depends on the way in which Russian political and intellectual leaders and Russians in general imagine their nation. The question of Russian identity and its geographic extent is of more than academic interest, as it influences issues of war and peace along Europe's eastern frontiers today and will influence them for generations to come.

Russia's problem in defining its political, cultural, and ethnic borders after the fall of the Soviet Union is not unique. Similar issues have faced a number of powers that were constrained to divorce themselves physically and psychologically from their imperial possessions in the twentieth century. The vast Habsburg Empire, which disintegrated in the wake of World War I, shrank to the size of the interwar Austrian and Hungarian states, which left many citizens of German and Hungarian nationality beyond their borders. When the even larger Ottoman Empire collapsed, it left many Turkic-speaking or Muslim inhabitants outside the new Turkish state in lands dominated by non-Turks and non-Muslims. Finally, the disintegration of the British and French Empires, which took place over a longer period after World War II, saw the imperial powers reluctant to abandon their possessions and brought about the formation of states dominated by the indigenous population of the former colonies as well as a mass exodus of descendants of British and French settlers and administrators to their ancestral homeland.

But Russia also faces a major issue that most former imperial powers, especially the maritime empires, did not encounter—the definition of the Russian nation per se. In the words of the British historian Geoffrey Hosking, "Britain had an empire, but Russia was an empire—and perhaps still is." The traditional view holds that Russia's problem with self-identification derives from the fact that it acquired an empire before it acquired a nation. This is probably true for a number of empires, including the British, the Spanish, and the Portuguese, but what makes the Russian situation unique is that none of those empires shared common historical roots and myths of origin with their foreign subjects, as had been the case with Russia throughout a good part of its imperial history.

Does the Russian nation, understood in ethnic and cultural terms, consist only of ethnic Russians within and outside of the borders of the Russian Federation, or does it also include fellow Eastern Slavs—Ukrainians and Belarusians? This is the key question faced today by the Russian elites and the public at large as they try to reinvent themselves and their nation in the post-Soviet world. This is also the core element of the research undertaken in this book. In a manner of speaking, it falls into the familiar category of studies in the "invention" of nations. Britain, France, Germany, Spain, and, last but not least, Russia all have such books about their history reaching to premodern times. My book differs from them by narrating the invention and life of a nation that does not exist in institutional terms. The pan-Russian nation described in these pages is not to be found on any map and never materialized as a political entity, but it exists in the minds of political and cultural elites and, if one trusts opinion polls, of tens of millions of Russians as well. Its political influence exceeds that of many very real nations easily located on the political map of the world.

My book is a history of Russian nationalism at its cross section with Russian imperialism. In chronological terms, it begins with the formation of an independent Russian state in the second half of the fifteenth century and continues all the way to the present, covering large swaths of Russian and East European history and territory. As discussed in Part I of the book, in the course of the eighteenth century Russian imperial rulers and intellectuals managed to combine the medieval concepts of dynasty and religion with an emerging national consciousness in a new construct of Russian imperial nationhood. As shown in Part II, that construct was strongly challenged by the modern European nationalism of the Poles: though defeated in battle, they defiantly refused to give up their claim to the Ukrainian and Belarusian territories annexed to the Russian Empire in the late eighteenth-century partitions of Poland.

By the second half of the nineteenth century, the empire had to adjust its model of national identity in order to suppress the rise of modern nationalism among the Eastern Slavs. As detailed in Part III, the Russian imperial authorities tried to accommodate rising Ukrainian nationalism by promoting the concept of a tripartite Russian nation consisting not of a monolithic Russian people but of three tribes: Great Russian, Little Russian (Ukrainian), and White Russian (Belarusian). The authorities also tried, not without success, to stop the development of non–Great Russian literary languages and high cultures.

The Russian revolutions of 1905 and 1917, the subject of Part IV of the book, destroyed the imperial model of a tripartite nation. Russians, Ukrainians, and Belarusians were recognized as separate nations and pitted against one another (this applied particularly to Russians and Ukrainians). It was the task of the Soviet leaders, whose policies are analyzed in Part V of the book, to establish a hierarchy and modus vivendi between the three nations that constituted the Slavic core of the Soviet Union. Their efforts ultimately proved unavailing, and the USSR disintegrated in 1991. In the final part of the book, I discuss Russia's post-Soviet attempts to forge a new national identity by reviving some of its imperial legacies—the attempts that eventually led to the Russo-Ukrainian war of 2014–2015.

From the rise of the independent Muscovite state on the ruins of the Mongol Empire to the reinvention of Russian nationhood after the fall of the USSR, my book follows the efforts of the Russian elites to restore the territorial unity of the "lost kingdom"—the medieval Kyivan state that provided all Eastern Slavs with much of their cultural legacy. The search for a "lost kingdom" as a phenomenon of European history is hardly unique to Russia. Charlemagne sought to reconstitute the Roman Empire in medieval times, as did the Habsburgs in the early modern era. But a particular feature of the Russian story is that its search for the "lost kingdom," coupled with its longing for imperial expansion and great-power status, is still going on. It is in the pursuit of that vision that Russia has lost its way to modern nationhood, and in that sense has become a "lost kingdom" in its own right.

LIST OF MAPS

1. The Lost Kingdom: Kyivan (Kievan) Rus' c. 1054. Source: Zenon E. Kohut, Bohdan Y. Nebesio, and Myroslav Yurkevich, *Historical Dictionary of Ukraine* (Lanham, Maryland; Toronto; Oxford, 2005).
2. Medieval Rus' Principalities. Source: *The Cambridge Encyclopedia of Russia and the Former Soviet Union* (Cambridge, 1994),
3. The Rise of Muscovy. Source: Ibid.
4. The Polish-Lithuanian Commonwealth. Source: *Encyclopedia of Ukraine*, ed. Volodymyr Kubijovyc and Danylo Husar Struk, vol. 4 (Toronto, 1993).
5. The Partitions of Poland (1772–1795). Source: Paul Robert Magocsi, *A History of Ukraine: The Land and Its People* (Toronto, 2010).
6. Eastern Europe at the End of World War I. Source: Timothy Snyder, *Bloodlands: Europe between Hitler and Stalin* (New York, 2010).
7. The USSR c. 1933. Source: Ibid.
8. European Boundaries, 1933. Source: Ibid.
9. USSR's New Borders, 1940. Source: Ibid.
10. The German-Soviet War (1941). Source: Ibid.
11. Western USSR and Eastern Europe c. 1945. Source: Ibid.
12. The Russo-Ukrainian War (2014–2017). Source: Serhii Plokhy, *The Gates of Europe: A History of Ukraine* (New York, 2015).

1. The Lost Kingdom: Kyivan (Kievan) Rus' c. 1054

2. Medieval Rus' Principalities

SWEDISH
EMPIRE

White Sea

REPUBLIC OF NOVGOROD

PERM

Gulf of Finland

● Ivangorod

Vologda ●

● Novgorod

VIATKA

Riga

PSKOV

Kostroma ●

Suzdal ●

● Kazan

● Vilnius

Smolensk ●

● Moscow

Nizhnii Novgorod

KAZAN KHANATE

Mensk ●

LITHUANIA

● Pinsk

● Kaluga

Kulikovo
Field

RIAZAN

NOGHAI HORDE

● Chernihiv

Kyiv ●

Sarai ●

CRIMEAN KHANATE

ASTRAKHAN
KHANATE

Azov ●

Astrakhan ●

*Caspian
Sea*

Black Sea

500 km

250 miles

Principality of Moscow by 1462

Further expansion of Muscovy
by 1533

Constantinople ●

3. The Rise of Muscovy

4. The Polish-Lithuanian Commonwealth

BALTIC
SEA

R U S S I A

1795

1772

Kaliningrad
(Königsberg)

Kaunas

Polatsk

Vitsebsk

Gdańsk
(Danzig)

Vilnius

Smolensk

1772

PRUSSIA

LITHUANIA

Mahilioŭ

1795

1793

1795

1793

Warsaw

Brest

Pripet

Chernihiv

Warta

B R E S T

Desna

1795

LUBLIN

V O L H Y N I A

1795

1793

Luts'k

Kïïov

Cracow

1772

L'viv

Zhytomyr

K

GALICIA

San

I

E

Southern

Ros'

V

Dniester

Buh

TRANSCARPATHIA

PODOLIA

Kamianets'

BRATSLAV

1774

BUKOVINA

AUSTRIA

MOLDAVIA

OTTOMAN EMPIRE

Copyright © by Paul Robert Magocsi

Acquisitions by 1795

0   50   100 miles

- · · International boundaries, 1770
········· Boundaries of the first and
second partitions, 1772, 1793
━━━ Boundary of Ukraine, 2005
1772 Date of
acquisition
of area

Austrian Empire

Russian Empire

Prussian Empire

0   50   100 kilometers
Scale 1 : 9,000,000

5. The Partitions of Poland (1772–1795)

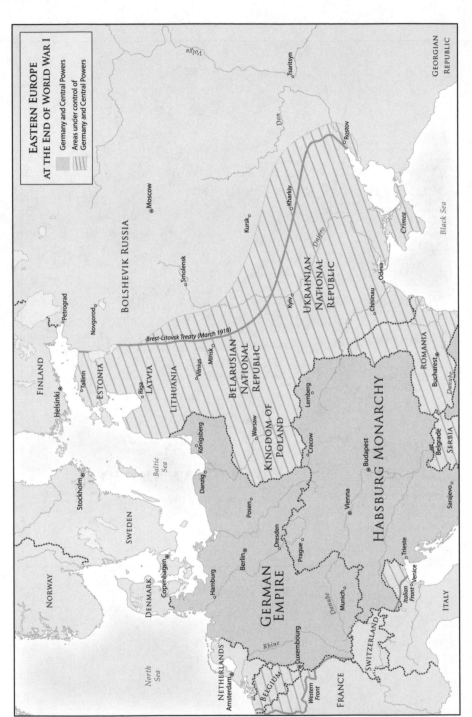

EASTERN EUROPE
AT THE END OF WORLD WAR I

Germany and Central Powers

Areas under control of
Germany and Central Powers

NORWAY

SWEDEN

North Sea

DENMARK
Copenhagen

Stockholm

Baltic Sea

FINLAND

Helsinki

Tallinn

ESTONIA

LATVIA
Riga

Petrograd

Novgorod

BOLSHEVIK RUSSIA

Moscow

Smolensk

Kursk

Volga

Don

Tsaritsyn

Brest-Litovsk Treaty (March 1918)

Vilnius

LITHUANIA

Minsk

BELARUSIAN
NATIONAL
REPUBLIC

Kharkiv

UKRAINIAN
NATIONAL
REPUBLIC

Dnipro

Kyiv

Königsberg

Danzig

KINGDOM OF POLAND

Warsaw

Cracow

Lemberg

Chisinau

Odesa

Crimea

Black Sea

GEORGIAN
REPUBLIC

Rostov

Posen

NETHERLANDS
Amsterdam

Hamburg

Berlin

Dresden

Prague

Munich

Vienna

Budapest

HABSBURG MONARCHY

Bucharest

ROMANIA

Danube

Belgrade

SERBIA

Sarajevo

GERMAN
EMPIRE

Rhine

Danube

Luxembourg

BELGIUM

Western
Front

FRANCE

SWITZERLAND

Italian
Front

Trieste

Venice

ITALY

6. Eastern Europe at the End of World War I

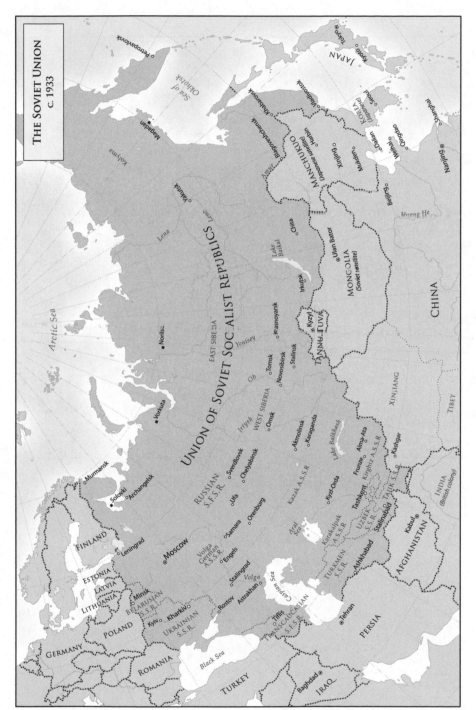

7. The USSR c. 1933

8. European Boundaries, 1933

9. USSR's New Borders, 1940

10. The German-Soviet War (1941)

11. Western USSR and Eastern Europe c. 1945

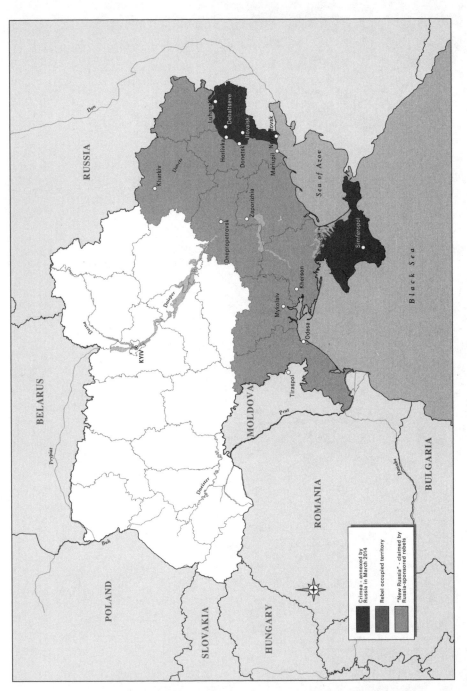

12. The Russo-Ukrainian War (2014–2017)

I

INVENTING RUSSIA

1

THE BIRTH OF THE TSARDOM

O N THE COLD AUTUMN DAY OF NOVEMBER 12, 1472, THE THIRTY-
two-year-old Grand Prince Ivan III of Moscow married the twenty-
three-year-old Sophia, the daughter of the despot of the Greek polity of
Morea, Thomas Palaiologos (Palaeologus). It was Ivan's second marriage
and Sophia's first. The ceremony took place in a wooden church in the
Kremlin next to the not yet completed Dormition Cathedral, and later
Russian chroniclers could not even agree whether the marriage service was
performed by the metropolitan or a regular archpriest. For all its modest appearance, the wedding had major symbolic significance: the ruler of Moscow
became a relative and continuator of the Byzantine emperors. Sophia's uncle, Constantine XI Palaiologos, had died in May 1453 defending Constantinople against the Ottoman assault. The Byzantine Empire died with him,
but not the imperial ambitions of Orthodox rulers. By marrying Sophia,
Ivan III of Moscow was putting on the mantle of the Byzantine emperors.

It was probably owing to Sophia's Roman connections that Ivan
brought to Moscow a group of Italian architects to build new walls for the

Kremlin—the seat of the grand princes that Ivan was now turning into an imperial castle. Marco Ruffo, who arrived in Moscow in 1485, built a number of Kremlin palaces and churches. Together with another Italian architect, Pietro Antonio Solari, he constructed the Palace of Facets, the tsar's richly decorated banqueting quarters. Solari, who came to Moscow in 1487, supervised the construction of the Kremlin towers, including the Spasskaia (Savior's) Tower. This iconic symbol of Moscow and Russia still bears an inscription commemorating the Italian architect who built it: the text on the inner gates is in Russian, the one on the outer gates in Latin. The former reads: "In the year 6999 [1491], in July, by God's grace, this tower was built by order of Ivan Vasilievich, sovereign and autocrat of all Rus' and grand prince of Vladimir and Moscow and Novgorod and Pskov and Tver and Yugra and Viatka and Perm and Bulgar and others in the thirtieth year of his reign, and it was built by Pietro Antonio Solari of the city of Milan."

Ivan's title listed his possessions, both old and new. While his marriage and ambitious construction project pointed to the imperial future, his title of ruler of "all Rus'" and claims to individual lands was rooted in the past—more specifically, the medieval origins of his dynasty and state. Scholars point out the dual origins of the power of the Muscovite prince, who functioned as both khan and *basileus* (the Byzantine emperor)—at once the secular and religious ruler of the realm. Often overlooked in this focus on dual origins is the continuing importance of the title of grand prince, which would remain central to the identity of Ivan III and his successors right up to the mid-sixteenth century. The title associated the princes of Moscow with the long-deceased rulers of Kyivan Rus', allowing the princes to claim supremacy over the Rus' lands—the former Kyivan possessions extending from the Black Sea in the south to the Baltic Sea in the north.

IVAN'S RIGHT TO RULE SUCH TOWNS AS VLADIMIR AND MOSCOW, as well as Novgorod and Pskov, was based on his claim of descent from the Scandinavian Rurikid dynasty, whose origins went back to the legendary figure of the Viking king (*konung*) Rurik.

The Rurikids had ruled Kyivan Rus' as a strong state whose power had reached its peak between the eleventh and early twelfth centuries. Among the most venerated princes of Kyiv was Volodymyr (Vladimir), who had ruled the realm from 980 to 1015 and brought Byzantine Christianity to the Rus' lands, an accomplishment for which the Orthodox Church made him a saint. Another major figure was Volodymyr's son, Yaroslav the Wise (1019–1054), the builder of St. Sophia's Cathedral in central Kyiv. According to established tradition, he issued the first Rus' law code and promoted chronicle writing. Finally, there was another Volodymyr, known as Monomakh because of his family connection to the Byzantine emperor Constantine IX Monomachos, who managed to restore the shaken unity of the Kyivan realm in the course of his twelve-year reign (1113–1125).

Rurikid rule over Kyivan Rus' came to an abrupt end in the mid-thirteenth century, when the Mongols, accompanied by Turkic steppe tribes known in Rus' as Tatars, attacked and subjugated the Rus' principalities. In the fall of 1237, Batu Khan, a grandson of Genghis Khan and founder of the easternmost realm of the Mongol Empire, sent envoys to Prince Yurii of Vladimir in northeastern Rus' to demand his surrender. The prince refused. Within the next few months, the Mongols besieged and devastated Riazan and a number of other Rus' towns. The prince himself died in battle in March 1238. In the winter of 1239, the Mongols sacked the towns of Chernihiv and Pereiaslav. The next year they appeared on the approaches to Kyiv, the center of a once huge polity. Because Kyiv would not surrender, the Mongols besieged it, using heavy beams to breach the city walls.

"Batu placed battering rams near the city by the Polish Gate," wrote the chronicler, referring to a location that is now in downtown Kyiv, "for a dense forest came up to there. Beating the walls unceasingly, day and night, he breached them." In early December, the Mongols rushed across a frozen creek that no longer presented a barrier and poured into the city. As the short winter day drew to a close, the Mongols took over the city walls and palisades, where they stayed overnight, waiting for dawn. That was probably the most dreadful night in the lives of the city's defenders. Historians believe that the Rus' warriors and the remaining inhabitants retreated to the Church of the Dormition. The first stone church in Kyiv, it became the last sanctuary for those who would not capitulate. "Meanwhile, people ran to the church and onto its roof with their possessions," wrote the chronicler about the events of December 7, 1240, the last day of Kyiv's defense, "[and] the walls of the church collapsed from the weight, and so the fortress was taken by the [Tatar] warriors."

Few of the inhabitants and defenders of Kyiv survived its fall. Batu and his armies moved westward, conquering the rest of the Rus' lands and invading Poland and Hungary. The Mongols succeeded in part because the Rus' lands, once united around Kyiv, no longer formed a coherent polity and were ruled by princes competing with one another for power and influence. At the time of the Mongol invasion, most of the northeastern Rus' princes, who ruled the lands of today's central Russia, recognized the suzerainty of the princes of Vladimir. Southwestern Rus', including the city of Kyiv, was ruled by the Galician-Volhynian princes, while the Republic of Novgorod in northeastern Rus' conducted its affairs quite independently of the other Rus' lands. If anything, the Mongol invasion worsened the political fragmentation of the Kyivan Rus' realm. Mongol rule over what are now the Ukrainian and Belarusian lands was largely indirect, lasting only a few decades. Those lands eventually found themselves under the control of the Grand Duchy of Lithuania and the Kingdom of Poland. Farther north and east, the situation was different. The Mongols established strict control over northeastern Rus', which in time would become a predominantly Russian land.

Although the unity of Rus' was very much a thing of the past, by the time of the Mongol invasion the princes throughout the Rus' lands, from Kyiv and Pereiaslav in the south to Novgorod and Vladimir in the north and east, shared a sense of dynastic origin. They were also heirs to Kyiv's impressive legacy in the realms of law, religion, literary language, and common Rus' identity. Nowhere did dynastic continuity with Kyivan Rus' play a more important role than in Muscovy, the polity that emerged in the northeastern realm of the former Kyivan Rus' under the suzerainty of the Mongols. To rule over their Rus' possessions, including Novgorod, the Mongols relied on subordinates holding the title of grand prince of Vladimir. A number of princely families competed with one another for the coveted title, which brought prestige, power, and income to those able to convince the khans of their loyalty and ability to do the job. The Mongol (later Kipchak) khans passed the title from one Rus' prince to another as a carrot to encourage the princes, who were obliged to collect tribute for the khans from their Rus' subjects.

The khans played off one princely line against another, trying to avoid the emergence of a strong political center, but eventually proved unable to sustain that strategy. In the course of the fourteenth century, the city of Moscow emerged as an important new center of power in the lands of Mongol Rus'. A small principality at the time of the Mongol invasion of northeastern Rus' in 1238, Moscow did not have even a princely family of its own. It acquired one only under the Mongols. The princes of Moscow belonged to a junior line of the Rurikids, but thanks to the location of their principality at the crossroads of various trade routes and to their political skills, they became the most powerful princely house in northeastern Rus'. In 1317, the prince of Moscow married a sister of the khan of the Golden Horde, thereby gaining the title of grand prince of Vladimir and the power inherent in the post of the khan's representative in Rus'.

The Muscovites' main rivals for the title of grand prince were the princes of Tver, a much more powerful principality than Moscow located between Muscovy and the Republic of Novgorod. But the junior princes of Moscow, whose capital was closer to Vladimir, the original seat of the grand princes, and to the Mongol-controlled steppe, effectively outmaneuvered their competitors. A significant factor in the unexpected and steady rise of Moscow was the policy of the metropolitan of all Rus', the head of the Orthodox Church, who had moved from Kyiv to Vladimir at the turn of the century. He now established himself in Moscow, making it the new capital of his vast metropolitanate, which covered all the lands of Mongol Rus' and extended into Lithuanian Rus' as well. The Moscow princes and the Rus' metropolitans both professed loyalty to the Golden Horde, and their alliance helped turn Moscow into the true capital of northeastern Rus'.

By the mid-fifteenth century, the princes of Moscow, as principal agents of the khans of the Golden Horde in the Rus' lands, were in a position to threaten their masters' continuing political dominance. With the Golden Horde weakened by internal rivalries and entering a period of disintegration, the Moscow princes pushed for the sovereignty of the Rus' realm. The first to do so was Prince Vasilii II, nicknamed the Blind—his enemies had plucked out his eyes in the vain hope of disqualifying him as a ruler. But it was only during the rule of his son, Ivan III, a man of true foresight who assumed the office of grand prince in 1462 and ruled until 1505, that the goal of independence was finally achieved.

Ivan established his control over the entire territory of Mongol Rus'. To secure his independence of the khans and rule the rebellious Rus' lands, he employed not only the military might of his realm but also powerful legal and historical arguments. Dynasty and patrimony—two concepts that the Muscovite rulers rooted in the Kyivan past—were key ideological foundations of the tsardom. The visions of the Rus' princely past and of an imperial future would prove mutually reinforcing in the course of the fifteenth and sixteenth centuries, which were crucial to the formation of Muscovite statehood and identity.

IN 1471, ONE YEAR BEFORE HIS MARRIAGE TO SOPHIA PALAIOLOGina, Ivan III had scored a major victory in the struggle to consolidate his power over the former Mongol Rus'. His troops had captured and subjugated the Republic of Novgorod, by far the largest and richest polity of the realm.

Many scholars have regarded the Novgorod republic as a democratic alternative to the authoritarian trend in Russian history embodied in the Grand Duchy of Moscow, which was ruled by strong princes. Since the twelfth century, Novgorod, with possessions extending from the Baltic Sea in the west to the White and Barents Seas in the north and the Ural Mountains in the east, had been ruled by officials elected by a popular assembly. The princes of Novgorod functioned as military commanders who served at the pleasure of the citizens, or, rather, their patrician elite. The republic's wealth came not only from landholdings but also from trade, as Novgorod was a major commercial power in the Baltic region, exporting furs and other forest products and importing textiles for itself and much of Rus'.

In 1470, a group of Novgorod patricians led by Marfa Boretskaia, the widow of a former mayor of the city and mother of its serving mayor, came to an agreement with Casimir IV, who was both grand duke of Lithuania and king of Poland (the two states had concluded a personal and then a dynastic union in 1385). Casimir sent Prince Mykhailo Olelkovych, a son and brother of the princes of Kyiv, to help Novgorod defend itself. But little more help came from the duke, and Mykhailo Olelkovych left the city in the following year. A Muscovite army, supported by Tatar cavalry in the service of Ivan III, attacked the Novgorodians in the summer of 1471. The inhabitants learned of the approaching danger when they saw their soldiers retreating from the field to the city walls with their noses and lips cut off. As the forces of Ivan III advanced, they mutilated their captives and sent them home to terrify the rest of the defending army and the local population.

The decisive battle, which took place on the Shelon River in July 1471, brought victory to the less numerous but more disciplined and experienced Muscovite forces. The Tatars played an important role, ambushing the Novgorodian army and helping to pursue, capture, and kill retreating troops. Muscovite and Novgorodian chroniclers disagreed on the details of the battle, but its outcome and significance were clear: Ivan III had crushed Novgorod's efforts to maintain its autonomy. Mayor Dmitrii Boretsky was captured in battle and executed on Ivan's orders. An estimated 12,000 Novgorodians died in battle or were killed in the course of the retreat. The Novgorodians were forced to pay a huge tribute, more than twice the amount that Muscovy had rendered to the Horde, and abandon their alliance with the Grand Duchy of Lithuania. The republic was on its knees.

The strength of Ivan's army allowed him to subjugate Novgorod and repel the Great Horde, the main successor to the Golden Horde. But the new status of the Grand Principality of Moscow and its constant acquisition of new territories required justification in the eyes of its subjects and neighbors. According to the Muscovite scribes, who conveniently produced a new rendition of the Russian chronicles in 1472, Ivan III had taken Novgorod and punished the republic for its insubordination on the basis of his patrimonial rights, which went back to Prince Volodymyr of Kyiv. "From antiquity you, the people of Novgorod, have been my patrimony," the Muscovite envoys allegedly said on behalf of Ivan III, "from our grandfathers and our ancestors, from Grand Prince Volodymyr, the great-grandson of Rurik, the first grand prince in our land, who baptized the Rus' land. And from that Rurik until this day, you have recognized only one ruling clan of those grand princes. . . . [W]e, their kin, have ruled over you, and we bestow [our mercy] upon you, and we protect you against [all adversaries], and we are free to punish you if you do not recognize us according to the old tradition."

The reference to "old tradition" was a fairly new feature of Muscovite political culture. The Kyivan lineage of the Muscovite princely line had hardly been mentioned by chroniclers before Ivan III took Novgorod. Until then, the princes of Moscow had competed for power with those of Tver and other centers by appealing to the khans of the Horde. References to Kyiv and the Rurikid origins of the ruling dynasty had no value in the eyes of the khans, who were the heirs of Genghis Khan, the founder of the Mongol Empire. But that situation changed with the continuing disintegration of the Horde. The same year Ivan consolidated his rule over Novgorod, he also turned back the Tatar armies of Ahmed, the khan of the Great Horde. Disturbed by the growing power of Moscow, Ahmed had moved his army toward the Muscovite borders, but the Muscovites had mounted an effective defense, preventing Ahmed's troops from crossing the Oka River. The Tatars turned back, and the Muscovites stopped paying tribute, letting their former overlords know that their dependence on the Horde was over. With Novgorod defeated and Tatar dominance thrown off, the foundations of Muscovite sovereignty had been laid.

But that was not the end of Ivan's troubles either with Novgorod or with the Mongols. Five years later, the scenario first played out in 1471–1472 was repeated. Once again, the three main actors were Muscovy, Novgorod, and the Horde. In October 1477, as the Novgorodians questioned the conditions of the new treaty imposed on them by Ivan III and his status as their sovereign, the grand prince besieged the city and forced a new loyalty oath on its citizens. In January 1478, Ivan III entered the city. Novgorod ceased to be a republic. The bell that had summoned citizens to council meetings—the symbol of Novgorodian democracy—was taken to Moscow. Marfa Boretskaia, the leader of republican resistance, was brought first to Moscow and then to Nizhnii Novgorod, where she was compelled to take monastic vows. The landed wealth of the metropolitan of Novgorod, of the monasteries, and of the city's elite was confiscated. The leaders of the resistance and their families were exiled in midwinter, and many did not survive the ordeal. Their lands were given to servitors of the Muscovite prince.

The conquest of Novgorod by Ivan III in 1478 was followed once again by a military confrontation with the Great Horde, which demanded tribute from its former Moscow subjects. This time, Khan Ahmed found an ally in Casimir IV, the king of Poland and grand duke of Lithuania, who was concerned by the fall of Novgorod and Muscovy's increasing power in the Lithuanian borderland. The Lithuanian army was supposed to join the Tatars in an attack on Moscow. In the fall of 1480, Ahmed showed up on the Ugra River on the borders of Muscovy, ready for battle, but the Lithuanians, who had allowed the Tatars to march through their territories, did not appear. They were prevented from doing so by an attack on their southern, largely Ukrainian lands by another heir to the Golden Horde, the Crimean Khanate. Without Lithuanian support, Ahmed would not risk crossing the Ugra and turned back. This retreat became known in Russian history as the final act in the long struggle to shake off the "Tatar yoke" and the first decisive assertion of Muscovite sovereignty. Muscovy, which got to keep Novgorod, began its history as a fully independent state by crushing a democratic rival that had sought to distance itself from the heirs of the Golden Horde.

BY 1480, IVAN HAD SUCCESSFULLY ESTABLISHED HIS SOVEREIGNTY over the lands of Mongol Rus', but his title, "sovereign and autocrat of all Rus'," inscribed by Italian architects on the gates of the Kremlin tower a decade later, suggested much more than that. In 1478, the year of the final subordination of Novgorod, Muscovite diplomats began to speak of Moscow's rights to some Lithuanian territories, including Polatsk and Smolensk. By 1490, Ivan's chancellery had begun to use the Kyivan descent of the Muscovite princes as grounds to extend his claim from those two principalities to Kyiv itself. In a letter to the Habsburg emperor Maximilian I, Ivan III spoke of undertaking, with God's grace, to "reconquer our patrimony, the Grand Duchy of Kyiv, which is ruled by Casimir, the Polish king, and his children." In 1494, the Lithuanian duke was compelled to recognize the new title of the Muscovite ruler, including its reference to "all Rus'." In 1503–1504, Muscovite envoys made their claims to the Kyivan patrimony known to their Lithuanian counterparts: "The towns and lands now in our possession are not all of our patrimony, [which extends to] the whole Rus' land, Kyiv and Smolensk and other towns. . . . [B]y God's grace, this is our patrimony from antiquity, from our forefathers."

The extension of Muscovite patrimonial claims to the Rus' lands of the Grand Duchy of Lithuania was the direct outcome of a series of successful Muscovite wars against Lithuania in the late fifteenth and early sixteenth centuries. They began with border skirmishes in the 1480s. The first actual war was waged in 1492–1494, to be followed by the wars of 1500–1503, 1507–1508, 1512–1522, and 1534–1537—altogether almost half a century of warfare. For most of that period, the Muscovites were on the offensive, their advance checked for the first time in the early sixteenth century. By that time, the Grand Principality of Moscow had extended its borders deep into the territory of the Grand Duchy, capturing Chernihiv and Smolensk. As in the case of Novgorod, many inhabitants of Smolensk were forcibly resettled to the east and replaced by subjects of the Muscovite prince.

The Muscovites were gaining the upper hand thanks to the strength of Ivan III's armies and the unwillingness of Ivan's rival, Casimir IV of Poland and Lithuania, to attract and accommodate the descendants of the princes of Kyiv in the lands that now constitute Ukraine and Belarus. As Ivan annexed one principality after another, using his family's Kyivan descent to legitimize the process, Casimir abolished the only principality still extant in the Grand Duchy of Lithuania—that of Kyiv. He did so in 1470, and his decision would bear directly on Lithuania's "loss" of Novgorod to Muscovy one year later. The Kyiv principality had been ruled by the Olelkovych family, which traced its origins to one of the first Lithuanian rulers, Algirdas, and whose dynastic status was close to, if not on a par with, that of the grand dukes of Lithuania. Prince Mykhailo Olelkovych, who came to Novgorod in 1470 to help defend the republic against Muscovy, was a member of the Kyivan branch of the family. His departure from Novgorod in 1471 was motivated in part by his hope of assuming his father's office in Kyiv. But he was in for a surprise. Not only did Casimir not allow him to become the next prince of Kyiv, but he abolished the office and the principality altogether, appointing his own representative to administer the region.

The Kyivan princes never forgave Casimir for doing away with their principality and putting an end to their dreams. In 1480, news reached Casimir that Mykhailo Olelkovych, the unsuccessful defender of Novgorod and candidate for the Kyiv principality, had entered into a conspiracy with other princes to kill him and take his place as grand duke. The conspirators were either arrested or fled to Muscovy, but the plot, together with a Crimean Tatar attack on the Grand Duchy, prevented Casimir from sending his army to help Khan Ahmed as he faced the Muscovite forces on the Ugra River. Casimir's earlier failure to support Novgorod for fear of strengthening the Rus' princes of the Grand Duchy was now compounded by his inability to help the Great Horde against Muscovy because of the revolt of the very same princes.

The death of Casimir in 1492 and the interregnum that followed it gave Moscow a perfect opportunity to advance Ivan III's claims to "all Rus'" and launch a full-blown war against the Grand Duchy. The borderland princes were left to their own devices, as Lithuanian troops were either unavailable or insufficiently strong to protect the vassals of the grand duke. Under these circumstances, the princes considered themselves no longer bound by loyalty to the Grand Duchy. "Your father, Sire, kissed the cross in my presence to affirm that it was the duty of your father, our lord, to stand up for our patrimony and defend it against all; but Your Grace, Sire, did not show favor to me . . . and did not stand up for my patrimony," wrote one of the "turncoats," Prince Semen Vorotynsky, to the new grand duke of Lithuania, Alexander. The new grand duke used both force and diplomacy in his efforts to stop the Muscovite advance. He succeeded only to a degree, as he found himself obliged to recognize Ivan's new title, which included a reference to "all Rus'," and lost significant territories, including the Chernihiv land near Kyiv.

Alexander's rule inaugurated an era in which the Lithuanian princes and Polish kings began to take the Muscovite eastern offensives more seriously than Casimir had done. Alexander had to abandon the centralizing reforms of Casimir IV and make an alliance with the princely clans of the Grand Duchy. He recognized the authority of the princely council and promised to consult with its members on all state appointments. He also established close relations with the Ruthenian (Ukrainian and Belarusian) princes. In 1514, the Muscovite troops were defeated in the Battle of Orsha by a Lithuanian-Ruthenian army led by one of those princes. The almost uninterrupted Muscovite westward march was finally checked. The war established, for the time being, the extent of the borders of "all Rus'" in the titles of the Moscow grand princes: those borders included Smolensk and Chernihiv but not Kyiv or Polatsk (in present-day Ukraine and Belarus, respectively), which remained within the borders of the Grand Duchy of Lithuania. Internal strife in Moscow following the death of Ivan III in 1505, and, in particular, of his son Vasilii III in 1533, halted the Muscovite westward advance, but the aspiration to extend the Muscovite "patrimony" at the expense of the Grand Duchy of Lithuania was by no means abandoned.

The Muscovite wars with Lithuania, triggered by the conflict over the fate of Novgorod and continued under the banner of gathering the patrimony of the Kyivan princes, made Muscovy a major actor on the East European scene. It was no longer just a country fighting for its independence, but one expanding beyond its "natural" Mongol borders.

IN THE 1520S, MUSCOVITE INTELLECTUALS PRODUCED A NEW genealogical tract, the *Tale of the Princes of Vladimir*, which associated the rulers in the Kremlin, the former grand princes of Vladimir, with Emperor Augustus, the founder of the Roman Empire. The link was established though a legendary personality called Prus, allegedly the brother of Augustus. Thus the founder of the Roman Empire and the rulers of Moscow had the same forefather. But how were the grand princes of Vladimir (and later, Moscow) related to Prus? The solution proposed by the Muscovite authors was quite simple: the missing link was another legendary figure, Prince Rurik, the founder of the Kyivan ruling clan. According to the Rus' chronicles, Rurik had come from the north, the part of the world allegedly assigned by Augustus to Prus.

Should that lineage be found wanting, the authors provided another connection to Rome with a much more solid historical foundation. It led to the eternal city through Byzantium. The princes of Vladimir and Moscow were heirs of Prince Volodymyr (Vladimir) Monomakh, the twelfth-century ruler of Kyiv who had received his name from his mother, a relative of the Byzantine emperor Constantine IX Monomachos, who in turn was related to Augustus. One way or another, all roads of the Muscovite imagination led to Rome. According to the *Tale*, Constantine had passed on his emperor's regalia to Volodymyr, and they had subsequently been inherited by the princes of Moscow. Among them was Monomakh's Cap, an Eastern equivalent of an emperor's crown. It was in fact a fourteenth-century gold filigree skullcap from Central Asia, possibly a gift from the khan of the Golden Horde, intended to symbolize the vassal status of the Muscovite princes. The Mongol gift was now reimagined as a symbol of imperial power.

The Monomakh Cap and the Augustus–Prus–Monomakh account of the origins of the Moscow rulers' sovereign and imperial power would have a spectacular career in Muscovite political thought. Both were included in the coronation of Ivan IV (the Terrible), the first Muscovite ruler to be installed with the title of tsar—a Slavic word derived from the Latin "Caesar," meaning emperor, or ruler of rulers. The ceremony took place in 1547, with Monomakh's Cap serving as Ivan's crown. Metropolitan Makarii, who devised the formalities, conferred divine power on the new ruler, stressing the Kyivan and ultimately Roman origins of the dynasty. In the next few decades, the Augustus legend would become central to the official genealogy of the Muscovite rulers as presented in the *Book of Royal Degrees*, the first official history of Muscovy. It was commissioned by Ivan the Terrible in 1560 and written at the metropolitan's court. The legend also made its way into the frescoes of Moscow palaces and cathedrals. Sigismund Herberstein, a Habsburg envoy who first visited Muscovy in 1519 and published an account of his voyages in 1549, during the rule of Ivan the Terrible, claimed that the Muscovites he met believed in the Roman origins of Rurik, as well as those of their current ruler.

The Roman connection served Ivan well both at home, by distinguishing the ruling dynasty from the rest of the princely elite, and abroad, by putting him on a par with Western rulers. Ivan's geopolitical objectives were significantly different from those of his father and grandfather. Unlike them, he switched the focus of his foreign policy from gathering the Rus' lands to taking over those of the Horde. In 1552, he defeated and annexed the Khanate of Kazan. The city's inhabitants were resettled and replaced by subjects of the tsar—the policy applied earlier in Novgorod and Smolensk. In 1556, Ivan's troops defeated another successor to the Horde, the Khanate of Astrakhan, and Muscovy took control of the all-important Volga trade route. In ideological terms, the tsar of Muscovy had defeated two Tatar rulers to whom the Muscovite chronicles referred consistently as "tsars." Ivan's authority was enhanced when he added their tsardoms to his. In his diplomatic correspondence, he would count separately the years of his rule over the Muscovite, Kazan, and Astrakhan tsardoms.

If Ivan's alleged descent from Augustus made him an equal of the Habsburgs in lineage, the conquest of the Volga khanates improved his geopolitical standing and gave substance to his claim to be an emperor. In 1557, the year after the conquest of Astrakhan, Ivan wrote to the supreme Orthodox authority, the patriarch of Constantinople, asking for recognition as tsar on the basis of his conquest of Kazan and Astrakhan. The same argument was used in dealings with Muscovy's Western counterparts. But reaction to Ivan's claim to the title of tsar, or Caesar, was mixed. The patriarch of Constantinople, eager to recognize a new Orthodox emperor and potential protector, assured Ivan in 1558 that "the tsar's name is invoked in the Universal Church every Sunday, like the names of the former Byzantine tsars [emperors]." The rulers of the Holy Roman Empire were more cautious, as the Muscovite ruler's new title undermined the universality of their authority. Thus the Holy Roman emperor Maximilian II suggested in 1576 that Ivan call himself eastern emperor—a possible reference to Byzantine tradition—or emperor of all Rus', a variation on the grand-princely title of Ivan and his predecessors.

In 1558, with his tsar's title recognized by the patriarch of Constantinople but not by Western rulers, Ivan turned his troops westward. The Livonian War, which would last a quarter of a century, until 1583, started with an attack on a declining regional power, the Livonian Order, a state established by Teutonic knights that encompassed parts of Estonian, Latvian, and, to a lesser extent, Lithuanian territories. The campaign began well, with victory for Ivan's troops, but the defeat and destruction of the order alerted its neighbors to the rising Muscovite threat. The Grand Duchy of Lithuania, which had borne the brunt of Muscovite offensives since the late fifteenth century, leaped into battle on the side of the order only to be badly defeated. In 1563, Ivan the Terrible took Polatsk, a city and territory in present-day Belarus first claimed by the Muscovites back in 1478, immediately after their takeover of Novgorod. In 1569, in the Polish city of Lublin, the Grand Duchy of Lithuania was forced to turn its previous dynastic union with the Kingdom of Poland into a permanent union of the two states, losing its independence and control over Ukrainian lands to Poland but maintaining its rule over Belarus. The combined Polish-Lithuanian troops were now able to withstand the Muscovite offensive, with additional assistance from Sweden.

The tsar of Muscovy found himself on the defensive. In 1571, taking advantage of his involvement in the west, the Crimean Tatars captured Moscow, forcing Ivan to end his ill-fated rule by terror known as the *oprichnina*, whereby he had divided his realm, cleansing part of it of aristocratic clans. But the war in the west continued to go badly. The new Polish king, Stephen Báthory, recaptured Polatsk at the head of Polish and Lithuanian armies in 1579. Two years later, the Swedes expelled Muscovite troops from Narva, an important trade center on the Baltic Sea controlled by Muscovy since 1558. In 1582, Ivan found himself obliged to make a peace treaty that ended his ambitions to acquire yet another "tsardom" on the Baltic. The tsar, regarded by some of his subjects as the protector of Orthodoxy throughout the world, was reduced to asking the pope to help negotiate peace with the Polish king. It was a most humiliating way of invoking Ivan's alleged Roman origins.

Ivan the Terrible died in 1584, one year after a peace with Sweden ended the Livonian War. He left his son and successor, Fedor Ivanovich, who would be the last Rurikid on the Muscovite throne, a country economically broken and devastated by war and terror but more centralized than under any previous Muscovite ruler. He also left Fedor the title of tsar, which was now recognized by foreign leaders, and Monomakh's Cap as the crown of the Tsardom of Muscovy. The cap and the legend attached to it embodied the complex identity of the tsardom and its elites as it had evolved in the course of the sixteenth century. Featuring Central Asian gold and jewels and Muscovite furs, the cap was swathed in invisible layers of historical mythology, first Kyivan, then Byzantine, and finally Roman. Whether the Muscovites sought a Roman connection by way of the Baltics and Prussia or the Black Sea and Constantinople, all ways led through Kyiv, the seat of the first Rurikid princes, without whom there could be no claim to anything but the Mongol tradition.

It was the Kyivan myth of origins that became the cornerstone of Muscovy's ideology as the polity evolved from a Mongol dependency to a sovereign state and then an empire. The ruling dynasty, which relied on Kyivan roots to legitimize its rule, would subsequently find it difficult, if not impossible, to divorce itself from that founding myth.

2

THE THIRD ROME

IN JUNE 1586, THE MUSCOVITE COURT WELCOMED AN UNUSUAL guest, Patriarch Joachim V of Antioch, who held one of the five ancient and most prestigious patriarchal seats of the Eastern Christian (Orthodox) world. Tsar Fedor, who had succeeded his father, Ivan the Terrible, as ruler of Muscovy two years earlier, met him in full regalia in the company of Muscovite aristocrats, called boyars, and scores of court officials. Rising from his throne to greet the honored guest, the tsar walked a full seven feet toward him—an ostentatious gesture of respect for the patriarch's exalted status. After receiving Joachim's blessings, Fedor invited him to dine at his table, another honor rarely bestowed on the tsar's visitors.

Moscow was accustomed to receiving Eastern hierarchs requesting financial support, but never before 1586 had it received a patriarch. The status of the Orthodox Church in Muscovy was lower than that of the ancient churches of Byzantium, as it was ruled by a metropolitan as opposed to a patriarch, who, to add insult to injury, was not even recognized by the "big four"—the patriarchs of Constantinople, Alexandria, Antioch, and Jerusalem. While Joachim's visit presented the tsar with an opportunity to enhance his status in the Orthodox world, the opportunity came with a challenge. How was he to demonstrate the superiority of the Muscovite church to those of the Eastern patriarchs? The tsar left that difficult task to his metropolitan, Dionisii. After inviting Joachim to dine, Fedor suggested that he first visit the metropolitan, who was awaiting him in the Kremlin's Dormition Cathedral. When the patriarch entered the cathedral, the metropolitan, violating every rule of Orthodox protocol, gave him his blessing. The patriarch, taken aback, stated that it would be more appropriate for Dionisii to accept his blessing first. But victory in this first round of diplomatic relations went to the metropolitan; the rest was handled by the tsar and his advisers.

They asked Joachim to elevate the metropolitan see of Moscow to a patriarchate. Apparently surprised by this request, the patriarch decided to play for time. On the one hand, he badly needed the tsar's alms and did not want to risk leaving Moscow empty-handed or with a nominal donation. On the other hand, the creation of a patriarchate was a matter for the Ecumenical Council, not for the patriarch's unilateral decision. Thus, according to Muscovite sources, Joachim responded that he thought it appropriate for Muscovy to have its own patriarchate but would have to speak with the other patriarchs, who would make a decision with the Ecumenical Council. He promised to lobby for the patriarchate once he returned to his see. Tsar Fedor sent Joachim off with rich gifts for him and the patriarchs of Constantinople and Alexandria.

The vision of Muscovy as successor to Byzantium and the only remaining Orthodox empire on the face of the earth was first developed in the early sixteenth century. That vision, centered on the figure of the Muscovite tsar, was incomplete as long as the country remained without a patriarch of its own—the tsars had to keep turning for spiritual support and legitimacy to the Eastern patriarchs. Ivan the Terrible had appealed to the patriarch of Constantinople for recognition of his tsarist title. In 1581, after the death of his son and heir apparent, Tsarevich Ivan—contemporaries claimed that the father had killed the son in a fit of rage—Ivan the Terrible sent emissaries to the Orthodox East, asking the hierarchs to pray for the repose of his son's soul.

Now it seemed that the vision of the true Orthodox empire was about to be realized. In Western and Central Europe, the sixteenth century would be marked by the Protestant Reformation, Catholic reform, and religious wars between Protestants and Catholics. For Muscovy, the ecclesiastical priorities were to win higher status for its Orthodox church. The first half of the seventeenth century would test established relations between the secular and spiritual authorities in Moscow as well as Muscovites' perceptions of themselves and the world around them.

RELATIONS BETWEEN THE MUSCOVITE CHURCH AND THE EASTern patriarchs had broken down in the mid-fifteenth century, when Isidore, the Greek metropolitan of Rus', was arrested and thrown into a Muscovite prison for attempting to introduce a church union with Rome.

Isidore first came to Moscow in 1437 but then left to attend the Council of Florence, where he was one of the most ardent supporters of the church union with Rome. The schism between the Catholics and the Orthodox went back to the eleventh century, when the Latin West, represented by the pope of Rome, and the Greek East, represented by the emperors and patriarchs of Byzantium, broke their communion. The theological differences between the two branches of Christianity concerned the Holy Spirit: Did it come from God the Father alone, as the easterners claimed, or from God the Father and God the Son in equal measure, as the westerners believed? Underlying this and many other theological disputes was the question of who should wield ultimate authority in the church—the hierarchs of Rome or Constantinople. Political and cultural differences also pulled the two parts of what had once been the Roman Empire in different directions. In the East, the church was subordinate to the emperor, who exercised both secular and spiritual power. In the West, the pope had to compete with secular rulers, a situation that produced a political culture much more pluralistic than that of the East. In time, the West would come to overshadow its Eastern rival.

The union, which placed the Orthodox Church under the tutelage of the pope, was discussed and approved by both sides at the Council of Florence in 1439. The Orthodox, who would be referred to in later texts as Uniates, accepted Catholic dogmas while maintaining their traditional Byzantine rite and the institution of the married clergy. The last Byzantine emperor, Constantine XI, had accepted a union between the two branches of Christianity in the vain hope that Rome would save him and his state from the Ottomans. Isidore returned to Moscow from the council in 1441 only to be arrested by Grand Prince Vasilii II the Blind, the father of Ivan III. Isidore managed to escape, and the Muscovite prince did not pursue him. Had he been caught, ecclesiastical ordinances would have obliged Vasilii to "burn him in flames or bury him alive" for his apostasy.

Why did Moscow reject church union in 1441? An explanation is to be found in letters signed by Grand Prince Vasilii and sent to the Byzantine emperor and the patriarch of Constantinople, citing theological differences between the Eastern and Western churches. But given that it was the grand prince, not the church hierarchs, who figured as the main actor on the Muscovite side, it may be assumed that at least part of the motivation lay in his own agenda and political aspirations. It is no accident that the rise of Muscovy as an independent state coincided with the declaration of independence of its church from Constantinople, which had been an ally of the Mongol Horde for decades, if not centuries. We know that Vasilii wanted the metropolitan of Rus' to be his own appointee and had actually sent his candidate to Constantinople for approval, but he had been rebuffed, and the post had gone to Isidore. After Isidore's arrest, Vasilii again asked Constantinople for the right to nominate his own candidate, but he was again refused.

The Union of Florence offered the ambitious ruler a perfect pretext to cut ties with Constantinople and assume the right to appoint metropolitans to the Moscow seat. In 1448, a council of Orthodox bishops elected Vasilii's candidate, Iona, to the metropolitan throne, and the Muscovite church broke all ties with Constantinople. Even before the fall of the Byzantine capital in 1453, the metropolitanate of Moscow would become autocephalous, or self-governing—an isolation from the rest of the Orthodox world that lasted almost a century and a half. But that did not prevent the Muscovite princes from claiming the legacy of Byzantium, or, indeed, from establishing advantageous relations with Rome, as Ivan's marriage to Sophia clearly attested.

The years 1448, when the Muscovite church broke relations with Constantinople, and 1472, when Ivan married Sophia, belong to different epochs in Russian history. In the first case, Muscovy was beset by internal strife, struggling to establish its autonomy from the Horde. In the second, it had achieved de facto independence from the khans and taken control of their Rus' possessions. Ivan's marriage to Sophia helped create an unprecedented opening to the Christian world outside Muscovy: the matchmaker was the pope himself, and the bride was Uniate. To be sure, Sophia returned to Orthodoxy, and Muscovy never accepted the Union of Florence. But for a Muscovite ruler to marry a Uniate with the support of Rome was a sign of recognition of his new independent status by the political and ecclesiastical elite of Western and Central Europe.

In the early 1490s, the Russian religious elite embraced several notions: that the Muscovite tsars were heirs of the Byzantine emperors, that Moscow was the second Constantinople, and that Muscovy and the Rus' land were successors to the Byzantine Empire. Those ideas were first fully expressed by Metropolitan Zosima of Moscow in 1492. In that year, as Christopher Columbus discovered the New World, the Orthodox believers of Moscow prepared for the world's end. According to the Orthodox calendar, which counted years from the creation of the world, 1492 was in fact the year 7000, which would mark the end of time. The Orthodox faithful in Muscovy believed that 1492 would be the last year of their lives and of humankind in general. They thanked God that they professed the true religion and were about to be saved.

To the surprise of the Muscovite churchmen, the world did not end in 1492. With the world continuing to exist, a new calendar problem emerged for the church of Rus'—how to calculate the ever-changing date of Easter. Metropolitan Zosima rose to the challenge and produced the *Exposition of the Easter Cycle*. For him, as for many other Muscovites, the new calendar and the new Orthodox era began with a change in the structure of the world hierarchy. At its top, the Orthodox empire of Byzantium was now replaced by Muscovy, and the Byzantine emperor was supplanted by the Muscovite tsar. According to Zosima, God had installed Ivan III as "a new Tsar Constantine for the new city of Constantine, sovereign of Moscow and the whole Rus' land and many other lands." Zosima presented Moscow as a new Constantinople, while referring to Constantinople as a new Rome (in some copies, a new Jerusalem).

In the course of the fifteenth and sixteenth centuries, Muscovy was imagined as both a new Jerusalem and a new Rome, but it is the notion of Moscow as the Third Rome that has attracted the most attention from historians, given the metaphor's inspiration of a new model of relations between church and sovereign. Moscow was called a Third Rome in a number of letters dating from the early sixteenth century and attributed to the monk Filofei, who resided in one of the Pskov monasteries on lands recently annexed by Moscow. Among the letters is one addressed to Grand Prince Vasilii, warning him against neglecting or even impairing the interests of the church. According to Filofei, the churches of Rome had fallen because of heresy, while those of Constantinople—the second Rome, to which imperial and spiritual power had migrated after the fall of the first Rome—had been taken over by the Muslims. Moscow was the third Rome, charged with saving the true faith. That idea was presented at the beginning of the letter attributed to Filofei and repeated at its end: "All Christian kingdoms have come together in yours alone: two Romes have fallen, the third stands, and a fourth there will never be; your Christian kingdom will not be replaced by another."

The representation of Moscow as the Third Rome, all but forgotten by the Muscovites during the rule of Ivan the Terrible, was dramatically revived after his death, in the midst of Moscow's efforts to elevate its metropolitanate to patriarchal status. In the summer of 1588, two years after Patriarch Joachim V of Antioch left Moscow, Tsar Fedor's court received an indication that its lobbying of the patriarch had had its intended effect. Smolensk officials reported a meeting with a new visitor from the East, Patriarch Jeremiah II of Constantinople. The tsar sent a court official to greet him and inquire about the decision of the Ecumenical Council on the proposed Moscow patriarchate. The Moscow officials were in for a disappointment, as Patriarch Jeremiah knew nothing about their request and had brought no council decision with him. The sole purpose of Jeremiah's mission, as it turned out, was to collect alms to improve the patriarchate's finances and build a new headquarters and patriarchal church, as the Ottoman Turks in Istanbul, the former Constantinople, had taken over the old ones.

Although the Muscovite authorities arranged for Jeremiah's solemn entrance into Moscow, the welcoming party did not include the metropolitan. The patriarch was not summoned to the tsar's court until eight days had passed. He was brought there mounted on an ass, supposedly a reenactment of Jesus's entry into Jerusalem, but the tsar walked only half the previous seven-foot distance to greet the new guest: either the Muscovites were uncertain that Jeremiah was a true patriarch, or displeased that he had brought no news about their request. The tsar did not invite Jeremiah to dine, asking instead that he meet with the court advisers, who inquired about the situation of the Orthodox Church in the Ottoman Empire. After that, Jeremiah was sent back to his quarters and told to wait.

The patriarch was now a prisoner in all but name. "In the place where they held Jeremiah, they would not let anyone from the local people come to see him, nor would they allow him to go out. Only the monks, if they so desired, would go out with the people of the tsar into the marketplace, and the Muscovites guarded the monks until they returned to their quarters," wrote a member of Jeremiah's party. Whereas Patriarch Joachim had spent less than two months in Moscow, Jeremiah was there for almost a year, from July 1588 until May 1589. He eventually did what the Muscovites wanted, creating a patriarchate and presiding over the consecration of the new patriarch of Moscow.

The consecration of a candidate elected by the local Orthodox council took place in early February 1589. To no one's surprise, it was Metropolitan Iov of Moscow. In May of that year, Tsar Fedor let Jeremiah go with a generous reward, given his original mission of collecting alms. But the price of his release had been the unintended creation of a patriarchate in violation of all existing church ordinances. A few years later, the Eastern patriarchs, impoverished and dependent on the tsar's alms, approved Jeremiah's actions.

Moscow was now the seat of an Orthodox patriarchate—a junior one, to be sure, which yielded precedence to the long-established patriarchates of Constantinople, Alexandria, Antioch, and Jerusalem. In real terms, however, it was the biggest, richest, and most powerful patriarchate in the Orthodox world. Its power came from the tsar, who was its true master, along with his courtiers. The newly installed Patriarch Iov not only had taken no part in the negotiations with Jeremiah but had not even seen him before the consecration. The decree establishing the patriarchate included an explicit reference to Moscow as the Third Rome: "For the old Rome fell through the Apollinarian heresy. The second Rome, which is Constantinople, is held by the grandsons of Hagar—the godless Turks. Pious Tsar!

Your great Rus' tsardom, the third Rome, has surpassed them all in piety, and all pious people have been united as one in your tsardom. And you alone in the firmament are called Christian tsar in the whole universe among all Christians."

In no other document did Jeremiah ever refer to Moscow as the Third Rome. There are strong indications that the decree was prepared by the Muscovite side, and Jeremiah was simply made to sign it. For the first time, a concept that had been developed much earlier in the century was being invoked to promote the goals of the Muscovite church and state. If the monk Filofei had sought to protect the church against secular encroachments, his notion of Moscow as the Third Rome was now being used to enhance the international status of the newly created Moscow Patriarchate and the tsar who ultimately controlled it. Moscow was preparing to assert its primacy in the Orthodox world.

THE KEY FIGURE BEHIND THE CREATION OF THE MOSCOW PATRI-
archate was not Tsar Fedor but his brother-in-law and éminence grise, Boris Godunov. It was Godunov who handled the visits of both Eastern patriarchs to Moscow, Joachim of Antioch in 1586 and Jeremiah of Constantinople in 1588–1589. And Metropolitan Iov of Moscow, who was personally close to Godunov, became the first Muscovite patriarch in 1589. The son of a petty provincial noble, Godunov had risen through the ranks of Ivan the Terrible's *oprichnina* servitors to become one of his closest aides.

Tsar Fedor died at the age of forty in January 1598, leaving his wife childless, the monarchy without heirs, and the country without a dynasty: Fedor's younger half-brother, Prince Dmitrii, had died under suspicious circumstances seven years earlier, in May 1591. On the tsar's death, power passed to Fedor's wife, Irina, and then to her brother, the powerful courtier Boris Godunov. The Rurikid dynasty, on which Ivan the Terrible had based his belief in his German origins, and which was the foundation of the Muscovite mythology that linked Moscow with Kyiv, Constantinople, and Rome, had now become extinct. Godunov's family legend associated him with Tatar servitors, not Kyivan rulers. But thanks to his political astuteness, the transition from one dynasty to what many believed was the beginning of a new one went rather smoothly. Godunov was elected to the tsardom by the Assembly of the Land, a consultative body made up of representatives of various strata of Muscovite society, first called into being by Ivan the Terrible.

On September 1, 1598, New Year's Day by the Muscovite calendar (Russia would switch to January 1 only in the early eighteenth century under Peter I), the Muscovite elite gathered in the Dormition Cathedral of the Kremlin for the installation of the new tsar. Godunov appeared with an entourage of courtiers. One of the boyars carried Monomakh's Cap, another the tsar's scepter, and yet another the golden orb, a sphere surmounted by a cross that was referred to as an "apple" in Muscovite documents of the time. Godunov mounted the throne, and Iov, his loyal patriarch, invested him with the royal insignia. Muscovy was ending the sixteenth century with a brand-new political and ecclesiastical team as well as the prospect of a ruling dynasty. The orderly transition seemed to augur a bright future: with the tsar and the patriarch in office, the leadership of the prospective Orthodox empire was complete.

But the early seventeenth century brought innumerable difficulties for the Muscovite elite. The unexpected death of Boris Godunov in April 1605, in the midst of social turmoil, plunged Muscovy into a long and bloody political crisis, civil war, and international conflict known as the Time of Troubles. It lasted eight long years that saw a succession of rulers on the Muscovite throne. First came the defrocked monk Georgii Otrepiev, who publicly assumed the identity of the deceased youngest son of Ivan the Terrible, Dmitrii. He held the Muscovite throne for less than a year, from June 1605 to May 1606, when he was killed by the supporters of a new tsar, Vasilii Shuisky, who was actually a descendant of the Rurikids. Shuisky was deposed in July 1610 by supporters of Władysław IV, a son of the Polish king Sigismund III, who desired the crown for himself, and whose troops occupied Moscow. The Time of Troubles ended in 1613 with the expulsion of the Poles from Moscow and the election to the throne of Mikhail Romanov, the progenitor of a new dynasty, in the following year.

The Time of Troubles posed new challenges to the Muscovite historical, political, and cultural identity that had taken shape in the previous century and a half, following the end of Mongol rule. On the one hand, the crisis began the process of separating the person of the tsar from the state over which he ruled, laying the foundations for the early modern Russian nation. On the other hand, the patriotic reaction to the Polish invasion that accompanied and exacerbated the crisis closely identified loyalty to the tsar with loyalty to church and fatherland. In official Muscovite discourse of the era, disloyalty to one came to mean disloyalty to all.

If one considers the main ideological arguments used to mobilize Muscovite resistance to the foreign invasion, religion and the idea of defending the Orthodox Church emerge as by far the most important. In a country without a ruling dynasty or a legitimate secular institution to run the state, the church took on particular importance. The office of head of the church emerged from the shadow of the political sovereign, where it had been since the early days of the Tsardom of Muscovy, to claim a central place in the country's symbolic politics. That role was played by Patriarch Hermogen, the third cleric to assume the patriarchal office and an unlikely agent of change. He became patriarch in July 1606, when he was seventy-five years old—ancient by the standards of the time.

In his pastoral letters, Hermogen presented the changing worldview of Muscovite religious and secular elites as they struggled to respond to the challenges of the Time of Troubles. Hermogen refused to treat those who rebelled against the newly installed Tsar Vasilii Shuisky as fully Christian. "I turn to you, former Orthodox Christians of every degree, age, and office," wrote the patriarch,

> but now we do not even know what to call you, for you have turned away from God, conceived hatred for the truth, fallen away from the universal and apostolic Church, turned away from Tsar Vasilii Ivanovich, who was given the wreath by God and anointed with holy oil; you have forgotten the vows of our Orthodox faith, in which we were born, baptized, raised and grew up; you have abandoned your kissing of the cross and your vow to stand to the death for the house of the Most Holy Mother of God and for the Muscovite state and have cleaved to that falsely pretending little tsar of yours.

Hermogen's insistence that a Muscovite patriot and a true Christian must be loyal to the tsar became a staple of Muscovite literature in the first decades of the seventeenth century.

The Time of Troubles came to an end in 1613, when the Assembly of the Land elected the sixteen-year-old Mikhail Romanov to the Muscovite throne. The head of the Romanov clan was the new tsar's father, Fedor, who had competed for the tsar's throne after the death of the last Rurikid tsar, also named Fedor. He lost, and after Boris Godunov's election he was tonsured as a monk and exiled to a northern monastery. As a victim of Godunov, he was later brought back to Moscow and consecrated metropolitan of Rostov under the name Filaret. He was arrested by the Poles in 1610 and spent the next eight years as a prisoner of honor in the Polish-Lithuanian Commonwealth.

Filaret returned to Moscow in 1619, after the signing of a Polish-Muscovite armistice and an exchange of prisoners. By that time, his son Mikhail Romanov had already been tsar of Muscovy for six years. The return of Filaret, who assumed the vacant position of patriarch of Moscow in the following year, created a unique situation in which the tsar was the son of a patriarch. Both had the designation "sovereign" in their respective titles, but it was quite apparent that the imperious patriarch dominated his meek son. The Byzantine model, in which the emperor held sway over the Orthodox patriarch, had been effectively reversed.

The new patriarch was not well disposed to all Orthodox outside the tsardom. During his Polish captivity, Filaret had become convinced that the Orthodox of Ukraine and Belarus were spiritually corrupt, as they were subject to a Catholic monarch and obliged to deal constantly with the non-Orthodox. There was also the grave issue of the church union concluded in the Commonwealth between the Catholic Church and part of the Orthodox Church. The new Uniate Church, created at the Council of Brest in 1596, recognized the supremacy of the pope and accepted Catholic dogma while maintaining its traditional Byzantine rite. Filaret accused the Uniates of "walking two paths" simultaneously and considered not only them but also the Orthodox of the Commonwealth as less than fully Orthodox and Christian, even if they rejected the union.

Under Patriarch Filaret, who was the de facto ruler of Muscovy from 1619 until his death in 1633, the Orthodox Church and the state itself fused into something of a last bastion of "true Orthodoxy." But while questioning the credentials of every Christian outside Muscovy, Filaret was eager to make political alliances with non-Orthodox rulers in order to defeat the hated Polish-Lithuanian Commonwealth and retake the lands lost to it during the Time of Troubles. He died in the midst of another war with the Polish-Lithuanian Commonwealth, which brought new defeats to Muscovy. Orphaned by the death of his domineering father, Mikhail Romanov was now the sole ruler of Muscovy. But the tradition of treating the patriarch as a sovereign and the chronic tension between the secular and spiritual authorities in Muscovy did not disappear overnight. It would not be fully resolved in favor of the tsar for another three decades.

WITH EUROPE EMBROILED IN THE THIRTY YEARS' WAR (1618–1648), which pitted Catholic countries against Protestant ones, Muscovy was eager to make alliances with the Protestant powers against the Catholic Poles, but was constrained by the refusal of its church to treat the rest of the Christian world as fully legitimate. That limitation became embarrassingly apparent in 1644, when the Muscovite elite welcomed Prince Valdemar of Denmark, who had come to marry Tsar Mikhail's daughter, Irina. The wedding was meant to set the seal on the alliance between Muscovy and Denmark, which was long in the making—Valdemar and Irina had been engaged since 1640. But the long-awaited wedding fell through. Under the influence of church hierarchs, the tsar insisted that Valdemar, who had no plans to stay in Muscovy or claim its throne, convert to Orthodoxy before marrying his daughter. The prince refused. The tsar, for his part, would not let him go. Valdemar was detained and allowed to leave the country only after the death of Tsar Mikhail and the coronation of his son, Aleksei Mikhailovich, in 1645.

The disrupted marriage of Irina, who was very close to Aleksei, indicated to the new tsar and his advisers that the Orthodox Church was becoming a political hindrance. Further evidence of this was the failure of Muscovite Orthodox theologians to hold their own against Valdemar's Lutheran preachers on issues of Christian dogma and marriage. But there was a reform movement growing within the church that aspired to raise the educational level of the clergy and eradicate corruption. The Zealots of Piety, as they came to be known, included Archimandrite Nikon, who became patriarch of Moscow in 1652 and, with the tsar's consent, included the word "sovereign" in his title. Nikon initiated an ambitious reform of the church, remodeling it along lines established not long before by the Orthodox metropolitan Peter Mohyla, who had reformed the Kyiv metropolitanate in the Polish-Lithuanian Commonwealth in response to challenges presented by the Protestant Reformation and Catholic reform.

Peter Mohyla, a son of the Moldavian ruler, became the metropolitan of Kyiv in 1633 and worked hard to reform Ukrainian and Belarusian Orthodoxy. He began with the education of the clergy. In 1632, he merged two existing schools for Orthodox youth, establishing a Kyivan college—the first Western-type educational institution in Ukraine, modeled in structure and curriculum on the Jesuit colleges of the era. The Catholic reform, launched by Rome at the Council of Trent (1545–1563), became the inspiration and model for Mohyla's reform of the Orthodox Church of the Commonwealth.

Catholic influences were apparent in the new metropolitan's liturgical innovations and in his Confession of Faith—an Eastern Christian catechism that the Orthodox had lacked. An Orthodox catechism was compiled in the 1640s by a circle of intellectuals working under Mohyla's supervision and approved by the Kyivan church council. In 1643, it was approved by the Eastern patriarchs. The confession that Mohyla and his learned circle composed became an official exposition of the dogmas and articles of the Orthodox faith throughout the Orthodox world, with the notable exception of Muscovy.

The rise of Kyiv as a center of Orthodox learning took place at a time when Muscovy and its church were in almost complete isolation, oblivious to the challenges that faced their fellow Orthodox abroad. But the desire of the young Tsar Aleksei to reform his church changed the attitude of the Muscovite state to Kyiv and its teachings. Nowhere was this more evident than in the sphere of publishing. In 1649, Moscow printers published a *Brief Compendium of Teachings on the Articles of Faith*, based on Peter Mohyla's Orthodox Confession of Faith. Muscovite Orthodoxy was rejoining the rest of the Orthodox world, now defined by the theological teachings of Kyiv.

There was a certain irony in that development. The Muscovites had sought to remedy problems arising from the self-imposed isolation of their church by returning to the basics of their faith as presented in the uncorrupted texts of the Eastern church fathers. But that required checking the old Muscovite translations of the Greek texts and, if necessary, producing revised ones. Since there were no qualified translators in Moscow, they were summoned from Kyiv, bringing along Kyiv's understanding of the Greek texts and of Orthodox Christianity in general. The conflict between the Kyivan vision of church reform and the traditionalist Muscovite view would bring about a profound schism (*Raskol*) in the Muscovite church and society.

The turn of the Muscovite clerics toward Kyiv, which seemed almost an accidental detour on their way to the Orthodox East, coincided with the emergence of a new force in Ukraine that was interested in close ties with Muscovy, not only in religion but also in politics. That force was Cossackdom and the state that it created—the Hetmanate. In the spring of 1648, Ukraine was shaken by a new Cossack uprising, the seventh since the end of the sixteenth century. The Cossacks, who had begun as trappers and brigands in the fifteenth century, were now emerging as a major fighting force and demanding special rights and privileges from the Commonwealth government. By 1648, they wanted a polity of their own.

In December 1648, the leader of the uprising, the veteran Cossack officer Bohdan Khmelnytsky, solemnly entered the city of Kyiv. He was hailed by the professors and students of the Kyivan College as the Moses of the Rus' people and their liberator from the Polish yoke. The Orthodox metropolitan of Kyiv also welcomed Khmelnytsky. More important, the metropolitan was accompanied by no less a hierarch than Patriarch Paisios of Jerusalem. The patriarch had been on his way to Moscow, where he had intended to ask the tsar for alms, when he was intercepted by the rebel Cossacks and brought to Kyiv on Khmelnytsky's orders in anticipation of his grand entrance into the ancient capital of the Rus' princes and Rus' Orthodoxy.

Paisios did not mind. He referred to Khmelnytsky as an illustrious *princeps* (prince), thereby granting his ecclesiastical blessing to the new ruler, and engaged him in a discussion about creating a world alliance of Orthodox powers, starting with Muscovy and Ukraine. Khmelnytsky needed little encouragement. When he wrote his first letter to the Muscovite tsar in June 1648, he presented the Cossack revolt as a struggle against the oppression of the "ancient Greek faith" and stated: "We would wish for ourselves such an autocratic ruler in our land as Your Tsarist Majesty, the

Orthodox Christian Tsar." Khmelnytsky wanted direct Muscovite military intervention in support of the Cossacks. He asked Patriarch Paisios, who was leaving Kyiv for Moscow, to intervene with the tsar on his behalf. Paisios, wishing to promote a new Orthodox alliance, obliged. He asked the tsar to "take the Cossacks under his high hand" and provide them with military assistance, all in the name of the Orthodox religion.

Tsar Aleksei Mikhailovich was cautious. It was explained to the confessionally minded patriarch that the tsar could not do as Khmelnytsky requested because, as a Christian ruler, he was bound by the peace treaty concluded with the Commonwealth in 1634. He could take the Cossacks under his protection only if they secured their own liberation. Otherwise, he could allow them to resettle to Muscovy if they were persecuted by the Poles because of their Orthodox faith. The tsar seemed to be caught in a religious dilemma—whether to violate the oath he had given to a fellow Christian—but not Orthodox—ruler, or to protect his fellow Orthodox Christians. For the next four years, he would stay out of the Ukrainian conflict. Muscovy was not prepared to make war on a country that had defeated it more than once in recent decades and had even managed to place a garrison in Moscow itself.

Muscovy began preparing for war with the Commonwealth in the spring of 1651, when the tsar realized that the Commonwealth was too weak to effectively suppress the Cossack uprising. It was then that Muscovite diplomats began preparing the ground for a breach with the Commonwealth, casting themselves as protectors of the Polish king's Orthodox subjects. They claimed that Khmelnytsky had risen in protest against religious persecution, as the Poles had forced the Cossacks to "accept their Roman faith, sealed godly churches, and imposed the Union on the Orthodox churches, and oppressed them in every way." The final decision to go to war with the king was made in the Assembly of the Land, which met in Moscow in a number of sessions between June and October 1653. The delegates concluded that the tsar was free to take the Cossacks and their lands under his high hand (protection) for the sake of "the Orthodox Christian Faith and the holy Churches of God."

An embassy was sent to Khmelnytsky to break the news: Muscovy was entering the war on the side of the Cossacks. The embassy's path through Ukrainian territory was marked by religious processions and church services celebrating the newfound unity of the two Orthodox peoples. At a Cossack officers' council convened by Khmelnytsky in the town of Pereiaslav southeast of Kyiv, the hetman presented three alternatives: go back under the rule of the Catholic king; recognize the suzerainty of the Muslim sultan, who ruled over the Crimea and was interested in extending his authority northward; or accept the protectorate of the Orthodox tsar. He called on his officers to accept protection from a ruler "of the same worship of the Greek rite, of the same faith." The gathering supported the hetman, shouting that they wanted the "eastern Orthodox tsar."

The Orthodox alliance had been born. But whereas the wars of religion in Western and Central Europe had ended with the conclusion of the Thirty Years' War in 1648, those between Orthodox and Catholics in Eastern Europe were expanding in scope. The Muscovites and the Cossacks disagreed on important elements of their alliance at the Pereiaslav negotiations, including the obligations of the tsar and the duties of his new subjects. There was a minor crisis when the Muscovite envoys refused to swear an oath on behalf of the tsar to ratify the conditions, but it was soon resolved, as Khmelnytsky did not want to jeopardize the alliance. The differences in the two parties' geopolitical agendas and political culture (the Cossacks were accustomed to Polish officials swearing an oath on behalf of the king, who was then obliged to keep his end of the bargain) were papered over by the rhetoric of Orthodox brotherhood.

THE METAPHOR OF THE THIRD ROME, WHICH FIRST ENTERED official Muscovite discourse with the elevation of the metropolitanate of Moscow to a patriarchate, was elastic enough to accommodate major changes in Muscovites' thinking about themselves and the world during the first half of the seventeenth century. At its core was the notion of the tsar's status as the only remaining Orthodox emperor after the fall of Byzantium. That trope could be used to declare Muscovy a fortress under siege, as the monk Filofei did in the early sixteenth century, or to insist on the special status or even primacy of the Muscovite church over any other Orthodox church. "The only pious tsar under the sun was in Constantinople," said a learned Muscovite monk to Patriarch Paisios in 1650, " . . . and now, in place of that tsar, we have a pious sovereign tsar in Moscow, the only pious tsar under the sun." A broader audience was reminded of Moscow's special role in the Orthodox world by the *Kormchaia kniga* of 1653 (a collection of ecclesiastical and civil laws), which included a reference to the Third Rome in Patriarch Jeremiah's address to the tsar on the creation of the Moscow patriarchate.

By the mid-seventeenth century, Muscovy had overcome the shock of the Time of Troubles. It returned to the international arena with new confidence in its mission in the Orthodox world. The "rehabilitation" of Orthodox Ukrainians and Belarusians as legitimate Orthodox faithful for whose sake Muscovy was making war on Poland-Lithuania indicated a major change in the country's dealings with the outside world. That change was in keeping with the demands of the new age of religious wars and confessionalization of international politics brought on by the Protestant Reformation and Catholic Reform. Moscow as the Third Rome was switching from a defensive to an offensive strategy, of which there would be a great deal more in the decades and centuries to come.

3

THE IMPERIAL NATION

On January 8, 1654, when the tsarist envoy Vasilii Buturlin accepted a loyalty oath from the Ukrainian hetman Bohdan Khmelnytsky and his officers in the city of Pereiaslav, he took a major step toward what Russian imperial historians would call the "reunification of Rus'" and their Soviet successors rendered as the "reunification of Ukraine and Russia." But the act later hailed as a "reunification" was accompanied by the signing of a document that stressed not unity but diversity. That day Bohdan Khmelnytsky wrote to the tsar, addressing him not as sovereign of all Rus', as was customary at the time, but as sovereign of Great and Little Rus'. This revision was probably discussed with Buturlin, as the tsar soon changed "all Rus'" to "Great and Little Rus'" in his official title.

These names had originated in the early fourteenth century, when the Metropolitanate of All Rus' was divided in the wake of the Mongol invasion and a new Metropolitanate of Little Rus' was established in the Ukrainian town of Halych. The "Great" and "Little" Rus' terminology was brought back to Eastern Europe in the late sixteenth century with the help of Middle Eastern hierarchs who traveled through the Rus' lands of the Commonwealth in search of alms from the tsar. Under the new circumstances, "Little Rus'" meant the Orthodox lands administered from Kyiv, while "Great Rus'" referred to the Muscovite realm. The religious terminology was transferred to the political realm at the time of the Pereiaslav Agreement.

White Rus' (Belarus) was added to the tsar's title in 1655. These changes marked a departure from the old religious terminology, reflecting the new military and political situation in the region. The name Little Rus', earlier applied to the territory of the Kyiv Metropolitanate, was now applied to Ukraine, or the Rus' lands of the Kingdom of Poland. They were either under the control of the Cossacks or claimed by them, and they enjoyed special rights and privileges granted by the tsar to the Cossack hetman. Those rights and privileges did not apply to White Rus', which was part of the Grand Duchy of Lithuania in the Polish-Lithuanian Commonwealth. When a successful Muscovite military campaign brought White Rus' under the rule of the tsar, no special rights were granted to its inhabitants. Nor did the Orthodox connection help the Belarusians secure such rights: the Orthodox parishes of White Rus' came under the jurisdiction of Moscow, while those of Ukraine remained subordinate to Kyiv.

Just as the tsarist scribes insisted on differentiating not only Great and Little Rus' but also White Rus', so the intellectuals of the latter two realms maintained that the identities of Little and White Rus' were separate from that of Great Rus'. Educated in the same Kyivan College under Metropolitan Peter Mohyla, those intellectuals considered themselves part of a distinct Rus' community, basing their view not only on dynastic and religious considerations but also on the new idea of nationality. In their minds, they constituted one Rus' nation. Curiously enough, from today's point of view, they were reluctant to extend membership in the nation that they called "Rossian" (in present-day English, "Russian") to the inhabitants of Great Rus'.

On July 5, 1656, one of the best-known alumni of the Kyivan College, Simeon of Polatsk, and his students welcomed a distinguished guest, Tsar and Grand Prince Aleksei Mikhailovich of Muscovy, to their city in northern Belarus. They greeted him as a true Eastern or Orthodox ruler and as the legitimate master of Rus' lands inherited from Prince Volodymyr of

Kyiv, but not as a member of the same nation. "Live, long-awaited solace of the nation / Granted to the persecuted Russian clan," declaimed one of the students, referring to the Rus' population of the former Commonwealth. Another student explained that his "Russia" consisted of two parts: "All Russia, White and Little, kisses [the tsar] / Having become enlightened with the light of faith under you." For the Polatsk students, Aleksei Mikhailovich was an Eastern or Orthodox tsar who had come to their "Russia" from abroad, a place called the "northern country."

Aleksei Mikhailovich and his entourage did not seem to mind that the citizens of Polatsk did not treat them as conationals. Ethnicity did not yet have the political significance that it would acquire in the age of national states. Muscovite thinking was monarchic, patrimonial, and increasingly confessional, but the Muscovite elites rarely thought of themselves in national terms, and to the extent that they did so, they did not include the Rus' population of the Commonwealth in their nation. The Ruthenian (Ukrainian and Belarusian) elites, by contrast, did think in national terms, but at this time they did not imagine themselves as part of the Muscovite nation.

IT TOOK BOTH GROUPS SOME TIME TO ADJUST THEIR THINKING TO the new political reality and come to think of their lands and peoples not only as a realm ruled by the same sovereign, but also as one nation. Nothing promoted that process more than the fierce struggle for the Ukrainian and Belarusian lands that pitted Muscovy against its two regional rivals, the Polish-Lithuanian Commonwealth and the Ottoman Empire.

Muscovy found it difficult to retain the Ukrainian and Belarusian lands captured in 1654–1655 in their entirety. According to the Truce of Andrusovo, signed in 1667 in a village near Smolensk after three years of negotiations, Muscovy lost eastern Belarus to the Polish-Lithuanian Commonwealth. Chernihiv in northeastern Ukraine remained under Muscovite control, but indirectly—it was part of the Cossack Hetmanate, which accepted the suzerainty of the tsar. Muscovite suggestions that the Cossacks subordinate Chernihiv directly to them fell on deaf ears, as the Cossacks were now in charge of Ukraine on the left or eastern bank of the Dnieper River. The rest of Ukraine, including most of the Kyiv region, Volhynia,

Podolia, and Galicia—all parts of what the Kyivans defined in political and ecclesiastical terms as Little Rus'—remained under Commonwealth rule.

Kyiv, the old capital of the Rus' princes and the center of Rossia/Russia as imagined by Simeon Polotsky and his Kyivan professors and classmates, found itself in a precarious position. The city was located on the Right Bank of the Dnieper, and so the tsar and his advisers were prepared to give it up to ensure peace with Warsaw. According to the Truce of Andrusovo, Kyiv was to be handed over to the Poles two years after the signing. That never happened, despite the difficulty of defending the Kyivan "bridgehead" on the other side of the river. The handover was prevented, in part, by the lobbying efforts of the city's Orthodox clergy, which wanted to maintain the tsar's military protection against Kyiv's enemies at all costs.

In 1674, faced with a possible Ottoman attack on the city, the Kyivan intellectuals recapitulated their arguments in favor of the city's remaining under the tsar in a historical text titled *Synopsis, or brief compendium of various chronicles about the origin of the Slavo-Rossian nation and the first princes of the divinely protected city of Kyiv and the life of the holy, pious grand prince of Kyiv and all Russia, the first autocrat Volodymyr, and about inheritors of his virtuous Rus' domain, even unto our illustrious and virtuous sovereign, Tsar and Grand Prince Aleksei Mikhailovich, autocrat of all Great, Little, and White Russia.*

The book was issued by the printshop of the Kyivan Cave Monastery and is usually attributed to the pen of Inokentii Gizel, the abbot—or, to give him his traditional Orthodox title, archimandrite—of the monastery. It represents a continuation of Kyivan chronicle writing and is preoccupied with questions of Kyivan history, the origins of the Rus' church, and issues of nationhood. The *Synopsis* was received with great interest by readers in Kyiv and beyond. New editions were published in 1678 and 1680. Not surprisingly, the *Synopsis* presented a highly Kyiv-centric vision of Rus' and its history. At its core was the presentation of Moscow as a second Kyiv—the city that had been crucial to the construction of the paradigm of Moscow as the Third Rome but remained in Constantinople's shadow until the publication of the *Synopsis*. The Kyivan monks were now insisting on their city's importance, stressing its centrality to Rus' and Muscovite history.

Kyiv emerges from the pages of the *Synopsis* as the birthplace of the Russian dynasty, state, and church. No less important to the author of the

Synopsis was the status of Kyiv as the birthplace of the "Rossian" nation. The section on the origins of Kyiv was titled "On the Most Renowned City of Kyiv, Supreme and Principal for the Whole Rossian Nation." What was that nation? In the *Synopsis*, it was counted as one of the Slavic nations and identified as "Slavo-Rossian." The Slavo-Rossian nation included those who were living in the territories of the medieval Kyivan state. This was a major departure from the established canon of Ukrainian chronicle writing, which had followed Polish historiography in distinguishing clearly between the two nations (*narody*) of Muscovy and Rus'.

The *Synopsis* became the first textbook of Russian history to be used in the eighteenth-century Russian Empire, and by the early nineteenth century sixteen reprints or new editions had appeared. As the numerous editions and reprints of the *Synopsis* educated the Muscovite public in the basics of its history, they prompted the Muscovites to think about themselves as a nation. That nation, however, was anything but purely Muscovite, as the history and nation of Muscovy described in the book were unimaginable without Kyiv and the lands then known as Little and White Rus'. The author(s) of the *Synopsis* encouraged readers to consider extending the tsar's possessions not primarily as a dynastic realm or an Orthodox state but as a nation. This was a revolutionary idea.

Although the new concept of a Russian nation historically centered in Kyiv, and uniting the Muscovite subjects of the tsar with those who, until recently, had been subjects of the Commonwealth, was widely publicized by the *Synopsis*, the acceptance of that model was by no means a given. In Muscovy, that concept had to compete with the alternative vision of Russia advanced by the Old Believers—traditionalists who rejected the Kyivan innovations in the Muscovite Orthodox Church and rebelled against the tsar, who supported the innovations.

One of the leaders of the schism, Archpriest Avvakum, called on the tsar to maintain and strengthen his traditional Rus' identity and use his native language: "After all, you are a Russian, not a Greek. Speak your native language; do not demean it in church, in your home, or in anything you say. God loves us no less than he loves the Greeks." Avvakum protested even more strongly against elements of Catholic practice brought to Muscovy by Kyivan intellectuals such as Simeon of Polatsk, who settled in Moscow in 1664 and became one of Avvakum's foremost opponents. "Oh, poor Rus', why did you desire Latin customs and practices but come to despise and reject your true Christian law?" wrote Avvakum in one of his missives.

If Avvakum's Russia rejected the tsar's authority, that of Simeon of Polatsk embraced it. Along with religious innovations and new national thinking, the Kyivans brought to Moscow elements of Western secular culture, embodied in education, literature, theater, and visual representation. There would be no stronger supporter of these new elements of Russian identity than Peter I, the tsar known in Russian and Western historiography as Peter the Great.

ON JUNE 27, 1709, ON A FIELD NEAR THE CITY OF POLTAVA IN Cossack Ukraine, a Swedish army of 24,000, supported by close to 6,000 Cossacks and Polish cavalrymen, confronted a Russian army of 52,000 supported by more than 20,000 Cossacks and Kalmyk horsemen. The Russians were led into battle by the energetic Tsar Pëtr (Peter) Alekseevich, who became the sole ruler of Muscovy in 1696 after outliving his half-brother and co-ruler Ivan V, while the Swedes were under the command of their young but already battle-hardened King Charles XII. The outcome of the battle would decide the fate of the Great Northern War (1700–1721), in which Sweden and Russia fought each other as members of ever-shifting alliances for access to and supremacy over the Baltic region. It would also define the future of Russia as a nation and as an empire.

In 1700, the first year of the war, Charles confronted a Muscovite army of close to 40,000 with a Swedish corps numbering barely more than 10,000 troops near the town of Narva. He emerged victorious, losing fewer than 1,000 men to Muscovy's 9,000 and taking more than 20,000 prisoners. In the summer of 1708, after defeating his enemies in Central Europe, Charles turned eastward once again. He began his march from Saxony to Muscovy, but with winter fast approaching, and supplies running out even faster, he turned south toward Ukraine, where he hoped to find plenty of supplies as well as winter quarters. Both were promised him by Hetman Ivan Mazepa, until then a loyal ally of the tsar, who had joined Charles and his staff in October 1708 because of his dissatisfaction with Peter's treatment of Cossack Ukraine. The rest of the Cossack army was supposed to follow him in a matter of weeks, if not days. But Peter sent troops to

Ukraine, captured the Hetmanate's capital of Baturyn, massacred its residents, and replaced Mazepa with a hetman loyal to himself.

Throughout the winter of 1708 and the spring of 1709, Charles and Peter and the two Ukrainian hetmans—the pro-Swedish Ivan Mazepa and the pro-Muscovite Ivan Skoropadsky—engaged in a war of manifestos intended to win over the Cossack army and the Ukrainian population at large. The war of manifestos revealed profound differences between the Russian and Ukrainian sides in definitions of values and presentation of goals. Tsar Peter presented Mazepa's action as a vassal's betrayal of his sovereign. Mazepa responded to the accusations of betrayal by pleading loyalty not to the tsar but to his homeland. As Mazepa defined it, the political conflict was a battle not between a suzerain and a vassal but between two nations. "Muscovy, that is, the Great Russian nation, has always been hateful to our Little Russian nation; in its malicious intentions it has long resolved to drive our nation to perdition," wrote Mazepa. Another object of Mazepa's loyalty was the "Little Russian fatherland." Peter and his scribes never referred to Muscovy in such terms. It looked as if only the Little Russians had a nation and a fatherland, while the tsar and his people, including those whom Mazepa called the "Great Russian nation," had none. That was about to change.

The change came with the Russian victory at Poltava in June 1709. This time the Russians had more than numbers in their favor. In the years preceding the showdown with Charles, Peter had built a much more professional army. It was well trained and fresh. The Swedes, for their part, were exhausted by the unusually cold winter they had spent in Ukraine, constantly harassed by pro-Muscovite Cossacks and peasants. Besides, Charles XII had been wounded during a reconnaissance mission a few days earlier and could not lead his regiments into battle. With a disorganized leadership, the Swedes lost their way and, eventually, the battle as well. Charles and Mazepa fled to the Ottoman dependency of Moldavia in the aftermath of the battle.

Peter would celebrate the Poltava victory more than once and devise elaborate commemoration ceremonies for those events. One of the first formal celebrations took place in Kyiv on July 24, 1709. There, in the ancient St. Sophia Cathedral, Peter was welcomed with a sermon delivered by the prefect of the Kyivan College, Teofan Prokopovych. Almost fifty years had passed since Simeon of Polatsk's address to Tsar Aleksei in Polatsk. The message delivered in 1709 by another alumnus of the Kyivan College, Prokopovych, to Aleksei's son Peter also included references to Russia and the Russian nation, but their meaning was much broader than Simeon's. Prokopovych's "Russia" referred to the tsar's entire realm, "starting from our Dnieper River to the shores of the Euxine [Sea] in the south, eastward from there to the Caspian or Khvalinian Sea, even to the borders of the Persian kingdom, and from there to the farthest reaches of the Sino-Chinese Kingdom . . . and to the shores of the Arctic Ocean."

Referring to the monarchy, state, and nation (*narod*), Prokopovych called all of them "Russian," an "all-national" (*obshchenarodnoe*) name. He also spoke of "all-Russian" joy on the occasion of the Poltava victory. For Prokopovych, Russia was also a fatherland no longer limited to the Little Russian fatherland of Mazepa and of Peter's pre-Poltava manifestos. More importantly, Prokopovych called Peter the father of that new fatherland. He had used the same appellation for Mazepa (father of the Little Russian fatherland) a few years earlier. According to Prokopovych's sermon, Peter, the "Russian Samson" (not Simeon's distant "Eastern Tsar"), had saved the Russian fatherland from mortal danger and now deserved gratitude for his achievement.

Peter doubtless appreciated what he heard. A few years later, he would invite Prokopovych to join him on a military campaign. By 1717, Prokopovych was already in St. Petersburg, delivering sermons to the tsar and becoming one of his main ideologues and promoters of Westernization. His influence at court eclipsed that of the other former Uniate adviser to the tsar, Simeon of Polatsk. Peter was a fast learner, and many of Prokopovych's concepts and ideas were not entirely unfamiliar to him. Peter's letters and decrees show an interesting transformation of his understanding of the term "fatherland" (*otechestvo*), which changed its meaning in the course of the first decades of the eighteenth century from the tsar's patrimony to a *patria* common to all Muscovites.

In 1721, on the occasion of the Russian victory in the Great Northern War, the Senate and the Synod—consultative bodies created by Peter himself—bestowed on him the title of "All-Russian Emperor" and the appellations "the Great" and "Father of the Fatherland." The "Tsar of All Russia" was now the "All-Russian Emperor." The two other appellations, "Great" and

"Father of the Fatherland," were officially justified as having been merited by the tsar's achievements. According to the document signed by the senators, "Your Majesty's labors for the advancement of our fatherland and your subject all-Russian people are known to the whole world." Peter responded with references to the nation and the common good. He declared: "One must labor for the general welfare and prosperity that God sets before our eyes, both internal and external, which will ease the people's lot."

Peter and his aides had clearly mastered the national discourse, with its emphasis on the fatherland, the nation, and the common good. Teofan Prokopovych, who was the first to introduce some of those notions to Russian officialdom, was not only present at the ceremonial conferral of the new titles on Peter, but also read out the text of the Nystad peace treaty with Sweden and delivered a sermon on that occasion. Another Kyivan cleric, Metropolitan Stefan Yavorsky, the interim head of the Moscow patriarchate, served the liturgy afterward. The Kyivans had successfully imparted their Western ideas to Peter and his court.

PETER DIED UNEXPECTEDLY IN 1725, HAVING ENDED THE LONG Northern War victoriously but scarcely begun the formation of the new imperial state and its nation-minded political elite. The court's almost immediate reaction was to undo some of his most drastic reforms. In 1728, the advisers to Peter's grandson, Peter II, decided to move the capital of the realm from St. Petersburg, the embodiment of Peter's Western aspirations, where he had established it in 1712, back to Moscow. Around the same time, the office of hetman was restored in Ukraine. These were indications that the Russian elite wanted to go back to pre-Petrine times. But there was no turning back, especially when it came to Russia's Western orientation. After the death of Peter's grandson, Peter II, in 1730, with no male heir in sight, the courtiers placed their bets on Duchess Anna Ioannovna of Courland, a daughter of Peter I's elder brother, Ivan. She was invited by the Supreme Privy Council, a consultative body to the tsars that was now in the business of choosing a new ruler, to assume the throne, but only on certain conditions.

Anna disappointed those who thought they could dictate conditions to the tsars. The authoritarian nature of the office was soon restored, as was the status of St. Petersburg as the imperial capital and the ruler's fascination with European political and cultural models. In Russian historical memory, Anna's ten-year rule (1730–1740) has been remembered as one dominated by foreign advisers, in particular Ernst Johann von Biren (Biron), who had been Anna's lover and court favorite since her time in Courland. Legends about Biron and crimes committed by him and his family survived long after the end of Anna's rule.

Anna's rule produced a widespread sense of resentment and anti-Western feeling among the imperial elites. With Anna's death and the ascension to the Russian throne of Peter I's daughter Elizabeth in 1741, the anti-Western attitude became a sea-change. Elizabeth was regarded and fashioned herself as a quintessentially Russian princess, and it was the "faithful sons of Russia," the guards officers, who brought her to power as a true Russian princess. A clear indication of the change was the simple fact that while Elizabeth, like Anna, remained officially unmarried, her favorite and morganatic husband was not a "German" but a "Russian." The son of a Ukrainian Cossack and, in the appellation of the time, a Little Russian, Oleksii Rozum made his way to St. Petersburg as a talented singer and became Elizabeth's favorite courtier before her ascension to the throne. Once she took the throne, the former Cossack became a count, and later field marshal under the name Aleksei Razumovsky. Having little interest in affairs of state, Razumovsky, unlike Biron, kept a low profile: court regulars referred to him as the "night emperor."

The rule of Elizabeth also witnessed a backlash against foreigners in the Russian service. What had begun as a trickle under Tsar Aleksei Mikhailovich became a flood during the rule of his son, Peter I, and continued under his successors. Resentment and distrust of foreigners in government were accompanied by an unprecedented growth of Russian national assertiveness. It was during Elizabeth's rule that key discussions took place about the empire's history and literary language—two major elements of all nation-building projects in early modern Europe. Peter's all-Russian empire was about to acquire an all-Russian nation, all-Russian history, and all-Russian language—all during the age of Elizabeth.

"Origines gentis et nominis Russorum," or "The Origins of the Russian People and Name," was the title of a talk given by Gerhard Friedrich Müller at a meeting of the St. Petersburg Academy of Sciences on August

23, 1749. Müller was an ethnic German who came to St. Petersburg in 1725, the year in which Tsar Peter I had founded the Imperial Academy of Sciences as a research and teaching institution. The presentation did not go well. Müller's research pointed to the Scandinavian origins of the Rus' name and dynasty. These conclusions would have been welcomed by many Muscovite rulers of previous centuries, including Ivan the Terrible, who traced his origins through the Rurikids to Emperor Augustus and considered himself a German. But in 1747, Müller's arguments were found not only unpatriotic but also damaging to Russia's prestige. The academy canceled his scheduled longer presentation and appointed a commission to look into his research. Müller's address set off the first academic debate in Russian historiography, and the outcome influenced its development for decades, if not centuries, to come.

Patriotic fever was running high in St. Petersburg in the wake of another Russian war with Sweden (1741–1743). But the academy's negative reaction to Müller's conclusions was more than a reflection of a short-lived patriotic upswing. Imperial officials had been greatly concerned about patriotism in the academy since the beginning of Elizabeth's rule. In the early 1740s, the academy was hit by defections—scholars, most of them German, were leaving the Russian service and going to Europe to publish research conducted in the Russian Empire. This was a blow to Russia's prestige, to say nothing of its academic potential. In 1744, the authorities posted guards in the academy's buildings, restricting access to its library, archives, and research materials. Foreigners were no longer to be trusted.

Two years later, the imperial court intervened in the affairs of the academy by appointing a new president. He was Kirill Razumovsky (Kyrylo Rozumovsky), the younger brother of the empress's favorite, Aleksei Razumovsky. A recent graduate of the University of Göttingen, he was only eighteen at the time of the appointment. His age seemed less important than his closeness to Elizabeth and the fact that he was the first "Russian" president of the academy, which had been chaired, controlled, and run largely by foreigners—four previous presidents had come from abroad.

It fell to Razumovsky and his close adviser Grigorii Teplov, a former disciple of Prokopovych and an adjunct at the academy, to deal with the "historiography crisis." They appointed a commission to investigate and debate Müller's findings. The debates in the academic commission took up twenty-nine meetings between the fall of 1749 and the spring of 1750. Müller's main opponent in the historiographic debates was an ethnic Russian, Mikhail Lomonosov. The son of a fisherman from Russia's north, Lomonosov was known largely for his accomplishments as a chemist. But the new age of national mobilization called for universality, and he branched out of the sciences into history and linguistics, becoming an amateurish but also forceful and influential supporter of the nativist approach to both. Lomonosov argued that Müller's work glorified "the Scandinavians or Swedes," while "doing almost nothing to illuminate our history." Kirill Razumovsky took Lomonosov's side in the historiographic debate on the origins of Rus'. The print run of Müller's dissertation on that subject was destroyed.

For Lomonosov, the main inspiration in his debates with Müller was the outdated and often inaccurate Kyivan *Synopsis* of 1674. But it was the ideas of the book rather than the facts that mattered most. This book on the origins of the Rus' nation had finally found not only publishers but also readers in Russia who appreciated its focus on the origins of the nation, as opposed to the state and dynasty. Lomonosov wanted the academy to adopt the *Synopsis* as its standard history textbook. In accepting its historical explanation of the origins of the Rus' people, Lomonosov embraced a historical myth that stressed the unity of the Great and Little Russian heirs to the medieval Kyiv state, separating them from the European West.

THE NEW ALL-RUSSIAN NATION NEEDED NOT ONLY A COMMON past but also a common language. The reforms of Peter I had opened Russia to direct Western influence, which manifested itself in the linguistic sphere in borrowings from Western languages (predominantly German). Another, less obvious, import from the West was the practice of basing the literary language on the vernacular. Until then it had been based largely on Church Slavonic, a language created by medieval Christian proselytizers to convert the Slavs and later used as the language of liturgy and belles lettres in the Orthodox Slavic lands, including Muscovy and the Ukrainian and Belarusian territories of the Polish-Lithuanian Commonwealth. It was a language that united Great, Little, and White Russia but belonged to the past, not to the future. The state bureaucracy created by Peter required a new secularized language to run the state. The chancery language of the Muscovite bureaucracy, also based largely on Church Slavonic, was not suited to that purpose. Thus, Peter introduced a simplified ("civil") script and often encouraged his subordinates and the translators of Western works to write as simply as possible, avoiding the high style of Church Slavonic.

It was only the upsurge of Russian patriotism in the era of Empress Elizabeth that abruptly halted the decline of Church Slavonic, which all of a sudden turned from a symbol of religious traditionalism and backwardness into a bulwark of national identity and a token of true Russianness. Like the controversy about the history of Rus', the debate on the future of the language began within the walls of the Academy of Sciences. It pitted two major Russian literary figures, the poets and playwrights Vasilii Trediakovsky and Aleksandr Sumarokov, against each other, with Mikhail Lomonosov as their judge. Trediakovsky, who had originally favored the trend toward modernization and vernacularization of the written Russian language, changed his mind during the rule of Elizabeth, asking: "Why should we voluntarily suffer the poverty and limitations of French when we have the multifarious richness and breadth of Slavo-Rossian?" Sumarokov, however, remained critical of the Church Slavonic—in fact, Kyivan—legacy in Russian literature. With regard to Prokopovych, he wrote: "The sage Teofan, whom nature / Endowed with the beauty of the Slavic people / As regards eloquence / Produced nothing decent in verse."

In the fall of 1748, Sumarokov submitted his drama *Hamlet* to the academy for prepublication review. Trediakovsky, who was a professor in the academy, cited stylistic flaws. "Unevenness of style is apparent throughout, that is, sometimes surpassing theatricality in Slavonic, elsewhere descending beneath tragedy into coarse marketplace jargon," wrote Trediakovsky. The review triggered open conflict between Sumarokov and Trediakovsky. At stake were their places at the top of the emerging Russian literary scene and the future of the Russian language in which new works would be written. Trediakovsky defended the high style rooted in Church Slavonic, while Sumarokov wanted the language to be as close to the Great Russian vernacular as possible.

A compromise position on the future of the Russian language was taken by Mikhail Lomonosov. He advocated the continuing use of Slavonic as a basis for the development of literary Russian. Like Trediakovsky, he sought the roots of Russian in Kyivan Rus' and hailed it as a rich, beautiful, and powerful language. Although Lomonosov defended Slavonic and the linguistic tradition associated with it, he also tried to accommodate the new Western-inspired trend toward the vernacular. He managed to reconcile the two approaches by developing a theory of three literary styles that assigned a different literary language to each: the high style, to be used for the composition of epics, odes, and poems, was supposed to employ the vocabulary common to Church Slavonic and literary Russian; the intermediate style, to be used in dramatic works, was to rely on the vernacular but avoid colloquialisms; and the third, lower style, which admitted the language of townsfolk and peasants, was reserved for comedy.

In the introduction to his Slavonic grammar of 1757, Lomonosov wrote that Russian had "the majesty of Spanish, the vivacity of French, the firmness of German, the delicacy of Italian, and the richness and concise imagery of Greek and Latin." This formula was hardly original: Lomonosov's praise of Russian was suspiciously close to the encomium to English in Richard Carew's *Epistle on the Excellencies of the English Tongue* (1605). Unlike Carew, however, Lomonosov was praising a language that was struggling to meet the challenges of the modern world, its grammar and vocabulary still underdeveloped. Whence, then, his optimism about the prospects for Russian? The answer is apparent from his comment on the history of German: "The German language remained poor, simple, and weak as long as Latin was the language of religious services. But once the German people began to read sacred books and hear the liturgy in their own language, its richness multiplied, and skillful writers appeared." The Russian language had avoided the tortuous development of German, one may infer, thanks to its close association with Church Slavonic, which had saved it from subordination to a foreign tongue and made it great.

The linguistic discussions of the mid-eighteenth century were directly related to the question of which linguistic tradition—the Great or the Little Russian, or, in present-day terms, Russian or Ukrainian—should prevail in imperial Russian culture. Thus Sumarokov accused Trediakovsky of spelling his surname in the Little Russian manner, not "Tred'iakovskoi" but "Tred'iakovskii." He claimed that Trediakovsky was giving "the name of his lineage a Little Russian ending." Another significant feature of the Russo-Ukrainian cultural encounter was the discussion on the correct pronunciation of the letter "г." The Church Slavonic pronunciation was closer to the Ukrainian /h/, while the Russian pronunciation favored the phoneme /g/. Lomonosov devoted a poem to the subject, trying to teach his reader which words should be pronounced with a /g/ and which with an /h/.

Like Lomonosov's other compromises, this one proved temporary in effect. The development of Great Russian syntax, vocabulary, and phonetics was slowly but surely making the Russian literary language a less hospitable home for Little Russians than it had been at the beginning of the eighteenth century. To be sure, such Ukrainians in the imperial service as Danylo Samoilovych, who advocated the creation of a Russian medical vocabulary, or Hryhorii Poletyka, who compiled a comparative dictionary of Russian, as well as other alumni of the Kyivan Academy, had no difficulty in mastering the new Russian literary language, but in doing so they had to abandon their own accustomed speech, thereby undermining the hitherto peaceful coexistence of the two linguistic traditions.

By the mid-eighteenth century, the Kyiv intellectuals had come a long way from the time when Simeon of Polatsk first greeted Tsar Aleksei in his city with references to the "Russian nation" being liberated by the "Eastern Tsar." In the course of a century, they had managed to instill elements of Western, often national or proto-national discourse into the official language and, eventually, into the thinking of the Muscovite elites. They also helped create a common "all-Russian" historical narrative and contributed to the formation of the "all-Russian" imperial language. They did so just as Muscovy was refashioning itself into the Russian Empire. The confusion between empire and nation, and the various peoples overshadowed by the umbrella of the "Russian nation," would last for centuries.

II

THE REUNIFICATION OF RUS'

4

THE ENLIGHTENED EMPRESS

Sophie Friederike Auguste von Anhalt-Zerbst-Dornburg became the Russian empress Catherine II on June 28, 1762. For her, that day began in the early morning with disturbing news about the arrest of one of the officers involved in the plot to depose her husband, Emperor Peter III, and bring her to power. Chances were that she would soon be arrested and possibly executed. She and her advisers decided to act immediately and launch the coup that had long been in the making. Peter was away from St. Petersburg, and Catherine immediately left her palace in the St. Petersburg suburb of Peterhof and drove to the capital. There she was welcomed by the guards regiments, whose commanders were involved in the plot. The army was on her side. A few days later, it would all be over. Peter III, Catherine's unfortunate husband, was surrounded by troops loyal to her and forced to abdicate. He died under suspicious circumstances less than ten days later.

Although the coup was well prepared and successful, it still badly needed justification and legitimization. Catherine had to show why she—a

German-born princess who had come to Russia at the age of fifteen, had never managed to shed her German accent, and had violated every rule of succession to the throne—was a better Russian than her husband, the grandson of Peter I. The manifesto issued on behalf of Catherine on June 28 claimed that she had assumed power to save Russia from mortal danger: "It was clearly apparent to all upright sons of the Russian Fatherland what a grave danger this presented to the whole Russian State." The authors of the manifesto relied mainly on the religious factor, claiming that Catherine was more genuinely Orthodox than Peter. He had allegedly planned to change Russia's state religion from Orthodoxy to Lutheranism. "Our Greek church was already utterly exposed to ultimate danger by the change of Orthodoxy, ancient in Russia, and the adoption of an infidel faith," read the manifesto.

According to Catherine, the manifesto was written on the fly. Some scholars think that it was prepared ahead of time. One way or another, it reflected important elements of Russian thinking at the time: given the close association of the Russian state with the Orthodox Church, a threat to either was deemed sufficient reason for the "sons of the Fatherland" to intervene and depose an otherwise legitimate ruler. It was now up to Catherine II to prove her loyalty and usefulness to Russia lest she suffer a similar fate. She accomplished the task admirably, becoming known in Russia and abroad as Catherine the Great.

DURING CATHERINE'S LONG REIGN OF ALMOST THIRTY-FIVE YEARS (1762–1796), the formation of the imperial Russian nation begun under Peter I and Elizabeth took on new impetus and new characteristics. As one would expect under the rule of a foreign-born princess, the civic elements of the new Russian identity became more important than the ethnic ones. The concepts of nation, state, and fatherland were disseminated far beyond the circle of the tsarina's Western-leaning and foreign-trained advisers. It was also during her rule that the idea of citizenship made its way into Russian discourse. The ethnocentric model of Russian identity formed under Elizabeth turned into one of civic loyalty to the empire. The ideas of the Enlightenment, of which Catherine was a student and admirer, transformed the understanding of empire from a patchwork of territories that maintained particular rights and privileges acquired over the centuries to a centralized state that relied on administrative uniformity even as it celebrated its ethnic and religious diversity.

Catherine presented her vision of the relation between empire and nation in another important document, a manifesto of 1785 that confirmed the right of the Russian imperial nobility to forgo obligatory service to the state. The manifesto read: "In the true glory and greatness of the empire we taste the fruits and recognize the results of the deeds of our subject, obedient, courageous, dauntless, enterprising, and mighty Russian people." The same manifesto left no doubt about the identity of the leading stratum of the nation and the true "sons of the Fatherland." "In the course of eight hundred years from the time of her founding," wrote Catherine, "Russia has found commanders and leaders among her sons. At all times it has been, is, and, with God's help, always will be characteristic of the Russian nobility to distinguish itself with qualities making for brilliant leadership." Thus the nobility was the vanguard of the Russian nation, and the Russian nation was the leading force of the empire.

Among the "true sons of the Fatherland" who brought Catherine to power in 1762 was the president of the Imperial Academy of Sciences and hetman of the autonomous Cossack state on the Left Bank of the Dnieper, known in history as the Hetmanate, Kirill Razumovsky. It was the printers of the academy who issued Catherine's first manifesto, leaving no doubt about Razumovsky's political allegiance. As the new empress showered her supporters with titles, gifts, and lands, Razumovsky was among the first in line. We do not know whether he made any requests on behalf of the academy, but his plans for the Hetmanate were quite extensive. Backed by local Cossack officers, he planned to strengthen its autonomy and institutions. Many in the Hetmanate were looking forward to a bright future for their autonomous polity.

In the fall of 1762, a few months after Catherine's coronation, Semen Divovych, a scribe in the Hetmanate's headquarters in the city of Hlukhiv on today's Russo-Ukrainian border, produced a long poem titled *A Conversation Between Great Russia and Little Russia*. One passage read as follows:

Great Russia:
Do you know with whom you are speaking, or have you forgotten?
I am Russia, after all: do you ignore me?

Little Russia:
I know that you are Russia; that is my name as well.
Why do you intimidate me? I myself am trying to put on a brave face.
I did not submit to you but to your sovereign,
Under whose auspices you were born of your ancestors.
Do not think that you are my master:
Your sovereign and mine is our common ruler.

These verses presented a vision of empire in which the little Hetmanate called Little Russia would be linked to the huge Russian Empire only by name and common ruler, undoing all that the Russian emperors, starting with Peter I, had done to limit the autonomy of the Hetmanate. That vision made scant provision for a common state, nation, or fatherland. Hopes were high in the capital of the Hetmanate, and at first they appeared to be justified. Catherine began her rule with a minor concession to her loyal hetman and the Little Russian elites, reinstating the Hetmanate's traditional court system in 1763. The Cossack officer council asked for more, and Razumovsky threw in an additional request: he wanted the hetman's office to become hereditary and stay in his family.

But Catherine's gratitude had its limits, and her reaction was swift. In 1764, she summoned Razumovsky to St. Petersburg and removed him as hetman, compensating him later with the title of field marshal. More important, she abolished the office of hetman altogether. It was the third and final liquidation of the office of Cossack leader, the first two having occurred under Peter and Anna Ioannovna. It would take Catherine another two decades to eliminate all the institutions of the Hetmanate, including its system of military regiments, but the empress took her time and stayed her course. At stake was the formation of an empire whose regions would all be governed from the center according to Enlightenment principles of rational governance and universal laws. The hodgepodge of long-established customs and special privileges accumulated in the course of history was to yield to well-ordered and homogeneous bureaucratic norms.

Even so, prudence called for a gradual transition to the new practices. In February 1764, a few months before the abolition of the hetman's office, Catherine wrote to the procurator-general of the Senate—the empire's legislative, judicial, and administrative body—and de facto chief of Catherine's political police ("secret expedition"), Prince Aleksandr Viazemsky: "Little Russia, Livonia, and Finland are provinces governed by confirmed privileges, and it would be improper to violate them by abolishing them all at once. To call them foreign and deal with them on that basis is more than erroneous—it would be sheer stupidity. These provinces, as well as Smolensk, should be Russified as gently as possible so that they cease looking to the forest like wolves. . . . When the hetmans are gone from Little Russia, every effort should be made to eradicate from memory the period and the hetmans, let alone promote anyone to that office."

Catherine first turned the Hetmanate into the province of Little Russia and then divided it into the vicegerencies of Kyiv, Chernihiv, and Novhorod-Siverskyi. The abolition of the Hetmanate and the gradual elimination of its institutions and military structure ended the notion of partnership and equality between Great and Little Russia imagined by generations of Ukrainian intellectuals. Once incorporated into the administrative system of the empire, the former Hetmanate was dwarfed by the huge Russian state. Out of close to fifty imperial vicegerencies at the end of the eighteenth century, only three represented the former Hetmanate. The special status of the former Cossack polity was gone, its officer class integrated, though not without difficulty, into the Russian nobility and expected to serve the interests of the all-Russian nation. The Little Russians maintained their attachment to their traditional homeland, which they continued to call a "fatherland," but for most of them there was no longer a contradiction between loyalty to their historical *patria* and to the Russian Empire.

Accordingly, the lands of the former Hetmanate continued to supply cadres for the empire. Young Cossack officers, such as Oleksandr Bezborodko and Petro Zavadovsky, enjoyed Catherine's support and made spectacular careers in St. Petersburg. Bezborodko served as her secretary, and eventually as one of the architects of imperial foreign policy; Zavadovsky became the highest official in the empire's educational system. The westward-looking alumni of the Kyivan Academy were needed as much by the empress, who proclaimed Russia a European state, as they had been by Peter I. But whereas Peter had summoned clerics to the capital, Catherine brought in secular elites. Given the Kyivan graduates' good knowledge of Latin, they were considered ideal candidates for training as medical doctors, and 60 percent of the empire's doctors in Catherine's time were Ukrainians.

Ukrainians constituted a significant part of the intellectual elite, with Hryhorii Kozytsky, Vasyl Ruban, and Fedir Tumansky, all natives of the Hetmanate, becoming publishers of some of the first Russian journals. Kozytsky, who was one of Catherine's secretaries, published the journal *Vsiakaia vsiachina* (Anything and Everything, 1769–1770) on her behalf; Ruban published *Starina i novizna* (Antiquity and Novelty, 1772–1773); and Tumansky served much later as the publisher of the first historical journal in the Russian Empire, *Rosiiskii magazin* (Russian Magazine, 1792–1794). They were among the early "nationalists" who helped form an emerging Russian identity that embraced the new Russian literary language and associated nation with empire more closely than ever before. According to some estimates, as many as half the "Russian" intellectuals promoting the idea of a Russian nation were in fact "Little Russians," or Ukrainians.

IN THE FALL OF 1772, THE RUSSIAN ARMY, UNDER THE DIRECTION of the president of the Military College, Zakhar Chernyshev, crossed the Polish-Russian border and took new positions along the Dnieper and Daugava Rivers. The towns of Polatsk, Vitsebsk, Mstsislaŭ, and Mahilioŭ, which had not seen Russian troops since the mid-seventeenth century, now found themselves under Russian control. The Russian takeover of eastern Belarus was part of what became known in historiography as the first partition of Poland, undertaken in 1772 by Russia, Austria, and Prussia.

The partitions of Poland had been foreshadowed in 1762, during the festivities accompanying the coronation of Catherine II in Moscow. Among the speakers was Archbishop Heorhii Konysky of Mahilioŭ, who had come to take part in the coronation from the Polish-Lithuanian Commonwealth, where his eparchy was located. Speaking on the last day of the coronation ceremonies (September 29, 1762), the hierarch of the last surviving Orthodox bishopric in the Commonwealth pleaded for his persecuted church, arguing that God had spared Catherine's life so that she could defend not only the faith and the fatherland in Russia but also her coreligionists outside the empire. "Among Your Imperial Majesty's subject peoples celebrating your most joyous coronation, the Belarusian nation, too, offers its most devoted greetings through me, a subject of Your Majesty," declared the hierarch. The idea of religious unity between the Orthodox of the Russian Empire and the Commonwealth was well established in Russian imperial discourse of the time. But the notion of the "Belarusian people" being among the real or potential subjects of the empress was something new and entirely different—it had not appeared in Russian discourse since the mid-seventeenth century, when the name "White Rus'" was added to the tsar's title.

Konysky's prayers for the protection of the "Belarusian nation" were unexpectedly answered when Russian troops took over eastern Belarus in 1772. In Mahiliou, church bells rang day and night to mark the swearing of the loyalty oath to Catherine. In March 1773, Konysky was in St. Petersburg, thanking Catherine for what he could hardly have expected a few months earlier. "Finding myself among this people now, it seems to me that I am among the Israelites making their way out of Egypt; among the captives of Zion returning from Babylon; among the Christians of the times of Constantine," Konysky told the empress. She had not only offered protection to the "Belarusian nation" under Polish control, but taken it under her rule, making Konysky and his countrymen Russian subjects. Konysky thanked the wrong ruler for the liberation of his people from "Egyptian captivity." His true redeemer was Frederick II of Prussia, not Catherine II of Russia.

Ever since the Battle of Poltava (1709), after which Peter I introduced de facto Russian control over Commonwealth affairs, the Polish-Lithuanian state had belonged to the Russian sphere of influence. Consequently, for a long time, the annexation of any of its territory by other powers was not in the interests of Russia. But the partition of Poland-Lithuania was certainly in the interests of other European powers. Prussian kings, who badly wanted Polish-held West Prussia in order to connect Brandenburg with East Prussia, made their first offers to divide the Commonwealth in the early eighteenth century. The weakness of the Polish-Lithuanian state was an irresistible temptation to the stronger European powers to settle their accounts at its expense, and the Russian Empire could resist the desires of the Commonwealth's neighbors only so long.

The turning point came in 1771. Once Austria, alarmed by Russian successes in a war with the Ottomans, allied itself with the Porte, St. Petersburg decided to succumb to Prussian pressure and agree to a three-way partition of Poland-Lithuania in order to avoid the looming conflict with Austria. On February 17, 1772, Prussia and Russia signed a treaty in St. Petersburg agreeing to annex parts of Polish territory. A tripartite agreement with Austria was signed in the Russian capital on August 5 of the same year. Prussia got what it most wanted—West Prussia. Austria annexed eastern Galicia, with its center in Lviv, to be renamed Lemberg. Russia got part of Lithuania and Belarusian territories.

Russia was also a reluctant participant in the second partition of Poland, which took place in 1793. Developments in the rump Commonwealth—the territories left under Warsaw's control in the 1780s and early 1790s—presented a clear threat to Russian interests in the country. In 1790, the Poles signed a defensive alliance with Prussia to the exclusion of Russia, and potentially against it. The alliance ended the de jure Russian protectorate over the Kingdom of Poland. To add insult to injury, the Four-Year Diet, which began its proceedings in Warsaw in 1788, launched a number of reforms intended to modernize the Polish state. Adopted by the pro-reform faction of the Diet, the Constitution of May 3, 1791, strengthened the position and powers of the king, made the Diet a more workable institution by getting rid of the *liberum veto*—the requirement that all decisions be made by unanimous vote—and establishing the separation of the executive, legislative, and judicial branches of government. None of that was good news for Russia, which saw the reforms not only as impairing its ability to manipulate the Polish political system but also as promoting the ideas of the French Revolution. The latter threat made Catherine forget many of her Enlightenment-era initiatives and take a reactionary view of anything that smacked of danger to her authoritarian rule.

The third partition took place in 1795, shortly after the second, as a reaction to the Polish revolt against the partitioning powers led by Tadeusz Kościuszko, a Polish military commander and a native of Belarus. Russia sent an army led by its best military commander, Aleksandr Suvorov, against the rebels. The Prussians also sent their troops, and the two powers defeated the Kościuszko Uprising. Russia, Prussia, and Austria divided the rest of the Polish territories between themselves and, once again, the Russian booty significantly exceeded that of Prussia and Austria—the latter two got less than 50,000 square kilometers each, whereas Russia's share was 120,000 square kilometers. Altogether, Russia took over more than 66 percent of the former Polish territories. Its new borders encompassed all of Lithuania, with its capital city of Vilnius and its Baltic coastline, as well as Brest in Belarus and the towns of Lutsk and Volodymyr in Ukraine's Volhynia region. Almost all the Ukrainian and Belarusian lands were now under St. Petersburg's control. The only exception was Ukrainian Galicia, which remained under Vienna.

In Russian imperial historiography, the partitions of Poland were often referred to as the reunification of Rus'—a term emphasizing that, with the exception of Lithuania, all the other lands annexed to the Russian Empire as a result of the partitions were settled by Eastern Slavs, who had been subjects of Kyivan princes centuries earlier. The ethnic selectivity of the Russian territorial acquisitions was by no means accidental and signaled changes in the Russian national imagination that would take place during Catherine's rule.

IF THE PARTITIONS PER SE WERE FORCED ON CATHERINE BY HER allies and changing circumstances, the territories that Russia annexed as a result offer insight into the historical, religious, and ethnic identity of the Russian elites.

The territory of Russia's first partition was defined not by any historical claims but by the desire of the Russian military to have clear-cut borders that would be easy to defend. The new line was drawn along the Dnieper and Daugava Rivers and their tributaries—a border first suggested by the president of the Military College, Zakhar Chernyshev, in the early 1760s. But the treaty on the first partition signed between Russia and Prussia in January 1772 referred to a historical rather than a strategic rationale for the partitions. "Her Royal Majesty the All-Russian Empress and His Royal Majesty the King of Prussia pledge the most positive mutual assistance to each other in their undertaking to take advantage of current conditions to obtain for themselves those districts of Poland to which they have ancient rights," read the Russo-Prussian convention on the partitioning of Poland.

Territorial claims based on history were also made by Empress Maria Theresa of Austria: "Her Royal Highness the Imperial Queen has ordered her army corps to enter Poland and instructed them to occupy the districts to which she asserts her previous rights." Maria Theresa hated the term "partition," which in her opinion implied the unlawful character of the whole enterprise, and sought historical justification of the new acquisition. She found it in the historical claims of the Hungarian kings to the medieval Principality of Galicia-Volhynia. As the Austrian emperors were considered heirs of the Hungarian kings, the new territories became known as the Kingdom of Galicia and Lodomeria—the latter term being the Latinized form of the word "Volodymeria," referring to the capital of Volhynia, the town of Volodymyr, which remained in Poland for the time being.

Curiously enough, references to historical rights disappeared from the manifestos that accompanied the second and third partitions. But those were precisely the partitions that Russia justified with intensive domestic propaganda stressing its historical rights. Where possible, the borders of the second and third partitions were drawn along rivers, but this time historical, religious, and ethnonational considerations were involved along with strategic ones. On the occasion of the second partition, Catherine ordered that a medal be struck depicting the double-headed eagle straight from the Russian imperial coat of arms holding in its clutches two maps, one with the territories attached to Russia in 1772, the other the territories attached in 1793, with an inscription at the top: "I restored what had been torn away." Thus Catherine was allegedly returning to Russia what had once belonged to it but had been taken away by force.

Catherine's understanding of what territories she had the right to claim was based on her study of Rus' history. In her *Notes on Russian History*, which she wrote for her two grandsons, Alexander (the future tsar of Russia) and Konstantin (the future king of Poland), Catherine covered a good part of the history of Kyivan Rus' and described in some detail the Rus' princes' relations with their Polish counterparts, including numerous wars between the two sides. There is little doubt that Catherine wanted all the former Kyivan territories, including Galicia, which Austria had taken in the first partition. Soon after the second partition, she commented, in the presence of one of her secretaries, "In time, we should obtain Galicia from the emperor in exchange: he has no need of it." Catherine never got Galicia but insisted on taking the town of Volodymyr in the third partition. In doing so, she prevented Emperor Joseph II of Austria from obtaining Volhynia—the land that the Austrians had claimed as part of their inheritance (Galicia and Lodomeria) from the Hungarian kings. The Austrians had to be satisfied with Little Poland, including Cracow and Lublin, claiming that those lands were in fact "Western Galicia."

Something important had changed in Catherine's mind between the first and second partitions. In the case of the first, she did not mind Austria getting Galicia; by the time of the second partition, she wanted Galicia for herself. A better knowledge of Rus' history could certainly have been one reason for this change of heart (the empress wrote her *Notes* sometime in the 1780s), but there may have been other reasons as well. Catherine began to think about the new lands not just in historical and religious terms, as she had earlier, but also in ethnic ones. In December 1792, once Catherine had decided in favor of the second partition, she wrote to her ambassador in Warsaw that her goal was "to deliver the lands and towns that once belonged to Russia, established and inhabited by our kinsmen and professing the same faith as ours, from the corruption and oppression with which they are threatened." Thus, she was not only claiming what had belonged to her predecessors on the Russian throne, but also saving coreligionists and people of the same ethnic background from persecution and from the temptation to rebel.

Much of Catherine's thinking on the subject became public knowledge and, indeed, official policy after the second partition, when the Russian army crushed Kościuszko's rebellion. The capture of Warsaw was lavishly celebrated in St. Petersburg, in stark contrast to the marking of the second partition, when liturgies were served but no gun salute ordered. Catherine II, who believed that the Orthodox population of the Commonwealth (the Ukrainians and Belarusians) belonged to the same tribe as the Russians, had no fraternal feelings toward the Poles. In the same letter of December 1792 to the Russian ambassador in which the empress wrote so positively about the fellow Eastern Slavs, she castigated the Poles: "The experience of the past and the current disposition of conditions and attitudes in Poland, that is, the inconstancy and frivolity of this people, the hostility and hatred it has shown us, and particularly the inclination it has shown toward the depravity and violence of the French, indicate that we shall never have in it either a peaceful or a secure neighbor unless we reduce it to utter weakness and impotence."

The view of the Poles as a hostile nation and Ukrainians and Belarusians as fraternal ones became dominant in Russian discourse after Suvorov's capture of Warsaw in November 1794. In December, the government issued a manifesto that had been written by Catherine's chief foreign-policy adviser, Oleksandr Bezborodko, but reflected, sometimes almost verbatim, the ideas expressed by Catherine in her letter of December 1792. "Her Imperial Majesty has restored to her empire lands that belonged to it from antiquity, torn away from it in troubled times with the same perfidy as that shown in our day by malevolent individuals among the Poles preparing to act to the detriment of Russia, and inhabited by people who are our kinfolk and coreligionists, oppressed because of their piety," read the manifesto. With regard to the Poles, Bezborodko wrote, "the treachery of the Poles was revealed to the utmost by their perfidious attempt to annihilate the Russian troops who were peacefully and securely posted in Warsaw under the terms of a treaty of alliance concluded in good faith. All of them, young and old, had a hand in perpetrating this villainous act."

The loyal poets were eager to adopt a new line. Vasilii Petrov, a poet who after the second partition had called Poles the "confidants of Russia," now turned them into bloodthirsty monsters:

> Having trampled on the sacred rights,
> They threaten to plunder and raze the temples,
> To take their fill of foreign property
> And satisfy their greedy hands, mouths, and stomachs.

FOR MOST OF CATHERINE'S RULE, THE UKRAINIANS AND BELARUsians of the Commonwealth were defined by religious terminology as adherents of the Greek-Russian—or simply Greek—Church, suggesting that they were Orthodox. But the absolute majority of the "Belarusian nation" that Russia acquired in the partitions was non-Orthodox. This was true not only of the Polish or Polonized nobility, which was Catholic, or the Jews, who were not Christian at all, but even of the majority of the Eastern Slavs—they were Uniates. In the lands annexed to Russia after the second partition, only 300,000 people were Orthodox. More than 2 million were Uniates, while the lands attached as a result of the third partition had almost no Orthodox believers.

In April 1794, Catherine decided to remedy that situation by launching an official campaign to convert the Uniates to Orthodoxy. Her decision was triggered by an appeal from representatives of twenty villages in Right-Bank Ukraine—the battleground between Orthodoxy and the Union since the time of the 1768 uprising—who wanted to abandon the Union and convert to Orthodoxy. Catherine not only granted the request but also suggested it as a model for the "return" to Orthodoxy of other Uniate parishes, by force if necessary. According to a pastoral letter issued at her request, "during the troubled times of Russia, a great part of its subjects who confessed the Greek Orthodox faith, having been torn from the true body to fall under the Polish yoke . . . witnessed the greatest oppression of the free worship of their faith." Catherine, claimed the pastoral letter, had returned "to her reign this people of the same tribe."

Catherine's own decree, addressed to the governor general of the annexed territories, was much more blunt and explicit than the pastoral letter about the goals of the new policies. She wrote about "the most suitable eradication of the Uniate faith" as a whole, not just the conversion of a few willing parishes. Catherine was prepared for major disturbances and protests against the liquidation of the established church and expected the governor to deal with it. With the support of the police force, he was to ensure that "any disorder and trouble be averted, and that none of the permanent or temporary landowners or spiritual and civil officials of the Roman and Uniate faith dare to cause even the smallest hindrance, oppression, or offense to those who are converting to Orthodoxy. Any such attempt directed against the dominant faith and indicating disobedience to Our will shall be regarded as a criminal offense, subject to trial and entailing confiscation of property until a court decision is reached."

The empress who had defended the Orthodox of the Commonwealth in the name of religious toleration and had been acclaimed for that by Voltaire suddenly turned into the persecutor of another religion. How to explain this? Although the reference in the pastoral letter to Uniates as people of the same tribe can elucidate the background to her thinking about the connection between religion and ethnicity, the immediate reason should be sought elsewhere. By 1794, in response to the French Revolution and to what she saw as a French-style attack on the authoritarian order coming from Poland and its new constitution, Catherine had abandoned many elements of her earlier beliefs. The decree ordering the eradication of the Uniate faith was issued at the time of the Kościuszko Uprising, whose leaders sought support among the Uniate peasantry. The eradication of the Uniate Church under such circumstances could be regarded as an anti-insurgency measure. Catherine could count on the loyalty of Orthodox priests in the former Commonwealth, but she could hardly trust the Uniate ones.

Catherine's erstwhile defense of religious toleration was not replaced with a justification of intolerance. What she now claimed to be doing was redressing the previous injustice done to the Orthodox. They had been forcibly converted to the Union by the Polish authorities, and now she was merely trying to bring them back to their ancestral faith. The return to "the faith of fathers and forefathers," as the conversion campaign was called in official pronouncements of the Russian church and state, proceeded with spectacular success in Right-Bank Ukraine, where almost no Uniate parishes remained by 1796. The farther one went west and northwest, however, the more Uniate priests and parishes refused to convert, despite the pressure applied by the secular and religious authorities. Central Belarus and Volhynia remained largely Uniate. The number of Uniates further increased after the third partition of Poland. Altogether, close to 1.4 million Ukrainians and Belarusians remained Uniate after Catherine's "reunification" campaign came to a halt following her death in 1796.

THE PROCESS OF MERGING EMPIRE AND NATION UNDER THE AUSpices of a powerful state began under Peter and was highly developed under Catherine, who employed Enlightenment practices of rational governance to eliminate regional and ethnic particularities, thereby strengthening central control over the empire's diverse lands. Besides reshaping the administrative structure and institutions of the state, empire-building involved the articulation of a historical mythology, the development of a common language, and the rethinking of the status of Orthodoxy in a multiethnic polity.

As for Russian identity and self-awareness, Catherine's rule brought about a new understanding of the Russian imperial nation. As increasing centralism broke down regional loyalties and autonomous enclaves such as the Hetmanate, an all-Russian identity emerged. Social norms were also changing: Russians were now not only "sons of the Fatherland" obediently serving the state but also citizens endowed with rights. The Russian imperial outlook was still as opposed to the West as it had been in Elizabeth's time, but it became less xenophobic.

The empress's role as protector of Orthodoxy prompted Russia to intervene more than ever before in the Catholic-Orthodox conflict in the Polish-Lithuanian Commonwealth, but Catherine regarded the Orthodox there as coreligionists, not ethnic compatriots of the Russians. For her, the borders of the Russian nation were coterminous with those of the Russian state. It was only toward the end of her reign that the partitions of Poland, which brought millions of largely non-Orthodox subjects into the Russian Empire, helped introduce ethnicity into official Russian discourse. Catherine and her advisers never accepted ethnicity as the main defining feature of the empire's new subjects, but those subjects helped lay the foundations for a new understanding of Russian identity in the next century.

The partitions challenged the Enlightenment-era model of Russian imperial identity. Not unlike Ivan III in the fifteenth century, Catherine II claimed new territories in the eighteenth by invoking the historical rights of Kyivan princes. But Catherine faced a much more difficult task than Ivan had when it came to the integration of those lands into the Russian state. The partitions brought into the empire millions of Eastern Slavs (Ukrainians and Belarusians) whom Catherine depicted in her letters and decrees not only as coreligionists but also as people of the same Russian tribe. As most of those prospective Russians turned out to be Uniates, the imperial government refused to adopt a multi-religious model of the Russian nation, launching instead a program of forcible conversion of the Uniates to the faith of their "fathers and forefathers."

Dictated largely by security concerns in the midst of the Polish uprising led by Tadeusz Kościuszko, the conversion campaign would provide an early model for the Russian authorities' treatment of the borderland Ukrainian and Belarusian population in the face of the Polish challenge to the stability and unity of the empire for generations to come.

5

THE POLISH CHALLENGE

"ONE POLE IS A CHARMER; TWO POLES—A BRAWL; THREE Poles—well, this is the Polish question," quipped Voltaire. The Russian Empire acquired more than three Poles as a result of the partitions enthusiastically supported by the French philosophe, and, as for the Polish question, it was presenting an ever greater challenge to its Russian overlord. Catherine II, who did not believe in special treatment of lands annexed to the empire, abandoned the traditional practice of the Russian tsars, who had tolerated broad autonomy for newly acquired territories, including the Hetmanate and the Baltic provinces, for decades or even centuries. The annexed Polish lands were given no special status, which created tension between the imperial center and its new periphery.

Many in the St. Petersburg imperial establishment, including some of those appointed to rule in Poland, were sympathetic to fellow aristocrats in that country and considered the partitions both unjust and imprudent as an assertion of Russian interests in Europe. The sense of guilt toward a conquered but not fully vanquished neighbor was something new for the

Russian imperial psyche and presented a special challenge to the rulers. Poland had been a regional power with a highly developed sense of its own imperial mission and an elite loyal to its state and fatherland. A full-fledged political nation, it was not prepared to give up the ideal of independent statehood. The resentment of the Polish nobility, which considered itself culturally superior to the conquerors (much more so than the elite of the Hetmanate had in the seventeenth century), created an additional problem for the traditional modus operandi of the Russian Empire. Its usual strategy had been to make a deal with local elites at the expense of the lower classes and thus establish its supremacy. A deal was made in this case as well, but the local elite was not fully cooperative and occasionally refused to cooperate at all.

The Russian Empire's Polish question never remained in the purely theoretical realm, limited to the soul-searching of intellectuals. More than once the Poles took arms in hand, not just to make their voices heard or negotiate a better deal with the empire, but to throw off Russian rule altogether and restore the Polish-Lithuanian Commonwealth in its pre-partition boundaries. They were marching forward with their heads turned back. For the Russian Empire, the Poles were dangerous enemies. The advent of nationalist ideology, with its emphasis on linguistic and ethnic particularism, created another obstacle to the successful integration of the annexed territories. The Polish nobles were not only bearers of a political culture opposed to absolutism, and adherents of a religion that the Russian Orthodox elites had always regarded with utmost suspicion, but as Western Slavs were ethnically distinct from the East Slavic core of the Russian imperial nation, and busily establishing the foundations of modern Polish identity based on a distinct history, political culture, language, literature, and religion.

The failure to resolve the Polish question by the traditional expedient of assimilating the elites of the conquered territories forced the Russian imperial elite to reexamine its own identity. It came up with a formula that combined its traditional loyalty to autocratic imperial rule and the dominance of the Orthodox Church with the new concept of nationality. In historiography, that triad came to be known as "official nationality." It would define Russian imperial nation-building projects for the rest of the century.

NAPOLEON'S INVASION OF RUSSIA IN 1812 WAS OFFICIALLY CALLED the Polish campaign—the second Polish campaign, to be precise. In the first (1806–1807), Napoleon had defeated the Russian, Prussian, and Austrian troops and carved the Duchy of Warsaw out of the Prussian share of the Polish partition. The official goal of the second campaign was to restore the Kingdom of Poland, now including lands from the Russian sphere of the partitions. The implicit and, many believe, primary goal was to stop the Russian Empire from trading with Britain and thereby tighten the French economic blockade of Napoleon's British enemy. But an economic issue could hardly serve as a battle cry for the French armies or for potential allies in the region, who were ordered or asked to invade the Russian Empire and march all the way to Moscow. The undoing of a major historical injustice through the restoration of the Polish state could and did rouse the martial spirit, inspiring mass Polish participation in Napoleon's invasion of Russia and lending international legitimacy to the war.

Although the third partition had wiped Poland off the political map of Europe, and the partitioning powers had agreed not to use the country's name in their titles or in the official names of the lands annexed as a result of the partitions, Poland had retained its place on the mental map of many Europeans—first and foremost, of course, the Poles themselves. Legend has it that upon his defeat at the hands of Russian troops in 1794, the leader of the Polish uprising, Tadeusz Kościuszko, exclaimed in desperation: "Finis Poloniae!" He later denied having said those words, and many Poles indeed refused to consider their country lost. Some of them joined Napoleon's revolutionary army, fighting in the West Indies, Italy, and Egypt alongside the future emperor. Their marching song, later to become the national anthem of the restored Polish state, began with the words: "Poland is not dead as long as we are alive."

Napoleon never forgot the loyalty of the Polish legionaries or the ultimate goal for which they were fighting. Addressing the Diet of the Duchy of Warsaw just before the invasion of Russia in June 1812, the emperor recalled the bravery of the Polish detachments in his army and his own readiness to fight for their cause. "I love your nation," declared the French emperor. "For sixteen years now, I have seen your warriors fighting along with me on the fields of Italy and Spain. I applaud your deeds. I approve of all the efforts that you intend to make, and I will do everything in my power to support your intentions. If your endeavors are unanimous, then you may nourish the hope of forcing your enemies to recognize your rights."

The intentions and rights Napoleon had in mind were reflected in the appeal prepared a few days earlier by the Polish Diet. It read:

> We are restoring Poland on the basis of the right given to us by nature; on the associations of our ancestors; on the sacred right, acknowledged by the whole world, that was the baptismal font of the human race. It is not we alone, tasting the sweetness of Poland's resurrection, who are restoring her, but all the inhabitants of various lands awaiting their liberation. . . . Regardless of their lengthy separation, the inhabitants of Lithuania, White Rus', Ukraine, Podolia, and Volhynia are our brethren. They are Poles, just as we are, and they have the right to call themselves Poles.

Napoleon told the deputies that he could not violate the promises he had given to Austria and the peace he had concluded with her; hence, restoring the Austrian partition to Poland was out of the question. But there seemed to be no problem with the Russian one. "Let Lithuania, Samogitia, Vitsebsk, Polatsk, Mahilioŭ, Volhynia, Ukraine, and Podolia," said Napoleon, "be inspired with the same spirit that I encountered in Great Poland, and Providence will crown your sacred cause with success."

Later that month, Napoleon's Grand Army crossed the Russian border and began its march through the territories annexed by Catherine II from Poland, aiming at the Russian hinterland. As far as the Warsaw Poles were concerned, the war for the restoration of their fatherland and reunification with their Polish brethren in the Russian partition was on. Close to 100,000 Poles entered Napoleon's army—every sixth soldier serving in his Russian campaign was a Pole. Not surprisingly, the first major military encounter, in late June 1812, took place not between French and Russian troops but between Polish and Russian detachments. What the outside observer saw as the first test of forces between Napoleon and Alexander was in fact a battle between Polish cavalrymen and Cossacks. They were continuing their age-old struggle on familiar turf—the eastern provinces of the former Commonwealth. Although the Cossacks won, they had to retreat. Their whole operation was meant to gain time for the main Russian armies to withdraw to the interior, eventually leading Napoleon to the gates of Moscow.

Napoleon's invasion and the Russian surrender of Moscow after the inconclusive Battle of Borodino in September 1812 aroused Russian patriotism and stirred anti-French and anti-Polish sentiments that had been building up in Russian society since the start of the Napoleonic Wars. Russian propaganda, spearheaded by the new state secretary and head of the "Russian party" at court, Admiral Aleksandr Shishkov, reached out for symbols of patriotism and found them in the struggle against the Polish invasion during the Time of Troubles. The manifesto on Napoleon's invasion issued by Emperor Alexander I called on the "faithful sons of Russia" and "the Russian people, valiant descendants of valiant Slavs," to rise against the aggressor. "In every noble, let him encounter a Pozharsky, in every religious a Palitsyn, in every citizen a Minin," wrote Shishkov, recalling the leaders of the resistance to the Polish invasion back in 1612. With Napoleon taking Moscow—the first presence of foreign troops in the capital since the Time of Troubles two hundred years earlier—parallels between the Polish capture of Moscow in 1612 and Napoleon's in 1812 became inescapable.

What seemed to be the end of Russia in September 1812—the surrender of Moscow to the French army—turned out to be the beginning of the end of Napoleon's empire. He had expected Russia's surrender and negotiations, but there was nothing of the kind. The Russians were repeating the strategy used in 512 by the Scythians against the army of Darius the Great of Persia, who chased the Scythian horsemen across the Pontic steppe without getting the chance to fight a decisive battle. The Russians also employed a scorched-earth policy extending from villages and small towns to Moscow itself. Russian agents set the city on fire, forcing the French to protect the Kremlin from the blaze. Napoleon was shocked by this lack of manners on the part of what he believed to be a vanquished enemy. In fact, he had fallen into a trap.

The Russian army was nowhere in sight for a decisive battle, supplies were short and eventually ran out, and the capital, St. Petersburg, was out of reach for a tired and significantly diminished army. Winter was approaching in Moscow, while the army's winter clothes were in Paris. In mid-October, Napoleon ordered the army to start retreating to the borders of Russia. The Russian commander, Mikhail Kutuzov, used his rested and well-supplied army to force Napoleon to follow the same route for the retreat that he had used for his advance on Moscow. That area had been burned and stripped of supplies during the original march. Hungry, cold, and harassed by Cossacks and partisan units, the conquerors of Moscow made their way out of Russia. In mid-December, three months after the capture of Moscow, a little more than 22,000 soldiers out of the Grand Army of 600,000 left Russia in regular formations. Others were killed, imprisoned, or retreated in small groups. The Grand Army was no more.

In December 1812, Emperor Alexander issued a manifesto in which he addressed the Poles as close relatives, almost brothers, offering amnesty to those who had fought against Russia in Napoleon's army. "We hope," declared Alexander, "that this philoprogenitive and altruistic forgiveness of Ours will bring the guilty to wholehearted repentance and prove to all residents of these regions in general that they, as a people of one language and kin with the Russians from ancient times, can nowhere and never be so happy and secure as in complete merging in one body with mighty and magnanimous Russia." The pan-Slavic idea of Russo-Polish brotherhood, first presented by the Russian court poet Vasilii Petrov on the occasion of the second partition of Poland in 1793, was now reiterated and strengthened by the notion of linguistic affinity.

Alexander believed that he knew how to redeem the Poles. His solution was to establish the Kingdom (in Russian, Tsardom) of Poland, and it was approved by the Congress of Vienna (1814–1815)—the international conference that defined the borders of post-Napoleonic Europe. The kingdom was created out of the Polish lands taken over by Prussia, with its capital in Warsaw. Without renouncing his title of emperor of Russia, Alexander thus assumed the new title of tsar of Poland, thereby creating the semblance of a dynastic union to justify Russia's continued domination of that country. This was also a step toward the realization of his old dream of becoming a constitutional monarch: if he could not become one in Russia, perhaps he could do so in Poland. He granted the kingdom quite a liberal constitution that provided for a Diet, a separate government and administrative structure, and even an army. Catherine's notion of making all parts of the empire homogeneous was discarded in favor of particularism, now under the banner of the Polish constitution. Alexander hoped that one day the rest of the empire would get its constitution as well. As things turned out, it would have to wait another ninety years.

Alexander was hailed in Warsaw as a restorer of the Polish statehood. The Poles retained most of the territories given to them under Napoleon. But their enthusiasm for Alexander was short-lived, as the Polish government had no control over the kingdom's budget, military forces, or international trade. Besides, the tsar's officials exceeded their mandate, while the tsar's brother, Grand Duke Constantine, who was commander in chief of the Polish army, acquired a bad reputation among the Polish elites for his abusive behavior. On top of that, Warsaw had no authority over the former Polish lands acquired by Russia in the course of the partitions. The younger generation of Polish activists began to create clandestine organizations whose goals included the restoration of Poland in its pre-partition boundaries. The Russian authorities cracked down on the conspirators, adding to the general sense of dissatisfaction in the kingdom.

ALEXANDER'S CONSTITUTIONAL EXPERIMENT WAS NOT GOING well, either in the Kingdom of Poland or in the rest of the empire. Conservative sections of Russian society opposed the idea of constitutionalism as such. Progressives who wanted a constitution complained that the Poles had gotten one while the Russians had not. Persistent rumors about Alexander's plans to transfer to the kingdom the territories annexed by Russia in the second and third partitions aroused protests from both camps.

In 1819, these concerns were voiced by Russia's most prominent historian of the day, Nikolai Karamzin. In a letter titled *The Opinion of a Russian Citizen*, Karamzin warned the tsar against what he saw as tantamount to a partition of Russia: "Will they say that she [Catherine] divided Poland illegally? But you would act even more illegally if you should think of smoothing over her illegality by partitioning Russia itself." He then pointed out how tricky the use of historical argument could be. "There are no old fortresses in politics," wrote Karamzin. "Otherwise we would be obliged to restore the kingdoms of Kazan and Astrakhan, the republic of Novgorod, the grand principality of Riazan, and so on. Moreover, even by virtue of their old fortresses, Belarus, Volhynia, and Podolia, along with Galicia, were once original possessions of Russia. If you give them back, they will also demand Kyiv, Chernihiv, and Smolensk of you: after all, they, too, belonged to hostile Lithuania for a long time."

Karamzin, the author of the multivolume *History of the Russian State*, published in St. Petersburg between 1816 and 1826, did not confine himself to historical arguments in his letter. He maintained that the tsar who ruled both Russia and Poland had to choose and take the side of "your true Fatherland—good, strong Russia." With reference to the Polish elites of the annexed territories, he wrote: "Lithuania and Volhynia want the Kingdom of Poland, but we want one Russian Empire." Ceding those territories to the Kingdom of Poland would create a threat to Russia: "Poles legally recognized as a separate and sovereign people are more dangerous to us than Pole-Russians." Finally, Karamzin wanted no part of the pan-Slavic discourse that was popular at the time: "No, Sire, the Poles will never be true brothers to us, nor faithful allies. Now they are weak and insignificant: the weak do not love the strong, and the strong hold the weak in contempt; if you strengthen them, they will want independence, and their first step will be to draw away from Russia— not in your reign, of course, but look beyond your own lifetime, Sire!"

Karamzin turned out to be a prophet of sorts. There was no revolt in the Kingdom of Poland as long as Alexander was alive. But five years after his death, which came in 1825, the Poles were up in arms. In November 1830, young Polish cadets tried to assassinate their Russian military commander, Grand Duke Constantine, sparking a revolt that would become known as the November Uprising. The grand duke survived the attempt, fleeing his residence in women's clothes, but the façade of dynastic union between Russia and Poland was now gone. The Polish Diet convoked by the rebels not only declared the secession of the Kingdom of Poland from the Russian Empire but also sought to regain the pre-partition Polish territories that were not part of the kingdom. The rebels sent troops and reinforcements to Lithuania, Belarus, and Ukraine and chose delegates to go to St. Petersburg to demand those territories.

Emperor Nicholas I, the new ruler of Russia, succeeded Alexander I in 1825 in the midst of the Decembrist revolt against the monarchy, which was led by liberal-minded Russian officers. Seeing the Polish revolt as a new threat to his authority and power, Nicholas refused to negotiate; instead, he sent his army against the rebels. To his surprise, the Polish army turned out to be a formidable opponent. After months of fighting, the Russian troops failed to take Warsaw. In Lithuania, the Russian army was barely holding Vilnius as it repelled Polish attacks. In Belarus, as well as in the Podolia and

Volhynia regions of Ukraine, the Polish nobility waged partisan warfare, harassing Russian detachments and breaking lines of communication.

In June 1831, Nicholas appointed a new commander of the Russian army on the Polish front—General Ivan Paskevich-Yerivansky (he acquired that honorific title for the capture of Yerevan from the Ottomans in 1827), a descendant of a Cossack officer family from the Hetmanate and commander in chief of Russian troops in the Caucasus. Paskevich, who had Nicholas's personal trust and received additional troops, managed to change the course of the war. In August 1831, he besieged Warsaw. The Poles showed heroic resistance and refused to surrender the city. One of their generals responded to Russian demands by saying, "A cannonball of yours tore off one of my legs at Borodino, and now I cannot take a single step backwards." He was referring, of course, to his participation in the Battle of Borodino on Napoleon's side. But Paskevich penetrated one line of Polish defenses after another, finally entering Warsaw on September 8, 1831. He wrote to the tsar: "Warsaw is at Your Majesty's feet." A month later, the last Polish military unit had been defeated. The question was what to do next. If the authorities could hope before the November Uprising that by bribing the Poles with broad autonomy and a constitution they could do away with their sovereignty, those illusions were now gone.

News of the fall of Warsaw caused jubilation in St. Petersburg, not just at the tsar's court or in government circles. The leading Russian poets took part, celebrating this major victory with the brochure *Na vziatie Varshavy* (On the Taking of Warsaw). It included a contribution by Russia's most respected poet, Vasilii Zhukovsky, and two poems by his younger colleague Aleksandr Pushkin, who was much more talented but also far less reliable from the official viewpoint. Before publication, Pushkin's poems were read and approved by Tsar Nicholas.

Zhukovsky praised the conquest of Warsaw by putting it into the context of previous Russian imperial triumphs. For him, the seizure of Warsaw was similar to the victories over Persia and the Ottoman Empire achieved by General Paskevich in the Caucasus a few years earlier. Pushkin's poems "To the Slanderers of Russia" and "The Anniversary of Borodino" had a different leitmotif, or, rather, two. The first was an attack on France and Europe as instigators of hatred toward Russia; the second had to do specifically with Poland. For Pushkin, the Polish question was also the Russian question. As far as Pushkin was concerned, the Polish rebels were claiming inalienable parts of Russian history and territory. These included Kyiv, imagined as the ancient Rus' capital and the mother of Rus' cities, and the Ukrainian lands attached to Muscovy in the time of Bohdan Khmelnytsky, the rebellious hetman who became a symbol of Russian unity. Pushkin asked his reader a number of questions:

> Whose will Volhynia be?
> And Bohdan's legacy?
> Right of rebellion recognized,
> Will Lithuania spurn our rule?
> And Kyiv, decrepit, golden-domed,
> This ancestor of Russian towns—
> Will it conjoin its sainted graves
> With reckless Warsaw?

Pushkin defined the November Uprising and the Russian suppression of it as "a quarrel of Slavs among themselves." At the center of that conflict was the Russian program of the unification of the Slavs. "Will the Slavic streams merge in the Russian sea? Will it dry up?"—that is how Pushkin formulated the main question to be resolved in the conflict between the "bumptious Pole" and the "faithful Russian." Unlike Zhukovsky, Pushkin was not just building the empire but also defending the pan-Russian nation and creating a pan-Slavic one. For him, the Russo-Polish struggle was about the future of Slavdom in general: all the Slavs eventually had to become politically Russian. In that regard, he echoed Vasilii Petrov's poetry from the times of the second partition—according to Petrov, the Poles were only the first to enter what Pushkin had called "the Russian sea."

THE POLISH NATIONAL MOBILIZATION OF THE NAPOLEONIC ERA, followed by the Polish revolt of 1830–1831, prompted the Russian search for the political, cultural, and ethnic roots of the empire's new identity. That process began during Napoleon's invasion of Russia, gained speed in the course of Alexander's constitutional experiment in the Kingdom of Poland, and received new impetus with the formulation of what historians subsequently called the "theory of official nationality" by the new imperial minister of education, Count Sergei Uvarov. Uvarov claimed that Russian education, and indeed Russian identity itself, should be based on three main principles: Orthodoxy, autocracy, and nationality. It was nationality (*narodnost'*) that represented Uvarov's principal innovation and eventually gave its name to the triad.

Uvarov formulated the main principles of Russian political ideology and of the country's new imperial identity in a memorandum first presented to Tsar Nicholas I in March 1832, when Uvarov was a deputy minister of education. Uvarov presented the final version of his text in November 1833, a few months after he was appointed to the post. In his memorandum, he formulated his goal as being nothing less than that of saving Russia from the same kind of collapse of social and religious institutions that Europe had experienced, which he associated with the French Revolution and its consequences. Russia had to restore and maintain its national values, which had allegedly been marginalized, if not actually destroyed, in the preceding decades. Those values also had to be adjusted to suit the "current intellectual disposition."

Where did Uvarov find his inspiration? A former Russian diplomat stationed in Paris before the Napoleonic Wars, he was an admirer of François Guizot, a key figure in the July Revolution of 1830 in France, which overthrew King Charles X and brought to power Louis Philippe I, and one of the leaders of the conservative wing in the French liberal camp. If Catherine II looked to Voltaire and other French *philosophes* for guidance on transforming her empire according to the universalist ideas of the Enlightenment, Uvarov found inspiration in Guizot for developing a position between the extremes of conservatism and revolution. He followed with great interest Guizot's efforts to establish a national system of education in France (the two happened to be ministers of education at the same time), but rejected what he considered the French claim to have produced a universally valid educational model.

Claiming that the French did not know or care about the rest of Europe, Uvarov turned to Germany for an alternative to French universalism. He found it in the works of the historian, philologist, and poet Karl Wilhelm Friedrich Schlegel, who emphasized national culture and tradition. Schlegel was among the first writers to promote a model of the nation based on common language and customs. He was influenced in that regard by the ideas of Johann Gottfried Herder, the creator of the Romantic concept of the nation, according to which the legitimacy of the state was based on the national spirit (*Volksgeist*), and every ethnic group had the right to a polity of its own. Schlegel envisioned a German national state united around Austria, which had best preserved the medieval institutions of dynasty, aristocracy, and religion. Uvarov and Schlegel had met in Vienna when Uvarov was stationed there in 1807–1809, a period in which Russia and Austria were closely allied against Napoleonic France.

Inspired by Guizot's creation of the French national educational system and by Schlegel's view of the particularity of ethnic nations, Uvarov set about formulating the principles of national education in Russia. Uvarov sought a formula whereby the best elements of the European tradition could be assimilated to Russia's benefit. "How to establish popular education here that corresponds to our sense of things but is not alien to the European spirit?" he wrote to the tsar. "What rule should we use in dealing with the European Enlightenment, with European ideas that we can no longer do without, but that threaten us with inevitable demise unless we adapt them skillfully?" Uvarov told the tsar that "in searching out the sources that constitute the essence of Russia (every land and every people has such a Palladium)," he had found them in the Orthodox faith, political autocracy, and nationality.

"Without love of its ancestors' faith, a people, like an individual, must perish," wrote Uvarov. This struck him as obvious and incontrovertible. He developed a much more elaborate argument concerning autocracy, a principle that was under attack not only abroad but also at home, especially in light of Alexander's idea of constitutional monarchy: "Autocracy is the basic condition of Russia's political existence in its current state. Let dreamers deceive themselves and find obscure manifestations of some order of things corresponding to their theories and prejudices: they may rest assured that they do not know Russia, do not know its condition, its needs, its desires." Uvarov claimed that attempts to limit the power of the tsar destabilized relations within the state and created obstacles to Russia's development. He was convinced that most Russians shared his views on the danger of tampering with the principle of autocracy.

While nationality was introduced as a new element of the official Russian belief system, it came in as a distant third in Uvarov's own thinking as expressed in his memorandum to the tsar, and he did not conceive of it as an equivalent of modern nationalism. He understood "nationality" as native tradition rooted in Russia's historical development, linking the throne and the church in order to ensure their stability.

Ironically, from today's standpoint, but quite normally for Uvarov's time, his program of Russian nation-building was written in French, which was still the prevailing idiom of the Russian elites. Uvarov defined his new principle as *nationalité*, which his clerks subsequently translated as *narodnost'*. The Russian term is best rendered in English as "national way of life." As far as we know today, the term *narodnost'* first appeared in 1819 in a letter from the Russian poet Petr Viazemsky, who wrote: "Why not translate *nationalité* as *narodnost'*? After all, the Poles have said *narodowość*. The Poles are not as squeamish as we are, and if words do not leap into their language of their own accord, they drag them in by the hair, and that is the end of the matter." The letter was sent from Warsaw, where Viazemsky was working on the constitutional projects of Alexander I.

The term *narodnost'* soon found acceptance in Russia. In 1825, Aleksandr Pushkin wrote about both the popularity of the term and its lack of a clear definition. "For some time we have been used to speaking of *narodnost'*, demanding *narodnost'* and complaining of the lack of *narodnost'* in literary works, but no one has thought to define what he means by the word *narodnost'*," he observed. "One of our critics seems to think that *narodnost'* consists in choosing objects from our country's history; others see *narodnost'* in words, that is, they are glad that in expressing themselves in Russian, they use Russian expressions."

According to Uvarov, nationality was the traditional way of life that was supposed to ensure the continuity of the other two key elements of Russian identity—religion and autocracy—in an age shaped by new European ideas. If in Europe the idea of nation, closely associated with the principle of popular representation, challenged political autocracy, in Russia it was supposed to support the traditional tsarist regime. Uvarov did not seek to justify the tsar's autocratic rule by claiming that it was based on divine right, as was customary at the time in the imperial capital; nor did he look to the church to legitimize it. Instead he linked autocracy with nationality, claiming that "one and the other flow from the same source and are conjoined on every page of the history of the Russian people." He stopped short, however, of suggesting that the Russian nation was the source of autocratic power.

Uvarov was clearly being selective in introducing the Western idea of nationality to Russia. He ignored Schlegel's emphasis on national language and culture, stressing attachment to traditional institutions. Since the Russian Empire was multiethnic, the idea of ethnic particularity threatened it with the kind of mobilization against Russian political dominance that the Poles had demonstrated in 1830. There was also the prospect that Russian nationalists might define their rights and interests differently from those of the monarchy. Uvarov sought to link empire and nationality in the hope that the latter would strengthen the former. He concluded his memorandum with a reference to the responsibility that he felt to "God, Sovereign, and Fatherland." This was a reprise of the triad enunciated by Admiral Shishkov, Russia's chief propagandist at the time of the Napoleonic Wars, indicating the link between Uvarov's formula and established imperial tradition.

Despite Uvarov's conservative intentions, the introduction of the term "nationality" into Russian politics meant that European nationalism had arrived in the Russian Empire. Peter I's chief ideologue, Teofan Prokopovych, had used the term "fatherland"; it had now been transmuted into "nation" (prefigured in the *Synopsis* of 1674, where "nation" was also used in a traditional rather than a revolutionary sense). What "nationality" would mean in practice was not yet clear, either to the author of the new ideological triad or to his addressee, the tsar himself. It would take generations to resolve the political issues implicit in the term. What were the borders of Russian nationality? Did it suffice for a subject of the empire to profess loyalty to the tsar and the Orthodox faith, or were there other essential elements of Russianness as well? Nowhere were these questions more pressing, in the wake of the Polish uprising of 1830–1831, than in the former territories of the Polish-Lithuanian Commonwealth annexed to the Russian Empire.

6

THE BATTLE FOR THE BORDERLANDS

I N THE SUMMER OF 1831, AT THE HEIGHT OF THE NOVEMBER Uprising, Nicholas I had offered Austria and Prussia some of the Polish lands beyond the Vistula, but now, with the uprising crushed, he changed course. His answer to the new Polish question came in February 1832 with the publication of the Organic Statute, which laid out his plans for the future of the Kingdom of Poland. The Organic Statute took away freedoms previously granted to Poland by Alexander I: the office of tsar of Poland was gone and the Diet abolished, as was the separate Polish army. General Field Marshal Count Ivan Paskevich was given the new title of Prince of Warsaw and appointed ruler of the former kingdom, which he was to integrate into the Russian Empire.

The decision to integrate the Kingdom of Poland with the empire had a major impact on imperial policy in what would become known in official parlance as the "western provinces"—the Ukrainian, Belarusian, and Lithuanian lands annexed by Catherine and located between the Kingdom of

Poland and core areas of the empire. For a long time before the November Uprising, the imperial rulers had vacillated on what to do with those territories. Nicholas was no exception. Like his father, Paul, and his brother and predecessor, Alexander, Nicholas did not believe that partitions served the interests of Russia, but, like them, he felt that he could not afford to turn those lands over to the Poles. "As long as I live, I can in no way allow ideas of annexing Lithuania to Poland to be encouraged," wrote Nicholas to his brother, Constantine, in 1827. He believed, however, that "this does not prevent me from being just as good a Pole as I am a good Russian." What he probably had in mind was the fulfillment of his duties as emperor of Russia and tsar of Poland. When the Polish revolt broke out in November 1830, the Polish minister of finance quipped that "Nicholas, Tsar of Poland, is waging war with Nicholas, Emperor of All Russia." With the defeat of the November Uprising, there was no longer any doubt about who had won that war. Poland would not get its former territories back.

On September 14, 1831, only a week after the fall of Warsaw, the imperial government created a special body that became known as the Committee on the Western Provinces, or "Western Committee." Established on the oral and secret order of Nicholas, the committee was charged with "examining various proposals concerning the provinces regained from Poland." For the first time since the partitions, the Russian government had created an authoritative body to deal systematically with the annexed territories. The goal was their speedy and complete integration into the empire, to be accomplished much more quickly than the integration of the Kingdom of Poland. Russification (*obrusenie*), the goal that Catherine II had formulated for Smolensk province and the Hetmanate back in 1763, now became official Russian policy with regard to the former Polish lands. It included administrative, legal, and social measures to bring those regions into line with the Russian provinces of the empire.

The model of imperial expansion and integration of new territories based on the principle of elite co-optation had failed to function in the case of the territories annexed from Poland, and the Polish uprising drove home to the Russian imperial elite this uncomfortable truth. The Polish elites had rebelled, and the government now had no choice but to change its policy. The popular masses at whose expense the deal with the Polish nobility was made were overwhelmingly Eastern Slavs, although their adherence to

Uniate Catholicism differentiated them from the Russian Orthodox. In its struggle with the imperial center, the Polish Catholic nobility had appealed for and often obtained support from its Ukrainian and Belarusian subjects because of this religious affinity. The government wanted to drive a wedge between the elites and the ruled. It employed every means at its disposal, including the concept of official nationality formulated by Count Uvarov, to that end.

In November 1832, the Western Committee issued a decree intended to diminish the number of people in the western provinces who could claim noble rights, including the right to buy land and serfs—a measure designed to undermine the status of Polish nobles. In the 1840s, Nicholas promoted initiatives to register and limit peasant obligations to landowners in order to support "Russian" peasants. To the degree that a noble-based empire could do so, it was taking the side of the Ukrainian and Belarusian peasantry against Polish nobility. Other policies included the liquidation of urban self-government and the abolition of the local law code, which went back to the times of Polish and Lithuanian rule over the region. Those policies were applied to the lands that had once belonged to the Polish-Lithuanian Commonwealth as a whole, including the former Hetmanate, whose loyalty was no longer in question.

The government also introduced policies to promote cultural Russification of the region. These included the creation of a new historical narrative, claiming the newly acquired lands for Russia, the establishment of new university and school districts, and the conversion of the Belarusian and Ukrainian Uniates to Orthodoxy and their incorporation into the ranks of the Russian Orthodox Church. It was these three sets of policies that had the most profound effect not only on the region but also on the way in which the Russian elite imagined itself and the geographic, social, and cultural borders of its nation.

THE RUSSIAN IMPERIAL ELITES HAD BEGUN TO THINK ABOUT THE future of the western provinces of the empire, which were settled largely by Eastern Slavs, during the period of Alexander's liberal reforms. A leader of the Decembrist Uprising (1825), Pavel Pestel, had fully recognized the complexity of the question when he sat down to write the rebels' manifesto of intentions—a constitution for the future Russian state that he called "Russian Justice," alluding to the law code of the medieval Kyivan state. He had to reconcile his concern for the preservation and strengthening of the Russian Empire with his belief that every nationality had a right to political independence. Clearly, the empire had no shortage of national homelands. Aside from Russia and Poland, Pestel's incomplete list included "Finland, Estland, Livland, Courland, Belarus, Little Russia, New Russia, Bessarabia, the Crimea, Georgia, the whole Caucasus, the lands of the Kirghiz, and all the Siberian peoples." Pestel's solution to the problem was simple: smaller nationalities would have to forgo their right to independence and become part of the larger and more powerful nationality. "They will find it better and more useful to themselves," wrote Pestel about the small nationalities, "if they unite in spirit and society with a large state and completely merge their nationality with that of the ruling people, constituting just one people with them, and ceasing to dream uselessly of a task that is impossible and unrealizable."

Pestel wanted to give independence to the Kingdom of Poland while Russifying most of the lands acquired during Catherine's partitions of Poland. He considered those lands to be settled by the Russian people, which he defined as a Slavic tribe united by a single language, religion, and social structure. He divided his Russian nation into five subgroups: the Great Russians of the core imperial provinces, the Little Russians on the Left Bank of the Dnieper, the Ukrainians of the region around Kharkiv called Sloboda Ukraine, the Rusyns on the Right Bank of the Dnieper as well as in Volhynia and Podolia, and the Belarusians of the lands annexed to Russia at the time of the first partition of Poland. (Pestel did not consider the inhabitants of the Grodno [Hrodna] and Minsk provinces to be part of the Russian nation and probably envisioned the transfer of those provinces to the enlarged Kingdom of Poland.) Pestel argued that the difference between the Russians of the core imperial provinces and those of today's Ukraine and Belarus lay in the special administrative status of the western provinces. "Hence it should be established as a rule," wrote Pestel, that all inhabitants of the Vitebsk [Vitsebsk], Mogilev [Mahilioŭ], Chernigov [Chernihiv], Poltava, Kursk, Kharkov [Kharkiv], Kiev [Kyiv], Podolia, and Volyn [Volhynia] provinces should be considered true Russians and not divided from the latter by any particular names."

It fell to Nicholas I's minister of education, Count Uvarov, to find ways of uniting the various branches of Pestel's "true Russians" in the wake of the Polish uprising. Uvarov was of one mind with Pestel when it came to treating the East Slavic population of the western provinces as Russians, but he did not share Pestel's belief that the differences were purely administrative. He must have thought that they were much more substantial, had to do with culture, and could be overcome only in another generation—and that even that would require a proper educational program. He wrote to the tsar: "All illustrious rulers from the Romans to Napoleon—those who intended to unite the tribes they conquered with the victorious tribe—invested all their hopes and all the fruits of their labors in future generations instead of the present generation."

Uvarov had good reason to be cautious and place his trust in the future. In the western provinces, he had to deal with a formidable obstacle in the shape of the Polish language, history, and culture: in the aftermath of the uprising of 1830, more people there read and wrote in Polish than in Russian. Like Pushkin and Pestel before him, Uvarov regarded the Polish question not as a conflict between an imperial center and a province, or between a multiethnic empire and one of its nationalities, but as a conflict between two nations, Russia and Poland, which ultimately had to be resolved in the sphere of education.

As early as 1831, Uvarov began looking for an author who could provide historical justification for the annexation and integration of the western provinces into the empire. His search was triggered by a letter to the Ministry of Education from one of its officials in the Grodno (Hrodna) province of what is now western Belarus. The official argued for the "resurrection, dissemination, and establishment in the western provinces of a nationality closely tied to the general Russian nationality." In his view, the problem of nationality in the region was to be solved by integrating its history into that of the empire and promoting linguistic assimilation by offering classes in Church Slavonic, a common literary language of the Eastern Slavs throughout most of the eighteenth century.

Uvarov took to heart the request for a new history. His vision of the region's past was not unlike that of Pavel Pestel. The Decembrist leader argued that the western provinces "belonged to Russia in ancient times and were torn away from it under unfavorable circumstances." According to Pestel, by "reuniting them with its body" under Catherine II, Russia had "restored its ancient dignity, all the dearer to it inasmuch as it can pay homage to the cradle of the Russian state—in the north, Novgorod and its adjoining provinces, and in the south, Kiev [Kyiv] with the Chernigov [Chernihiv], Kiev [Kyiv], Poltava, Podolia, and Volyn provinces, that most ancient nucleus of the Russian state."

This line of argument followed the tradition established by Catherine II and Prince Oleksandr Bezborodko after the second partition of Poland but called into question during the liberal rule of Alexander I. It was during the latter's rule that the statist interpretation of Russian history, presented by Nikolai Karamzin in his *History of the Russian State*, was challenged by the nationality principle advocated by the Polish and Russian historians. One of the leading Russian historians and journalists of the period, Nikolai Polevoi, published a six-volume history of the Russian *narod* (people or nation) between 1829 and 1833—a clear contrast to Karamzin's earlier multivolume work. This challenge to the statist interpretation coincided with the Polish uprising, which dramatically changed the Russian historiographic scene and placed on the agenda the task of uncovering and substantiating the "Russian" past of the western provinces.

Uvarov's first choice for writing a history text integrating the western provinces into the empire was Mikhail Pogodin, a professor of history at Moscow University who enthusiastically embraced the task. Pogodin, who assured the minister that he would fight the Polish historians as General Paskevich had fought the Polish insurgents in 1831, was approached in November 1834 and submitted his text a year later—Uvarov reported directly to the tsar about the scholar's progress. But Pogodin turned out to be too good a historian to satisfy the minister's demands. His book presented the history of northeastern Rus', or Russia, as distinct—indeed, separate—from that of southwestern Rus' (Ukraine and Belarus), undermining the project's main goal of linking the western provinces with Russia in a seamless historical narrative. Uvarov explained the failure to the tsar by citing the novelty of presenting the history of the Russian, Polish, and Lithuanian provinces as a single narrative.

But Pogodin's failure did not discourage Uvarov. He established a special prize of 10,000 rubles for an author who could present the history of the western provinces as part of Russian history, then asked another history professor, this time from St. Petersburg University, to attempt the task. His name was Nikolai Ustrialov, and he set to work on a four-volume history of Russia. In December 1836, Ustrialov submitted the first volume of his work. Uvarov approved it a month later, recommending the volume as a standard textbook to his subordinates in educational districts throughout the empire. In 1839, Ustrialov produced a one-volume synthesis of his larger work, which Uvarov presented to the tsar. The next year, Uvarov closed the competition for the best textbook of Russian history. The task accomplished, the award eventually went to Ustrialov.

What attracted Uvarov so much in Ustrialov's compendium, titled *Russian History*, was Ustrialov's presentation of the reclamation of the Kyivan lands, which had been lost through treachery to foreign powers, as the leitmotif of Russian history. Ustrialov wrote: "The major fact in the history of the Russian tsardom was the gradual development of the idea of the need to reestablish the Russian land within the borders it had under Yaroslav [the Wise]. . . . [A]ll our conflicts with Poland, the Livonian Order, and the Swedes . . . stem from this fact." In Ustrialov's interpretation, the Lithuanian state was a dynastic rather than a national rival of Moscow, and he claimed that difficulties in relations between Lithuanian rulers and their "Russian" subjects had begun only with the arrival of the Poles in the fourteenth century. Ustrialov wrote three versions of his survey, which was printed a total of twenty-six times.

In the 1857 edition, Ustrialov claimed that the population of Kyivan Rus' had constituted one nation, thereby completing the process of supplementing Karamzin's statist approach with one based on the principle of nationality and extending the scope of Russian history not only in institutional but also in geographic terms. As Ustrialov conceived it, Russian history was now something more than just the history of the Russian state. It also included historically Russian lands that did not belong to that state.

APART FROM HISTORY, RUSSIAN LANGUAGE AND CULTURE EMERGED as the principal tools of the government's new policy in the borderlands. Education with Russian as the language of instruction was meant to suppress a sense of separate nationality among Polish youth. To that end, new educational institutions and policies were established in the western provinces of the empire.

The empire needed new people to introduce those policies. In 1802, when the empire created its first ministry of education, it was entrusted to Petro Zavadovsky, a former Cossack official and, more importantly, a graduate of the Kyivan Academy and a Jesuit seminary in the Belarusian town of Orsha, which had then belonged to the Polish-Lithuanian Commonwealth. Zavadovsky's subordinates who headed educational institutions in the western borderlands of the empire were Polish aristocrats. Adam Jerzy Czartoryski, an adviser to Alexander I and for some time foreign minister of the Russian Empire, also ran the Vilnius educational district between 1803 and 1817. The district included Lithuanian, Ukrainian, and Belarusian provinces annexed from the Commonwealth. The Kharkiv educational district, which encompassed eastern Ukraine, was administered during the same period by a fellow Polish aristocrat, Seweryn Potocki. The Poles had more experience than Russian educators because of the pioneering activities of the Polish Educational Commission, created in 1773 in the partitioned Commonwealth to establish a system of public education in the country, including its Ukrainian and Belarusian provinces.

The Polish-run universities and schools turned out to be something more than institutions of general education. They also popularized Polish culture and spread anti-imperial ideas, as became obvious in 1830, when the University of Vilnius became a recruiting ground for the Polish insurrection. In May 1832, the imperial authorities closed the university (it would not reopen until the fall of the Romanov dynasty) and dissolved the Vilnius educational district. But shutdowns and prohibitions could take the empire only so far. The void left by the closure of the Polish institutions had to be filled with imperial ones. In November 1833, Nicholas I approved Sergei Uvarov's proposal to open a new university in the city of Kyiv, which Pushkin had feared a few years earlier might fall into Polish hands. In fact, if one did not count the Kyivan Cave Monastery and Orthodox churches, the city was already dominated by Polish culture. Visitors heard more Polish spoken in the streets of Kyiv than Russian or Ukrainian. In Kyiv province there were 43,000 Polish nobles as against slightly more than 1,000 Russian ones, and it was Poles who defined the public face of Kyiv.

The first attempt to open a Russian university in Kyiv was made in 1805, when Petro Zavadovsky sought to convince the city's metropolitan to help him turn the Kyivan Academy into a university. The minister did not get much support from the hierarch. Also nonsupportive were the Polish nobles, the only group with enough money to fund the institution. One of the best Polish educators of the period, Tadeusz Czacki, was working hard to obtain donations from the nobility for a Polish institution of higher learning. To avoid competition with Kyiv, he called it a gymnasium rather than a university and proposed to open it in the Volhynian town of Kremianets. Backed by the curator of the district of Volhynia, Adam Czartoryski, and donations from Polish nobles, Czacki succeeded in opening the Kremianets school, which became a lyceum in 1819. The lyceum, a hotbed of insurgency during the uprising of 1830, was swiftly closed by the authorities. Kyiv's time had come. The lyceum's library, which had close to 35,000 volumes, its chemical laboratory, and its botanical garden were shipped to Kyiv for the new university. Some of the professors also came along.

The story of the Polish lyceum was effectively over, while that of the Russian university in Kyiv was about to begin. It was named after St. Volodymyr, the tenth-century prince who was regarded as the founder of the Russian state and its first Orthodox ruler. The opening took place on July 15, 1834, St. Volodymyr's Day according to the Orthodox calendar. In symbolic terms, the imperial authorities were reclaiming Volodymyr's city. In his decree on the opening of the university, Nicholas I called Kyiv "precious to all Russia, the cradle of the holy faith of our ancestors and first witness of their civic individuality." The minister of education, Count Uvarov, dubbed the university a "mental fortress." There was no doubt whom it was supposed to protect, and who the enemy was. According to the minister, the new university was "to smooth over, as much as possible, the sharp characteristics whereby Polish youth is distinguished from the Russian, and particularly to suppress the idea of a separate nationality among them, to bring them closer and closer to Russian ideas and customs, to imbue them with the common spirit of the Russian people."

The first rector of the university was Mykhailo Maksymovych, a native of the former Hetmanate. He came to Kyiv from Moscow University, where he had been a professor of botany. A man of many talents, at Uvarov's personal request he now took on the much more politically important position of professor of Russian philology. Maksymovych's appointment exemplified the strategy chosen by St. Petersburg to Russify the educational system in the newly annexed territories. The foot soldiers of the new policy—and, indeed, some of their field commanders—were cadres from the former Hetmanate. This seemed an obvious choice: they knew the local language, culture, and conditions, and they were as anti-Polish as one could imagine at the time.

In time, however, the government's reliance on natives of the Hetmanate would become problematic. By the late 1840s, the inhabitants of that region would acquire a national agenda of their own, presenting an unexpected challenge to the empire. For the time being, however, the Ukrainians from the former Hetmanate did their best to fight Polish influences.

Kyiv, with its new university, became a construction site of the new imperial Russian identity. Pilgrimages of Russian intellectuals and officials to that city had begun in the early nineteenth century, with travelers looking for the origins of Russian history as presented in the Rus' chronicles. By the 1820s, little remained of Kyiv's princely past except a few churches, so enthusiasts undertook archeological digs to uncover the city's lost heritage. In 1832–1833, the local amateur archeologist Kondratii Lokhvitsky conducted excavations of Kyiv's Golden Gate—the main entrance to the city, built by Prince Yaroslav the Wise in the first half of the eleventh century in an attempt to emulate the Golden Gates of Constantinople. The excavations were visited by Emperor Nicholas I himself, who gave Lokhvitsky an award for his work and provided funds for more excavations.

At that time, Kyiv was a predominantly Polish and Jewish city. Its Russification was literally proceeding from below as ancient ruins, accurately or inaccurately dated to princely times, emerged from beneath the surface of the earth. The first rector of Kyiv University, Mykhailo Maksymovych, became among other things a guide to the world of "Russian antiquities" for scores of prominent guests, starting with Nikolai Gogol (Mykola Hohol') and the professor of Russian history at Moscow University, Mikhail Pogodin, and ending with the future tsar Alexander II, who was accompanied by his tutor, Vasilii Zhukovsky, Russia's best-known poet of the pre-Pushkin era.

In 1853, the Kyiv authorities celebrated a special event in the history of their city—the unveiling of a monument to Prince Volodymyr. This was the culmination of a project that had taken twenty years: the first proposal to erect the statue had been submitted to the tsar by the governor general of Kyiv back in 1833. It was unveiled on the same day as the opening of a chain-link bridge across the Dnieper connecting the city's Left Bank with its rebellious Right Bank. By that time, Kyiv already had a special institution charged with the task of substantiating Russia's claim to the entire Right Bank of Ukraine. The Archeographic Commission, established in 1843 under the supervision of the governor general, went on two years later to issue its first collection of documents from local depositories that were intended to demonstrate the inalienably Russian identity of the region. In decades to come, it would issue hundreds of volumes of valuable sources that ultimately supported local inhabitants' claims to an identity distinct from the Russian.

WITH THE POLISH UPRISING CRUSHED, THE EMPIRE ONCE AGAIN had to address the question of the Uniate Church, which numbered 1.5 million followers, mainly in territories that had been annexed to the Russian Empire after the third partition of Poland. Most of the Uniates who lived on lands taken over in the second partition had been converted to Orthodoxy during the time of Catherine II.

When leaders of the Polish nobility in the western provinces issued a call to arms in 1830 and 1831, it was met with understanding and even enthusiasm by many Uniate priests, with monastics offering particularly strong support. According to government estimates, close to two-thirds of those belonging to the Uniate Order of St. Basil in the Lithuanian province were Roman Catholics. Among those who fully supported the insurrection were the Basilian monks of the Pochaiv Monastery in Volhynia—a former stronghold of Orthodoxy that had converted to the Union in the early eighteenth century. The monastery's printing shop published an appeal to the inhabitants of Ukraine, asking them to join the uprising. Not only did the monks welcome a Polish military unit to the monastery in April 1831, but eight of them joined the rebels. They rode on horseback in monastic garb, swords at their side, calling on the crowds to join the fight for the fatherland. Forty-five members of the monastery joined the insurgent ranks. The loyalty of the Uniate peasants was clearly at stake, and the government acted without delay. In September 1831, at the request of the military and civil authorities, Nicholas I signed a decree dissolving the Uniate monastery in Pochaiv. Its buildings were turned over to the Orthodox Church, which opened its own monastery there. Altogether, about half the ninety-five Uniate monasteries that had existed in the empire before 1830 were shut down in the wake of the Polish uprising.

Nicholas I also accelerated his earlier plans to convert the entire Uniate population to Orthodoxy by devising an institutional unification of Orthodox and Uniate churches. Like many members of the Russian imperial elite, he considered the Uniate Ukrainian and Belarusian peasants to be quintessential Russians who had been forced to abandon their native Orthodox faith by Polish pressure and intrigue, which now endangered their national identity. While stationed with his military unit in the western provinces of the empire before his ascension to the throne, the future tsar had been struck by the poverty of the Uniate priests and their churches. Lacking support from the state or from Catholic landowners, some Uniate clergymen had sought ways of "returning" the Uniates to the Orthodox Church even before the Polish uprising. Nicholas found a perfect candidate to achieve that goal in the twenty-nine-year-old Iosif Semashko, a Uniate priest and member of the Spiritual College in St. Petersburg, an institution charged with supervising the activities of the Roman Catholic and Uniate churches in the empire.

Semashko, a native of Right-Bank Ukraine, was born in 1798, a few years after the region came under Russian control as a result of the second partition of Poland. His father was a Uniate priest who had refused to accept Orthodoxy and lost his parish. As a child, the young Semashko more often attended Orthodox services in his native village than Roman Catholic ones farther away, as there were few Uniate churches remaining in his neighborhood. A talented youth, he was first sent to study at a school in the town of Nemyriv in Podolia and then at the joint Roman Catholic–Uniate seminary in Vilnius University. Both institutions were centers of Polish education and culture under the patronage of the inspector of the Vilnius educational district, Adam Czartoryski. The young Semashko had to master Polish and later remembered the privileged status of the sons of the Polish nobility at the Nemyriv school and the atmosphere of Polish patriotism and anti-Russian sentiment in Vilnius, where his reading of a Russian journal with a fellow student was regarded as an act of national treason.

But it was not until Semashko was sent to serve as an officer of the Spiritual College in St. Petersburg that he decided to link his future with the Orthodox Church. He was impressed by the grandeur of the imperial capital and the richness of St. Petersburg's Orthodox churches, but appalled by the patronizing attitude of the Roman Catholic clergy toward Uniates. Compelled to choose either a Polish or a Russian identity (he saw no other option), Semashko decided that he was a Russian and, as such, had to belong to the Russian church. To achieve that, he had to make his Uniate Church Russian, which meant Orthodox.

"Immeasurable Russia, bound by one faith and one language, directed by a single will toward a blessed goal, became for me a great attractive fatherland. I considered it my sacred duty to serve it and promote its welfare," remembered Semashko later. In 1827, he prepared a memorandum for the government outlining his plan for the gradual conversion of the Uniates to Orthodoxy, which caught the emperor's eye and won his full approval.

Semashko's plan was in many ways a continuation of the official policy toward Uniates during the liberal rule of Alexander I. The forcible conversion of Uniates to Orthodoxy that had marked the rule of Catherine II was no longer practiced. The change of policy was due not only to the tsar's ideological preference for toleration but also to the failure of the pressure applied to the Uniates to yield the desired result. Indeed, it had produced an unwanted result: rather than becoming Orthodox, some 200,000 Uniate peasants had joined the Roman Catholic Church in the late eighteenth and early nineteenth centuries. In 1805, on Alexander's orders, a special Uniate department was created within the Spiritual College, which had previously overseen the activities of Roman Catholics only. The Uniate metropolitan welcomed this official recognition of his church and, with government support, embarked on an effort to free the Uniate liturgy from Latin borrowings and influences.

Semashko, however, wanted much more than just to stop the conversion of Uniates to Roman Catholicism. In preparation for the unification of the Uniate and Orthodox churches, he suggested the establishment of a Uniate Spiritual College separate from the Catholic one, as well as a Uniate seminary to train Uniate priests in an Orthodox spirit, thereby preparing cadres for future unification. The Uniate Basilian monastic order, which Semashko considered the main instrument of Latin and Polish influence in the region, was to be subordinated to the Uniate bishops in order to prevent Roman Catholics from joining the order. In April 1828, Nicholas I issued a decree that closely followed Semashko's recommendations. Semashko himself was consecrated a Uniate bishop in the following year and put in charge of one of the two Uniate eparchies remaining in the empire.

The Polish uprising brought the Uniate question closer to the center of the government's concerns and, for the first time, made it the object of public attention and debate. Semashko felt that he had to speed up the realization of his original plan. In 1832, Nicholas I approved Semashko's idea of subordinating the Uniate College, now independent from that of the Catholics, to the Orthodox Synod, but that measure was not realized. The Orthodox authorities, backed by public opinion, made it a priority to convert individual Uniate parishes rather than the entire Uniate Church to their faith. Disheartened, Semashko requested permission to convert to Orthodoxy himself, but he was prevented from doing so by the Orthodox hierarchs, who now promised to assist him in his efforts to prepare the ground for the future conversion of the entire church.

Semashko redoubled his efforts. His promotion of the "Orthodoxization" of Uniate parishes went hand in hand with their cultural Russification. He would later assert that he had been guided by one thought: "how to turn Uniates into born-again Russian Orthodox." Semashko busied himself convincing priests to erect an Orthodox-style iconostasis—a high screen or wall of icons separating the nave from the sanctuary—in Uniate churches that had eliminated them under Catholic influence, replacing old Uniate service books with Russian ones, and encouraging Uniate priests to grow beards, as was customary among their Orthodox counterparts. The use of Russian service books also meant introducing the Russian language into spheres where it had not previously been present. It was an uphill battle, as the priests were much more comfortable with Polish, the language in which they corresponded with Semashko. He himself was mortified by what he considered his inadequate mastery of Russian, even though he regarded himself as more Russian than many native speakers of that language.

Semashko also conducted a campaign of anti-Polish propaganda among his priests, trying to turn their Ruthenian (Ukrainian and Belarusian) identity into a Russian one. "In order to warm the hearts of the Uniate clergy with the Russian spirit, every possible opportunity was taken to revive the memory of their origins, the Polish repressions that they had suffered, and the paternal concern of the Russian government for their welfare," wrote Semashko in 1837. He thought his efforts were bringing some results: "The previously alien notion of taking pride in the Russian name and heritage," he wrote, "is now treasured by a very considerable portion of the clergy subordinate to me."

Generally speaking, however, Semashko felt overwhelmed by the difficulties that his project encountered. The Orthodox authorities were suspicious of him as someone who opposed direct conversions and was trying to build up the Uniate Church, while the Roman Catholic clergy regarded him as their sworn enemy. More importantly, the Uniate priests whom Semashko was trying to bring back to their "Russian" roots, even if they sympathized with him, were caught between the Roman Catholic landowners, who controlled resources in the village, and the conservative peasants, who wanted no change at all. The one power Semashko had was that of appointing Uniate priests to their parishes and removing those whom he considered opponents of his policy, thereby denying income to the malcontents and their families. He used that power extensively, working together with the civil authorities and the police to crush resistance among the Uniate clergy. He was a zealot who apparently had no regrets or doubts about what he was doing, and he finally obtained the full support of the authorities.

By the mid-1830s, Nicholas I and his government had become more serious than ever in their efforts to eliminate the Uniate Church. In 1835, Semashko was invited to join a secret government committee charged with bringing about unification. Two years later, Semashko's old idea of subordinating the Uniate hierarchy to the Orthodox Synod, which the tsar had approved in 1832, was finally implemented. Two deaths—that of an elderly Uniate metropolitan, Iosafat Bulhak, and that of a bishop who had opposed unification—resulted in Semashko being put in charge of church administration, opening the way for the realization of his old dream of the religious reunification of the Russian nation.

With the support of the Orthodox authorities and the backing of the civil administration, Semashko convoked a Uniate Church council to consider the issue. The synod was supposed to issue an appeal to the tsar drafted by Semashko. "With Lithuania's detachment of Russian provinces in troubled times and their subsequent annexation to Poland, their Russian Orthodox inhabitants were subjected [to persecution]," Semashko wrote. "Since then, those people, separated from the broad Russian masses, have constantly been subjected to all the devices of a policy of fanaticism intended to make them alien to Russia." Semashko continued: "A million and a half Uniates, Russian by language and origin . . . would have remained somewhat alien to the broad mass of their actual brethren, the Russians."

The synod took place in February 1839 in the Belarusian town of Polatsk, the home of the seventeenth-century Westernizer of Muscovy Simeon of Polatsk. In preparation for the event, with the help of the authorities, Semashko collected 1,305 statements from Uniate priests indicating their readiness to join the Orthodox Church. Despite pressure, arrests, and exile of opponents of the "reverse Union," 593 priests refused to sign the statement. To forestall possible peasant riots, the authorities sent a Cossack regiment to Vitsebsk province. On February 12, 1839, the Polatsk synod adopted the Act of Union and issued an appeal to the tsar prepared by Semashko, asking him to accept close to 1,600 Uniate parishes and close to 1.5 million parishioners into the body of imperial Orthodoxy. Semashko served an Orthodox liturgy in the St. Sophia Cathedral in Polatsk before taking the document to the imperial capital. The St. Petersburg Synod—the ruling body of the Orthodox Church—was glad to approve the request. The imperial hierarchs celebrated not only the adherence of the Uniates but also the return of part of the Russian tribe to its brethren. The Synod welcomed "the reconsolidation of the ancient interrupted union and the reestablishment of perfect unity" with the Uniates, who had been "united with us for ages by unity of kin, fatherland, language, faith, liturgy, and church hierarchy."

Nicholas I offered a token of approval in the spirit of Catherine II by having a special medal struck for the occasion. Its inscription echoed the one on the medal that she had issued upon the second partition of Poland: "Torn away by force (1596), reunited by love (1839)." Like Catherine, Nicholas was reacting to a Polish insurrection and trying to prevent Ukrainian and Belarusian peasants from joining it by converting them to Orthodoxy. But there was also an important new element in Nicholas's policy. He was not just returning what he believed historically belonged to the Romanov dynasty, but also striving to restore the broken unity of the Russian nation. Autocracy, Orthodoxy, and nationality were to be mutually reinforcing elements of an attempt to integrate the western provinces into the empire. But the fait accompli of 1839 contained the seeds of future problems. The provinces reunited "by love" with the Orthodox Church and the Russian nation under the tsarist scepter would soon challenge the model of nationality promoted by the authors of the Polatsk synod.

III

THE TRIPARTITE NATION

7

THE ADVENT OF UKRAINE

THEY PLANNED THE WEDDING FOR SUNDAY, MARCH 30, 1847, but two days earlier police officials unexpectedly showed up at the groom's apartment and arrested him, postponing the wedding for twenty-eight long years. The arrested man was a twenty-nine-year-old professor of history at Kyiv University, Mykola (Nikolai) Kostomarov. On the evening of March 31, a day after his wedding was supposed to take place, Kostomarov was sent under police escort to St. Petersburg: the order for his arrest had come from the very top of the imperial hierarchy.

It was given by Count Aleksei Orlov, head of the Third Section of the Imperial Chancellery—the body responsible for political surveillance. The heir to the throne, the future Tsar Alexander II, was briefed on the case, which involved a number of Kyivan intellectuals—government officials, teachers, and students. One of them, Taras Shevchenko, an artist and popular poet who wrote in Ukrainian, was arrested on April 5, upon his arrival in Kyiv, and also escorted to St. Petersburg. There were further arrests and more deportations to the capital, where the liberal public was at a loss to explain the authorities' actions.

The governor general of Kyiv, Podolia, and Volhynia, Dmitrii Bibikov, was then in St. Petersburg, reporting on, among other things, a proclamation that had been found on the wall of a building in Kyiv. It read: "Brothers! A great hour is upon us, an hour in which you are being given the opportunity to wash off the dishonor inflicted on the dust of our ancestors, on our native Ukraine, by the base hand of our eternal foes. Who among you will not lend a hand to this great undertaking? God and good people are with us! The ever loyal sons of Ukraine, foes of the *katsapy* [derogatory term for Russians]."

The appeal was as anti-Russian as could be imagined, but it was written in Russian, not Polish, and not addressed to the Polish nobles who then dominated Kyiv society. It was directed to "the faithful sons of Ukraine"—people whom the imperial government considered Russian by nationality. Bibikov was sent back to Kyiv with orders to take over supervision of the Kyiv educational district. At a meeting with faculty and students of the university, he warned them against "loose thinking," threatening, "If I managed to bring 5 million people to heel, then I will do it to you as well: either I will burst, or all of you will explode!" The reference was to the millions of the inhabitants of Right-Bank Ukraine, entrusted to Bibikov but claimed as followers by the Polish insurgents.

There was no doubt that this manifestation of disloyalty came from the very institutions that had been created to ensure the loyalty of the region's inhabitants to tsar and empire. Mykola Kostomarov taught at the university, while Taras Shevchenko, who had just been appointed instructor of drawing there, had earlier been employed by the Archeographic Commission, which aimed to document the Russian identity of Right-Bank Ukraine. Official policy appeared to have backfired. Instead of solidifying a common front between the government and the "Russian" population of the western provinces against the Polish threat, it had contributed to dividing the imperial Russian nation and promoted the development of a separate nation that would claim equal rights with the Great Russians in the core areas of the empire in the course of the next few decades. A new Ukrainian nation was emerging from the cocoon of the old Little Russian identity. The imperial government would do everything in its power to stop its development and put the Ukrainian genie back into the Little Russian bottle.

THE THIRD SECTION'S INVESTIGATION INTO THE ACTIVITIES OF Kostomarov, Shevchenko, and others uncovered the existence of a clandestine organization, the Brotherhood of Saints Cyril and Methodius. Its goal was the creation of a voluntary federation of Slavic nations, with Ukraine at its core. The brotherhood became known in government circles as the Slavic Society, later renamed the Ukrainian Slavic Society.

There was reason for the authorities' initial view of the case as part of a broad intellectual movement. As employed by government officials of the 1840s, the designation "Slavophiles" was applied to a group of intellectuals, located mainly in Moscow, who took the issue of nationality—Slavic in general, and Russian in particular—very seriously. Their views coincided only in part with the government's understanding of the principle of nationality as presented in Count Sergei Uvarov's triad of Orthodoxy, autocracy, and nationality. The Slavophiles held Orthodoxy in great esteem but were much less enthusiastic about the government. Moreover, they believed that with the introduction of Western practices by Peter I, Russia had almost lost its unique character.

The Slavophile movement emerged in opposition to the "Westernizers" among the Russian intellectual and political elite, who saw Western Europe as a model for Russia's development. Their viewpoint was first fully articulated in the *Philosophical Letters* of Petr Chaadaev, who criticized the Russian social and intellectual scene, claiming that his country was lagging behind the West. Written in the years following the Decembrist Uprising, the letters were first published in 1836 and provoked a negative reaction not only from the government, which closed the journal that published the letters, but also from the nascent Slavophile movement, led by the prominent theologian, philosopher, and poet Aleksei Khomiakov. Khomiakov's followers were influenced by the ideas of Friedrich Schelling, a friend and later rival of G. W. F. Hegel, whose vision of society as a living organism appealed to them. Their texts emphasized the Russian historical tradition, the importance of the church, and differences between Russia and the West.

Among the key figures of the Slavophile movement mentioned by investigators of the Brotherhood of Saints Cyril and Methodius in their reports were two Moscow University professors, Mikhail Pogodin and Stepan Shevyrev. Pogodin, whom Uvarov had rejected as the prospective author of a Russian history textbook integrating the western provinces into the empire, taught history at Moscow University; Shevyrev lectured there on philology and literature. The two also served as copublishers of the journal *Moskvitianin* (The Muscovite), which became a mouthpiece of the Slavophile movement in the 1840s. Pogodin was a leading figure in the emerging pan-Slavic movement, which regarded all Slavs as a single family. By stressing the uniqueness (*samobytnost'*) and self-awareness (*samosoznanie*) of the Russian nation, the Slavophiles, for all their pan-Slavic ecumenism, set an example to non-Russian Slavs who wished to celebrate the distinctiveness of their own peoples and, consequently, their right to autonomy and independence.

Early on, Ukraine took a special place in the Slavophile imagination. Pogodin and Shevyrev in particular showed great interest in the culture and history of Ukraine, or, as they called it, Little Russia. In the 1830s, Mykola Kostomarov, then a student at Kharkiv University in eastern Ukraine, had been strongly influenced by Stepan Shevyrev, whose lectures he attended. Shevyrev, who referred to Little Russia as Great Russia's elder sister, put a strong emphasis on nationality and encouraged the study of popular culture. But there was a problem, since "nationality" meant different things in Moscow and Kharkiv. When Kostomarov went to the people to collect their lore, he had to speak to them in Ukrainian, and by 1839 he was already writing in that language. Kostomarov was not the first admirer of nationality to bring back texts from his field trips that were written in a language difficult to understand, if not entirely foreign, to enthusiasts of nationality in Moscow and St. Petersburg.

The first major literary work in vernacular Ukrainian was published in 1798. It appeared in St. Petersburg, where a printshop issued the first three parts of a six-part travesty of Virgil's *Aeneid*, titled *Eneïda*. The Greek characters of the original epic were turned into Ukrainian-speaking Zaporozhian Cossacks. The author, Ivan Kotliarevsky, was descended from a Cossack officer family residing in the former Hetmanate. Employed as a schoolteacher and military officer, he also served as artistic director of a

Poltava theater between 1812 and 1821. During that time, he wrote the first modern Ukrainian-language play, *Natalka from Poltava*. By then the Ukrainian language had already acquired its first grammar, and the first collection of Ukrainian folk songs had seen the light of day.

In the 1830s, Kharkiv became the center of the Ukrainian Romantic movement, with a promising Russian philologist, Izmail Sreznevsky, and the descendant of a local noble family, Hryhorii Kvitka-Osnovianenko, among others, writing on Ukrainian topics and trying their hand at expressing themselves in Ukrainian. In 1833, Kvitka-Osnovianenko produced the first Ukrainian-language short story. Five years later, Kostomarov made his contribution by writing a Ukrainian-language drama on a subject from the Cossack past and then publishing collections of his Ukrainian poems.

But the most important contribution to Ukrainian literature in the late 1830s was made by Kostomarov's future co-conspirator, Taras Shevchenko. Like Kostomarov, Shevchenko was born a serf, but whereas Kostomarov was recognized as a free man at the age of fifteen—his mother was a serf, but his father had been a nobleman—Shevchenko had to wait for his freedom until he was twenty-four. He owed it to the Russian artistic community and, improbably enough, to the generosity of the imperial court. Shevchenko was brought to St. Petersburg by his landlord in the early 1830s, where his artistic talent was noted by the most prominent figures in the Russian artistic and intellectual world. They wanted to set the young artist free and eventually achieved their goal. Kirill Briullov, one of the best painters of the Russian Empire, produced a portrait of Vasilii Zhukovsky, one of the most prominent Russian poets of the era and a tutor of the future Tsar Alexander II. At an auction held in 1838, the portrait went to a member of the imperial family who knew that the proceeds would buy the freedom of a twenty-four-year-old artist born into serfdom.

It was Shevchenko's aptitude for drawing and painting that was recognized at the time. In 1838, after becoming a free man, Shevchenko entered the Imperial Academy of Fine Arts and joined the class of his savior, Briullov. But Shevchenko's real talent lay in poetry and writing. He wrote prose in Russian and poetry in Ukrainian, and it was the latter that both made him famous and got him into trouble, first with the Russian critics and then with the imperial authorities. His collection of Ukrainian-language poetry was first published in 1840 under the title *Kobzar* (Minstrel). It was widely reviewed in Russian literary journals and newspapers: while some critics welcomed the appearance of a collection of Ukrainian poetry, others questioned the legitimacy of such an enterprise, expressing regret over the decision of a gifted poet to waste his talent by writing in Ukrainian.

"It seems to us," wrote one of the critics in a popular journal, *Biblioteka dlia chteniia* (Library for Reading), "that the Little Russian poets pay insufficient attention to the fact that they often write in such a dialect as does not exist even in Russia: they unceremoniously rework Great Russian words and phrases in Little Russian fashion, creating a language for themselves that has never existed, that none of all possible Russias—neither great, nor middle, nor little, nor white, nor black, nor red—could call its own." Another critic proposed that Shevchenko switch to Russian. "We would advise him," wrote this contributor to *Severnaia pchela* (Northern Bee), "to convey his exquisite feelings in Russian. Then his little flowers, as he calls his verses, would be richer and more fragrant and, above all, longer-lasting."

Shevchenko was not the only author attacked by Russian reviewers for his use of Ukrainian as opposed to Russian. When Kotliarevsky's *Eneïda* was first fully published in 1842, it met with a similar reaction. "For Russian readers who have not had the opportunity to live in Little Russia or its neighboring lands," wrote a contributor to *Biblioteka dlia chteniia*, "Mr. Kotliarevsky's poem is incomprehensible, even with the help of a dictionary." Not all Russian critics shared that view, but those who did were not inventing difficulties: the Ukrainian language was indeed hard for Russian readers to understand. Even Gogol's Russian-language writings on Ukrainian subjects were supplied with glossaries.

The differences between the Russian and Ukrainian nationalities did not manifest themselves in language alone. History became another point of contention. After Nikolai Polevoi, the author of a multivolume history of the Russian people, had criticized one of the imperial historians, Dmitrii Bantysh-Kamensky, for failing to take account of a distinct Ukrainian identity in his *History of Little Russia* (1822), the Ukrainian Mykola Markevych embarked on the writing of a new kind of Ukrainian history. His *History of Little Russia* was published in five volumes in 1842–1843. As a template for his work, Markevych used the anonymous manuscript "History of the Rus'" (ca. 1818), which treated Cossack history as the annals of a separate nation. The anonymous work was popularized by Izmail Sreznevsky in Kharkiv and widely read by Kostomarov and his circle, shaping their perception of the Ukrainian past as distinct from the Russian.

In 1846, the 1818 manuscript was published in Moscow by Osyp Bodiansky, a Ukrainian-born professor of Slavic studies at Moscow University who was also a member of the Slavophile circle mentioned in the investigation of the Brotherhood of Saints Cyril and Methodius. Another potential suspect, Mikhail Pogodin, saw cultural differences between Russians and Ukrainians that went beyond language and history. He wrote in 1845, "The Great Russians live side by side with the Little Russians, profess one faith, have shared one fate and, for many years, one history. But how many differences there are between the Great Russians and the Little Russians!"

By the mid-nineteenth century, the Slavophiles' belief in the unity of Great and Little Russia and their treatment of the latter as the fountainhead of Russian culture was being challenged by the Little Russians' search for a nationality of their own. Encouraged by like-minded individuals in Moscow and St. Petersburg to investigate and embrace issues of nationality, the Ukrainians brought to the salons of St. Petersburg and Moscow not only a language quite different from Russian but also a history distinct from that of the Russian people and state. It would soon become clear that language, history, and culture could be used not only to construct a past separate from that of the Great Russians but also a different future. In that new vision, Little Russia would turn into Ukraine, an entity still close to Russia but also very different and quite separate from it.

THE INVESTIGATION INTO THE ACTIVITIES OF THE BROTHERHOOD of Saints Cyril and Methodius was complete in May 1847, when the chief of gendarmes and head of the Third Section of the Imperial Chancellery, Count Aleksei Orlov, reported his findings to the tsar. "The uncovering of a Slavic, or, more correctly, a Ukrainian-Slavic, society began with a student at Kyiv University, Aleksei Petrov," wrote Orlov. Petrov was the impoverished son of a former police official. He rented a room in the same building as one of the active participants in the brotherhood, overheard its members' discussions, and was invited to attend some of their meetings. What he heard at those meetings made him to go to the authorities and denounce his neighbors. According to Petrov, the members were discussing preparations for a popular revolt against the imperial authorities with the goal of uniting all of the Slavic nations and establishing a government based on popular representation. To achieve their goal, he said, they were prepared to do away with the imperial family.

But, in Orlov's view, the interrogation of participants in the brotherhood and the analysis of its programmatic documents showed only that the original fears and concerns had been exaggerated. The brotherhood consisted of only three members, including Kostomarov. Acquaintances, such as Shevchenko, occasionally participated in the discussions, but even those petered out after a few months. The members of the brotherhood and their circle of friends were not preparing an uprising, and they allegedly only wanted to achieve the unification of the Slavic tribes under the auspices of the Russian tsar. "The political evil per se, fortunately, had not managed to develop to the extent suggested by the preliminary reports," wrote Orlov to the tsar.

Historians later claimed that Orlov either deliberately or inadvertently underestimated the threat presented by the brotherhood and thus misrepresented or misunderstood the nature of its program. The "political evil" that the authorities were concerned about was expressed in a number of texts, the most elaborate of which was *The Law of God, or Books of the Genesis of the Ukrainian People*. Orlov called it a reworking of a text by the Polish poet Adam Mickiewicz, while Kostomarov claimed at his interrogation that it had been composed by Poles in the early 1830s. In actual fact, Kostomarov was its main author, and the *Books of the Genesis* presented many of the ideas discussed by the members of the brotherhood.

The political goal put forward in the work was indeed, as the authorities had feared at the start of the investigation, the creation of a Slavic confederation based on the principle of popular representation, with no role envisioned for the tsar. The members of the imperial family were treated as German usurpers imposing their autocratic rule on the freedom-loving Slavs. The social order of the future Slavic state was supposed to be based on equality and Christian ethics. According to the text, there was no tsar but the ruler of the heavens. Kostomarov accepted only two elements of Uvarov's tripartite formula, religion and nationality, rejecting autocracy. But religion was interpreted in non-autocratic form, and the nationality endorsed in the *Books* was Ukrainian, not Russian.

The *Books* characterized the Ukrainians as a people distinct from both the Russians and the Poles who were destined to lead the future Slavic federation. The Ukrainians had a special role because they were the most egalitarian and democratic of all the Slavs. If the Russians were ruled by an autocratic tsar and the Poles had an overbearing caste of noble landowners, the Ukrainians were a peasant nation that cherished its democratic Cossack traditions. What were the distinguishing characteristics of the Ukrainians, aside from their egalitarian social structure? According to Kostomarov's friend and fellow suspect Panteleimon Kulish, those characteristics were language and customs. Another co-conspirator, Heorhii Andruzky, envisioned Ukraine as encompassing not only the lands settled by Ukrainians in the Russian Empire but also territory extending into Austrian Galicia. Kostomarov saw the future Ukrainian state as a republic in a union of equals with other Slavic states. He concluded the *Books* with the following statement: "Ukraine will become an independent republic in a Slavic union. Then all the peoples will say, indicating the place where Ukraine will be drawn on the map, 'Here is the stone rejected by the builder: it will be the cornerstone.'"

Orlov recommended punishing the Ukrainophiles—a term that he invented to denote the core members of the brotherhood and their acquaintances—with imprisonment, internal exile, and, in the case of Taras Shevchenko, forced military service. The authorities did not believe that Shevchenko was a member of the society but were disturbed by his verses, in which he not only extolled Ukraine but also attacked the emperor and empress for exploiting his native land. They were appalled by his lack of gratitude to the ruling dynasty: Shevchenko had been born a serf and redeemed with money paid by a member of the royal family.

Orlov was also concerned about the impact that Shevchenko's glorification of the Cossack past could have on readers. "Along with favorite poems, ideas may have been sown and subsequently have taken root in Little Russia about the supposedly happy times of the hetmans, the felicity of restoring those times, and Ukraine's capacity to exist as a separate state," Orlov wrote. The same applied to the prose of Panteleimon Kulish. Heorhii Andruzky entertained the idea of restoring the Hetmanate—one of the main concerns of the authorities, who, in the opinion of some scholars, mistook the new threat of cultural nationalism for the old one of Cossack separatism.

In order to avoid publicizing the brotherhood's program, the authorities convinced Kostomarov and others to change their original testimonies in order to fit the official narrative of the case. According to that version, the brotherhood had wanted nothing more than to unite the Slavs under the scepter of the Russian tsar. But that did not mean absolving the members of their misdeeds: the authorities made public the fact of the brotherhood's existence and the punishment meted out to its members. Orlov recommended a certain level of publicity "so that all may know the fate prepared for themselves by those who occupy themselves with Slavdom in a spirit contrary to our government, and even to divert other Slavophiles from such a path." The sentences were not excessively harsh. Kostomarov, the key figure of the brotherhood, was given a one-year term in the prison of the Peter and Paul Fortress in St. Petersburg, followed by internal exile in the provincial town of Saratov on the Volga River. Others received sentences of one to three years' imprisonment and internal exile. Most of those involved were simply exiled from Ukraine or transferred to Russia.

The authorities viewed the brotherhood's activities through the prism of their ongoing struggle with the Polish nobility for the loyalty of Right-Bank Ukraine. "Obviously the work of that general propaganda from Paris," commented Nicholas I on the investigative reports. "For a long time we did not believe that such work was going on in Ukraine, but now there can be no doubt about it." A memorandum prepared by an officer of the Third Section developed the same theme while arguing against harsh punishment of the suspects: "Harsh measures will make forbidden thoughts even dearer to them and may cause the hitherto submissive Little Russians to adopt the nervous attitude against our government in which the Kingdom of Poland finds itself after the revolt. It would be more expedient and just not even to give any appearance to the Little Russians that the government had any reason to suspect that harmful ideas had been sown among them."

Not showing that the government was unduly concerned was one thing; dealing with the newly uncovered problem of Little Russian disloyalty was another. A memorandum prepared by officers of the Third Section suggested measures to curb the future spread of Ukrainophile ideas. It read: "Through the minister of popular education, to warn all those dealing with Slavdom, antiquity, and nationality, as well as professors, teachers, and censors, that in their books and lectures they sedulously avoid any mention of Little Russia, Poland, and other lands subject to Russia that may be understood in a sense dangerous to the integrity and peace of the empire, and that, on the contrary, they strive as much as possible to incline all lessons of scholarship and history toward the true loyalty of all those tribes to Russia." In 1854, Uvarov, in turn, reminded the minister of the interior of an imperial decree suggesting that "writers should be most careful when handling the question of Little Russian ethnicity and language, lest love for Little Russia outweigh affection for the fatherland—the Empire."

Faced with the Polish threat in the western provinces, and using the idea of Russian nationality as a weapon in the struggle for control of the region, the government had to be careful not to allow the idea of nationality to undermine the principle of autocracy and the unity of the empire. It was a difficult balancing act, but the authorities understood the complexity of the task.

ALTHOUGH THE PUBLIC WAS ALLOWED TO KNOW NOTHING ABOUT these and other "destructive ideas," the rumor mill was doing its job. Aleksandr Nikitenko, a literary censor in St. Petersburg, recorded in his diary: "In the south, in Kyiv, a society has been uncovered whose goal was a confederal union of all Slavs in Europe on democratic foundations, on the model of the North American States.... It is said that all this was brought to light by the representations of the Austrian government."

The Russian Westernizers had a field day. They had always regarded the Little Russian project with suspicion, considering it an intrigue designed to force Russia off the road of European progress and drag it back into the pre-Petrine past, and were constantly polemicizing with the Slavophiles. One leading Westernizer, the literary critic Vissarion Belinsky, in expressing his solidarity with the regime, wrote: "Shevchenko was sent to the Caucasus as a soldier. I have no pity for him: if I were his judge, I would do no less. I hold a personal grudge against liberals of that sort. They are the enemies of achievement of any kind. With their impertinent idiocies they irritate the government and make it suspicious, ready to see rebellion where there is nothing of the kind, and provoke harsh measures that are deadly to literature and education."

Commenting on Panteleimon Kulish's suggestion that Ukraine should separate from Russia, Belinsky continued his line of attack: "Oh, those topknots [*khokhly*, a derogatory term for Ukrainians]! They are just dumb sheep, but they liberalize in the name of dumplings with pig fat! And now that it is forbidden to write anything, they befoul everything. But on the other hand, how can one blame the government? What government would allow the advocacy in print of separating one of its provinces?"

The official investigation of the brotherhood exonerated the Moscow Slavophiles. The Slavophile writer and activist Fedor Chizhov, originally suspected of membership in the brotherhood, escaped persecution not only because he was found to have had no contacts with it, but also because, according to Orlov, he "turned out to be only a Slavophile, a champion of Russian nationality in the spirit of Moscow scholars." According to a report filed by an agent of the Third Section, the Russian Slavophiles were united only by "some kind of murky and mystical premonitions of the intellectual victory of the East over the West, by attachment to antiquity, by love for Moscow, and, consequently, by some kind of malevolence toward Petersburg." He continued: "No one suspects a political aim, although the desire and expectation is expressed that Russia, casting aside foreign elements of development, take an exclusively national path of development." He was right. One of the leaders of the Slavophile movement, Aleksei Khomiakov, upon hearing about the goals of the brotherhood, wrote, "The Little Russians were eventually affected with political stupidity. It is sad and painful to see such nonsense and backwardness. . . . Moral struggle—this is what we have to think about today."

The arrests and sentences made the Russian Slavophiles distance themselves from their Ukrainian brethren. This was true even of such "Ukrainophiles" among the Moscow intellectuals as Mikhail Pogodin. According to the report of a government informer, Pogodin began to speak differently about the Slavophile idea after the arrests. What that meant in practice was demonstrated by his review of the *History of the Rus'*, the anonymous text that Osyp Bodiansky had published in Moscow in 1846 presenting the exploits of the Ukrainian Cossacks as the history of a separate nation, which influenced the thinking of Kostomarov and his circle. In 1849, in a review that appeared in the journal *Moskvitianin*, of which he was a copublisher, Pogodin noted that the *History* "passed over in silence all the advantages that accrued to [Little Russia] from unification with mighty Great Rus', the heart of the Russian state." His earlier reading of the *History*, whose authorship was attributed at the time to Archbishop Heorhii Konysky, had been quite different. "I read Konysky with satisfaction," wrote Pogodin in 1846, a year before the arrests. He went on to express his approval of the way in which the author of the *History of the Rus'* portrayed the cruelty of Peter I and his assistants in Ukraine.

In 1851, Pogodin wrote a text styled as a letter to the distinguished philologist Izmail Sreznevsky, a former member of the circle of Kharkiv Romantics. There, Pogodin claimed for Great Russia the history of Kyivan Rus', which he had earlier regarded as part of the history of Little Russia. This claim marked the beginning of a prolonged Russo-Ukrainian debate over the legacy of Kyivan Rus', but for Pogodin it was a natural development of his earlier views on the Slavic nationalities and their histories. He believed that history was a product of the activities of nationalities, and each nationality had a history of its own. As long as the (Great) Russians and Ukrainians (Little Russians) were distinct Slavic nationalities (such as the Bulgarians, Serbs, and Czechs), the Kyivan past had to belong to one of them. Pogodin decided that it belonged to Great Russia.

Already in the mid-1830s, Pogodin had had trouble satisfying Uvarov's request to combine the history of northeastern and southwestern Rus' into a single narrative. In the mid-1840s, Pogodin suggested that there had been linguistic differences among the population as early as Kyivan times, and that they coincided with nineteenth-century distinctions between Great Russians, Little Russians, and White Russians. Thus the population of Kyiv, Chernihiv, and Halych spoke Little Russian, that of Minsk and Vitsebsk spoke White Russian (Belarusian), and that of Vladimir and Moscow spoke Great Russian. He considered the Kyivan princes, including even a major figure of Russian history, Andrei Bogoliubsky, to have been Little Russian. It was only Bogoliubsky's descendants, argued Pogodin, who had "gone native" in the northeastern lands and become Great Russians. Bogoliubsky himself, like his father and the founder of Moscow, Yurii Dolgoruky, had been a Little Russian.

Pogodin's account of Kyivan Rus' history deprived the early Great Russian narrative of its most prized element—the Kyivan period. In his letter to Sreznevsky, Pogodin decided to correct that problem with another twist of his linguistic argument. He asserted that, in reading the early Kyivan chronicles, he had detected no trace of the Little Russian language, but that there were clear connections between the chronicle entries and the Great Russian language. Equating language with nation, Pogodin suggested that it was Great Russians, not Little Russians, who had inhabited Kyiv during its golden age and created its history and annals. The Little Russians, he went on to argue, had appeared in the region only after the Mongol invasion, which pushed the Great Russians farther north.

Pogodin published his letter in 1856, five years after writing it. It provoked an immediate critical response from his old acquaintance Mykhailo Maksymovych, who explained to his friend in a series of published letters that the language of the Kyivan chroniclers was Church Slavonic, based on South Slavic dialects. As such, it bore little relation to the spoken language of the population of Kyivan Rus'. Maksymovych acknowledged the existence of differences between the Great Russian and Little Russian languages prior to the Mongol invasion, but said they were closely related to each other. He also regarded the histories of northern and southern Rus' before the Mongol invasion as being closely related. In effect, Maksymovych rebuffed Pogodin's Great Russian claim to Kyiv and defended the Little Russian (Ukrainian) character of Kyivan Rus' history. But Maksymovych was not a separatist: for him, the Little Russian ethnic group was part of a larger bipartite all-Russian nation. He wrote to Pogodin: "The fact that I love Kyiv, the city of our first throne, more than you is also natural, since, in cultivating an all-Russian love for it, and a closer Little Russian love for it as well, I also love it as the homeland of my kinsmen."

With the members of the Cyrillo-Methodian Brotherhood in internal exile or lying low after the arrests, the impulse to separate the histories of the Great and Little Russians now began to originate from Moscow, not Kyiv. The bone of contention was no longer the Cossack past, as it had been for Kostomarov, but the Kyivan Rus' past, which both sides considered their own. There is no indication that Maksymovych was able to convince Pogodin to change his opinion. Instead, Pogodin rejected his old view concerning the Little Russian nationality of the Kyivan princes and claimed them, along with Rus' history as a whole, for the Great Russians. In his history of pre-Mongol Rus', published in 1871, Pogodin wrote: "The supposed Little Russians moved north, to the Suzdal land, with Yurii Dolgoruky and

Andrei Bogoliubsky. It would seem that they should have left their Little Russian influence on something—in customs, in language. But no—we see no change in the north at that time; consequently, it was not Little Russians but the selfsame Great Russians who went there."

Judging by his other works and the reports he made to the government on the results of his travels in the Slavic lands, Pogodin regarded the Great and Little Russians as separate nationalities (he wrote that the latter had "all the distinguishing marks of a separate tribe") belonging to the same Russian group. Depending on circumstances, he considered the Galician inhabitants of Austria-Hungary as either a separate group or part of the Little Russian nationality, but he also considered them constituents of a larger Russian nation. In both word and deed, Pogodin supported the development of what he called the Little Russian dialect, but he objected to elevating it to a level equal to Russian. Arguing in the mid-1850s for autonomous status for Poland within the Russian Empire, Pogodin suggested that the boundary should recognize only two languages, Russian and Polish. "Language—that is the true boundary between peoples," he wrote. "Poland is where Polish is spoken. Russia is where Russian is spoken. What principle could be more right or just?"

The Pogodin-Maksymovych debate opened the question of how to divide the historical narrative between Russia and Ukraine. It challenged the model that had dominated the thinking of Russian elites in the first half of the nineteenth century—a model in which Kyivan Rus' was considered to belong to the all-Russian past. More clearly than any of his predecessors, Pogodin divided that past into Great Russian and Little Russian parts. Besides the Great and Little Russians, he recognized the White Russians (Belarusians) as a distinct group, while Maksymovych maintained the established division of the all-Russian nationality into Great (northern) Russians and Little (southern) Russians. Although this difference in the treatment of the all-Russian nationality was not contested in their debate, it would come to the fore in the next decade, the tumultuous 1860s.

Pogodin's letter appeared in print in 1856, the first full year of the rule of the new emperor, Alexander II, a student of Vasilii Zhukovsky known for his liberal leanings. Alexander's rule would begin in an atmosphere of great expectations and bring major political, social, and cultural changes, creating new opportunities for a Russo-Ukrainian intellectual encounter.

A few years later, the members of the Brotherhood of Saints Cyril and Methodius were allowed to return from internal exile. They now moved their activities from Kyiv to St. Petersburg. Shevchenko went there after his release from military service and exile, as did Kostomarov, who in 1859 became a professor of Russian history at St. Petersburg University. Ironically, that was a position that had once been held by the father of the "reunification of Rus'" paradigm, Nikolai Ustrialov.

If Ustrialov was the favorite court historian, Kostomarov now became the favorite of the radical students and liberal public of St. Petersburg. After his inaugural lecture, "he was carried out on their arms," recalled a contemporary. "The great hall of the university was so crowded that listeners sat on the windowsills or two to a seat." In the lecture, Kostomarov set new terms for the debate on nationality, shifting attention to the popular masses, whom he regarded as the main object of historical study. "No law, no institution will be important to us in themselves, but only their application to the people's lives," argued Kostomarov. "Features unimportant to the historian who puts the life of the state first will be a matter of the first importance to us." The debate was clearly entering a new stage.

8

GREAT, LITTLE, AND WHITE

S EPTEMBER 11, 1854, BECAME A DAY OF HUMILIATION FOR THE
Russian navy, later to be recast as a day of Russian glory and sacrifice.
On that late summer day, the commanders of the Russian Black Sea Fleet
were ordered to sink five battleships and two frigates in Sevastopol harbor, their home base. That was just the beginning. In August 1855, all the
remaining Russian ships went to the bottom of the harbor. The Russian
army soon left Sevastopol, marking the empire's defeat in the Crimean War
of 1853–1856.

The Russian fleet was sunk because it turned out to be of little use in
stopping the joint French-British-Ottoman invasion of the Crimea—sails
were no match for the steam engines of the British and French battleships,
and the empire had no steam-powered battleships on the Black Sea. On
the day of the allied landing there in September 1854, there was no wind
to fill the sails, and the Russian ships could not move. All that remained
was to sink them in order to block the access of the allied fleet to Sevastopol harbor. To the embarrassment of the rulers of the empire and the

amazement of future historians, the occupying powers got around that problem by building the first railroad in the Crimea, so that they could bring supplies from the port of Balaklava to the town of Sevastopol.

The peace treaty signed in Paris in 1856 was viewed in Russia as humiliation at the hands of the West. The conquerors of Paris in 1814, the Russians returned to that city forty years later to sign an arrangement that violated the territorial integrity of their empire. St. Petersburg was forced to abandon imperial possessions in the Caucasus and the Danube area, and eleven years later, the cash-strapped government sold Alaska to the United States, lacking the resources to defend it. It kept the Crimea but was banned from maintaining a fleet or fortifications on the Black Sea littoral. Even more significant was the empire's loss of face as a great power.

Something had to be done to restore Russia's international status. The government's priorities were building a new navy and reforming the army, but those tasks required large-scale social reforms. The new emperor, Alexander II, believed that this vast undertaking could be achieved without relinquishing much of his autocratic power. Nevertheless, he and his advisers understood that some liberalization of the previous regime's policies was inevitable. Nowhere was this more obvious than in the case of the Polish question—the empire's relations with its most mobilized and independently minded nationality.

Russia's loss of the Crimean War and the worsening of its international position, coupled with the uncertainty and internal turmoil caused by the emancipation of the serfs in February 1861, emboldened Polish society in its demands for the return of previously lost freedoms. In the former Kingdom of Poland and among the Polish nobility in the western provinces of the empire, hopes ran high that Alexander II would return to the policies of Alexander I, his uncle and namesake, by restoring liberties and the constitution. The kingdom, which had lost its sovereignty after the November Uprising of 1830, retained a degree of autonomy. But the government had no such plans, and the disillusioned Poles rebelled once again.

The new Polish revolt, which began in January 1863, became known as the January Uprising. Young Poles attacked Russian military units in the cities of the Kingdom of Poland, and the revolt soon spread to the Lithuanian, Belarusian, and Ukrainian provinces of the empire. It took more than a year for the Russian army to crush it. The fighting was followed by repression of the leaders and participants in the uprising, as well as a new campaign to Russify the borderlands. It soon occurred to the government that solving the Polish question was all but impossible without reimagining the Russian nation itself. It was during the public debate of the first years of Alexander II's rule that Russia first began to take on the character of a tripartite nation of Great, Little, and White Russians.

FROM THE VERY BEGINNING OF THE POLISH CRISIS, THE FUTURE of the former Polish territories outside the Kingdom of Poland was the principal concern of the imperial government and the general public. Alexander II had begun his rule with concessions to Polish public opinion, canceling his father's directives requiring Polish officials to serve in the Russian provinces before they could take government offices in the former Polish lands. Alexander II also lifted restrictions on the employment of non-Orthodox officials in the former Polish lands of the empire. But the question of "de-Polonizing" the region did not disappear from the government's agenda.

With the start of Alexander's reforms in the late 1850s, the supporters of Metropolitan Iosif Semashko—who had finally managed to bring most of the Uniates in the empire under the umbrella of Russian Orthodoxy, and believed in one indivisible Russian nation as a bulwark against Polish domination—spotted a new threat from the Polish side. A group of *khlopomany*, or "peasant-lovers," appeared among the young nobles of the Right-Bank Ukraine, causing a split in the Polish camp and threatening an even greater one in imperial Russia. The *khlopomany* renounced their Polish Catholic upbringing and embraced the Orthodox faith of the peasants. This would have been good news for the authorities if the *khlopomany* had declared themselves Russian, but they chose to identify themselves as South Russians, or Ukrainians. Among them was Włodzimierz Antonowicz, who changed his name to Volodymyr Antonovych: in time, he would become a prominent Ukrainian historian.

Semashko's supporters claimed that Ukrainophilism was nothing but a Polish intrigue. In 1859, Sylvestr Gogotsky, a professor at Kyiv University and one of the leading lights of the pan-Russian movement, put forward a program to stop the advance of the Ukrainian movement. Gogotsky's program was as follows:

> a) We should immediately take measures to educate the people on both sides of the Dnieper; b) From now on we should support the idea of the unity of the three Russian tribes; without that unity, we shall perish very quickly; c) The Russian literary language should be the same for all in primers. Faith and language should be binding elements. But it will do no harm to add something in our simple language as well; d) By no means should we promote discord between Great Russia and ourselves. The desire for change can be expressed in other ways. Do not forget that our enemies are the Poles and Rome!

The three Russian tribes that Gogotsky had in mind were the Great Russians, Little Russians, and White Russians. This tripartite model of the Russian nation had deep historical roots. Its origins could be traced back to 1656–1721, when the tsars had been called the sovereigns of Great, Little, and White Russia. By the time Peter I changed his title in 1721, becoming all-Russian emperor, only Great Russia and parts of Little Russia remained under Russian control—White Russia, or Belarus, had been lost to the Poles more than fifty years earlier under the terms of the Truce of Andrusovo (1667). When Russia regained eastern Belarus after the first partition of Poland in 1772, there was no change in the emperor's title or in official discourse, and in the second and third partitions of Poland, the new "Russian" lands, including Right-Bank Ukraine, Volhynia, Podolia, and western or Black Belarus, were annexed to the empire. There were simply too many Rus' nationalities to count. In 1823, when the leader of the Decembrist movement, Pavel Pestel, sat down to write his rebel constitution, he counted five rather than three groups of Russians to be merged into one Russian nation.

The rise of interest in local folklore and language that began in the western borderlands of the empire in the 1820s and developed in the 1830s did not make it any easier to answer the question of how many distinct groups Russia contained. There were numerous dialects of what imperial scholars considered to be the Russian language, even among the Great Russians themselves. Ivan Sakharov, a medical doctor and an alumnus of Moscow

University, counted four major Great Russian dialects, divided into numerous subdialects, in his *Sayings of the Russian People About the Family Life of Their Ancestors* (1836). The Little Russian dialect was said to consist of three subdialects. Numerous dialects would also be recorded in Belarus, where in the 1850s Russian military officers found, apart from Belarusian, a Black Russian dialect and identified southern Belarusian groups speaking the Little Russian dialect. Few participants in this ethnographic study of the imperial borderlands had any doubt that all those dialects were Russian and that their speakers constituted one Russian nation. But the newly discovered linguistic diversity of the "Russian tribe" raised the question of how many dialects there were, and— as the early ethnographers believed that every language corresponded to a nationality—how many Russian nationalities and subnationalities in fact existed.

The first to suggest that the Russian nation consisted of three subgroups was probably Nikolai Nadezhdin, a strong believer in both the diversity and the unity of the Russian nation. In 1841, fresh from internal exile after publishing the explosive *Philosophical Letters* of Petr Chaadaev (1836), and on his way to becoming editor of the journal of the Ministry of the Interior, Nadezhdin published a review of a work by the Vienna Slavist Jernej Kopitar. In the review he presented a historical scheme of the development of the Russian dialects and identified three of them: Pontic Slavic, or Little Russian; Baltic Slavic, or Belarusian; and Great Russian. According to Nadezhdin, the first two dialects were the oldest. The third, the Great Russian dialect, was a mixture of the first two and had developed in newly colonized areas east of the original settlements where the first two dialects were spoken.

Nadezhdin's brief review, published in German, and outside of the Russian Empire, remained largely unknown at home, but the same tripartite division of the Russian language and people would soon be introduced to a Russian readership. In 1842, the forty-seven-year-old Slovak censor Pavol Jozef Šafárik published a book titled *Slovanský národopis* (Slavic Ethnography) in Prague. Šafárik, reputed to be the foremost Slavist of his era, presented, in meticulous detail, a scheme of Russian dialects very similar to what Nadezhdin had proposed; in fact, Nadezhdin, in one of his own articles, identified himself as one of Šafárik's consultants. These mentions of a tripartite division of what was then considered a single "Russian world" were the first shocks of a linguistic earthquake that would eventually change the political map of Eastern Europe.

Šafárik's three dialects included Great Russian, which he said included the Novgorodian subdialect; Little Russian, which encompassed not only the population of Russian-ruled Ukraine but also the populations of Austrian Galicia and Hungarian Transcarpathia; and White Russian, spoken in eastern and western Belarus. Šafárik believed language and nationality were closely connected, so he wrote not only about linguistic groups but also about the Great, Little, and White Russians. Although Šafárik never conducted ethnographic or linguistic research on the "Russian" dialects, he closely followed the literature coming from the Russian Empire and was in touch with some of the leading Russian Slavists of the era. He met Mikhail Pogodin in Prague in 1835, and Pogodin subsequently gave him financial support.

Šafárik was also acquainted with Osyp Bodiansky, the Ukrainian-born professor of Slavic studies at Moscow University who had published *History of the Rus'*. Bodiansky supplied Šafárik with linguistic materials and in 1837 sent him a copy of the Belarusian "remake" of Kotliarevsky's *Eneïda*. He also provided Šafárik with a map of Ukrainian and Belarusian dialects. In November 1842, Bodiansky wrote to one of his colleagues, the Kharkiv professor Izmail Sreznevsky, "I have always been of the opinion that the latter river (the Prypiat) is the natural boundary between the White Russians and the Little Russians, especially as the so-called Black Russians or Pinchuks live on both sides of the river and constitute a transition from the Khokhols [Ukrainians] to the Belarusians, and if I indicated our boundary differently to Šafárik in this instance, then I did so as a result of accounts given by Belarusians themselves who had earlier become Polonized." Šafárik enjoyed unquestioned authority as a linguist among the Moscow-based Slavophiles, and as soon as *Slovanský národopis* appeared in print, Bodiansky, who had just returned to Moscow from trips abroad—he spent some time in Prague, where he consulted with Šafárik—sat down to produce a Russian translation of the book.

A year later, in 1843, Bodiansky's translation was published in the journal *Moskvitianin* (The Muscovite), edited by Pogodin. Šafárik's tripartite division of the Russian language—and consequently, of the Russian nation—became the basis of Pogodin's reinterpretation of Russian history.

In the 1850s, he employed the division of the Russian people into Great, Little, and White Russians in his polemics with his Kyivan friend and intellectual opponent Mykhailo Maksymovych. But despite the broad popularity of Šafárik's tripartite model, its acceptance in the empire was by no means assured. It was easy to see in it an attempt to undermine the notion of the unity of the Russian nation and state that was so cherished by the government and its supporters. Yet surprisingly, resistance to the model came not from the Great Russians, but from the Little Russian and White Russian sides.

At Kharkiv University, Izmail Sreznevsky, Bodiansky's correspondent and the empire's most respected linguistic authority of the period, came up with his own division of "Russian" languages. In 1843, the year in which the translation of Šafárik's work was published—and one year after returning from his own extensive journey to the Slavic lands—Sreznevsky postulated a division of Russian into two groups: Southern Russian (or Little Russian) and Northern Russian (or Great Russian). He was following in the footsteps of Mykhailo Maksymovych, who had made a similar division of the Russian nation in 1837. Yurii Venelin, a native of Transcarpathia who was an expert on the Bulgarian language and culture, suggested the same division around the same time. Sreznevsky admitted the existence of the Belarusian dialect, but he considered it a variant of Great Russian.

Translated into the language of ethnography, labeling the Belarusian dialect a variant of Great Russian meant that the Belarusians were a subgroup of the Great Russians, not a distinct nationality. According to police records, that was exactly what some members of the Cyrillo-Methodian Brotherhood in Kyiv also thought. More importantly, on the eve of the Polish uprising some of the former members of the brotherhood began to talk about the Ukrainians, also known as Little or South Russians, as a nationality separate from the Great Russians.

THE RETURN OF THE "POLISH QUESTION" IN THE RUSSIAN EMPIRE gave new urgency to the "Ukrainian question" in imperial politics and culture. Aleksandr Herzen, a writer and intellectual known today as the father of Russian populism and socialism, introduced the notion of Ukraine as an independent factor in the contest for the territories between

Russia and Poland. In the January 1859 issue of his Russian-language journal, *Kolokol* (The Bell), which was published in London, Herzen wrote: "Well, and what if, after all our considerations, Ukraine, remembering all the oppressions of the Muscovites, and the condition of serfdom, and the draft, and the lawlessness, and the pillage, and the knout on the one side, and not forgetting, on the other, how it fared under the Commonwealth with the soldiers, lords, and Crown officials, should not wish to be either Polish or Russian? As I see it, the question is to be decided very simply. In that case, Ukraine should be recognized as a free and independent country."

The genie was out of the bottle. In writing openly about the possibility of Ukrainian independence, which had so alarmed the authorities when they investigated the Brotherhood of Saints Cyril and Methodius, Herzen said what Mykola Kostomarov had never dared to say in his *Books of the Genesis of the Ukrainian People*, where he had been the first to address the question. And yet Herzen's suggestion of Ukrainian independence was only a rhetorical tool—a point in the heat of argument over the future of the Russo-Polish borderlands, and an assertion of the right of the region's inhabitants to decide their fate as they pleased. When it came to practical politics, both Herzen and Kostomarov preferred a federal solution to the nationality problem, and Herzen wrote as much in his article in *Kolokol*.

Kostomarov was very appreciative of Herzen's position and wrote to *Kolokol* endorsing the position its publisher had taken. His contribution, titled "Ukraine," appeared anonymously in *Kolokol* in January 1860. Kostomarov began with an expression of gratitude to Herzen: "You have expressed an opinion about Ukraine that the thinking part of the South Russian people has long treasured as a precious and sacred possession of its heart." He referred to his homeland as Ukraine, called its people Ukrainians, or the South Russian nation (*narod*), and expressed reservations about the term "Little Russians." Kostomarov's article was in many ways a development of his earlier ideas. By emphasizing the democratic nature of Ukraine's Cossack past, he provided historical justification for treating the Ukrainians as a distinct people.

Kostomarov developed his ideas further in an article titled "The Two Rus' Nationalities," which appeared in print in St. Petersburg in 1861 in the journal *Osnova* (Foundation), published by Panteleimon Kulish. In this piece, Kostomarov demolished the cocoon of the all-Russian nationality, declaring that in fact there were two separate Rus' nationalities: "Besides the Rus' nationality that holds sway in the outer world, another one now makes its appearance, claiming equal civil rights in the sphere of word and intellect." He argued that the name "Rus'" had effectively been stolen from its original owners, the South (or Little) Russians, by their northern neighbors. Kostomarov maintained that the distinct histories of the two Rus' nationalities had shaped their characters differently. Whereas the South Russians valued individual freedom and the principles of collegiality and federalism, the North Russians valued collectivism, the state, and authoritarian rule. In choosing between Polish and Russian orientations for the nascent South Russian nation, Kostomarov argued in favor of the latter. He believed that the South Russians had a better chance of establishing equal relations with the Great Russians than they did with the Poles.

This article would become a rallying point for the Ukrainian movement in the Russian Empire for generations to come. Since "The Two Rus' Nationalities" was signed and published in the empire, Kostomarov did not use the terms "Ukraine" and "Ukrainians," as he had done a year earlier in the anonymous *Kolokol* publication, leaving future generations of Ukrainian activists to sort out the confusion between the two Russias and the two Russian nations. But the article clearly declared, for the first time in the public press, the birth of a separate nationality on a par with the Great Russian nationality. Kostomarov was nominally following in the tradition established by Mykhailo Maksymovych in the 1830s. Maksymovych had divided Rus' into two parts: northern and southern. Kostomarov's scheme had two parts also, but unlike Maksymovych, Kostomarov did not consider them parts of the same entity. As far as Kostomarov was concerned, they were separate. Moreover, he argued that in some respects the South Russians were closer to the Poles than to the Russians. "If the South Russian nation is farther from the Poles than from the Great Russians in the structure of its language, it is nevertheless much closer to them in national traits and fundamentals of national character," he wrote.

Kostomarov considered the Belarusians a branch of the Great Russian nation, but that proposition did not sit well with many of his readers, either in the imperial capitals or in Belarus itself.

THE TERM "BELARUS," WHICH HAD FIGURED IN THE TSAR'S SHORT title in the second half of the seventeenth century and was dropped from it in the first decades of the eighteenth, returned to the official imperial vocabulary in the aftermath of the first partition of Poland in 1772, when the eastern Belarusian lands were annexed to the Russian Empire. The Belarusian eparchy of the Roman Catholic Church was also created at that time, and in 1797, after Catherine's death, the Russian Orthodox Church established its Belarusian archbishopric. "Belarus" was considered a wholly legitimate term until the Polish uprising of 1830–1831.

In 1828, that name was given to the Uniate eparchy of the region, and in 1829 it was applied to the educational district that included both the eastern and the western lands of Belarus. But the uprising of 1830–1831 changed the political connotation of the term. Polish intellectuals who had earlier referred to their homeland as Lithuania, such as the poet Adam Mickiewicz, a native of the Brest region, adopted the name "Belarus" after the revolt. Spelled "Białoruś" in Polish, it was applied to the region east of the core Polish territory that was also considered historically, culturally, and lingustically Polish. The new interest in the language and customs of the simple folk no longer allowed culturally conscious Polish nationalists to refer to Belarus as "Lithuania," whose inhabitants spoke a language profoundly different from Slavic.

This ethnographic turn was fully apparent in a talk on folk culture that Aleksander Rypiński, a native of the Vitsebsk region of Belarus, delivered in Paris in 1839. Rypiński had taken part in the uprising of 1830 and, like many of his compatriots, had found refuge in France. He defined the territory of Belarus as the part of Polish lands extending from the Prypiat River and the Pinsk marshes in the south to Pskov and Velikie Luki in the north. The language of the inhabitants of this region, he asserted, was different from the languages spoken in Russia, Russian-ruled Ukraine, and Austrian Galicia, and was closer to Polish than to any of those languages. According to Rypiński, speakers of Belarusian had been blood relatives of the Poles since time immemorial. The talk received such a warm response from Polish émigrés that Rypiński published an expanded version of it in Paris in the following year.

In 1840, the same year Rypiński published his brochure, Nicholas I banned the use of the words "Belarusian" and "Lithuanian" in government documents, but the measure could not be enforced outside official circles. It was too little, too late. In 1835, Roman Catholics issued a Belarusian-dialect catechism written in the Polish alphabet for the local peasantry. By the end of the decade, a Polish-alphabet Belarusian version of Ivan Kotliarevsky's *Eneïda* began to circulate among the local nobility. In 1844–1846, a native of the Polatsk region of Belarus, Jan Barszczewski, published his four-volume collection of literary works, where he tried his hand at writing in Belarusian, employing the Polish alphabet. The 1850s witnessed a small explosion of similarly written texts when Wincenty Dunin-Marcinkiewicz, one of the Polish promoters (and creators) of a bilingual Belarusian culture, published prose works for the common people in Belarusian and prepared a translation into that language of Adam Mickiewicz's classic poem *Pan Tadeusz*.

The Russian Orthodox hierarchs and some government officials became increasingly concerned about what they regarded as a "Polish intrigue" intended to corrupt the "Russian" peasantry. The Polish-inspired project of producing and distributing Belarusian-language literature in the Polish alphabet for the common reader faced a setback in 1859. There had been Austrian and Polish attempts to switch Ruthenian publications in Austrian Galicia from the Cyrillic to the Latin alphabet, and Russian authorities responded by banning the import of these texts. Similar publications in the empire were also stopped in their tracks, but Belarusian literature in Cyrillic did not fill the resulting vacuum. Back in 1846, the Russian Academy of Sciences had turned down the manuscript of a Cyrillic-alphabet Belarusian grammar prepared by the ethnographer Pavel Shpilevsky on grounds of poor academic quality. In 1862, the first grammar of Belarusian was finally published with the support of a local marshal of the nobility, but the Polish uprising of 1863 put an end to further Belarusian publications in the empire.

In 1862, there had been discussions among those in the inner circle of the governor general of Vilnius, Vladimir Nazimov, about publishing a journal in the local Belarusian dialect. Differences arose over the language to be used—Russian, slightly adapted to local usage, or the Belarusian dialect—with the governor backing the latter option. Nazimov petitioned the imperial minister of education, arguing that the religious education of Belarusian Catholics—former "Russian" Uniates who had converted to Roman Catholicism—should be conducted in the "local Belarusian language." The journal, he wrote, should be published in a language that he defined as "Russian or, better, Belarusian, consisting of the writing of the local Ruthenian dialect on paper in Russian script." The governor was desperate to overcome his Polish opponents, led by Wincenty Konstanty Kalinowski, who in their publication *The Peasant Truth*, addressed to the peasantry, were using local Belarusian dialects written in the Polish alphabet to appeal to the local peasant population.

Neither Nazimov and his advisers, who argued for the use of the Belarusian language, nor the Polish publishers of *The Peasant Truth* equated Belarusian with any particular nationality or considered the Belarusians a distinct ethnic group. Nazimov regarded the local peasants as members of the Russian nation, while Kalinowski called on them to fight for the Polish cause. Neither man appeared to take the Belarusians seriously as independent political actors, and both hoped to manipulate them by making effective use of the local Belarusian dialect. While Kalinowski managed to publish in Belarusian, Governor Nazimov's proposal to establish a Cyrillic-alphabet Belarusian journal was never approved by St. Petersburg. Even so, Nazimov's proposal indicated that the authorities could no longer ignore the rise of Belarusian cultural assertiveness.

How to handle that unexpected rise remained a highly controversial issue. No one contributed more to the debate than Mikhail Koialovich, a native of western Belarus and the son of a Uniate priest who had studied with Iosif Semashko. Mikhail Koialovich was eleven years old in 1839 when Semashko engineered the "reunification" of the Uniates. Educated in Orthodox schools, he became a professor of history at the St. Petersburg Theological Academy and took an active part in Russian debates before and during the Polish uprising of 1863. He believed in the unity of the Russian nation while recognizing the existence of a Belarusian "tribe" that spoke the Belarusian "dialect," but he did not regard language and ethnicity as criteria for defining a separate group within the big Russian nation. In his opinion, nationality was defined in social terms and shaped by common historical experience. Thus, he divided the Russian nation into two parts, but unlike Kostomarov, who had divided Rus' into northern and southern branches, Koialovich posited an east-west division.

Today, Koialovich is considered the father of a trend in Belarusian political thought that imagined Belarus as part of a broader entity called

Western Rus'. This view had deep historical roots, as it was based on the division of the Rus' lands in the decades and centuries following the Mongol invasion. By the fourteenth century, most of the Ukrainian and Belarusian lands had ended up within the Grand Duchy of Lithuania, and those were the territories that, for Koialovich, constituted Western Rus'. He defined its inhabitants in social terms, not in the ethnic or religious ones accepted by the other nation-builders of the era. Koialovich was an early populist who lumped together the lower classes of society irrespective of whether they were Slavs or Lithuanians.

Populism was an orientation that Koialovich shared with Kostomarov, but Kostomarov's populism did not cross ethnonational boundaries. The two writers were at odds with regard to the definition of their respective nationalities, and they debated their views in the press before and during the Polish insurrection. On the one hand, Koialovich considered the Ukrainophiles the only true public activists of Western Rus', given their readiness to work with the people. On the other, he was disappointed by what he considered their narrow-mindedness.

Koialovich wrote that the Ukrainophiles were "strong in numbers, popular education, and energy. . . . But it must be acknowledged with regret that one can hardly expect any great service from them for the people of all Western Rus'. To all appearances, they are great egoists (not all of them, of course): in actual fact, Little Rus' does not suffer so much from Polonism and Jesuits, and the people there are able to stand up for themselves." Kostomarov, who thought in ethnolinguistic terms, maintained that the Little Russians and Belarusians belonged to different nations. In fact, he argued that the Belarusians were descended from the North Russian or Great Russian tribe—an idea that can be traced back to the testimonies of members of the Cyrillo-Methodian Brotherhood in 1847. Koialovich was outraged and, in response to Kostomarov's argument, wrote, with reference to the proto-Belarusian Krivichian tribe of the Kyivan Rus' era, "The children of the old Krivichians cannot be represented by the young historical children of the Northern Rus' tribe."

Kostomarov's Ukrainophilism was just one of the obstacles that Koialovich had to address in his struggle for the recognition of the Western Rus' branch of the big Russian nation. The other front was represented by Russian Slavophiles, whom Koialovich accused of the mindless

"Russification" of Western Rus'/Russia. He called on his Great Russian colleagues "to restrain all foolish Great Russian passions in encounters with the West Russian people and win their love with good humane deeds." This appeal did not mollify his Russian opponents, who were alarmed by what they regarded as the rise of Belarusian separatism, a local counterpart of Ukrainophilism.

The Russian Slavophile Konstantin Aksakov wrote to Koialovich, "Russia is now saving Belarus from mortal danger: the point is to destroy Polonism, but Belarus, as if it were already safe from the threat, is concerned not with deliverance from the Polish yoke but with the preservation of local particularities! And yet those basic particularities are few in number." Mikhail Katkov, a former professor of philosophy at Moscow University and editor of the influential newspaper *Moskovskie vedomosti* (Moscow News), was even more outspoken: "They write to us from St. Petersburg that some kind of Belarusophile party is being born. Petersburg is so overloaded with social forces that it wants to fertilize all our dialects at all costs and create as many Russian nationalities and languages as there are lands suitable for chopping off." He envisioned the Polish "nationalists" rejoicing over "this new attempt to divide the Belarusian land mentally from Russia."

Thus, Koialovich's idea of a bipartite Russian nation divided into east and west was rejected on all fronts. Kostomarov maintained his concept of a north-south divide, while Aksakov and other Russian Slavophiles thought in terms of three branches, leaving Koialovich a Belarusian niche within the Russian nation. He would not settle for it but was unable to make his view prevail. The tripartite nationality advocated by Katkov was endorsed by the imperial authorities, providing justification for the empire's eventual transformation into a nation-state.

THE TRIPARTITE RUSSIAN NATIONALITY EMERGED AS THE DOMInant model of Russian nation-building in the wake of the Polish uprising of 1863–1864. In political terms, it was a means of dealing with Polish nationalism while accommodating the cultural demands of the growing Ukrainian national movement. In purely conceptual terms, it was a way of reconciling the principle of Russian nationality formulated by Uvarov back in 1832 with the growing realization that the big Russian nation was in fact diverse and could be imagined in a number of ways. Whereas Pavel Pestel counted five Russian nationalities to be merged in a pan-Russian entity, the Russian Slavophiles and imperial nationalists of the post-1863 era agreed on three. The vernacular languages spoken by the three branches were termed "dialects," and there was to be one literary language, Russian or all-Russian, allegedly created by all three groups. The union of the three branches was justified by *raison d'état*: the Russian Empire had to be a politically viable unit like the nationalizing states of Europe.

In historical terms, the tripartite model harked back to the mid-seventeenth century, when, after attaching Cossack Ukraine and conquering eastern Belarus, the Muscovite tsar added the names of Great, Little, and White Rus' to his title. This was a two-stage process. The terms "Great" and "Little" Rus' were the first to come into use, reflecting Muscovite expansion into the Ukrainian-Belarusian lands of the Polish-Lithuanian Commonwealth. "Little Rus'" was then divided into two parts: the "Little Rus'" that denoted the Ukrainian lands, and "White Rus'," which included the lands of eastern Belarus. This nomenclature denoted the different statuses of the two territories—one, Ukrainian, taken under Muscovite protection on the basis of the agreement reached with Hetman Bohdan Khmelnytsky in 1654; the other, Belarusian, conquered with no grant of special rights or privileges. Now, in the mid-nineteenth century, the tripartite division of Rus'/Russia was recognized once again, but this time on linguistic rather than political grounds. But the recognition of differences was not intended to prepare for a federal arrangement, with local autonomy for Russia's constituent parts. The goal was to unite the three branches, not only in dynastic and religious terms but also under the cultural cloak of the Russian tsars.

9

KILLING THE LANGUAGE

O N July 18, 1863, the minister of the interior of the Russian Empire, Petr Valuev, spelled out the new imperial policy on the development of the East Slavic languages. He did so in a seemingly routine document—an instruction to the censors—whose significance was heightened by the sovereign's approval. Known subsequently as the Valuev circular, the instruction would have a strong impact on Russian nation-building. The very fact that the minister of the interior was involved in defining the empire's language policy indicated that by now, in the opinion of St. Petersburg officials, the development of non-Russian languages and cultures could pose a threat to the security of the tsarist realm.

Valuev's circular was directed mainly against the Ukrainian intellectuals, whose efforts to introduce their language into churches and schools he regarded as part of a Polish intrigue to undermine the empire. "That phenomenon is all the more deplorable and deserving of attention," stated the circular, "because it coincides with the designs of the Poles and is all but obliged to them for its origin, judging by the manuscripts received by the censors and by the fact that most of the Little Russian compositions actually come from the Poles." Valuev claimed that the "adherents of the Little Russian nationality" were turning to the common people for political reasons. He noted that many of them had already been investigated by the government and were being accused by their own compatriots of "separatist designs hostile to Russia and fatal for Little Russia."

The circular directed the censors' attention to the development of publications in Ukrainian (Little Russian), ranging from writings by and for a narrow circle of intellectuals to literature for the masses. Valuev sided with the Ukrainian officials of the all-Russian persuasion. "They show quite fundamentally," wrote the minister, "that there has never been, is not, and cannot be any separate Little Russian language, and that their dialect, spoken by the common people, is the selfsame Russian language, only spoiled by the influence of Poland; that the all-Russian language is as comprehensible to Little Russians as to Great Russians, in fact much more comprehensible than the one now being devised for them by some Little Russians and, in particular, by the Poles—the so-called Ukrainian language."

The Valuev circular aimed to prevent the distribution of Ukrainian-language texts among the peasantry and common folk. It prohibited the publication of educational and religious texts in Ukrainian, with the sole exception of belles lettres. Although the circular was introduced as a temporary measure, it had profound effects on the development of the Ukrainian culture and identity. In 1863, when Valuev signed his circular, thirty-three Ukrainian-language publications had appeared in print; by 1868, when he stepped down as minister, their number had been reduced to one. The government had effectively arrested the development of the alternative Rus' language, literature, and high culture in the western borderlands envisioned by Ukraine's leading political thinker of the time, Mykola Kostomarov. Nor did any Belarusian-language publications appear after 1863.

"In our time, the question of whether one can or should write in South Russian, which is to say, in Ukrainian, is decided by practice itself," argued the publishers of *Osnova* (Foundation), the Ukrainophile journal published in St. Petersburg in Russian in 1862. What they still found questionable was the "practical significance of the people's speech in teaching and preaching." This was an understatement. In fact, bringing the Ukrainian language into the church and school had become the main political goal of the Ukrainophile movement. The Russian socialist writer and critic Nikolai Chernyshevsky endorsed that program when he welcomed the appearance of the first issue of *Osnova*: "Teaching the Little Russian people in the Little Russian language and developing popular Little Russian literature is, in our view, the goal toward which it will be most convenient and useful for the Little Russians to strive initially."

The Ukrainophiles had been busy implementing that program long before it was formulated in print. By 1862, there were six Ukrainian primers on sale in the cities of the empire, one of them compiled by Taras Shevchenko, another by Panteleimon Kulish. Mykola Kostomarov was collecting funds among the Ukrainian and Russian public in St. Petersburg to publish more books in Ukrainian for the common folk, and a Ukrainian translation of Scripture was making its way through the Scylla and Charybdis of the Russian government and church censorship. The government was at a loss, lacking a clear idea of what to do with Ukrainian-language publications. The old restrictions on the activities of the Cyrillo-Methodian Brotherhood had been removed, and the peasants were being set free, but the question of how to educate the masses hung in the air. In 1859, the government had prohibited the publication or import of Latin-alphabet texts written in the Slavic languages, seeking to prevent Polish cultural expansion, but what to do with texts in the Russian "dialects," which now also included White Russian (the first grammar of Belarusian appeared in 1862), was anyone's guess.

In 1861, when the Ukrainophiles approached Metropolitan Arsenii (Fedor Moskvin) of Kyiv for help in distributing Shevchenko's primer, he turned to the government for advice. The Censorship Committee recommended that he turn down the request, arguing that publications in Little Russian could produce a schism between the two Slavic peoples and undermine the stability of the state. But generally, in the eyes of the censors, the Ukrainophile project was a pipe dream: they assumed that it would wither if they left it alone. No restrictions or prosecutions were needed, but one had to beware of providing it with government support. The change in government policy that led Valuev to issue his circular was set off by a letter sent to the Third Section of the Imperial Chancellery in March 1863, shortly after the start of the Polish uprising. It was unsigned but penned on behalf of a group of unidentified Little Russian Orthodox clerics who demanded a ban on the publication of a Ukrainian translation of the Gospels then being reviewed by the Holy Synod in St. Petersburg.

The letter was forwarded to the governor general of Kyiv, Nikolai Annenkov, who supported the petitioners' request. He was concerned that the translation would elevate Ukrainian from a dialect to the status of an independent language and produce political repercussions. Annenkov wrote: "Debate continues in the literature on the question of whether the Little Russian dialect is only a particular feature of the Russian language or an independent language. Having obtained the translation of Holy Scripture into the Little Russian dialect, the supporters of the Little Russian party will attain, so to speak, recognition of the independence of the Little Russian language, and then, of course, they will not stop at that but, basing themselves on the uniqueness of the language, will start making claims for the autonomy of Little Russia."

Annenkov's opinion was reported to Emperor Alexander II, who instructed the head of the Third Section to contact the appropriate officials in the central government. This meant that the emperor himself considered the concerns expressed by the governor general of Kyiv legitimate and his proposal worth consideration. The matter was passed on to Valuev, who in turn contacted the Holy Synod. As a result, the plans to publish the Ukrainian translation of the Gospels, prepared by the Ukrainian cultural activist Pylyp Morachevsky, were canceled, and publications in Ukrainian intended for the popular masses were banned. The new policies were spelled out in the Valuev circular of July 18, 1863. In the months leading up to the circular, Valuev apparently underwent an evolution, turning from a reluctant executor of the tsar's will into a strong supporter of the prohibitive measures the circular introduced. It took him three months to report to the Third Section that he fully agreed with the governor general's proposal in Kyiv to ban the publication of the New Testament in Ukrainian. But once he made his decision, Valuev stood by it.

In the Russian government of the 1860s, Petr Valuev was a liberal—a cautious reformer who wanted to strengthen the autocracy by creating a rudimentary system of popular representation on an ad hoc basis. Valuev's hand on the question of Ukrainian publications was forced by a media campaign organized by the Third Section at the suggestion of

Nikolai Annenkov, the same governor general of Kyiv who had proposed harsh measures against the Ukrainophiles. The key figure in that media campaign was an academic turned journalist, Mikhail Katkov. An intellectual who was at home with the conservative leaders of the Slavophile movement, Katkov had at first taken a condescending and even indulgent attitude toward the Ukrainian project, thinking that it was doomed to fail. But his position changed radically with the outbreak of the Polish uprising.

On June 21, 1863, about a month before Valuev signed his circular, Katkov added his voice to the discussion on prohibiting Ukrainian-language publications in an article with a telling title, "The Coincidence of Ukrainophile Interests with Polish Interests." In complete agreement with the adherents of pan-Russian Orthodoxy in Iosif Semashko's camp, Katkov accused the Ukrainophiles of being instruments not only of Polish but also of Jesuit intrigue. In doing so, Katkov not only politicized the question of Ukrainian-language publications but in fact criminalized it, opening the door to the politically damaging treatment of the Polish-Ukrainian connection in Valuev's circular. More importantly in the long run, Katkov provided intellectual foundations for the repressive policies vis-à-vis the Ukrainian cultural and political movement that would be adopted by the imperial government and last for decades. Katkov argued that "Ukraine has never had its own history, never been a separate state; the Ukrainian people are an authentic Russian people, an indigenous Russian people, an essential part of the Russian people, without which it can hardly remain what it is now." Although he recognized linguistic and cultural differences between the branches of the "Russian nation," he considered them only locally significant. If the big Russian nation was to develop and prevail, the cultivation of local dialects would have to be arrested.

Comparing the Russian Empire to France, Italy, and Germany, Katkov concluded that the differences between the local dialects of the "Russian" groups were slighter than those within the West European nations. Throughout the "Russian land," he argued, the Russian traveler could understand local speech without much difficulty. As Katkov saw it, the unity of the one and indivisible Russian nation was based on the unity of its literary language. He attacked Kostomarov's idea of two Rus' nationalities: "Outrageous and ridiculous sophistry! As if there could be two Russian nationalities and two Russian languages; as if there could be two French nationalities and two French languages!" He attacked Kostomarov and the Ukrainophiles in the strongest possible terms: "Out of nothing there suddenly appeared heroes and demigods, objects of worship, great symbols of a nationality that is being newly created. New Cyrils and Methodiuses with the most outlandish alphabets made their appearance, and the phantasm of some nonexistent Little Russian language was loosed upon God's creation."

The argument Katkov developed in the debate on the prohibition of Ukrainian publications would constitute the basis for the imperial authorities' handling of the Ukrainian question for generations to come. He was the first public intellectual to establish a close bond between language, ethnicity, national unity, and the strategic interests of the Russian state. While continuing to blame differences between the Eastern Slavs on Polish and other foreign subjugation, as the creator of the pan-Russian historical narrative, Nikolai Ustrialov, had done in his historical writings of the 1830s and 1840s, Katkov brought ethnic and linguistic elements into the discussion. He did so not to distinguish Great and Little Russians from each other, as Mikhail Pogodin had done in his debate with Mykhailo Maksymovych on the ethnic identity of Kyiv in the 1850s, but to bring them together as one linguistic, ethnic, and cultural entity for the sake of the unity of the Russian state.

Russian censors and political and cultural commentators such as Katkov placed their recommendation to ban Ukrainian-language publications in a broad international context, pointing to similar challenges facing the German, French, and British governments with regard to their own unofficial languages and dialects, including Occitan in France and Scottish Gaelic and Irish in Britain. But the comparison serves to emphasize the difference in the policies adopted by the Russian and West European governments. Whereas the British and French did not limit the development of "rival" languages with restrictive measures, instead relying on their school systems to promote the use of official languages, the Russian authorities resorted to repression, "forgetting" about any positive action that would have required the investment of major resources, such as developing a system of Russian-language elementary schools throughout the empire. They would maintain this cheap but one-sided policy, losing their battle on the same linguistic terrain as the one on which the Germans, French, and British had won theirs.

THE FIRST VISIBLE CRACKS IN THE OFFICIAL POLICY OF SUPPRESS-ing the Ukrainian language appeared in the early 1870s, a decade after the Valuev circular had appeared. If they had been applied broadly, the strictures in the circular could have wiped out Ukrainian-language publications in the Russian Empire, as happened in 1868, when only one Ukrainian title appeared in print. But Valuev's resignation that year allowed Ukrainian-language publications to make a comeback. It began slowly, but in 1874 alone thirty-two publications were approved by the censors, only one less than in 1862, the last "pre-circular" year. With Valuev gone, the censors were freer to decide whether Ukrainian-language books were literary works, which were allowed, or fell into the prohibited category of books for the common folk. Academic publications, which fit neither category, fell through the cracks. Besides, some censors could be persuaded to turn a blind eye to possible violations, sometimes with the help of bribes, as was the case with Ilia Puzyrevsky in the Kyiv office, which cleared the lion's share of Ukrainian-language books proposed for publication in the 1870s.

The Ukrainophiles were growing ever bolder, declaring that the *entr'acte* in the development of their movement was over. The key figure on the Ukrainophile side of the new debate was a young and ambitious historian, Mykhailo Drahomanov. A professor of ancient history at Kyiv University, Drahomanov spent the early 1870s in Europe, studying his subject and nationality problems on the continent. He celebrated the publication of a few Ukrainian-language titles in the Russian Empire as a sign of good things to come and believed that the reforms of Alexander II would promote public activism. Soon Drahomanov found himself a target of a new attack on the Ukrainophiles.

As in 1863, Mikhail Katkov supported and endorsed the attack: in February 1875, he published in his *Russian Herald* a long article by Nikolai Rigelman, the head of the Kyiv Slavic Benevolent Society. Rigelman took particular issue with a recent article by Drahomanov that had appeared in Galicia under the title "Russian, Great Russian, Ukrainian, and

Galician Literature," where Drahomanov suggested that along with the common Russian literary language and high culture, their Great and Little Russian counterparts should also be developed, mainly to provide for the educational and cultural needs of the common folk. Rigelman smelled a rat.

He accused Drahomanov of providing nothing but a smoke screen for the continuing development of a separate Little Russian language and culture. "You, Messrs. Ukrainophiles, are so concerned about your people, so afraid of its ignorance, and want to enlighten it. For that purpose you choose such a circuitous route: you want to forge its dialect into a learned literary language, to create a whole literature that would divide it from the Russian people of 60 million; that is, you want to create a spiritual particularism for it in the Russian world." He concluded: "As for true Russians, as well as Slavs with any understanding of their true interests, they should fight you with all their might."

And fight they did. In May 1875, three months after Rigelman's article appeared in Katkov's *Russian Herald*, the deputy minister of education sent a letter to the head of the Kyiv educational district, attaching a copy of Drahomanov's article and Rigelman's criticism and asking for the names of Ukrainophile professors. This led to Drahomanov's dismissal from the university. But the leader of the Kyivan proponents of Little Russian identity, a retired military officer and educational official named Mikhail Yuzefovich, and his supporters wanted total victory. Yuzefovich sent his complaints directly to the head of the Third Section, General Aleksandr Potapov. Whatever he said in his letter, which has not yet been found by researchers, it made a strong impression on the head of the secret police, who reported Yuzefovich's concerns to the tsar. In August 1875, Alexander II ordered the creation of a Special Council to examine the continuing activities of the Ukrainophiles and the publication of Ukrainian literature. In addition to Potapov and the general procurator of the Holy Synod, the council included the ministers of the interior and education and, last but not least, Yuzefovich himself.

The Special Council, which began its deliberations in April 1876, interpreted the continuing activities of the Ukrainophiles as an attack on the unity of the tripartite Russian nation. The journal of the council's proceedings included the following passage:

Also obvious is the ultimate goal toward which the efforts of the Ukrainophiles are directed: they are now attempting to separate the Little Russians by the gradual but to some extent accurate method of separating
Little Russian speech and literature. Allowing the creation of a separate
popular literature in the Ukrainian dialect would mean establishing a
firm basis for the development of the conviction that the alienation of
Ukraine from Russia might be possible in the future, however distant. If
the government were to take an indulgent attitude to the currently developing feeble impulse to separate the Ukrainian dialect by elevating it to
the status of a literary language, then it would have no basis not to allow
the same separation for the dialect of the Belarusians, who constitute a
tribe as significant as that of the Little Russians. Ukraine, Little Russia,
and Western Russia, inhabited by Belarusians . . . constitute one great
political body inseparable from and united with Russia.

The council's position was informed by ideas first expressed in 1863
by Mikhail Katkov. They included the interpretation of the Ukrainophile
movement as both a Polish intrigue and a threat to the unity of Russia,
posed both directly and through the example offered to the Belarusians.
Katkov's thinking prevailed once again among the liberals and pragmatists
in the imperial government. Not only Slavophile activists, such as Pogodin,
or nationalist journalists, such as Katkov, but also key ministers were rallying to the defense of the indivisible Russian nation.

On May 18, 1876, Alexander II, vacationing at the German spa of
Bad Ems, signed a decree prepared by the Special Council that became
known as the Edict of Ems. It began with a resolution to "put a stop to
the activity of the Ukrainophiles, which is a danger to the state." The prohibitions imposed by the Valuev circular were made permanent and new
ones introduced. The edict banned the import of all Ukrainian-language
publications into the empire and prohibited the publication not only of
religious texts, grammars, and books for the common people, but also of
belles lettres addressed to the upper strata. This measure was intended
to arrest the development of Ukrainian literature on all levels. Existing
Ukrainian-language publications were to be removed from school librar-
ies. But the prohibition went beyond the written word: also banned were
theatrical performances, songs, and poetry readings in Ukrainian, "which

are in the nature of Ukrainophile manifestations at the present time." The only exception was for the publication of folklore, but it had to be done in Russian orthography.

Alexander II also ordered repressive measures against leading Ukrainophiles. Drahomanov and another Ukrainophile leader, Pavlo Chubynsky, were to be exiled from Ukraine, and the Kyiv branch of the Imperial Geographic Society—the locus of intellectual and cultural activity in the city and the hotbed of the Ukrainophile movement—closed, along with the newspaper *Kyivan Telegraph*. The heads of the Kyiv, Kharkiv, and Odesa educational districts were ordered to watch for unreliable Ukrainophiles on their faculty and report them to the authorities. New teaching positions were now to be filled exclusively by Great Russians, while Little Russians were to apply for positions in Great Russian schools and universities. This was an all-out attack on the Ukrainophile movement and its current and potential members. The treatment of Drahomanov and Chubynsky was not as harsh as that of the members of the Cyrillo-Methodian Brotherhood, but the approach was much more systematic and broader in scope than ever before. It was no longer limited to a handful of rogue intellectuals, as in 1847, or to restrictions on publishing, as in 1863, but aimed against Ukrainian cultural expression in general, both written and spoken.

THE EDICT OF EMS HAD A SINGLE PURPOSE—TO ARREST THE development of the Ukrainian cultural and political movement. What it offered was a mix of repressions, prohibitions, and restrictions. There was no positive program to build up an alternative all-Russian project; consequently, no additional funds were allocated for the development of Russian-language schools, publications, or societies. The only exception was the section of the edict dealing with the newspaper *Slovo* (Word), which was published, of all places, in Lviv, the capital of the Galician province of neighboring Austria-Hungary. Russia was "to support the newspaper *Slovo*, which is being published in Galicia with an orientation hostile to that of the Ukrainophiles, by providing it at least with a constant subsidy, however small, without which it could not continue to exist and would have to cease publication," stated the edict. The measure was justified as a response to Polish propaganda. The authors of the edict added, in parentheses: "The Ukrainophile organ in Galicia, the newspaper *Pravda* [Truth], which is completely hostile to Russian interests, is published with significant assistance from the Poles."

The subsidy, which amounted to 2,000 guldens, was suggested by Yuzefovich and approved by the tsar. It was the first time that the Russian imperial government had decided to allocate resources abroad not to support fellow Slavs but to influence a contest between two trends in the Slavic movement beyond the borders of the empire and support the Russophiles in their conflict with the Ukrainophiles. The dominant population of Galicia, or Red Rus', called itself "Rusyn" (in present-day English, "Ruthenian") and was considered by Russophile authors to be Russian, or, more specifically, Little Russian. That view began to gain ground after the publication in the empire of a Russian translation of Pavol Šafárik's *Slovanský národopis* in 1843. It was certainly the view of Mikhail Pogodin, who had visited Galicia, established close ties with local Russophile activists, and provided financial support for their activities. The Slavic Benevolent Society, especially its Kyivan branch, which was headed by Nikolai Rigelman, worked for the same cause, channeling mostly private funds to the region, but the government showed little interest until the signing of the edict of 1876.

Until then, developments in Galicia had been considered a matter for the imperial Ministry of Foreign Affairs, and Russian diplomats had advised their superiors to stay away from involvement in the region. In 1866, ten years before the Edict of Ems, and in the midst of Austria's disastrous Seven Weeks' War with Prussia, the Russian ambassador in Vienna, Ernst Shtakelberg, advised the foreign minister, Prince Aleksandr Gorchakov, against the possible partitioning of Austria and annexation of the province to Russia. As defeat in the Austro-Prussian war forced the Habsburgs to turn their empire into a dual monarchy and share power with the Hungarians on the national level, and with Poles and other nationalities in local administration, Galicia came under de facto Polish control, arousing great discontent among the Ruthenian elites.

Once again, Shtakelberg advised caution. He argued against a media campaign in defense of the Ruthenians in order to avoid directing "Austria's attention to the Ruthenians, who might perhaps drop into our hands like ripe fruit as a result of the Vienna cabinet's careless toleration of Polonism." Prince Gorchakov agreed with the ambassador's reasoning. Although the

Slavophile media in the Russian Empire sided with the Ruthenians against the Poles, the government once again did nothing. Shtakelberg was right in predicting the evolution of Ruthenian attitudes toward the monarchy. The transformation of the Habsburg Empire into a dual monarchy in which Hungarians wielded power along with Austrians, and the appointment of a Polish governor to rule Galicia on behalf of Vienna, were widely regarded by the Ruthenian elite as a betrayal, making a turn toward Russia and Russian identity almost inevitable.

The movement that came to be known as Muscophile or Russophile was born. Among its leaders was Bohdan Didytsky, the editor of *Slovo*, the movement's official mouthpiece. Didytsky was an alumnus of the University of Vienna, where he had studied Slavic languages and literatures under the supervision of Franz von Miklosich (Franc Miklošič), a close colleague of another prominent Slavist, Jernej Bartol Kopitar. (It was in a review of one of Kopitar's works that Nikolai Nadezhdin had first formulated the idea of a tripartite Russian nation in 1841.) Didytsky was originally attracted to Ukrainian literature under the influence of Ivan Kotliarevsky's *Eneïda*—the first major literary work written in vernacular Ukrainian in Russian-ruled Ukraine, but then, fascinated by the writings of Pushkin and Gogol, had opted for the Russian solution of the Ruthenian identity problem, seeing the Austrian Ruthenians as part of the Russian rather than the Ukrainian nation.

In 1871, in the wake of the constitutional reforms, another Russophile, Adolf Dobriansky, produced a political program for the Russophile movement that was adopted by its leading body, the Rus' Council. For Dobriansky, the Rus' nation (*russkii narod*) that the council represented and on whose behalf he spoke was not limited to Galician Rus' but also included the Ruthenians of Bukovyna and Transcarpathia, as well as Ruthenian settlements in the Austrian Balkan possessions. Dobriansky insisted that the Ruthenians of Austria-Hungary not only constituted one nation but were also part of a larger Russian nation: "Our Ruthenian people of 3 million, living under the Austrian scepter, is just one part of one and the same Russian (*russkii*) people, Little, White, and Great Russian, and has the same history as they do, the same traditions, the same literature, and the same folk customs; consequently, it has all the characteristics and conditions of complete national unity with the whole

Russian people and is therefore in a position (in that regard) to realize and proclaim its true national status."

Dobriansky pledged his allegiance to the Habsburg Empire, dismissing Polish accusations that by claiming membership in a larger Russian nation the Ruthenians were casting doubt on their loyalty to the Habsburgs. Dobriansky, however, saved most of his polemical zeal for his fellow Ruthenians, particularly those who had lost their way and subscribed to the Ukrainian project. Commenting on the foundations of the Ukrainophile movement, he wrote: "The Ukrainian question, presented in its current form, is based on the historical argument of the former independence of Cossack Ukraine and is more closely defined by the antiquity of the Little Russian dialect and the independence of recent Little Russian literature. Its ultimate goal is the independence of Ukraine." He considered the Ukrainophiles' historical and linguistic argument flawed and their political program of either joining a pan-Slavic federation or gaining complete independence a threat to the international order.

The rise to prominence of the Polish aristocracy in Galicia in the late 1860s—after the Habsburg Empire had lost the war with Prussia and reinvented itself as Austria-Hungary, making a deal with the former masters of Galicia, the Poles—provoked different responses from the Russophiles and Ukrainophiles. Whereas the Russophiles placed their hopes in the powerful Orthodox tsar and hoped to join the big Russian nation, the Ukrainophiles turned their attention to the Ukrainophile movement in Russian-ruled Ukraine, imagining themselves not as part of a 60-million-strong Russian people, as did Didytsky and Dobriansky, but as a Ukrainian people of 15 million. If the Russophiles subscribed to a conservative social agenda and were closely allied with the church, the Ukrainophiles, who were also known as populists (narodovtsi), had a more radical following that included the secular intelligentsia. They rejected both the conservative agenda of Slovo and the artificial language used by that newspaper. They wanted the literary language of the Ruthenians to be as close as possible to the one spoken by the popular masses, which they identified as Ukrainian.

The late 1860s and early 1870s saw the institutionalization of the Ukrainophile movement in Austria-Hungary. In 1868, the Ukrainophiles created a cultural society called Prosvita (Enlightenment) to disseminate their brand of Ruthenian nationalism among the peasantry. This was followed in 1873 by the establishment of a Ukrainophile literary society named after Taras Shevchenko. The initiative for the literary society and the money to make it possible came from Dnieper Ukraine—a donation from Yelysaveta Myloradovych-Skoropadska, a descendant of a prominent Cossack family that counted numerous colonels and hetmans in its ranks. Ukrainophiles in Russian-ruled Ukraine invested not only their money but also, and predominantly, their ideas in Galicia. The prohibitions on Ukrainian-language publications in the Russian Empire turned Austrian Galicia into an attractive market for Ukrainophile writers and activists. The Russian Ukrainophiles helped the Galician Ukrainophiles create new publications. Thus the Ukrainophile newspaper *Pravda* was established in Galicia in 1867 through the efforts of Panteleimon Kulish, one of the leading members of the Brotherhood of Saints Cyril and Methodius and a key figure in the Ukrainian cultural revival of the late 1850s and early 1860s. After his exile from the Russian Empire, Mykhailo Drahomanov was one of the many Ukrainophile activists who wrote for *Pravda*.

Mikhail Yuzefovich and the authors of the Edict of Ems had good reason to be concerned about the impact of *Pravda* on political and social thought in Galicia and Dnieper Ukraine. They strove to undermine the influence of the newspaper and the development of the Ukrainophile movement on both sides of the imperial border by introducing new prohibitions on Ukrainian publications in Russia and funding pro-Russian publications in Galicia, but their attempts proved unsuccessful. With new prohibitions in place, more Ukrainian writers turned to the Galician press as an outlet for their works, strengthening the appeal of the Ukrainophile project in Galicia.

By contrast, the subsidy for the newspaper *Slovo* decreed by the tsar did not reach the Russophiles for a number of years, either through bureaucratic incompetence or owing to corruption. The editor of *Slovo* informed his alleged benefactors in 1879 that he had never seen the money allegedly sent to him through diplomatic channels. When the Russian government resumed its support for the Russophiles in the 1880s, it was too late. Pro-Russian activists in Austria found themselves under increasing pressure from the government: in view of growing tensions with Russia, Vienna considered the Russophiles a more serious threat than the Ukrainophiles, with their dreams of an independent or autonomous Ukraine and its place in a future pan-Slavic federation.

The Russian authorities welcomed refugee Russophiles from Austria-Hungary, which was becoming increasingly hostile toward them, but preferred to keep the ideologically motivated arrivals away from the contested lands of Right-Bank Ukraine. The Galician Russophiles were welcome in the northwestern provinces and in the Kholm region of the former Kingdom of Poland. That had been the homeland of the last large group of Greek Catholics in the Russian Empire, who by living in this area had been shielded from the Orthodox zeal of Iosif Semashko and his supporters prior to 1863. They were "reunited" with the imperial Orthodox Church in 1875.

The Russophile priests and seminarians from Galicia, who had been born, raised, and educated as Greek Catholics but became Orthodox out of a desire to join the imperial Russian nation, effectively propagated imperial Russian identity among the former Uniates, who were forced to change their religion. In 1881, out of 291 Orthodox priests in the Kholm eparchy, 143—almost half—were former Greek Catholics from Galicia. Their salary from the imperial government was significantly higher than their previous income in Galicia—another incentive to leave the Galician battlefield to the Ukrainophiles and join the winning side in a Polish province of the "Russian world."

THE INCREASING NUMBER OF RUSSOPHILE MIGRANTS FROM GALIcia indicated a simple fact: the Russian Empire was losing the battle in that Austrian province. The emerging winners were the Galician Ukrainophiles, whom the Russian authorities were unwittingly strengthening by instituting repressive measures against the Ukrainian language and culture in their own empire. Such policies had their drawbacks, and some in the imperial government understood that better than others. Among them was the new liberal minister of the interior, Mikhail Loris-Melikov. Soon after taking office in August 1880, Loris-Melikov and his advisers got busy preparing either the complete abolition of the Edict of Ems or significant modifications to it in order to ease the pressure on Ukrainian cultural activities and

Ukrainian-language publications. Loris-Melikov wanted to restore trust in the government. That could not be achieved in the Ukrainian lands if the edict were left in place: its provisions made it illegal even to sing Ukrainian songs on a theater stage, which alienated many perfectly loyal members of the Little Russian elite.

Some historians have referred to this attempt to reconcile growing tensions between Ukrainian nationalism and the demands of all-Russian unity as a Scottish model. In Great Britain, the authorities had allowed the flourishing of a distinct Scottish identity and culture while ensuring the political loyalty of the Scottish elites. In the Russian Empire, an equivalent "Little Russian" solution would have accommodated Ukrainian identity and culture within a tripartite all-Russian nation. This would have involved the teaching of the Ukrainian language in elementary schools and the development of the Ukrainian language and culture alongside their dominant all-Russian (in fact, Great Russian) counterparts, leading to the creation of a bilingual educational system and a bicultural public sphere in the Ukrainian provinces of the empire. Some of the compromise ideas underlying the Little Russian educational program had been suggested by leading Ukrainophiles, including Mykola Kostomarov, and won the favor of some reform-minded officials in the 1870s and early 1880s.

Many expected that the restrictions would soon be lifted. But March 1881 brought the assassination of Alexander II—a sea change in Russian politics. Gone were not only exaggerated expectations in Russian society for movement toward a form of Russian constitutionalism, but also the no less exaggerated expectations of Ukrainian society for eliminating the ban on its language and culture. The proposals of government officials to amend the Edict of Ems were minimal, and they were indeed adopted under the new tsar. On October 8, 1881, Alexander III signed a decree permitting theatrical performances in Ukrainian with the special permission of provincial governors but forbade the creation of a separate Ukrainian theater—every Ukrainian play had to be accompanied by a Russian one.

The edict would remain in force for another twenty-four years. The continuing prohibitions made Galicia even more attractive to Ukrainophiles in the Russian Empire as a place of publication and cultural activity—a development that sealed the victory of Ukrainophile circles in Galicia over their Russophile opponents, despite Russian financial support for the latter in the 1880s. Inside the Russian Empire, the prohibitions made it completely impossible for the Ukrainophiles to find any common ground with the government and the proponents of the Little Russian idea. Over the next few decades, representatives of the Little Russian group would help turn Ukraine into a hotbed of Russian nationalism. One way or another, the times of the Little Russian compromise as a solution to the Ukrainian question were gone, and with them the hope of accommodating Little Russia in the all-Russian cultural and political space as a distinct component of a tripartite Russian nation. From then on, Little Russian intellectuals were left with only two choices—to become "true Russians," or to embrace an independent Ukrainian identity.

IV

THE REVOLUTION OF NATIONS

10

THE PEOPLE'S SONG

IT WAS A HUGE DISASTER AND A BAD OMEN FOR THE MONARCHY. Festivities organized to celebrate the coronation of the new Russian emperor, the twenty-eight-year-old Nicholas II, turned into a stampede that killed close to 2,000 men, women, and children.

On May 18, 1896, an estimated half million people gathered on the Khodynka Field near Moscow to celebrate the ascension of a new Romanov to the throne. Many were attracted by the promise of gifts from the tsar that included bread, sausage, and sweets. When the officials began to give out the gifts, the crowd rushed toward the shops, crushing everything in its way and stampeding those who fell—the field was full of ditches covered with wooden boards that gave way under the pressure. The young emperor wanted to cancel the celebrations, but his courtiers insisted that they go on. Most of those who gathered at the Khodynka Field were attracted not by the promise of food and drink at the tsar's expense but by the possibility of getting a commemorative cup with the double-headed eagle—the imperial coat of arms—depicted on it. The cups were put on display in Moscow shops on the eve of the celebrations, and enthusiasm for the monarchy ran high in Russian society. Once the corpses were removed, the crowd greeted the arriving emperor by singing of "God Save the Tsar," a hymn that had become known as the "people's song." The monarchy had survived the accident almost without a scratch.

The imperial regime was not so lucky in surviving another instance of popular adoration of the tsar and belief in his power to change the lives of his subjects for the better. It took place eight and a half years later, on Sunday, January 9, 1905. On that day, close to 20,000 St. Petersburg workers and members of their families marched from the outskirts of the city to the tsar's winter palace (now the Hermitage Museum) in the center. Singing the "people's song," they carried Orthodox icons and portraits of the emperor. They did not ask for free food packages. But a petition prepared by the leader of the march, the Orthodox priest Grigorii Gapon, read: "We working men of St. Petersburg, our wives and children, and our parents, helpless, aged men and women, have come to you, O Tsar, in quest of justice and protection." The factory workers wanted civil rights, higher wages, an eight-hour workday, and the right to strike. They also wanted responsible government. "Demolish the wall between yourself and the people, and let them govern the country together with you," read the petition.

The government responded by firing at the demonstrators. Bad news was coming from the Far East, where the army of the mighty Russian Empire was losing the war with tiny Japan: on January 2, Russian troops had left Port Arthur. Revolutionaries were becoming bolder, and the demonstration before the tsar's palace was taken as proof of that. The decision was made to show strength and resolve by using the army to disperse the demonstrators and stop the revolution that they were thought to be demanding. As the soldiers began to shoot, dozens of people were killed and hundreds wounded. The event, which became known as "Bloody Sunday," shattered the highly idealized relations between the tsar and his people— the leader of the demonstration, Father Gapon, would call the tsar a beast and cry for vengeance. The events of January 9, 1905, in St. Petersburg launched the first Russian Revolution.

In the following days the St. Petersburg workers, already on strike, were joined by workers all over the empire. The peasants followed suit, refusing to pay their debts to the state and the landowners and rising in revolt. A mutiny on the battleship *Potemkin* in the summer of 1905 carried the wave of disturbances into the army and navy. As early as February 1905, Nicholas ordered his interior minister to prepare a convocation of the Duma—the precursor of the first Russian parliament—which was to be given not legislative but advisory functions. Elections to the Duma were announced in August. But society remained dissatisfied, and the disturbances continued. On October 17, 1905, in the midst of an all-empire workers' strike, Nicholas issued a manifesto granting his subjects basic civil rights, introducing universal male suffrage, giving the Duma legislative powers, and pledging that no new law would be adopted without the Duma's consent.

The Russian Empire was launched on a new era of mass politics that saw workers' rebellions, peasant revolts, military mutinies, and the birth of parliamentarism, which challenged the absolute power of the tsars. The regime managed to survive the revolutionary upheaval but had to change its modus operandi, looking for new sources of legitimacy and support. Nowhere was that more obvious than in the sphere of nationality policy, where the imperial throne required the ideological backing of Russian nationalism.

THE REVOLUTION THAT BEGAN WITH WORKERS' DEMONSTRATIONS and strikes awakened the leaders of non-Russian political parties throughout the empire. As always, the Poles were in the lead. In the former Kingdom of Poland, which had become one of the main industrial hubs of the empire in the decades leading up to the revolution, workers' strikes were accompanied by the destruction of imperial symbols. The workers were followed by the students, who went on a prolonged strike, demanding the return of Polish-language education in the former kingdom.

The conservative Polish elites wanted equality—in particular, the introduction of local and municipal self-government—which had long been instituted in other parts of the empire but not in Polish-dominated areas, where the imperial government did not trust the upper social strata. The more radical leaders insisted on broad autonomy for the former Kingdom of Poland. That was the program of the Polish National Democrats, led by Roman Dmowski. His main political rival, the head of the Polish socialists, Józef Piłsudski, wanted a new uprising and complete independence.

The outbreak of the Russo-Japanese War in February 1904 had given Polish politicians new opportunities to advance their agendas. While St. Petersburg fought the Japanese over their influence in Manchuria and Korea, the western parts of the empire grew ever more restless. Piłsudski traveled to Japan to ask for support, and in the summer of 1905 his followers led a workers' uprising in Łódź, the center of the Polish industrial region and working class. The uprising was crushed, but the idea of territorial autonomy for the imperial regions found support among Russian liberals in the Duma and would become a major factor in reformulating the Russian national question during the Revolution of 1905–1907 and afterward.

If Poland gained autonomy, where would its borders be? That question was on the minds of many Russian politicians and intellectuals, especially leaders and supporters of the government campaign of previous decades to Russify the Polish lands. This time the center of attention was not Right-Bank Ukraine or western Belarus but the Kholm (Chełm) region of the former Kingdom of Poland, which constituted the eastern perimeter of Lublin and Siedlce provinces. The region had originally belonged to the Rus' princes and was settled by people who had been defined since the nineteenth century as Little Russians or Ukrainians, but after centuries of Polish rule it had become an ethnic, religious, and cultural borderland.

The event that launched the Kholm crisis and kept the city's name in newspaper headlines for the next seven years came on April 17, 1905, the first day of Orthodox Easter. It was the proclamation of an imperial edict on freedom of worship—one of the decrees that attempted to appease society in the face of growing civic unrest. The edict, which stated that subjects of the tsar could now freely choose their religion and, more importantly, leave the Russian Orthodox Church if they chose, with no political penalty, created a religious upheaval in the Kholm region, where thirty years earlier the authorities had forcibly converted hundreds of thousands of local Ukrainians from Uniate Catholicism to Orthodoxy. Government officials in St. Petersburg had foreseen that turn of events. Preliminary estimates suggested that anywhere between 100,000 and 150,000 people, or roughly one-third of the nominal Orthodox in the region, would bid farewell to the Orthodox Synod in St. Petersburg and pledge allegiance to the pope. The forecast was on the mark, as recent estimates put the actual number of converts exactly between the two projected figures.

But whereas the central government believed that it could not avoid paying that price in order to bring imperial policy into line with current standards of religious toleration, regional officials and Orthodox clergymen who had dedicated their lives to propagating Orthodoxy and Russian identity felt betrayed. Among those who felt that way was the Orthodox bishop of Kholm, Evlogii (Georgievsky), an ethnic Russian. He expressed his frustration in a letter to the general procurator of the Holy Synod, the government official overseeing the Russian Orthodox Church and its affairs. That post was occupied by Konstantin Pobedonostsev, one of the architects of the policies of Russification and Orthodoxization in the borderlands. Evlogii wrote: "The very credit of our priests has been undermined. For thirty years they repeated to the people that the Kholm-Podliashie [Podlachia] country will always be Orthodox and Russian, and now the people see, on the contrary, the complete, willful takeover of the enemies of the Orthodox Russian cause in that country."

Soon after he sent the letter, Evlogii and his supporters went to St. Petersburg to meet with Pobedonostsev and discuss how to deal with the threat to Russian interests in the region. They wanted to redraw the borders of the imperial provinces, dividing the Kholm region from the lands of the former Kingdom of Poland. The new Kholm province was to have a "Russian" core consisting of more than 300,000 ethnic Ukrainians—those who had said Little Russian was their native language in the 1897 census. Officials in the Ministry of the Interior got busy planning for the administrative change. The bill was sent to the Duma. Debates on the measure continued until 1912, leading eventually to the creation of a new province and mobilizing Russian nationalist forces in parliament and beyond.

The Kholm debate brought together Ukrainophiles and proponents of Russia, one and indivisible, in common cause against Polish influence, but their alliance was situational and limited to a single goal. In almost every other case, Ukrainophiles and Russian nationalists found themselves engaged in a life-or-death struggle for the future of a land that both considered their own. The language issue had traditionally been central to the Ukrainophile agenda. In December 1904, with the war against Japan going badly and social discontent rising precipitously, the imperial government had agreed to revisit the question of the prohibitions imposed on Ukrainian-language publications by the Edict of Ems. Once again, discussion focused on translation of the Gospels, but this time the atmosphere was different. The president of the Imperial Academy of Sciences himself, Grand Duke Konstantin Konstantinovich, advocated the abolition of the ban on publishing the Scriptures in Ukrainian.

In March 1905, a commission of the Academy of Sciences also discussed the issue of ending the ban on Ukrainian-language publications generally. The discussion was held at the behest of the government, which also solicited the opinions of the universities of Kyiv, Kharkiv, and Odesa. All four institutions advised lifting the restrictions, with the Academy of Sciences making the strongest statement. Its memorandum, prepared by the philologists Aleksei Shakhmatov and Fedor Korsh and signed by many other liberal academicians in April 1905, not only recommended doing away with the ban but also opened the door to the recognition of Ukrainian as a separate language.

The authors of the Academy of Sciences' memorandum did not say explicitly that Ukrainian was a separate language, but their reasoning left little doubt that it was on a par with Russian. They achieved that effect by discarding the notion of an "all-Russian language." The academics claimed that the efforts of Russian authors to bring their literary language closer to the vernacular "had already made the all-Russian literary language fully Great Russian by the late eighteenth and early nineteenth centuries, and our literary speech, the speech of the educated classes and written language of every kind, should be considered fully Great Russian." The authors of the memorandum used not only historical and linguistic but also political arguments to make their case. "A state that does not know how to guarantee one of the most elementary civil rights—the right to speak and publish in one's mother tongue—arouses neither respect nor love in the citizen but a nameless fear for his existence," wrote Shakhmatov and Korsh before delivering their ultimate warning: "That fear gives rise to dissatisfaction and revolutionary aspirations." Their timing was perfect: shocked by the revolutionary upheaval of the previous few months, the government was prepared to listen.

The memorandum was published in a limited number of copies (exclusively for government use) in April 1905 and immediately had a major impact on political debates within the Russian Empire and beyond its borders. The lifting of restrictions on Ukrainian-language publications began in February 1905, with permission to publish religious texts in Ukrainian, for which Grand Duke Konstantin Konstantinovich had lobbied. All prohibitions were abolished with the introduction of new censorship regulations in the spring of 1906. By that time the abolition was a mere formality, given that the prohibitions on Ukrainian-language newspapers had been done away with in October 1905, the month that also saw the publication of the tsar's manifesto granting his subjects basic civil rights, including "freedom of the word." By the end of the year, three Ukrainian-language newspapers were being published in the empire, one in Kyiv and two in Poltava province.

Among the beneficiaries of the changes in official language policy were Belarusian activists. In September 1906, the first Belarusian daily, *Nasha dolia* (Our Destiny), began publication in Vilnius. After being closed for its radical leftist content, it was replaced in November 1906 by the more centrist newspaper *Nasha niva* (Our Field), which would continue publication until 1915. It formed a new Belarusian literary canon and helped popularize Belarusian-language literature. Between 1906 and 1915, the number of books published in Belarusian increased from almost zero to 80 titles, attaining a cumulative print run of 220,000 copies.

Although these figures represented a breakthrough for the Belarusian language and literature, they were very modest in comparison to publications in other languages of the empire. In 1911 alone there were 25,526 titles published in Russian, 1,664 in Polish, and 965 in Yiddish and Hebrew. The Ukrainians trailed those front-runners with 242 items. The Belarusians, who had never waged a prolonged struggle against the discrimination of their language or mobilized around that issue, were even further behind.

THE APPEARANCE OF A UKRAINIAN- AND BELARUSIAN-LANGUAGE press coincided with the beginning of the parliamentary period in the history of the Russian Empire. In the 1906 elections to the First Duma, the Ukrainian provinces of the empire elected sixty-two deputies, and forty-four of them joined the Ukrainian parliamentary club, agreeing to promote the Ukrainian political and cultural agenda in the capital. The Belarusian deputies attempted to do the same. "Infectious foolishness," wrote

one of Russia's most popular journalists and a leading Russian nationalist, Mikhail Menshikov. "The Belarusians, too, are following the *khokhly* in
speaking of a 'circle' of their own in the State Duma. There are Belarusian
separatists as well, you see. It's enough to make a cat laugh." The Belarusians
failed to create their own club and, depending on their political orientation,
supported either the liberal or the Russian nationalist agenda promoted by
other parties and caucuses.

The Ukrainian agenda in the Duma was formulated largely by
Mykhailo Hrushevsky, a professor of history at the University of Lviv and a
leading figure of the Ukrainian movement in Austrian Galicia. An alumnus
of Kyiv University, he closely followed political and cultural developments
in Russian-ruled Ukraine and refused to renounce his Russian citizenship.
He arrived in St. Petersburg in the spring of 1906 to edit the *Ukraïns'kyi
visnyk* (Ukrainian Herald), the mouthpiece of the Ukrainian parliamentary club. The *Herald* was published in Russian, reflecting not only the
everyday speech of most members of the club but also the need to disseminate the Ukrainian viewpoint and political agenda among the Russian
or Russian-speaking parliamentarians and public. By the time the First
Duma met for deliberations in May 1906, the program of the Ukrainian
movement, as formulated by Hrushevsky, had advanced from introducing
Ukrainian as the language of instruction in schools to achieving territorial
autonomy for Ukraine.

By the end of the nineteenth century, the idea of Ukrainian independence had gained support in Austrian Galicia, and in 1900 it was
introduced in Russian-ruled Ukraine as the program of the short-lived
Ukrainian Revolutionary Party. But Hrushevsky and the mainstream
Ukrainian leaders regarded autonomy, not independence, as their political goal. As far as Hrushevsky was concerned, Ukrainian needs could
only be met through a federal restructuring of the empire. He placed the
question of Ukrainian territorial autonomy within the broader context of
the "liberation of Russia"—a broad liberal movement seeking to turn the
Russian Empire into a constitutional state. For Hrushevsky, the Ukrainian
question was not part of the Russian ethnic question (he adduced the
opinion of the Imperial Academy of Sciences on the nonexistence of an all-
Russian language as a political argument) but an aspect of the empire's nationality problem in general, equal in importance to the Polish and Finnish

questions—the leaders of those peoples were demanding broad autonomy within the empire—and deserving of the same kind of resolution.

Not surprisingly, Hrushevsky and his followers in the Duma found a sympathetic ear among representatives of other non-Russian regions of the empire. Thus, the Ukrainian deputies joined the parliamentary "Union of Autonomist Federalists," which included members of various nationalities. It was a curious group of deputies that extended from Russian Cossack autonomists, who insisted on regional rights irrespective of nationality, to non-Russian federalists who wanted a federation of nationalities within the framework of the Russian Empire. The Polish deputies, organized in their own circle (koło), demanded autonomy for their former kingdom. Hrushevsky was ready to follow suit. He prepared a parliamentary resolution on Ukrainian autonomy but was unable to present it, as the imperial authorities dissolved the First Duma on July 8, 1906, only seventy-two days after its opening.

The tsar found the ideas and actions of the deputies destructive. "The representatives of the nation, instead of applying themselves to the work of productive legislation, have strayed into spheres beyond their competence and have been making inquiries into the acts of local authorities established by ourselves, and have been making comments on the imperfections of the fundamental laws, which can only be modified by our imperial will," read the tsar's manifesto on the dissolution of the Duma. The Ukrainian deputies were able to form a caucus of forty-seven in the short-lived Second Duma (February–June 1907), where they again raised the banner of Ukrainian autonomy. But the change of electoral legislation accompanying the dissolution of the Second Duma—the tsar found it even less agreeable than the first—favored large landowners and made it difficult to elect Ukrainophile deputies, who were often supported by peasants, to the Third Duma.

Neither the Third Duma (1907–1912) nor the Fourth (1912–1917) had a Ukrainian caucus. That put an end not only to Ukrainian autonomist plans but also to much more modest attempts to bring the Ukrainian language into the public sphere. In 1908, a Duma majority rejected a proposal to introduce the Ukrainian language into the school system and, in 1909, to allow its use in the courts. The Ukrainophile leaders had no choice but to work with and through the other parties, if not to advance their agenda, then at least to protect the achievements of the revolutionary period. They invested their hopes mainly in the Constitutional Democrats, a party of liberal representatives of the Russian urban intelligentsia.

The Constitutional Democrats gained strong support from the Polish and Jewish intelligentsia in the western borderlands and were the only party open to the autonomist aspirations of the minorities. The party was popular in the Ukrainian provinces, and many pro-Ukrainian activists joined its ranks, but the party program, published in Kyiv in 1905, made no mention of Ukraine or the Ukrainian question. The Constitutional Democrats were prepared to accommodate the autonomist aspirations of the Poles and Finns but distanced themselves from the similar aspirations of Ukrainians and other nationalities.

In a number of polemical articles published in 1911 and 1912, one of the leaders of the party, Petr Struve, formulated his (and, as many believed, his party's) position on the Ukrainian question. He first presented his views on the issue in January 1911, responding to an article by a Zionist leader and native of Odesa, Vladimir Jabotinsky, who questioned Struve's treatment of the Russian Empire as a Russian nation-state. With only 43 percent of the population consisting of Great Russians, Russia was nothing but a multiethnic empire, argued Jabotinsky. Struve, who included the Ukrainians and Belarusians in the Great Russian camp, disagreed: for him, the key was not ethnicity but culture. Struve considered Russia to be a work in progress, like the United States and Great Britain. The Russian nation that Struve had in mind was to be held together not by ethnicity but by culture—Russian culture. He insisted that that culture was not Great Russian but all-Russian, and thus included the Little and White Russians along with Great Russians as core members.

The Ukrainian activists, who had welcomed the demise of the concept of an all-Russian language in the memorandum issued by the Imperial Academy of Sciences, now found a more formidable obstacle to the development of their nation in Struve's vision of an all-Russian culture. In May 1911, Struve's journal, *Russkaia mysl'* (Russian Thought), published a letter from Struve's old acquaintance Bohdan Kistiakovsky, a prominent Ukrainian lawyer who disagreed with Struve and argued for the distinctiveness of the Ukrainian language and culture. In January 1912, Struve responded to Kistiakovsky with a long exposé of his views on the subject.

Struve wrote: "I am profoundly convinced that vis-à-vis the all-Russian culture and the all-Russian language, the Little Russian or Ukrainian culture is a local or provincial culture. This status of the 'Little Russian' culture and the 'Little Russian' language has been determined by the whole course of Russia's historical development and can be changed only by the complete collapse of the historically shaped structure not only of Russian statehood but also of Russian society." He went on to define the threat more precisely: "If the 'Ukrainian' idea of the intelligentsia strikes root among the people and inflames them with its 'Ukrainianness,' that threatens the Russian nation with a huge and unheard-of schism."

While Struve warned against that scenario, he did not consider it likely. He envisioned a two-level structure of imperial culture, the higher one to be served by the "all-Russian" language and culture, the lower one by local cultures, including that of Little Russia. Of the two options that he envisioned for the Ukrainian and Belarusian cultures—functioning either as local or as fully developed high cultures—Struve considered the first option more realistic. Ukrainian and Belarusian high cultures had yet to be developed, he maintained. Meanwhile, their languages could be used for elementary education of the masses, who would gain access to high culture and advanced education through the medium of the Russian language.

This was a throwback to the decade after the Edict of Ems, when Mykhailo Drahomanov had seen the Ukrainian language function in the imperial educational system as auxiliary to Russian, and Struve was happy to present some of his arguments as corollaries to Drahomanov's thinking about the all-Russian language and culture. But the times when Ukrainian activists would accept a subordinate position for their language and culture were gone. The Edict of Ems was no longer in force, and Struve's position soon began to create difficulties for the Constitutional Democratic leaders, who relied on the support of Ukrainophile activists. They officially dissociated themselves from Struve's concept of all-Russian culture, declaring that it represented only his private opinion.

The official position of the Constitutional Democratic Party on the Ukrainian question was formulated by none other than its leader, the prominent historian Pavel Miliukov. In 1912, in preparation for elections to the Fourth Duma, he had visited Kyiv and met with the Ukrainian leaders, including Hrushevsky, to discuss an electoral alliance. What Miliukov

offered the Ukrainian leaders in 1912 was the principle of cultural autonomy: the right of citizens of all nationalities to develop their culture and
use their language in dealings with the state. That meant the Constitutional
Democratic Party's support for the introduction of the Ukrainian language
in the educational and judicial systems. Hrushevsky assured Miliukov that
the Ukrainian movement was not pursuing separatist goals: "We are not
guided by the aspirations of aggressive nationalism and do not think that
the Ukrainian nationality will assume a position of sovereignty." He did
not budge, however, on the issue of territorial autonomy and federalism,
indicating the Ukrainian activists' goal of "restructuring everything on fed-
eralist foundations." That was the goal for the future, he told Miliukov.

Cultural autonomy—the intermediate goal of Hrushevsky and his
supporters and the biggest concession that Miliukov was prepared to offer
in order to accommodate Ukrainian aspirations—became a common platform on which they would work together on the eve of World War I. Their
cooperation was symbolized by a speech that Miliukov would deliver in the
Duma in February 1914, protesting the government's decision to prohibit a
celebration of the centenary of Taras Shevchenko's birth in Kyiv.

THE MAIN POLITICAL COMPETITORS OF MILIUKOV'S CONSTITU-
tional Democrats and the Ukrainian activists in the pre–World War I era
were the Russian monarchists and nationalists, who effectively dominated
the Third and Fourth Dumas. In the western provinces, the Russian nationalists had originally mobilized against the threat posed to the regime
by the Polish landowning class. By the turn of the twentieth century, the
political and cultural Russification of the western borderlands was under
way, but Polish landowners remained the true masters of the region. Their
influence became fully apparent in the elections to the First Duma, when
they managed to elect significantly more deputies than their own votes
could account for; meanwhile, Russian nationalist candidates in the region
were defeated by the combined Polish and liberal vote.

It was the desire to prevent the Polish nobility from using the new
electoral system to its advantage in the elections to the Second Duma
that prompted the Russian nationalists to launch their own electoral
campaign. Their problem was not only the traditionally high level of po-

litical mobilization of the Polish regional elite—some of its members came all the way from Paris to vote—but also the fact that the electoral law privileged large landowners. The small landowners, who were mainly Ukrainian peasants, could fight back only by combining their votes. The Russian nationalists had to go to the peasants and organize them if they were to overcome the Polish landowners. They soon managed to find an infrastructure and organizational base in the Russian Orthodox Church, which was engaged in an ongoing struggle with its Catholic competitor, as well as in numerous nationalist organizations established in the region with church and government support.

The most popular Russian nationalist organization to come into existence during the Revolution of 1905 was the Union of the Russian People. The first rally the Union organized in Moscow attracted close to 20,000 people. In December 1905, Nicholas received a delegation of leaders of the Union and gave his blessing to its activities. Backed by the authorities, the Union played a key role in mobilizing support for the monarchy under the banner of modern nationalism. According to the Union's statute, "the good of the motherland lies in the firm preservation of Orthodoxy, unlimited Russian autocracy, and the national way of life." Count Sergei Uvarov's formula of the 1830s—autocracy, Orthodoxy, and nationality—had been revived, now inspiring not only imperial bureaucrats but also rank-and-file subjects.

The Russia represented by the Union was not limited to Great Russians. "The Union makes no distinction between Great Russians, White Russians, and Little Russians," read the statute. In fact, the western provinces, and Ukraine in particular, became the Union's main base of operations. Its largest branch, located in the Ukrainian province of Volhynia, was centered on the Pochaiv Monastery. According to a report of 1907, the Union counted more than 1,000 chapters in Volhynia, with a membership of more than 100,000. If one trusts the report, compiled by the governor of Volhynia, that province alone accounted for one-quarter of the Union's membership throughout the empire. Not far behind were other Right-Bank Ukrainian provinces, especially the Kyiv gubernia.

What accounted for the truly impressive number of Union members in the western provinces was that, as in Volhynia, individual chapters were organized and led by priests, who enlisted their parishioners into the Union.

A police report described its functioning in Volhynia as follows: "The members are local Orthodox parishioners, as well as semiliterate and even completely illiterate people in the villages, who show no initiative themselves. The heads of the Union's local branches, mostly elected from among parish priests, instill patriotic feelings in the population by conversing with the peasants and preaching to them in order to strengthen Russia's foundations."

The translation of religious loyalty into loyalty to the empire and the adoption of an all-Russian identity by the Ukrainian peasantry was only one reason for the Union's success in the region. But its success was also rooted in the growing social and economic demands of the peasantry. The average landholding in Volhynia and Podolia amounted to only nine acres, compared to forty acres in the southern provinces. Land hunger drove peasants to leave the region for eastern parts of the empire. But those who stayed were prepared to mobilize in support of their economic interests, and the Union of the Russian People provided a ready framework.

Orthodox priests and propagandists of the Union were there to point to the main "culprits" of the peasants' troubles: Polish landowners and Jewish middlemen to whom the peasants sold their produce. According to a police report on Union activists, "sowing enmity among the peasants toward all non-Russians and landowners, those individuals impressed upon the peasants the need to join the Union, which alone was in a position to make the peasants' dreams come true by endowing them with lands forcibly taken from the landlords, freeing them from all dependence on the government, etc."

The peasants clearly regarded branches of the Union as institutions representing their interests, and on a number of occasions they refused to follow the orders of government officials, saying that they would follow only those given by leaders of the Union. This metamorphosis of the Union into an instrument of agrarian revolution caused concern among the authorities, who became less interested in nationalist mobilization of the masses in support of the monarchy and more concerned with the task of maintaining order and stability in the borderlands. Police officials ordered their underlings in the provinces to close chapters of the Union if that became necessary.

The symbolic union between the monarchy and the peasants, glued by xenophobia, anti-Semitism, and Russian nationalism, was beginning to crack only a few years after its establishment in the midst of the 1905 revolution. The stumbling block was the land issue. The leaders of Russian nationalist organizations, often large landowners themselves, wanted the authorities to buy land from the landowners and distribute it among the peasants, but government funds were insufficient for that purpose. Russian nationalism was becoming mired in the agrarian question. In a country inhabited mainly by peasants, that was a major impediment to those seeking to turn patriarchal loyalty to the tsar into national feeling. Years later, Vladimir Lenin, the leader of the most radical (Bolshevik) faction of the Russian Social Democrats, discovered a silver lining in the activities of the Russian nationalist organizations, to which he referred in general as "Black Hundreds": "The Black Hundred political organization first united the peasants and involved them in organizing. And those aroused peasants made Black Hundred demands one day and demanded all the land from the landowners the next."

For the Russian nationalists from the western provinces, the list of enemies and competitors was not limited to Poles and Jews but also included activists of the Ukrainian movement, which had gained strength from the Revolution of 1905. In 1907, those opposing the recognition of Ukrainian as a distinct language published a number of brochures, written by the philologists Timofei Florinsky and Anton Budilovich, seeking to prove that Ukrainian was nothing but a branch of the all-Russian language. The battle became heated in 1911 when Prime Minister Petr Stolypin was assassinated in Kyiv. Elections to the Fourth Duma were coming up, and it was also the year in which Petr Struve began his polemics on the Ukrainian question. Leading Constitutional Democrats, meanwhile, noted the growing popularity of Ukrainian parties and slogans among the urban intelligentsia of the Ukrainian provinces.

In November 1911, the Kyivan club of Russian nationalists, the largest such club in the empire, held a discussion about a number of papers dealing with the importance of Little Russian folklore, tradition, and patriotism in the worldview and ideology of Russian nationalism. This was a sticky issue, given the origins of the Russian nationalist movement in Ukraine as a reaction to the Ukrainian/Little Russian awakening of the 1840s. The debate showed that the Russian nationalists in Kyiv were not prepared to give up their claim to the local political, cultural, and even linguistic tradition. One of the leaders of the club, Anatolii Savenko, professed his love for Ukraine as part of his Little Russian identity. He wrote, "I am a Little Russian, and nothing Little Russian is foreign to me. I ardently love my homeland, Ukraine, and in essence I am a Ukrainophile in the old sense of the word. The nature of Ukraine, her history, language, and everyday life, are dear to me." He concluded his testimony with a quotation from Taras Shevchenko.

If the Russian nationalists in Kyiv were proclaiming their profound attachment to Ukraine, what was their view of the leaders of the Ukrainian movement? They referred to the latter as "separatists" and, more and more often, as Mazepists, after the name of the Cossack hetman Ivan Mazepa, who had led an uprising in 1708 against Peter I and joined the advancing armies of Charles XII of Sweden. In 1909, the empire had lavishly celebrated the bicentennial of Peter I's victory at Poltava—a commemoration that helped focus public attention on Mazepa and eighteenth-century separatism. In reality, most Ukrainian political leaders of the pre–World War I era did not see national independence as their goal and worked instead for Ukrainian autonomy within the Russian Empire. But the Russian nationalist ideologues were looking ahead. "The Mazepists are well aware that if the notion of Little Russians as a wholly independent people enters public consciousness, then ineluctable historical evolution will do the rest," wrote Savenko. According to him, the outcome might be a schism within the Russian nation and a fratricidal war that would destroy the empire.

While portraying the Ukrainian movement as a major threat to the unity of the Russian nation and state, the Russian nationalist leaders also pointed to its weaknesses: it was limited to students and intellectuals, with little following among the popular masses, especially the peasantry. After 1905, Ukrainian activists made inroads into the countryside, opening *Prosvita* cultural societies modeled on those in Galicia and conducting a campaign of socialist propaganda among the peasants. They also launched Ukrainian-language newspapers for the peasantry. But with the end of the active phase of the revolution in 1907, Ukrainian influence in the village was severely curbed by the government, while Russian nationalism swept the countryside, achieving a popularity that the non-Russian parties could only dream of.

THE RUSSIAN REVOLUTION OF 1905 RAISED THE HOPES OF non-Russian activists, most of whom considered the social and national liberation of their peoples to be closely connected issues. In the Ukrainian and Belarusian cases, radical social demands and national aspirations went hand in hand, as most younger activists of both movements held socialist views. Their opponents exploited that fact to discredit Ukrainian activists in the eyes of the authorities and shut down the first Belarusian-language newspaper. The revolution allowed the Ukrainians to organize in the Duma, mobilize their supporters in parliamentary elections, raise the banner of autonomy and federalism, launch magazines and newspapers, and spread their ideas among the intelligentsia of the empire's western provinces.

But activists of the Ukrainian—and especially of the Belarusian—movement garnered little understanding and less support from the mainstream Russian political parties. Even the liberal Constitutional Democrats, the most sympathetic of the Russian parties to the aspirations of the non-Russians, were split on the "Russian question" between adherents of Struve and the more pragmatically oriented group represented by Miliukov. Struve needed the Ukrainians and Belarusians as part of a larger Russian cultural nation to realize his vision of turning the Russian Empire into a "normal" European state. Miliukov, for his part, opted for a civic model of the Russian nation that would allow sufficient autonomy for the development of non-Russian cultures. But even Miliukov and his supporters offered no more than symbolic support for the main tactical goal of the Ukrainian movement of the time—the introduction of the Ukrainian language into the school system. The Duma never passed the bill that would have allowed teachers to use Ukrainian in the classrooms of the Ukrainian provinces of the empire.

By 1914, it looked as if the monarchy had successfully survived the revolution and adjusted itself to the new political and economic realities. The transition to constitutional monarchy had been made, a parliament established, and a way discovered to fill it with deputies generally loyal to the regime. The non-Russian nationalities were taken under control after receiving some cultural concessions, and Russian nationalism had created an unprecedented bond between the monarchy and most of its subjects. Fears that allowing the Ukrainians and Belarusians to publish in their languages would split the East Slavic core of the empire never materialized.

Popular support for one indivisible Russian state and nation was as strong as ever and was gaining new ground in the traditionally troublesome western provinces.

If anything, the outbreak of the Great War in August 1914 would strengthen the unity of that virtual nation and create conditions for its expansion beyond the borders of the empire.

11

THE FALL OF THE MONARCHY

O N August 31, 1914, Emperor Nicholas II signed a decree renaming the Russian capital from St. Petersburg, the name given to it by its founder, Peter the Great, to Petrograd. The reference to the saint was gone, replaced with the name of the tsar who had founded the city. More importantly, the German "burg" was replaced with the Russian "grad," signaling that Russia was turning its back on its close links to Central Europe and embarking on a process of gradual isolation from the West. That process would gather strength in the 1920s, when Petrograd was renamed Leningrad to honor the leader of the Bolshevik revolution, and would reach its peak in the next decade under Lenin's heir, Joseph Stalin.

The original change from the German to the Russian name was made in the early days of the World War I, which pitted Russia against Germany and Austria-Hungary, and was inspired by an upsurge of Russian patriotism. It was made by Tsar Nicholas himself, without much consultation with his chief ministers. He was clearly responding to the expectations of the masses as opposed to those of his cabinet. The Great War was not the first military conflict with a Western power, of which there had been many in the eighteenth and nineteenth centuries, but no one had suggested altering the name of the capital in those days. Times were changing. On both sides of the freshly drawn front lines, nationalism was on the rise, and nothing fed it better than war. This one was supposed to be short and victorious, but the change of name was by no means provisional and aroused jubilation among Russian nationalists. "A great historical fact has come to pass," wrote a newspaper at the time. "The capital of the Russian Empire, Petersburg, which bore that name for more than two centuries, has been renamed Petrograd by imperial decree. That which the finest Slavophiles dreamed of has been realized in the great epoch of struggle against Germanism."

A few weeks earlier, on August 2, tens of thousands of citizens had poured into the square in front of the Winter Palace, where the Revolution of 1905 had begun nine years earlier. This time they came not to protest and demand but to manifest their patriotism and loyalty to the monarchy. Russia's world-renowned opera singer Fedor Shaliapin (Chaliapin) led the crowd in the hymn "God Save the Tsar." People knelt when Nicholas II came onto the balcony to greet them and read his manifesto on the start of the war, which Russia had officially declared on Austria the previous day. Nicholas explained the government's decision as a response to Austria's attack on Serbia, a fraternal Slavic and Orthodox state. "True to its historical precepts, Russia, one in faith and blood with the Slavic peoples, has never regarded their fate with indifference," read the manifesto. He then explained that with the German declaration of war on Russia, more was now at stake than Slavic solidarity. "WE unshakably believe," continued Nicholas, "that all OUR faithful subjects will rise concordantly and selflessly to the defense of the Russian Land. Let internal disputes be forgotten at this terrible hour of trial. May the union of the TSAR with HIS people be consolidated even more firmly."

The war was presented not as a struggle of one European empire against another but as a contest of the Russian people and the Slavic world they led with the Germanic race. The crowds in front of the palace, bearing banners and portraits of the tsar, were most receptive. At the very center were two banners, one calling for "Victory for Russia and all Slavdom," the other demanding "Freedom for Carpathian Rus'." Although war was declared in Petrograd under the pan-Slavic banner, the Russian question was profoundly involved from the start. Among the immediate war aims was that of taking under the tsar's high hand the last remaining patrimony of Kyivan Rus'—the "Carpathian Rus'" of Austrian and Hungarian Galicia, Bukovyna, and Transcarpathia. That would complete the reunification of the "Russian" lands.

On August 17, Russian forces crossed the Russo-German border into East Prussia. Official rhetoric focused on the need to crush aggressive Teutonic might. On the following day, Russian commanders led their troops across the border with Austria, proclaiming the goal of liberating long-suffering "Russians" oppressed by the Habsburgs. The war on the southern sector of the Russian front was supposed to solve the Russian question once and for all, uniting all Russians under the emperor's rule. It also offered a unique opportunity to crush rising Ukrainian and Belarusian movements within the empire, ensuring the complete unity of the reconstituted Russian nation.

THE FIRST MONTHS OF THE WAR WITNESSED AN UNPRECEDENTED upsurge of Russian nationalism, fueling the high expectations of the leaders of Russian nationalist organizations. They had long argued for support of the Russophile movement in Austrian Galicia and fought against Ukrainian activists, who were branded as traitors to the Russian nation within the empire. Their time had finally come.

The manifesto issued by the Russian commander in chief, Grand Duke Nikolai Nikolaevich, on the eve of the Russian invasion of Galicia in August 1914, presented the Russian advance as the liberation of a long-suffering branch of the Russian people. "Brothers!" read the manifesto. "The judgment of God is upon us! Patiently, with Christian humility, the Russian people languished for centuries beneath the foreign yoke, but neither cajolery nor persecution could break its hope for freedom. As an impetuous stream breaks rocks in order to merge with the sea, so there is no force that could stop the Russian people in its drive for unification. Let there be no more Subjugated Rus'!" The manifesto also sought to justify the Russian incursion in more traditional, historical terms: "May the domain of St. Vladimir, the land of Yaroslav Osmomysl and Princes Daniil and Roman, throwing off the yoke, raise the flag of Russia, one, great, and indivisible." Finally, it appealed to the Ukrainian subjects of the Habsburgs, urging them to rebel against their government for the sake of a bright future in the Russian Empire. "And you, long-suffering fraternal Rus', rise to greet Russian arms. Liberated Russian brethren! You will all find a place in the bosom of Mother Russia."

The slogan of the unification, or, rather, reunification, of the virtual Russian nation divided by the border with Austria gained prominence during the early days of the war, serving to justify the conflict in ethnonational terms, mobilize public support for the war within the empire, and turn "Russians" abroad against the Habsburgs. If Austrian officials had ever doubted that Russia would play the Russophile card against them in the coming war, the Russian manifesto eliminated all doubt and provided formal justification for the roundup and detention of Russophiles.

In the first weeks of the war, thousands of real and alleged Russophiles—intellectuals, priests, and village leaders—were sent to Talerhof, a detention camp in an open field near the town of Graz in Styria. Out of its 20,000 inmates, some 3,000 would die of malnutrition and disease. Many of those who ended up in Talerhof and the other Austrian detention camp of Terezin were in fact not Russophile but Ukrainophile activists. In the commotion created by the war, those who were politically engaged often took advantage of the situation to denounce their opponents to the authorities. Ukrainian activists believed that they had been denounced by the Poles. Some were, while others were accused by their own, or were overheard saying the wrong thing at the wrong time. The typical accusation was that someone had been heard claiming that living conditions would improve once the Russians came to the region. Most inhabitants of Galicia and Bukovyna would soon find out for themselves whether that was true or not. Many were disappointed.

To Russia, the first months of the war brought not only high expectations but also early disappointment. The bad news came from the northern sector of the front. After initial successes in East Prussia, one of the Russian armies there suffered a major defeat in late August 1914. Another army had to retreat as well. But in Galicia, on the Austrian front, Russian military operations met with continuing success. On September 3, Russian formations entered Lviv, which was renamed from the German Lemberg to the Russian Lvov. Later that month, Russian troops approached Peremyshl, an ancient Rus' center with a strong fortress that was doggedly defended by the Austrian army for almost half a year. In March 1915, the exhausted Austrian garrison ran out of ammunition and was forced to surrender. Galicia and Bukovyna were now completely under Russian control. Plans were made for a major new offensive through the Hungarian plain to take Budapest and Vienna, knocking Austria-Hungary out of the war. Few people doubted that Peremyshl and the rest of Galicia would now be Russian forever. Transcarpathia, or, in the imperial parlance of the time, Subcarpathian Rus'—a region of the Austro-Hungarian Empire under Hungarian rule—was to come next, completing the "gathering" of the Rus' lands initiated, according to Russian historiography, in the fifteenth century by the first Russian ruler to call himself tsar, Ivan III.

In the fall of 1914, the newly conquered region was placed under the administration of the governor general of Galicia, Count Georgii Bobrinsky, an ethnic Russian who saw Russification as his main task. Upon assuming office, he declared, "I shall establish the Russian language, law, and system here." The governor's close assistant in promoting that agenda was his nephew, Vladimir Bobrinsky, a member of the Duma and a leader of the "moderate right." Since 1907, Vladimir Bobrinsky had headed the Galician Benevolent Society, which supported the Russophile movement and publications in Galicia and Volhynia and lobbied the Russian government to do the same. He argued that by fighting for the Russian cause on the San River—a tributary of the Vistula and one of the main waterways in Austrian-ruled Ukraine—the government could successfully defend that cause on the Dnieper, as the collapse of the Russophile movement in Galicia would only strengthen Ukrainophile propaganda in Little Russia. Now Bobrinsky and his Duma allies, including Archbishop Evlogii (Georgievsky) of Kholm, who was placed in charge of the Orthodox mission in Galicia, gained a unique opportunity to put their ideas for the Russification of Galicia into practice.

Not only was the name of the city of Lemberg changed to the Russian Lvov, but the names of streets and squares in Galician and Bukovynian towns were also changed. They were now meant to popularize Aleksandr Pushkin and other Russian cultural and political figures. The Russian language was introduced into the educational system with the goal of replacing Ukrainian. Special courses were instituted for local "Russian" teachers to master the Russian language. Ukrainian newspapers were closed and the sale of books published outside the Russian Empire in the "Little Russian dialect" prohibited. Even Ukrainian-language correspondence was banned. Ukrainophile organizations were closed and dozens of their activists arrested. The head of the Greek Catholic Church, Metropolitan Andrei Sheptytsky, was detained in September 1914 and exiled to central Russia, where he spent most of the war in an Orthodox monastery.

By contrast, Russophile leaders and organizations were supported. Vladimir Bobrinsky personally traveled from one prison to another in the newly occupied territories to release Russophile activists imprisoned by the Austrian authorities. Russophiles who avoided detention by the Austrians or were released from prison by Bobrinsky actively propagandized the population in support of the "White tsar" who had finally extended his protection to the long-suffering population of "Red Rus'," the medieval name for Galicia. Russian philanthropic societies, which had been active in the region even before the war, now moved into Galicia and Bukovyna to provide assistance to the peasants in the name of the all-Russian idea.

But wartime conditions limited the Russification program of Vladimir Bobrinsky and his supporters. The military command, especially Grand Duke Nikolai Nikolaevich, whose popularity in the army did not sit well with the emperor himself, believed that Galicia and Bukovyna should be integrated into the empire right away. The government, for its part, wanted to postpone integration until the signing of the peace treaty. A compromise was reached whereby full integration was postponed until the end of the war, but the needs of the military were to take precedence until then. The authorities wanted stability behind their lines, not a radical reform that could produce discontent and resistance. Limits were therefore imposed on the Orthodox mission in the region, allowing Archbishop Evlogii to take over Greek Catholic parishes only if they lacked a Greek Catholic priest (many had fled the region or had been arrested by the Austrians) and if a clear majority (at least 75 percent) of the parishioners approved. That was a remarkable change from the first months of the occupation, when the media reported 30,000 converts to Orthodoxy from the ranks of the Uniate Church.

Among the Galicians who suffered the most from the policies of the occupying administration were the Jews. The espionage mania that engulfed the Russian army and society after the first defeats on the German front led the military to regard Jews as a major security risk and argue for declaring the Jews of Galicia and Bukovyna Russian subjects and deporting them from the area. Since the government refused to go along with appeals for the immediate incorporation of the region into the empire, the military command prohibited all movement by Jews in the zone adjoining the front, effectively putting a stop to Jewish commerce there and undermining the economic foundation of Jewish communities in the region. As the ill-supplied Russian army resorted to requisitions and even plunder to replenish its food reserves, Jews topped the list of victims. The property of those who had left before the arrival of the Russian army was confiscated, as was that of Austrians and Poles who had fled the region.

The Russian policy of playing the national card against Germany and Austria-Hungary was full of contradictions. In the case of Galicia, two sets of policies came into direct conflict—one that promised support for Polish national aspirations and another that treated Galicia as a primordially Russian land. The Poles were promised reunification of Polish ethnic territory and a state of their own, to be augmented by the Polish territories belonging to Austria. "Let the borders that cut the Polish people into pieces be wiped out. Let it reunite itself as a whole under the scepter of the Russian tsar," read the manifesto addressed by Grand Duke Nikolai Nikolaevich to the Poles on the eve of the Russian invasion of Austria and East Prussia. "Under that scepter Poland will be reborn, free in its faith, language, and self-government." As the Russian authorities in Galicia tried to show the Poles that they meant what they said, the Polish-controlled court system remained in effect in some places. The administration that had first closed all Polish schools in Galicia was forced to reopen them and allow the use of Polish as a language of instruction along with Russian.

The Galician Russophiles felt betrayed. They were not allowed to take positions in the occupation administration, which were often filled by unqualified officials from the Russian Empire. On top of that, the treasonous Poles were now allies of Russia, while the "Russian people" of Galicia were once again being treated as second-class citizens.

RUSSOPHILE CONCERNS WERE TAKEN SERIOUSLY BY THEIR ALLIES in the Russian nationalist camp and often aired in the Duma. Rightist and nationalist deputies saw the occupation of Galicia in Russian nationalist terms and opposed everything that did not correspond to their vision of that development as a reunification of the Russian land after a millennium of struggle against the hostile West, represented by Germans, Austrians, and Poles. By contrast, the Russian liberals, represented first and foremost by the Constitutional Democrats, saluted the tolerant attitude of government officials toward the Poles of Galicia and Bukovyna. They were divided on the Ukrainian question, as they had been before the war.

Petr Struve, an influential figure in the liberal Constitutional Democratic Party, believed that the clampdown on the Ukrainian movement in Galicia spelled the end of the movement in Russian-ruled Ukraine. Pavel Miliukov, the leader of the Constitutional Democrats, disagreed with his party comrade, suggesting that he educate himself on the Ukrainian movement in Galicia and read the literature of the Ukrainian cooperative movement there—such phenomena could not be eliminated by means of military occupation. He presented a resolution to the Central Committee of his party demanding "an end to the anti-state system of Russifying occupied territory, the reestablishment of closed national institutions, and strict observance of the personal and property rights of the population." But the resolution was never passed. Some scholars argue that Miliukov's intention in sponsoring it was mainly to calm Ukrainophile supporters and allies of his party: if so, it proved futile.

In any case, Ukrainian activists in the Russian Empire could do little about the Russian nationalist offensive in Galicia. They were on the defensive, doing their best to prove their loyalty to the empire, which was questioned by their enemies in the Russian nationalist camp, who portrayed the Ukrainian movement as the product of a German-Polish-Jewish conspiracy. The Russian nationalists argued that Austrian Galicia was the center of the Ukrainian movement. Long before the war, the Russian nationalists in Kyiv had warned about the possibility of Ukraine leaving Russia and joining Austria-Hungary. With the start of the war, the authorities had acted on the worry and paranoia of the Russian nationalist camp, closing down Ukrainian-language publications such as the Kyiv-based newspaper *Rada* (Council) and harassing Ukrainian organizations and activists. Branded "Mazepists" by the government, they had little opportunity to express their views to the general public.

Symbolic of the fate of the Ukrainian movement on both sides of the Russo-Austrian border at the start of the Great War was the fate of Mykhailo Hrushevsky, one of the leaders of the Ukrainians in Galicia and, in the eyes of the Russian nationalists, their main opponent. The Austrian authorities, who suspected him of pro-Russian sentiments (he never gave up his Russian citizenship), ordered him to go west, away from the front line, at the beginning of hostilities. In Vienna, where he spent some time, Hrushevsky was under police surveillance. He left Austria a few days after an order was issued for his arrest. Hrushevsky arrived in Kyiv in November 1914 only to be arrested by the Russian police on charges of pro-Austrian sympathies. The "proof" of his alleged guilt was found in his luggage, which included a Ukrainian-language brochure titled *How the Tsar Deceives the People*. But that was a mere formality—the order for Hrushevsky's arrest had been issued soon after the Russian takeover of Lviv. There the authorities found photographs of Hrushevsky together with Ukrainian activists who, according to information received by the Russian police, were working for the Austrian government and against Russia.

Police officials considered Hrushevsky to be the leader of the Galician "Mazepists" and planned his exile to Siberia. Only the intervention of the Russian liberal intelligentsia—including such diverse figures as Aleksei Shakhmatov, one of the coauthors of the Academy of Sciences' memorandum on the Ukrainian language, and Petr Struve, a liberal opponent of the Ukrainophiles—made the government change its mind. Instead of Siberia, Hrushevsky was exiled to the town of Simbirsk. The joke went that his supporters had slipped a few letters into the word "Siberia," turning it into "Simbirsk," a town on the Volga closer to Moscow but still far from Ukraine. Not only Hrushevsky but the entire Ukrainian movement was effectively silenced. The government and its "true Russian" supporters got a free hand to carry out their own nation-building agenda within the old imperial borders and beyond.

IN MARCH 1915, AS HRUSHEVSKY WAS SETTLING DOWN TO HIS Simbirsk exile, Emperor Nicholas II was planning his visit to the recently conquered Galicia. The fall of Peremyshl on March 9 gave him an opportunity to bask in military glory. It would not be his first visit to the vicinity of the front but his first wartime venture outside the old imperial frontiers—a fact that caused panic among his bodyguards. Also opposed to the idea of the tsar's visit to Galicia was the military brass, run by Grand Duke Nikolai Nikolaevich—the Russian commanders were not sure that they could hold the freshly conquered territory, and the tsar's presence in what the press hailed as part of the Russian land might force them to put politics ahead of military considerations in what they knew would be the difficult summer campaign of 1915.

But Nicholas insisted, and his bodyguards and the military went along. It was a media coup for the tsar, who was much less popular with the army than his relative, Nikolai Nikolaevich. The Russian nationalist press celebrated Nicholas's visit to the "ancient Russian land" as a victory not only for Russian arms but also for the Russian national idea. The inspection of the occupation administration and troops in Galicia included visits to Lviv, Peremyshl, and Brody. It took place in early April, during the Easter season, when the emperor traditionally demonstrated his closeness to the people by exchanging Easter eggs (and kisses) with officers and rank-and-file soldiers and sailors of units attached to the court. He would present them with porcelain Easter eggs—not of Fabergé manufacture, which were reserved for members of the imperial family, but still a major luxury by the standards of the time—in exchange for red-colored boiled eggs offered by the soldiers. Now that same tradition was being brought to the troops in Galicia, extending the sacred space of the empire westward.

On his trip, Nicholas often felt as if he were at home, within the borders of the empire. "The farther we traveled, the more beautiful the country became. The appearance of the settlements and inhabitants strongly recalled Little Russia," reads the tsar's diary of the time. After visiting Lviv, he noted: "A very beautiful city slightly reminiscent of Warsaw, a wealth of gardens and monuments, full of armies and Russian people." In the city, Nicholas was welcomed not only by the governor general of Galicia, Count Bobrinsky, but also by the principal Orthodox hierarch of the land, Archbishop Evlogii.

On the eve of the visit, Evlogii received a request from Grand Duke Nikolai Nikolaevich not to bring up "politics" in his welcoming speech to the tsar. He was nonplussed. "Can I really not say, for example, 'You enter here as the sovereign master of this land'?" he asked the chief military chaplain who delivered the request. "No," came the answer, "the war is not over yet, and no one knows whether the tsar will remain the master of that land." Evlogii refused to follow the grand duke's advice. "Your Imperial Highness," he said in addressing the tsar upon his arrival in Lviv, "you are the first to enter this ancient Russian land, the patrimony of the old Russian princes Roman and Daniil, where no Russian monarch has ever been. This subjugated, long-suffering Rus', from which sighs and groans were heard for ages, now raises a triumphant hosanna to you."

Nicholas was delighted by the speech. He was also impressed by the reception the local Russophiles gave him. During dinner at the governor general's mansion, a group of Evlogii's Orthodox parishioners broke through the security perimeter around the building and showed up on the adjacent square with icons and church banners, singing the "people's song," "God Save the Tsar." Nicholas addressed the crowd from the balcony, as he had done on the Senate Square in St. Petersburg in August 1914. He thanked the crowd for the warm reception and concluded his brief speech with words dear to the heart of Evlogii and other Russian nationalists: "Let there be one mighty, indivisible Rus'!" The tsar's sister Olga, who was in the city with the military hospital, remembered the reception offered to her brother in Lviv with great warmth. "For the last time I felt the mysterious bond that united our family with the people," she wrote later.

NICHOLAS'S EASTER 1915 VISIT TO GALICIA WAS FILMED BY A Russian crew, and the celebration of Orthodox Easter in Galicia became a subject of paintings and postcards. It was a symbolic high point in the long campaign of Russian nationalists to gather the lands of the former Kyivan Rus', construct a big Russian nation, including Russians, Ukrainians, and Belarusians, and bring together monarchy, religion, and nation in the service of the state. For anyone looking out of the governor general's palace in Lviv on April 9, 1915, there would have been little doubt that the Russian Empire had finally succeeded in making its long transition to a Russian nation-state. Instead of succumbing to the rising ethnic nationalism that threatened to divide the empire, it had risen to the challenge by expanding its borders to incorporate all the Russias.

The hopes and dreams of the Russian "unifiers" were crushed even more quickly than they had been raised by the victories over the Austro-Hungarian forces. In May 1915, barely a month after the tsar's triumphal entrance into Lviv, the Germans brought their divisions to the Austrian front and began their attack on the Russian armies in Galicia, retaking Peremyshl and forcing the imperial army out of Lviv. By the end of September the Russian armies had lost most of Galicia, a good part of Volhynia, all of Poland, western Belarus, and most of the Baltic provinces.

In August 1915, an indignant Nicholas assumed personal command of the army, helping to raise morale but also taking direct responsibility for the conduct of the war. The fighting continued to go badly, exhausting Russia's economic and human resources. In the summer of 1915, soon after the spring and summer defeats of the Russian army in Galicia, the Russian nationalists in Duma had joined forces with Miliukov's Constitutional Democrats and monarchists from the "Union of October 17" in a Progressive Bloc that demanded a government responsible to the people, meaning one composed of Duma deputies. The tsar refused to create such a government. For the rest of 1915 and all of 1916, as Russian troops exhausted themselves and the empire in a positional war with the Germans and Austrians, the court remained in conflict with the Duma.

February 1917 brought a food shortage in the capital, long bread lines, and popular protests, as well as mutiny in the army, which refused to suppress the revolt. The socialists created a soviet (council) that became the real power in the city, making the tsarist government all but irrelevant. The leaders of the Duma, who formed a government of their own, were unable to calm the masses and bring the situation under control. Eventually they decided that the only way to save the country was to engineer the resignation of the tsar. They got the support of the generals, who believed, as did many courtiers and Duma deputies, that the tsar had lost touch with reality and was a puppet in the hands of his German-born wife, Alexandra, who was in favor of signing a peace treaty with Germany without the participation of Britain and France, Russia's Entente Allies.

The generals, led by Chief of Staff Mikhail Alekseev, believed that signing a separate peace would not only violate Russia's duties as an ally but also lead to the dismemberment of the empire, as a good part of its prewar territory would remain under German control. They were also concerned about the morale of the army and potential revolts behind the lines. Now, with rebellion in the streets and a soldiers' mutiny in Petrograd, they knew that Nicholas had to go. The leaders of the Duma agreed. On March 2, 1917, the Duma sent a delegation to Nicholas II, who was outside the capital, with the thankless task of telling the tsar that he was no longer welcome on the throne. The two men entrusted with the mission were the prominent Duma deputy Vasilii Shulgin and the newly appointed minister of the army and navy in the Duma-created government, Aleksandr Guchkov.

NICHOLAS II AND HIS ENTOURAGE, WHOM THE REVOLUTIONARY events in Petrograd found at army headquarters in the Belarusian city of Mahilioŭ (Mogilev), and who were now desperately trying to get back to the capital by rail via Pskov, learned of the Duma delegation beforehand. Some believed that Vasilii Shulgin's presence in it was a good sign for the tsar and the future of the monarchy.

Shulgin was well known not only as a leading Russian nationalist ideologue but also as a devoted monarchist, and the monarchy needed all the support it could muster. A graduate of the Kyiv University law school, Shulgin had been born into the family of Vitalii Shulgin, the publisher of the newspaper *Kievlianin* (The Kyivan), a mouthpiece of the all-Russian party in Ukraine. He had been raised by the newspaper's other editor, Dmitrii Pikhno, and had assumed its editorship himself in 1913. Shulgin's first foray into politics had taken place during elections to the Second Duma in the fall of 1906. In the Duma, Shulgin had become one of the leaders of the Russian nationalists and rightists. He was also a leader of the All-Russian Nationalist Union, a mass organization created in early 1910.

In March 1917, Shulgin volunteered for the Duma mission to the tsar. He felt that by asking Nicholas to resign he would save the monarchy. His companion, Aleksandr Guchkov, shared that view. Like other members of the government, such as the new minister of foreign affairs, Pavel Miliukov, Guchkov believed that the tsar's abdication in favor of his son and heir, the twelve-year-old Tsarevich Aleksei, would calm the people and allow the Duma and the Provisional Government to retake the initiative from the Petrograd Soviet. The monarchy would survive at the price of becoming constitutional.

Late in the evening of March 2, 1917, when Shulgin and Guchkov arrived in Pskov, where Nicholas and his entourage were stationed, they asked to see General Nikolai Ruzsky, the commander of the northern front. Chief of Staff Mikhail Alekseev had already consulted with the commanders of the military fronts and obtained their go-ahead for what amounted to a coup. Ruzsky, the master of Pskov, had been ordered to use his powers of persuasion to convince the tsar to resign. He was in close contact with the Duma leadership and, like other top generals, wanted the tsar to go. He succeeded admirably. Upon their arrival at the Pskov train station, Shulgin and Guchkov did not have a chance to see Ruzsky and were immediately ushered into the tsar's train car. When Ruzsky joined the meeting, he whispered to Shulgin that the question of resignation was already resolved.

Calm and composed as always, Nicholas informed Shulgin and Guchkov that he had decided in favor of abdication, but not, as they expected, in favor of his son, Aleksei, whose serious health problems made it necessary for him to stay with his parents. Nicholas would relinquish power to his brother Mikhail. After some hesitation, the guests agreed to the tsar's proposal. Shulgin even decided that it was a better solution, as the underage Aleksei could not legally swear allegiance to the constitution— an important element of Shulgin's vision for the future of the Russian monarchy—while Mikhail, as an adult, could do so. Shulgin asked the tsar to make one amendment to the resignation manifesto, indicating that Mikhail would swear "to the whole people" to work with their representative institutions, meaning the Duma. Nicholas agreed but replaced "oath to the whole people" with "inviolable oath." He was still struggling to define relations between the monarchy and the people.

The people, for their part—or, at least, those who had revolted in Petrograd—were more than clear about their attitude toward the monarchy. As Shulgin and Guchkov found out on their return to the capital, the people wanted neither Nicholas nor the monarchy. The government formed by the Duma had little choice but to accept the people's will, as did the heir apparent, Mikhail. On the day after Nicholas's resignation, Mikhail signed a document of his own, stating that he would accept the throne only if asked to do so by the Constitutional Assembly, which was to be elected by the people in order to decide Russia's form of government. The resignation of a second Romanov in as many days had the desired effect. With the agreement of the Petrograd Soviet, the Duma government was installed as the Provisional Government of Russia and charged with organizing elections to the Constitutional Assembly. The government issued a decree declaring an end to political persecution, introducing democratic freedoms, and promising the abolition of "all estate, religious, and national restrictions," which meant the equality of all Russian subjects in the eyes of the law. The monarchy was now gone in all but name.

Shulgin, his Duma colleagues, and the generals were disappointed, but they had to accept reality. More immediately important to them was the failure of the Provisional Government to say anything in its declaration about peace with Germany, separate or general. It became clear that the government was prepared to continue fighting the war in order to restore the territorial unity of the empire. It had the full support of those in the political and military elite who put the unity and indivisibility of Russia above all other values. They would soon learn that the main threat to the unity of the empire, and, indeed, of the hoped-for big Russian nation, was posed not so much by the German and Austrian armies as by revolutionary forces within the empire itself.

THE FALL OF THE MONARCHY AND THE VACUUM OF POWER IN Petrograd, which resulted from competition between the liberals in the Provisional Government and the socialists in the Petrograd Soviet, created an opening for the leaders of the national movements, which had been in retreat since the outbreak of the war. The first to take advantage of the new revolutionary situation were the leaders of nations that had experienced some form of self-rule in the course of the nineteenth century. Thus the Finns, who had enjoyed autonomy between 1809 and 1899, immediately demanded that their constitution be restored. The Provisional Government complied on March 20, 1917, less than three weeks after Nicholas's abdication. Nine days later, the Poles were promised an independent state in military alliance with Russia. The final decision on the Polish and Finnish questions was postponed until the convocation of the Constitutional Assembly, although, in the case of Poland, this was merely pro forma. "Recognizing the independence of Poland is like granting independence to the moon," people quipped in Petrograd in those days. The country had been lost in the summer of 1915 and was now under German occupation.

When it came to the western provinces of the empire, the Polish question had never existed in a vacuum. Each of the Polish uprisings, as well as Polish political achievements in the Habsburg monarchy, had chipped away at the imagined monolith of the big Russian nation by encouraging the Ukrainians and Belarusians to raise demands of their own. In the spring of 1917, the Ukrainians and Belarusians did not ask for independence, but they were eager to demand cultural and then territorial autonomy and the federal restructuring of the Russian state, which, according to the Provisional Government, now consisted not of imperial subjects but of Russian (*rossiiskii*) citizens.

The Provisional Government was reluctant to give the two lesser branches of the imperial Russian nation what they wanted. The reason was not only that it wished to postpone all decisions on the government and structure of the state until the Constitutional Assembly, but also that it was beholden to the Constitutional Democrats, the most influential party in the government in the early spring of 1917. Some of them, such as Petr Struve, still opposed the very idea of dividing a Russian nation held together by language and culture rather than by ethnicity. Others, like Pavel Miliukov, were prepared to grant the non-Russians personal autonomy, which allowed for the development of language and culture, but not autonomous territory or government.

But that was exactly what the Ukrainian leaders, and some of the Belarusian ones, were demanding from the Petrograd government. They would make their voices heard as never before and get further than they had ever dreamed as the political, social, and economic turmoil, known in history as the Russian Revolution, gained speed in the subsequent months of 1917.

12

THE RUSSIAN REVOLUTION

THERE IS PROBABLY NO MORE IMPORTANT, THOUGH CONVO-
luted and often confusing, term for understanding Russian history
than "Russian Revolution." To begin with, there were three revolutions in
Russia between 1905 and 1917. In 1917 alone, two revolutions took place:
the February 1917 overthrow of the tsarist government and the October
1917 takeover of state power by Vladimir Lenin's Bolsheviks. As if that
were not enough, the dates of those two revolutions are usually given according to the ancient Julian calendar used in the Russian Empire, and are
thus known as the February and October revolutions. However, according to the Gregorian calendar adopted in the former imperial territories
in 1918, they took place respectively in March and November 1917. Then
there is the issue of the revolutions' chronology. Under the capacious umbrella of the "Russian Revolution," historians usually include the civil war
in Russia and the international conflicts within the former imperial borders that took place from 1917 to 1921 and claimed millions of lives of

combatants and innocent victims. Some scholars extend the term to a good part of the 1920s, or even the entire Soviet period.

The most confusing aspect of the term "Russian Revolution" is that it obscures what actually took place in the multiethnic Russian Empire—a revolution of nations, of which the Russians were only one. Thus, historians have spoken for decades about the Ukrainian and other non-Russian revolutions as part of or coinciding with the revolutionary events in Russia proper. Whatever meaning one ascribes to "Russian Revolution," it fundamentally changed not only the economic, social, and cultural life of the former subjects of the Romanovs, but also relations among the nationalities. Nowhere were those revolutionary changes more dramatic than in the triangle of imperial Russian national identity—its "Great," "Little," and "White" components. Thus, the "Russian Revolution" was indeed "Russian" in more than one way.

As the Provisional Government that came to power in March 1917 did its best to maintain the façade of one all-Russian nationality, one political party in Russia seemingly had no problem with recognizing Ukrainians and Belarusians as distinct peoples and acknowledging their autonomy or even independence. That party was Vladimir Lenin's Bolsheviks, a small branch of the Russian Social Democrats that was rapidly increasing in popularity and numbers. Like most Marxists of that day, the Bolsheviks denounced capitalism, rejected private property, and believed that the future belonged to the proletariat—the industrial working class, whose vanguard they aspired to be. But unlike their European counterparts, the Bolsheviks, who established themselves as a separate political force in 1903, believed not in an evolutionary but a revolutionary ascension of the proletariat to political power. They needed state power to establish the dictatorship of the proletariat and lead the world to socialism. They knew that a proletarian revolution was all but doomed to failure in the largely peasant Russian Empire unless they ignited the fire of world revolution in Central and Western Europe, which had a well-developed proletariat and was thus supposedly ready for the advent of socialism.

Lenin and his cohort were internationalist in composition and outlook and in their conception of the forthcoming revolution. Russian imperial nationalism was anathema to them, and they declared themselves prepared to recognize the separate identity of the Ukrainians and Belarusians. What

Lenin and the Bolsheviks thought about the nationality question in general and the Russian question in particular took on unexpected importance after the night of November 7 (October 25 by the Julian calendar), 1917, when they deposed the Provisional Government in a largely bloodless coup and declared themselves the new government of the Russian republic. The extent of that republic's borders was as yet unspecified.

For Lenin and the Bolsheviks, who insisted on the political primacy of social classes, the nationality question was of secondary importance, and for a long time they had all but ignored it. Only the rise of national movements in the Russian Empire and Austria-Hungary on the eve of World War I forced Lenin and his allies to articulate their view of the nationality question. In 1912, Lenin commissioned the Georgian Bolshevik Joseph Stalin, who read no languages other than Russian and Georgian and was largely unknown outside the Caucasus, to formulate the party's position on the matter. That position was to be defined in debate with the views of the Austrian Marxists, whose works Stalin could not read in the original. Relying on Lenin's support and advice, he fully incorporated his leader's views on the subject of nationalities into a long article published in 1913 that subsequently appeared as a separate pamphlet under the title *Marxism and the National Question*.

The ideas first presented by Lenin and then spelled out in Stalin's pamphlet were further developed in Lenin's own articles published during the first months of the war. Lenin declared the right of all nations of the Russian Empire to self-determination, up to and including secession, but there was one caveat. In the final analysis, it was up to the working class of every nation—or, more prosaically, up to the Bolshevik Party—to determine whether "self-determination" meant secession or not. If secession was in the interest of the proletariat, as understood by the party, then the nation could leave the empire; otherwise, it would have to stay in order to ensure the victory of the working class over its enemies.

The principles looked quite clear on paper, but could they be implemented in practice? The first test came immediately after the Bolsheviks took power in Petrograd. In reaction to the coup, the Kyivan politicians declared Ukrainian statehood, claiming not only the provinces of central Ukraine but also the traditionally Ukrainian-settled territories of Kharkiv, Odesa, and the Donets River Basin in eastern Ukraine that many in Petrograd considered part of Russia. More importantly, the Ukrainians refused to cooperate with the new government in Petrograd, which Lenin and the Bolsheviks considered evidence of counterrevolution.

THE UKRAINIAN ACTIVISTS HAD ORGANIZED THEMSELVES ON March 4, 1917, into a Central Council, or, in Ukrainian, a Central Rada. Its mandate was to coordinate the activities of all Ukrainian organizations, political and otherwise. In political terms, its composition resembled that of the Provisional Government in Petrograd—the Rada consisted of activists close to the Constitutional Democrats as well as increasingly more influential socialists of various stripes. Its initial demands were quite moderate and compatible with the Constitutional Democrats' program on the nationality question. The Rada wanted finally to achieve something that the Ukrainian activists had demanded for decades—to bring the Ukrainian language into the school system. But Mykhailo Hrushevsky, the newly elected leader of the Rada, who had returned to Kyiv in mid-March after years of exile in Russia, had his eyes on a higher prize—the territorial autonomy of Ukraine.

In late March 1917, Hrushevsky wrote a programmatic article titled "No Turning Back," in which he threatened the Provisional Government with the prospect of complete independence if it did not agree to grant Ukraine territorial autonomy. He wrote:

Broad autonomy for Ukraine with sovereign rights for the Ukrainian people—that is the program of the given moment from which there can be no turning back. Any obstacles, any vacillation in satisfying it on the part of the leaders of the Russian state or the ruling circles of Russian society will tip the scales in the direction of Ukrainian independentism. . . . At the present moment, those who support an independent, or, more precisely, a self-sufficient, Ukraine agree to remain on a common platform of broad national-territorial autonomy and federal guarantees of Ukraine's sovereign right. The flag of independent Ukraine remains folded. But will it be unfurled the moment all-Russian centralists might wish to tear the banner of broad Ukrainian autonomy in a federal, democratic Russian republic?

Hrushevsky's program soon became that of the Central Rada and was supported by numerous congresses of peasants' and soldiers' deputies—the true source of legitimacy and power in the months following the February Revolution. Whereas in the Russian provinces of the empire the revolution brought about peasant revolts against the local nobility, and in the Caucasus and Central Asia it took the form of an insurgency of autochthonous populations against Russian colonists, in Ukraine the peasants were mobilized by Ukrainian activists in support of territorial autonomy. Having played his role in the abdication of Nicholas II, Vasilii Shulgin returned to his native Kyiv, complaining that Ukrainian activists were stirring up the peasants by telling them that if they assumed a Ukrainian identity and supported Ukrainian autonomy, they would assure themselves of the right to obtain land of their own and prevent foreigners, especially Russian peasants, from claiming the rich Ukrainian soil. The soldiers, who had been allowed to form Ukrainian units since June 1917, also supported the Rada, seeing it as the only institution that could end the war and send them back home in time for the redistribution of the land.

Encouraged by such popular support, Hrushevsky and the Rada unilaterally declared the territorial autonomy of Ukraine in June 1917. The genie of the federal restructuring of the Russian Empire and the concomitant partitioning of the big Russian nation was out of the bottle. The Provisional Government tried to put it back by sending its ministers to Kyiv, hoping to convince the Rada to withdraw its declaration of autonomy. Faced with the Rada's refusal, which was backed by Ukraine's minorities, including Jewish and Polish socialists, the ministers negotiated a deal in which they recognized the Rada and its government, the General Secretariat, as representatives of the Provisional Government in Ukraine. Thus Ukrainian autonomy, in curtailed form, survived its first encounter with the central government in Petrograd.

The Russian nationalists were outraged by what they interpreted as a surrender of Russian national interests by the socialist ministers of the Provisional Government. Vasilii Shulgin led the charge. In early April 1917, Shulgin had published an article in *Kievlianin* arguing that if the old regime had persecuted the non-Russians, the new one would go after the Russians, turning the state into a prison for them. Shulgin was prepared to tolerate the rule of the Central Rada, which he called "the despotism of an organized band," but only if its leaders supported the war effort. The Rada, however, opted for peace. It also wanted autonomy, which in Shulgin's eyes was tantamount to treason and stabbing Russia in the back in its war against Germany and Austria. He argued that an autonomous Ukraine would become easy prey for Germany.

But Shulgin's key issue remained the unity of the big Russian nation. He regarded the Provisional Government's recognition of curtailed Ukrainian autonomy as a betrayal of the Russian nation, of which Ukraine (Little Russia) and its inhabitants were an integral part. Shulgin insisted that Russians constituted the majority in Ukraine. He defined Russianness on the basis of the written rather than the spoken language, and if one could judge by the number of readers of the Kyivan press, it was the Ukrainians, not the Russians, who were in the minority. For Shulgin, the most important question was not the future structure of the Russian state, but the "reclassification" of Little Russians as Ukrainians and Little Russia as Ukraine.

VLADIMIR LENIN NEVER SHARED SHULGIN'S CONCERNS ABOUT the unity of the Russian nation. In June 1917, he went out of his way to manifest his support for the Rada, not only recognizing the Ukrainians as a distinct nation but also endorsing their right to autonomy, or even independence. "The Socialist Revolutionaries and Mensheviks tolerated the fact that the Provisional Government of the Constitutional Democrats, that is, of the counterrevolutionary bourgeois, did not fulfill its elementary democratic duty by failing to announce that it was for the autonomy of Ukraine and its complete freedom to separate," wrote Lenin.

Lenin saw the Rada as a potential ally in his assault on the Provisional Government, and in November 1917 the Bolsheviks and the Rada did indeed cooperate to expel the government's supporters from the city. But the situation changed dramatically after the Bolshevik takeover. The Kyiv Bolsheviks tried to gain a majority in the Ukrainian Congress of Soviets convened in Kyiv in December 1917 in order to repeat the Petrograd scenario and seize power in Ukraine in the name of the Soviets, but they found themselves in the minority. The Rada was no longer an ally but an enemy. The Kyiv Bolsheviks moved to Kharkiv, an industrial center close to the border with Russia, and declared the creation of the Ukrainian Socialist Soviet Republic. It claimed the same territory as the Ukrainian People's Republic, whose formation was declared by the Rada after the Bolshevik coup.

The Rada, as the government of the Ukrainian People's Republic, refused to recognize the Bolshevik clone or to support Lenin in his struggle against anti-Bolshevik forces, which was more than Lenin and his party comrades could take. As far as they were concerned, the Rada had abused the right of the Ukrainian people to self-determination. In the "Manifesto to the Ukrainian People with an Ultimatum to the Central Rada," drafted by Lenin along with Leon Trotsky, the second most powerful party and government official, and Joseph Stalin, the commissar for nationalities, the Bolshevik leaders made a contradictory argument, simultaneously recognizing the right of the Ukrainian people to self-determination and denying it in the name of the revolution. They began by asserting their recognition of "the Ukrainian People's Republic and its right to separate completely from Russia or enter into an agreement with the Russian Republic on federative or similar mutual relations between them." They then revoked their recognition of the Ukrainian government, claiming that it had an "ambiguous policy, which makes it impossible for us to recognize the Rada as a plenipotentiary representative of the workers and exploited masses of the Ukrainian Republic."

At stake was the Central Rada's neutrality with regard to the conflict between the Bolshevik government in Petrograd and commanders of the former Russian imperial army who had remained loyal to the Provisional Government and established their base of operations in the Don region of southern Russia. Lenin wanted the Rada to stop disarming Bolshevik formations in Ukraine, block the access of the anti-Bolshevik forces to the Don region, and join his government in a war against the opponents of the Bolshevik regime in Ukraine. That was the extent of the "self-determination" permitted by Lenin, who was no longer in opposition to the Provisional Government but in power. The Rada refused. Lacking strength in Ukraine itself, Lenin sent Russian military units to Kyiv led by the former security chief of the Provisional Government and commander of the Petrograd garrison, Lieutenant Colonel Mikhail Muraviev.

In January 1918, Muraviev's troops began their advance on Kyiv. In early February, he took the Ukrainian capital after firing 15,000 artillery shells at the city. Among other targets, the gunners bombarded the house of Mykhailo Hrushevsky, setting it on fire and causing the death of the elderly mother of the head of the Ukrainian movement. Hrushevsky and the Central Rada left the city, but not before proclaiming Ukraine's complete independence from Bolshevik Russia. In formal terms, Muraviev was acting on behalf of the Soviet Ukrainian government formed in Kharkiv in December 1917. Its commissar for military affairs was Yurii Kotsiubynsky, a son of the prominent Ukrainian modernist writer Mykhailo Kotsiubynsky. But the army that theoretically reported to that scion of the Ukrainian cultural elite was shooting people on the streets of Kyiv simply for using the Ukrainian language, which Muraviev's Russian troops considered evidence of nationalist counterrevolution. In February 1918, Volodymyr Zatonsky, the minister of education of the Soviet Ukrainian government, who had earlier served as a personal secretary to Lenin, was arrested on the streets of Kyiv by Muraviev's soldiers for speaking Ukrainian. Only a paper signed by Lenin that was found in his pocket saved him from execution.

The entire population of Kyiv was subjected to weeks of arbitrary arrests and executions, the kind of "Red terror" that served as a template for subsequent Bolshevik atrocities. After entering the city, Muraviev demanded 5 million rubles to supply his army. He also ordered his troops "mercilessly to destroy all officers and cadets, *haidamakas* [members of Ukrainian military formations], monarchists, and enemies of the revolution in Kyiv." According to some estimates, close to 5,000 people suspected of allegiance either to the old regime or to the Central Rada were killed by Muraviev's thugs. Among them was Metropolitan Vladimir (Bogoiavlensky) of Kyiv. In early February 1918, Muraviev sent a report to Lenin stating that "order has been reestablished in Kyiv, and revolutionary authority in the form of the People's Secretariat, the Soviet of Workers' and Peasants' Deputies, which has arrived from Kharkiv, and the Military Revolutionary Committee is working energetically."

The new Bolshevik masters of Kyiv arrested Vasilii Shulgin, who had returned to his native city in the spring of 1917, simply on the basis of his earlier political activity. He was lucky to survive the ordeal. The plan was to send him to Moscow, but that turned out to be impossible because of the changing situation at the front, where the Germans and Austrians were beginning their advance into Ukraine. One day he was called to the head of the investigative unit and informed that he would be released on condition that he return to prison at the first summons. He promised to do so and was released. The reason for this bizarre demand was simple: the Bolsheviks were leaving the city in haste before the advance of German forces and were not sure what to do with their prisoners. Eventually they would develop the practice of executing those whom they could not evacuate, but these were the early days of the Bolshevik regime, and Shulgin not only stayed alive but was set free. Along with him, the all-Russian project would gain a new lease on life.

Shulgin considered the Bolshevik coup of October 1917 in Petrograd a national catastrophe. In an article published in *Kievlianin* upon receiving the news from the capital, he had treated the Bolshevik revolution as a pro-German coup. As far as he was concerned, the foreign enemy was no longer making inroads into the periphery of the empire but had seized its capital. Shulgin suggested that if a German government were established in Petrograd, then a Russian government would have to be set up somewhere else. Before the end of the year, Shulgin left Kyiv for the Don region of southern Russia, where General Mikhail Alekseev, the former chief of staff of the imperial army, and General Lavr Kornilov were gathering forces to fight the Bolsheviks and continue the war on the German front.

THE WHITE MOVEMENT—THE NAME UNDER WHICH THE DON EXiles became known in opposition to the Red Army of the Bolsheviks—had its origins in the military coup staged by General Lavr Kornilov in August 1917 in an attempt to dissolve the Petrograd Soviet, which was then gaining strength in its competition for political power with the ever weaker Provisional Government. The coup failed, helping the Bolsheviks take control of the soviets in Petrograd and Moscow and stage their own coup in October 1917.

Kornilov's supporters among the imperial officer corps were imprisoned by supporters of the Provisional Government in the Belarusian town of Bykhaŭ, and it was there, while incarcerated, that they began to discuss their strategy and tactics in detail. Their overall objective was to prevent the disintegration of Russia, which they considered imminent in case of a separate peace with Germany. Escaping from Bykhaŭ in the wake of the

Bolshevik coup and the chaos created by the fall of the Provisional Government, the officers made their way to the Don region, where they reached an accommodation with the Don and Kuban Cossacks, whose leaders opposed the Bolshevik coup. A new power center was thus formed to restore the unity of Russia. It was easier said than done.

If 1917 ended with the triumph of the Bolsheviks, 1918 brought in the Germans and Austrians. They occupied the western provinces of the former Russian Empire on the basis of treaties signed first with the leaders of the Central Rada and then with the Bolsheviks in February and March 1918 in the city of Brest-Litovsk. The first treaty allowed the Germans and Austrians to occupy the territory of the formally independent Ukrainian state and exact payment for their nation-building services in the form of agricultural products. As the Austro-German forces began their eastward march, the Bolsheviks, whose army was unable to resist the well-oiled German military machine, withdrew, leaving Kyiv on March 1. Two days later, the Bolsheviks signed their own treaty with Germany and Austria-Hungary. According to that treaty, they ceded control of half the Russian Empire's European possessions, from the Baltics in the north to Ukraine in the south, to the German and Austrian High Command and undertook to pay 6 billion rubles to Berlin and Vienna. The Germans marched all the way to Taganrog in southern Russia, taking control of all Ukraine and the Crimea.

Erich Ludendorff, the chief architect of the German war effort and Eastern policy, considered that support for nationalist movements and the creation of a belt of client states adjoining Germany on the territory of the former Russian Empire would secure a territorially extended German Reich and keep a future Russia, Bolshevik or not, at bay. In December 1917, Finland had declared its independence from Russia and established close ties with Germany, to be sealed ten months later by the election of a German prince to the Finnish throne. The same happened in Lithuania, where an independent state was declared in December 1917 and a German prince elected to rule it eight months later. A separate United Baltic Duchy was created on the territory of Estonia and Lithuania, again in close alliance with Germany.

In February and March 1918, Ukraine became one more nation-building project supported by the Germans. Austria-Hungary, which had its own plans vis-à-vis Ukraine, joined in and dispatched a member of the imperial family, Archduke Wilhelm, who had long been preparing to become king of a future Ukrainian state closely allied with Austria. He learned Ukrainian and commanded Ukrainian units in the Austrian army. In Ukraine, Wilhelm Habsburg became known as the red prince, gaining the friendship of local elites and protecting the Ukrainian peasantry from the excesses of the Austro-German occupation. The Germans wanted him gone, fearing a coup in the interests of Austria, but Wilhelm, known locally as Prince Vasyl, stayed on.

The German High Command initially tolerated the socialist Central Rada, but in April 1918, frustrated by the Rada's inability to supply agricultural products to the German army, the High Command engineered a coup, replacing the socialists with conservatives led by a Russian aristocrat of Ukrainian origin, General Pavlo (Pavel) Skoropadsky. Back in June 1917, Vasilii Shulgin had listed Skoropadsky among the Russians of Little Russian origin who were not Ukrainians. But Skoropadsky eagerly took the leadership of the Ukrainian state from German hands, delivering a major blow to Shulgin's definition of Russian identity by language alone.

Skoropadsky, in fact, was not unique in his political choice, representing a growing group of Russian-speaking Ukrainians who combined allegiance to Russian culture with loyalty to the Ukrainian state and nation. Upon taking power, Skoropadsky proclaimed himself hetman of the Ukrainian state and declared everyone living in Ukraine a Ukrainian citizen. This inclusive approach to Ukrainian citizenship met with a formal protest filed by Vasilii Shulgin and two of his like-minded associates.

Not all proponents of Russian unity were as stringent as Vasilii Shulgin. Skoropadsky's Ukraine became a safe haven for former imperial government officials, politicians, and officers of the imperial army—anyone trying to escape the Bolshevik regime, which had established itself in central Russia. Many members of the Constitutional Democratic Party supported the hetman's regime or even joined his government. Since Russia had been taken over by the Bolsheviks, they saw the Ukrainian state led by a former Russian aristocrat as a base from which the traditional Russia might be restored. Independent Ukraine was supposed to save Russia and then trade its independence for a form of federative relationship with Russia. "If Ukraine remains indifferent to the struggle with the Bolsheviks, it

202 - LOST KINGDOM

will never be forgiven by its neighbors. If, on the other hand, it helps Russia defeat the Bolsheviks, it can be assured of free development in alliance with Russia," read a statement issued by Constitutional Democrats in the hetman's government in October 1918.

In November 1918, faced with the imminent withdrawal of German troops from Ukraine after the end of World War I, Skoropadsky indeed opted for federation with a future anti-Bolshevik Russia. "The former vigor and strength of the all-Russian state must be restored on the basis of the federal principle," read Skoropadsky's decree surrendering Ukrainian independence. "Ukraine deserves a leading role in the federation because it was from Ukraine that law and order spread throughout the country, and it was within its borders that for the first time the citizens of the former Russia, humiliated and oppressed, found refuge." Now Russian nationalists in Ukraine, initially skeptical about Skoropadsky's aspirations, joined his army. Among them was Vasilii Shulgin's own son, Vasilko, who was killed on the outskirts of Kyiv, defending Skoropadsky's dying regime against the advancing forces of the Ukrainian People's Republic.

GERMAN NATION-BUILDING INITIATIVES IN EASTERN EUROPE were not limited to support for a Ukrainian state independent of Russia. They also had a major impact on the articulation and development of the Belarusian project, whose rise created additional cracks in the imagined monolith of the imperial Russian nation.

The imperial government lost western Belarus after the disastrous spring and summer campaign of 1915. At first the German occupation authorities were unaware of the Belarusians as a distinct nationality and of their national organizations. They discovered both a few months after the start of the occupation, as they looked for local cadres to limit the influence of the dominant Polish elites in the region. A German report on ethnic policy in the region, now called *Ober Ost*, blamed the Poles for arresting the national development of the Belarusians and living "off this disoriented group parasitically, drawing upon it for recruits for their own nationality." The author of the report suggested that "the German future in this land depends on the *Weissruthenen* [White Ruthenians] experiencing a renaissance and confronting the Poles."

There was indeed a renaissance. The German commanding officer in the region, General Erich Ludendorff, ordered the creation of Belarusian-language schools to replace the Russian ones. By the end of 1917, the school system in western Belarus had 1,700 teachers educating about 73,000 schoolchildren in Belarusian. In February 1916, with German support and financial assistance (they supplied the paper), the Belarusian-language newspaper *Homan* (Echo) was launched with a press run of 3,000 copies, astonishing for a non-Russian and non-Polish publication in that time and place. The German military command, seeing Belarus as a nation in the making, also helped organize a Belarusian theater, which was characterized in a German newspaper in a paternalistic and condescending manner as representing "the earliest stages of dramatic sensibility."

German Orientalist paternalism notwithstanding, the military command's perception was accurate. The formation of the modern Belarusian nation was retarded in western Belarus, then under German occupation, by a mass exodus of ethnic Belarusians. They left the region, often under the guidance of their Orthodox priests, who were active participants in Russian nationalist organizations. These priests portrayed the Germans as Teutonic barbarians with no other purpose than that of killing and torturing Orthodox Slavs. With almost a million and a half Orthodox Belarusians gone, the national project had difficulty extending its base: political, intellectual, and economic power in the countryside was mainly in the hands of the Polish nobility, and a good part of the urban population was Jewish. Under the circumstances, Belarusian activists were reluctant to declare the creation of a Belarusian state as their political goal. They opted instead for the idea of a joint Belarusian-Lithuanian polity.

Belarusian national mobilization on the Russian side of the World War I front line began in earnest only after the February Revolution of 1917, when it emerged from the cocoon of the all-Russian nationalist project promoted by the imperial government during the war. The Bolshevik coup in Petrograd forced the Belarusian activists and socialist opponents of the Bolshevik regime (many of them ethnic Russians) to mobilize in support of Belarusian statehood. In December 1917, they convened the First All-Belarusian Congress, which recognized Soviet rule in Russia but not in Belarus. The Great Belarusian Rada elected by the congress declared itself the only legitimate authority in the land (meaning Belarusian territory not under German control) and announced plans for the creation of a Belarusian army. That was easier said than done.

The Bolsheviks, in power in Petrograd and Moscow and enjoying strong backing from soldiers' committees in the Belarusian sector of the Russo-German front, dissolved the congress. They saw no need for a Belarusian government not controlled from Moscow. They barely saw the need for a Belarusian government at all. Instead they formed the Soviet of Commissars of the Western Region, which included not only Belarus but also the Baltic provinces of the former empire. As in Kyiv, however, the Bolshevik triumph in Minsk was short-lived. After signing the Treaty of Brest-Litovsk with the Ukrainian Rada and imposing their conditions on Bolshevik Russia, the Germans occupied central Belarus, including the city of Minsk.

Now all Ukraine and most of Belarus (with the exception of its eastern lands) was under German or Austrian control. But the Germans treated the two nationalities differently: whereas the Ukrainian Rada had signed a separate peace with the Central Powers at Brest, the Belarusian Rada was not invited to the negotiating table. Whereas Ukraine had a government recognized by Berlin and Vienna, the Belarusian lands were simply occupied by German troops with no provision for a separate state or government—the Brest treaty explicitly prohibited the recognition of any new state on the territory of the former Russian Empire. It was something of a repetition of the mid-seventeenth-century situation in which Ukraine became part of the tsar's realm on the basis of special rights and conditions negotiated by the Cossacks, while Belarus was merely occupied by Muscovite troops with no such provisions.

After the German forces took Minsk in late February 1918, two groups of Belarusian activists—one that had worked with the Germans from the outset, and another that had been formed on the Russian side of the border in the previous year—got together and decided, after heated debates, on the formation not of a Lithuanian-Belarusian but a separate Belarusian state independent of Russia. Their declaration of March 25, 1918, read as follows: "Today we, the Rada of the Belarusian National Republic, cast off our country the last chains of political servitude imposed by Russian tsarism upon our free and independent land." The decision to declare Belarusian independence was passed by a slim majority of the Belarusian

Rada—the supreme governing body of the newly formed Belarusian Democratic Republic—and its significance was more symbolic than practical. The Belarusians were no longer claiming national-cultural autonomy or federal status in a future Russian state but outright independence.

The German occupation authorities approved the Rada's declaration, but the Kaiser's government in Berlin refused to recognize either the creation of a Belarusian state or the Rada as its representative. The Rada now found itself in legal limbo. In a move reminiscent of the installation of the conservative Skoropadsky regime in Ukraine, the Germans helped to put a conservative landowner, Raman Skirmunt, at the helm of the Belarusian Rada. No significant powers were delegated to the Rada, which served as an intermediary between the occupation authorities and the local population, advising German military commanders and running self-government at the local level. Tolerated but not officially recognized by the Germans as a governing body, the Belarusian Rada was neither popularly elected nor supported by the occupation authorities, although its very existence helped promote the idea of an independent Belarus.

It was in this period that Belarus acquired its insignia of statehood: a national flag with white stripes at the top and bottom and a red one in between, and a coat of arms featuring a mounted knight with a sword and shield—a symbol dating from the times of the Grand Duchy of Lithuania. The Rada dispatched diplomatic missions to Vilnius, Kyiv, Berlin, and other European capitals, issued Belarusian postage stamps, and supported cultural and publishing projects. A leader of the Belarusian movement, Vatslaŭ Lastoŭski, presented the basics of the Belarusian national "faith" in a book titled *What Every Belarusian Needs to Know*. In fact, the book was nothing if not an attack on religion, as it sought to replace the old confessional identity of the Belarusian peasantry with a new ethnonational one.

"The first important question to answer," wrote Lastoŭski, "is who are we? When we ask our brother 'Of what faith are you?' then the parishioner of the Catholic Church answers: 'I am a Pole,' and the Orthodox parishioner answers: 'I am a Russian.'" "Is that really true?" continued Lastoŭski. His answer was negative. "All those . . . who go to the Catholic chapel are Catholics—not Polish, not French, not Italian, but Catholic. And he who goes to the [Orthodox] church does not belong to the Russian faith but to the Orthodox faith. . . . When somebody asks: what people do you belong to, what nationality do you have, you ought to answer: we are Belarusians!—since our language is Belarusian." Apart from language, other markers of Belarusian identity, according to Lastoŭski, were blood, Belarusian ancestry, and sharing the nation's land. When it came to blood, one of Lastoŭski's fellow activists, the author of the first Belarusian geography, Arkadz Smolich, considered his countrymen the purest of Slavs, since Russian blood was contaminated by the Mongols and Finns, and Ukrainian blood by the Tatars.

In the course of just one year, from March 1917 to March 1918, the Belarusian national movement, like the Ukrainian one, made a huge leap from demands for cultural autonomy to full independence. Despite differences in strength—the Ukrainian movement was much stronger and more mature—both benefited from German occupation policies. They were dismissed as mere German intrigue by the leaders of Russian nationalist circles as well as by liberal politicians, both of whom found safe haven in the Don region of southern Russia in late 1917 and early 1918. With the German withdrawal from Ukraine and Belarus at the end of World War I, the proponents of Russia, one and indivisible, in the North Caucasus were presented with their last chance to restore the unity of the Russian state. They took full advantage of the new situation.

IN JANUARY 1919, THE VOLUNTEER ARMY—THE MILITARY ARM OF the White movement, formed in the Don region by Russian generals in late 1917—began its advance on Ukraine and central Russia. It was led by General Anton Denikin, who took first military and then political control of the White movement after the deaths of Generals Lavr Kornilov and Mikhail Alekseev in the course of 1918.

Denikin, who happened to be half-Polish by birth, was a strong proponent of an indivisible Russia. He hated the Bolsheviks for various reasons, blaming them for signing the Brest-Litovsk treaty with Germany and thereby giving up some of Russia's historical territories. He also opposed his former fellow imperial officer Pavlo Skoropadsky for his alliance with Germany. To Denikin, the Ukrainian movement was a threat, whether based in Ukraine or in his own backyard, the Kuban region of southern Russia originally settled by Ukrainian Cossacks who now dreamed of unity with Ukraine. In the summer of 1918, Denikin sent his troops to the

Kuban in order to prevent a takeover by the Bolsheviks or by the Skoro-padsky regime. In the fall of 1918, Denikin dissolved the Kuban Cossack Rada and executed its pro-Ukrainian leaders, thereby solving his internal Ukrainian question.

In theory, the leaders of the White movement were not associated with any particular party and took no position on the form of government in a future Russian state. In reality, those leaders were close to former members of the Progressive Bloc in the Duma and relied on their polit-ical and intellectual support. The bloc had included not only Constitu-tional Democrats but also monarchists such as Vasilii Shulgin, who had returned to the Don region in the fall of 1918. He became a key political adviser to General Denikin. Shulgin helped not only to formulate but also to execute the White movement's policy on the Ukrainian question.

When Denikin took Kyiv in August 1919, Shulgin got an opportu-nity to apply his solution to the Ukrainian question to the rest of Ukraine. He was the principal drafter of Denikin's programmatic appeal "To the Inhabitants of Little Russia" on the eve of his entrance into Kyiv. The ap-peal proclaimed Russian as the language of state institutions and the ed-ucational system but did not outlaw the "Little Russian language." It was to be allowed only in elementary schools to help students master Russian, as well as in private secondary schools. Its use in the court system was also permitted. This approach was very much in line with the program advocated by the Constitutional Democrats before the war and, in par-ticular, with the thinking of Petr Struve, who opposed prohibition of the Ukrainian language and culture but envisioned them as serving the lower classes of society, reserving the higher cultural spheres for the Russian language alone.

The official policy on the Ukrainian question formulated by Shulgin and sanctioned by Denikin was a major blow to the Ukrainian cultural program, especially in light of its positive treatment by the Central Rada and the subsequent Skoropadsky regime. Meanwhile, the leaders of the White movement were not willing or able to deliver to the Ukrainian public even the minimal freedom to use the Ukrainian language that was guaranteed by Denikin's appeal. In Kyiv and other cities under its control, the Volunteer Army busied itself with closing Ukrainian-language news-papers, schools, and institutions. With the help of Shulgin's longtime ally

Anatolii Savenko, who was put in charge of the local government's propaganda efforts, Ukrainian-language signs were peremptorily replaced with Russian-language ones, and owners of buildings who refused the change were threatened with fines.

As Ukrainian complaints about the violation of their cultural rights reached the capitals of France and Britain, which supported Denikin's efforts against the Bolsheviks, the Western powers tried to restrain the anti-Ukrainian zeal of Volunteer Army commanders. Their overriding goal was to promote a joint Ukrainian and White struggle against the Bolsheviks. They needed a united anti-Bolshevik front, as the Volunteer Army was in retreat after having failed to take Moscow from the Bolsheviks in November 1919. It eventually found refuge from the advancing Bolsheviks in the Crimea and adjacent regions of southern Ukraine. General Petr Wrangel, who succeeded General Denikin as commander in chief in March 1920, castigated his predecessor for trying to wage war simultaneously on various fronts against Bolshevik armies and Ukrainian detachments. Under Wrangel, the best that the beleaguered Whites would offer their potential allies territorial autonomy modeled on that which had been granted to the Don Cossacks—ethnic Russians who had a strong sense of historical and social identity distinct from that of the Russian mainstream. In the fall of 1920, Wrangel's government, which by that time controlled little more than the Crimean Peninsula, would concede no more to the Ukrainians than its willingness to abide by the decision of the Ukrainian question rendered by the future Ukrainian Constitutional Assembly. That concession meant little in political and military terms.

In November 1920, Bolshevik troops entered the Crimea, forcing Wrangel and 150,000 of his troops to seek refuge in Istanbul. Those who decided to stay, close to 50,000 officers and soldiers of the Volunteer Army, were massacred by the Bolsheviks. Those who left the Crimea took with them the idea of Russia, one and indivisible. The political, ideological, and ethnonational project launched by members of the Progressive Bloc in the Duma in March 1917 was now a dead letter. It was up to the victorious Bolsheviks to solve the Russian question on the diminished but still enormous territory of the multiethnic state under their control.

V

THE UNBREAKABLE UNION

13

LENIN'S VICTORY

O N THE COLD WINTER DAY OF DECEMBER 30, 1922, MORE THAN 2,000 men and women from all over the former Russian Empire gathered in the main hall of the Bolshoi Theater in Moscow. That year, after lengthy discussion, the Bolshevik government of Vladimir Lenin had decided against shutting down the theater. The key argument was not the need to continue ballet and opera performances, branded as products of decadent bourgeois if not downright tsarist culture, but the need for large buildings to accommodate party and Soviet congresses. The congress that gathered at the Bolshoi in the last days of 1922 was by far the largest yet convened there. On its agenda was the truly historic task of creating a brand-new country, the Union of Soviet Socialist Republics.

Most of the participants were in their twenties—the generation shaped by World War I and the recent revolutionary upheavals. Almost 95 percent of them were communists—members or candidate members of the All-Russian Social Democratic Labor Party (Bolshevik). The delegates represented the four formally independent Soviet republics. Three of them—the Russian Federation and the Ukrainian and Belarusian republics—had belonged to the imperial Russian nation of prerevolutionary times. The Russian delegates, who accounted for 1,727 of the total of 2,215 delegates, constituted the overwhelming majority: the gathering, called the First All-Union Congress of Soviets, was in fact a Russian congress joined by delegations from the non-Russian republics. The delegates of the First All-Union Congress came to Moscow to rubber-stamp a decision already made by the Central Committee of the party: to declare the creation of a new federal state that claimed most of what had been the Russian Empire. They did as they were bidden, and December 30 became the birthday of the Soviet Union.

The congress elected Lenin as its honorary chairman and sent him greetings from the delegates, but Lenin himself was nowhere in sight. The fifty-two-year-old leader of the Bolsheviks, who in the previous months had fought tooth and nail for the creation of the Union, stayed put in his Kremlin apartment, a short walk from the Bolshoi. It was a walk that he was unable to make. Eight days earlier, on December 22, he had suffered a major stroke and lost control of his right hand and leg. Two days later, a commission composed of party officials, led by Joseph Stalin, had placed strict limitations on his activities, effectively isolating him. The restrictions were designed to prevent the worsening of Lenin's health. But they also served a political purpose.

Lenin had been taking an ever more aggressive stand against Stalin, general secretary of the party and people's commissar (minister) of nationalities, who delivered two main reports to the congress, one on the creation of the Union, the other on the Union treaty. The reports followed Lenin's guidelines, but Lenin still did not trust Stalin, suspecting him of being soft on what Lenin dubbed Russian "great-power chauvinism." In the months leading up to the convocation of the congress, Stalin had wanted Ukraine, Belarus, and Transcaucasia—the federation of Armenia, Azerbaijan, and Georgia—to join the Russian Federation as autonomous republics like Bashkiria and the Crimea, which had already been incorporated with that status. They were to be subordinate to the Russian government in Moscow. Stalin had had to abandon his plan because of protests from the prospective republics and pressure from Lenin, who insisted on the creation of a federal union of equal republics, including Russia.

Barred from attending the congress by his illness and distrusting Stalin to fully implement his line, the paralyzed Lenin resolved to dictate his thoughts on the nationality question in a document to be passed on to the party leadership. On December 30, the day the delegates voted to create the Soviet Union, Lenin began dictating his last work on the nationality question. Titled "On the Question of Nationalities or 'Autonomization,'" it took the form of a letter and was completed the next day, December 31. It contained an attack on Stalin's policies on the subject and criticized the rights provided to the republics by the Union treaty as inadequate to stop the rise of Great Russian nationalism. As far as Lenin was concerned, Russian imperial nationalism constituted the main threat to the future of the Union and the proletarian revolution. He wanted to establish a government structure that would divest Russia of its imperial role in form, if not in substance.

LENIN'S THINKING ON THE UNION WAS ROOTED IN HIS IDEAS ON dominant and oppressed nationalities that he first formulated in the World War I era, and they were very much in response to Russian imperial mobilization under the banners of the Union of the Russian People and other nationalist organizations. Lenin, never a strong believer in the all-Russian nation, was prepared to treat the Russians, Ukrainians, and Belarusians as distinct peoples. According to him, the Great Russians were dominant, while the Ukrainians and Belarusians, former members of the privileged big Russian nation, were among the oppressed.

Lenin's nationality policies and pronouncements before October 1917 were designed with an eye to rallying support from the non-Russian nationalities for the overthrow of the existing regime, not for running the multiethnic country of which the Bolsheviks took control in the fall of 1917. However, it was one thing to proclaim the right of non-Russians to self-determination while the Bolsheviks were in opposition, and another to keep the promise when they seized power.

Lenin's stand on the Central Rada and its policies reflected the change that had taken place in his thinking on the nationality question over the course of 1917. In the summer of that year, with the Bolsheviks in opposition, he raised his voice in support of the Central Rada against what he perceived as the great-power chauvinism of the Provisional Government. In December, with the Bolsheviks in power, Lenin dismissed the Central Rada's proclamation of its right to self-determination and separation from Russia, accusing it of relying on bourgeois policies and refusing to recognize it as a legitimate representative of the toiling masses.

It took a while for Lenin and his comrades to figure out what their nationalities policy would be. It was a difficult process for a party whose intellectual leadership was composed largely of non-Russians. Leon Trotsky, who had been born into a Jewish family in Ukraine, and Joseph Stalin, a Georgian who had begun his literary career writing in his mother tongue, were the most prominent Bolshevik leaders of non-Russian origin to embrace the internationalist Marxist project, choosing it over the nationalist alternatives offered by the local anti-imperial movements. But there were others as well, and for them to go back on their internationalist beliefs was a difficult task. Lenin, a practiced tactician, charted a new course for the party and its supporters.

Responding to developments in Ukraine in 1919, he formulated a new approach to Bolshevik nationality policy. In the summer of that year, the Bolsheviks had been driven out of Ukraine by the combined forces of General Anton Denikin and the Ukrainian armies of the Directory, a successor to the Central Rada. The Ukrainian Bolsheviks called it "the cruel lesson of 1919," blaming their military and political defeats on deficiencies in nationality policy. When the Bolsheviks returned to Ukraine at the end of 1919, they felt that they had to change their policies to keep it under control. The smoke screen of an independent Soviet Ukraine was brought back, but the "cruel lesson" suggested that something more should be done to pacify the restive Ukrainian countryside and gain its trust. The Bolsheviks had support among the Russian or Russified proletariat of the big cities, but the Ukrainian-speaking villages were traditionally hostile toward the proletarian revolution.

The Ukrainian peasantry had undergone rapid ethnic mobilization during the first years of the revolution. The Central Rada and then the Directory—the government of the Ukrainian People's Republic—managed to convert the Little Russian identity of the prerevolutionary peasantry into the Ukrainian identity of the revolutionary period. The same regions of Right-Bank Ukraine that had sent Russian nationalist deputies to the imperial Duma before the war were now sending their sons to fight in the Ukrainian army against the Bolsheviks. The Bolsheviks wanted them under their own banner. They found out that the peasants cared about Ukraine and wanted to be addressed in Ukrainian, but few Bolshevik commissars could speak the language. The Bolsheviks in Ukraine were mainly Russian or Jewish, with largely Russified Ukrainians constituting only a quarter of the party membership. As Lenin saw it, the party would have to involve Ukrainians and take a positive attitude toward their language and culture if it was to gain their support.

The party that spoke Bolshevik now had to speak Ukrainian as well. Lenin spelled out the new policy in early December 1919 in a special resolution of the Central Committee on Soviet rule in Ukraine. He reminded his comrades that the Ukrainians had been persecuted and discriminated against under the tsarist regime and called on them to make it possible for the peasantry to speak Ukrainian in all governmental institutions. There was to be no further discrimination. "Measures should be taken immediately to ensure that there is a sufficient number of Ukrainian-speaking personnel in all Soviet institutions, and that in future all personnel are able to make themselves understood in Ukrainian," wrote Lenin.

Of course, that was easier said than done, given the ethnic composition of the party. To make things worse, the same resolution prohibited staffing government institutions with representatives of the Ukrainian urban middle class—whose devotion to communism was questioned—probably in an attempt to stop Ukrainian socialists from taking control of local government agencies. But in the countryside, Lenin welcomed the inclusion of the poorest peasants—the party's traditional base of support—as well as the inclusion of owners of medium-sized plots—who accounted for most of the rural population—in the new government institutions. "Soviet institutions must have the closest possible bond with the indigenous peasant population of the country, and to that end it should be taken as a rule at the very beginning, when revolutionary committees and soviets are first introduced, that they enlist a majority of representatives of the toiling peasantry, ensuring a deciding influence for representatives of the poor peasantry," wrote Lenin.

Formal recognition of Soviet Ukraine as a separate republic, the staffing of local institutions with Ukrainian peasant cadres, and concessions on language and culture did not mean, however, that Lenin was prepared to yield on the key issue of Ukrainian independence. In his "Letter to the Workers and Peasants of Ukraine on the Occasion of the Victories over Denikin," drafted in late December 1919 and published in the main Bolshevik newspaper, *Pravda*, in January 1920, Lenin did not attempt to conceal the fact that independence for Ukraine was not his preference: he supported the "voluntary union of peoples." But for now, he was not going to quarrel over that issue with his new allies in Ukraine, the *Borot'ba* (Struggle) faction of the Ukrainian Socialist Revolutionary Party that had joined the Bolsheviks in their fight against Denikin. "Among Bolsheviks there are those who favor complete independence for Ukraine, or a more or less close federative bond, or a complete merger of Ukraine with Russia," wrote Lenin. "Divergence over those questions is impermissible. Those questions will be decided by the All-Ukrainian Congress of Soviets."

Lenin was prepared to leave the question of Ukrainian independence open so as to avoid creating conflicts within the anti-Denikin front in Ukraine. But once the situation became more stable, he used the first available opportunity to crush the pro-independence movement among his allies. In early February 1920, Lenin drafted a Central Committee resolution that ordered the allegedly independent government (Revolutionary Committee, or Revcom) of Soviet Ukraine to prepare for the liquidation of the Borotbist faction, which was now branded as a nationalist political organization. The resolution said the Borotbists were to be regarded "as a party that violates the fundamental principles of communism with its propaganda of dividing military forces and supporting banditry, that plays directly into the hands of the Whites and international imperialism." Moreover, it declared, "their struggle against the slogan of close and closer union with the RSFSR [Russian Soviet Federative Socialist Republic] is also contrary to the interests of the proletariat. All policy must be directed systematically and unwaveringly toward the forthcoming liquidation of the Borotbists in the near future."

The order for liquidation was given the following month, in March 1920, when the Borotbist faction was dissolved and 4,000 of its members, roughly a quarter of the original membership, joined the Ukrainian Bolsheviks, not as a group but as individuals completely subordinate to Moscow. Behind the façade of an independent Ukrainian republic and the federal structure of Russo-Ukrainian relations was the highly centralized Bolshevik Party, whose members took orders from Moscow. Although the republican communist parties had central committees of their own, they had little more say in matters of general party policy than regional organizations in the Russian provinces. Lenin was prepared to maintain the trappings of Ukrainian statehood and grant the locals, especially peasants, linguistic and cultural rights in order to integrate them into Bolshevik institutions. The Bolsheviks would "go native" if that was what it took to turn the actual natives into Bolsheviks, but they would not allow differences in their ranks concerning the integrity of the state. The principles Lenin formulated in his writings of late 1919 and early 1920 would become the cornerstones of Bolshevik policy on the nationality question, and they would inform both Lenin's and Stalin's thinking on the formation of the Soviet Union.

THE ROAD TO THE FORMATION OF THE SOVIET UNION BEGAN IN April 1922 in Rapallo, an Italian resort town half an hour's drive from Genoa. Rapallo was home to the Soviet delegation to an international conference in Genoa at which representatives of thirty-four countries agreed that their banks would make a partial return to the gold standard in an attempt to curb postwar inflation and promote the rebuilding of their war-torn economies. The conference began on April 10. Six days later, on the night of April 16, the telephone rang in the residence of the German delegation. On the line was a Soviet diplomat who suggested that the Germans and Soviets sign a treaty renouncing financial claims on each other and opening the way to trade and economic cooperation. The Germans spent a sleepless night discussing the proposal, and the next day they came to the Soviet headquarters in Rapallo and signed the deal. It was a major coup for the Bolshevik government, which had now been recognized for the first time as the legitimate successor to what remained of the Russian Empire. Diplomatic recognition would follow, starting with Britain and France in 1924; the United States didn't follow suit until 1933.

The Rapallo agreement was a personal success for Georgii Chicherin, the Soviet Russian commissar for foreign relations. The obstacles he had to overcome were not only international but also domestic. Chicherin signed the deal on behalf of Russia, but he also attempted to sign on behalf of other formally independent republics. This strategy backfired, causing a conflict between the Soviet Ukrainian government in Kharkiv and the Russian government in Moscow. According to their agreement on military union, the Russian authorities had no right to give orders to Ukrainian institutions without the approval of the Ukrainian government. Nevertheless, they did so constantly, not only in the spheres of defense, economy, transportation, and finance, which were prerogatives of the center, but also in other areas, including trade, agriculture, justice, and, last but not least, international affairs.

The Ukrainian communist leaders protested. A commission was formed in Moscow to investigate the complaints and, finding them warranted, it issued resolutions attacking Chicherin's commissariat. As part of a special arrangement, Ukraine and Belarus, which were formally independent states, along with Georgia, Armenia, and Azerbaijan, united in the Transcaucasian Federation, joined the Treaty of Rapallo in November 1922. The situation in which formally independent republics had control over their foreign relations but none over their own economies and financial affairs was confusing to outsiders and insiders alike. The head of the commission that looked into the Ukrainian complaints about Chicherin's actions, the Soviet military commander Mikhail Frunze, later considered that incident the starting point of the process that eventually led to the formation of the Soviet Union.

After the revolution and the Bolshevik victory in the civil war, the Ukrainian question replaced the Polish one as the most critical issue for the nationality policy of the central government. The Ukrainians, with more than 20 percent of the population of the Moscow-controlled space, were the largest ethnic group after the Russians and constituted almost half the non-Russian population of the Union, with the next-largest nationality, the Belarusians, accounting for slightly less than 3 percent of the entire Soviet population. The Ukrainians also showed a strong desire for independence, and there were pro-independence Ukrainian cadres even among members of the Moscow-led Bolshevik Party.

In the summer of 1922, however, it was not only the Ukrainians who were in revolt against the policies that treated other republics as mere extensions of the Russian Federation. The Georgian communists were also insisting on their rights as the members of an independent republic, and it was this conflict that ultimately triggered the negotiations that resulted in the formation of the USSR. The Georgians protested their inclusion in the Transcaucasian Federation, which Lenin had initiated in order to link Baku oil production with the Georgian transportation system. In August 1920, Stalin and his right-hand man in the Caucasus, Sergo Ordzhonikidze, formed a special commission to recommend a new model of relations between Russia and the republics to the Central Committee. Stalin, who was both general secretary of the party and people's commissar for nationalities, chaired the commission. As one would expect of a central government official who was dismayed by the lack of clarity in relations between the Russian and republican governments and deeply involved in the conflict between them, Stalin did his best to produce a model that would not only dispel the confusion but also strengthen the center.

Stalin's proposal for the "autonomization of the republics" was quite simple. The formally independent republics would be incorporated into the Russian Federation with rights of autonomy like those already possessed by the autonomous republics of the Crimea and Bashkiria. The government bodies of the Russian Federation would become the central institutions of Soviet rule, issuing orders directly to the republics. The republics rebelled. The charge against Stalin's model was led by the Georgians, who claimed that the whole idea of unification was premature, and the Ukrainians, who preferred the status quo. The Belarusians said they would be satisfied with whatever model was developed for relations between the Russians and the Ukrainians.

Stalin refused to budge and pushed ahead with his plan for autonomization only to be stopped by Lenin. Despite this clash, their treatment of the nationality question revealed more similarities than differences between them. Neither questioned the highly centralized structure of the Bolshevik Party, which remained the main governing institution, no matter what official policy was adopted. Both agreed that concessions had to be made to the rising nationalism of the non-Russians, allowing a merger of nationalism and communism within the ranks of the Bolshevik Party. They differed more on tactics than on strategy. Stalin insisted on the principle of autonomy for non-Russians within the Russian republic, which would give them a measure of self-rule—an option not very different from the one offered the Ukrainians, Don Cossacks, and others by the government of General Petr Wrangel. Lenin was prepared to go a step further and offer the nationalities a federal state with Russia as one of the autonomous republics, more or less along the lines advocated by Mykhailo Hrushevsky and Ukraine's Central Rada in 1917.

In the debates between communist officials in the summer of 1922 on the rights of the republics, Lenin decided to side with the Georgians and Ukrainians. As far as he was concerned, the inclusion of the republics into the Russian Federation, especially against the will of their leaders, put the Russians in the position of imperial masters, thereby undermining the idea of the voluntary union of nations. Lenin's thinking about the future of the republics was influenced by his concern about the worldwide unity of the working classes of all nationalities. The survival of Soviet rule was closely linked in his mind with the success of world revolution, which depended on the rise of the working class in Germany, France, and Britain, and then on the nationalist movements in China, India, and Western colonies in Asia. The desire of those peoples for self-rule would have to be satisfied if the revolution was to triumph on a global scale.

Instead of an enlarged Russian Federation, Lenin proposed the creation of a Union of Soviet Republics of Europe and Asia. It was supposed to be a union establishing Russia and the existing formally independent republics as equals and creating all-Union government bodies. Stalin, recognizing that an enlarged Russian Federation would create a poor image for the multinational communist state as a community of equals, proposed simply to turn the Russian government bodies into all-Union ones. As he saw it, there was no need for another level of bureaucracy. But Lenin would not back down: for him, the Union was a matter of principle, not expediency. Some way had to be found to accommodate rising non-Russian nationalism, but Stalin's model proposed a return to the ethnic inequality of the past, which had already brought down the Russian Empire and might topple the Soviet state as well.

In September 1922, alarmed by the growing conflict between Stalin and the republics, Lenin met with a number of officials, including Stalin and the leader of the Georgian communists, Polikarp Mdivani, to discuss plans for normalizing relations. He managed to convince Stalin to go along with his Union plan. In a letter to one of the Bolshevik leaders, Lev Kamenev, Lenin described his motivation: "It is important that we not give sustenance to the 'independentists,' that we do not destroy their independence but create yet another level, a federation of republics with equal rights." In early October 1922, he sent Kamenev another note: "Comrade Kamenev, I declare a struggle against Great Russian chauvinism not for life, but to the death. . . . There must be absolute insistence that the all-Union Central Executive Committee be chaired in turn by a Russian, a Ukrainian, a Georgian, and so on." Stalin, Kamenev, and others agreed to adopt Lenin's ideas as the basis for the creation of the Union, which was officially declared at the First All-Union Congress of Soviets on December 30, 1922.

ALTHOUGH THE APPROVAL OF LENIN'S VISION OF THE UNION BY the delegates to the congress was a major victory for the Soviet leader, he was in no position to celebrate. On December 30, 1922, confined to his bed, he feverishly dictated his notes on the subject of nationality, questioning whether the Union would manage to keep the republics together. The reason was simple: despite Stalin's apparent compliance with his wishes, Lenin detected in the party secretary's actions a threat not only to the basic principles of the Union but also to his own power.

Stalin was enforcing his control over the rebellious Georgian communists not only with party resolutions but also with fists. His point man in the Caucasus, Sergo Ordzhonikidze, had beaten up one of his Georgian opponents. When the Georgians complained, Stalin appointed a commission headed by his client Feliks Dzerzhinsky, the head of the secret police, which exonerated Ordzhonikidze. After a long talk with Dzerzhinsky on December 12, 1922, the highly agitated Lenin suffered a stroke that led to his partial paralysis a few days later. He was now lying in bed, trying to explain to the party leadership what was wrong with Stalin's policies and how they could be neutralized by reforming the Union that he had proposed and that had just been approved by the congress.

This was the theme of the notes on the nationality question that the half-paralyzed Lenin dictated to his secretaries on December 30 and 31. For Lenin, the main threat to the unity of his state was coming not from the local nationalists, whom he hoped to accommodate by creating a federal framework for the future Union, but from the Great Russian nationalism

that threatened to derail his plans. He referred to it as great-power chauvinism, arguing that Russified non-Russians such as Ordzhonikidze (this
was also a dig at Stalin) could be much more ardent promoters of such
chauvinism than the Russians themselves. "The Georgian who takes a careless attitude toward that aspect of the matter," dictated Lenin with reference to the national question, "who carelessly throws around accusations of
'social nationalism' (when he himself is not only a true-blue 'social nationalist' but a crude Great Russian bully), that Georgian is in fact harming
the interests of proletarian class solidarity," dictated Lenin. The fact that
Ordzhonikidze and Stalin, both Georgians, were assaulting the national
feelings and limiting the national rights of other Georgians did not seem
to matter to Lenin. For him, both represented the center and could thus be
guilty of Russian chauvinism.

Given the danger that the Russian bureaucracy, which dominated the
party and state apparatus, might use its powers to oppress the non-Russian
nationalities, Lenin regarded Russian chauvinism as the main threat to the
unity of the country. Dictating his thoughts, he argued for positive discrimination in favor of the non-Russian republics: "Internationalism on
the part of the oppressor or so-called 'great' nation (although it is great
only in its coercion, great only in the sense of being a great bully) should
consist not only in observing the formal equality of nations but also in the
kind of inequality that would redress, on the part of the oppressor nation,
the great nation, the inequality that develops in actual practice."

Lenin attacked the government apparatus, which was largely controlled
by Stalin, claiming that it was mainly inherited from the old regime and
permeated with Russian great-power chauvinism. The way to keep it in
check was to take powers from the center and transfer them to the republics. Lenin was prepared to replace the Union he proposed and the model
approved by the First All-Union Congress with a looser union, one in which
the powers of the center might be limited to defense and international relations alone. He felt that the republics' right of secession, which was guaranteed by the Union treaty, might be an insufficient counterweight to Russian
nationalism, and proposed that at the next congress the Union could be
reformed to leave the center only with the aforementioned functions. The
Union just approved by the congress gave the central government control

over the economy, finance, and communications on top of military and international affairs.

"On the Question of Nationalities or 'Autonomization'" turned out to be not only Lenin's last work on the nationality issue but also one of his last letters to members of the party leadership. The "letters" were not made public until March 1923. Stalin did his best to isolate Lenin from the rest of the leadership, coming into conflict even with Lenin's wife, Nadezhda Krupskaia, whom he accused of passing political news on to Lenin, and thereby threatening Lenin's peace of mind, and ultimately his health. Stalin insulted Krupskaia at one point by telling her, "We shall see what sort of wife of Lenin you are," apparently hinting at Lenin's past extramarital ties. When Lenin heard of it, he became furious and demanded an apology. Stalin wrote back saying he apologized but did not know what Lenin wanted of him—he had just been protecting the leader from unnecessary stress. Lenin's stress level clearly increased when he learned that Stalin was stuffing the Chamber of Nationalities of the newly created Council of the Union with his Russian supporters. Enraged, Lenin tried to enlist Leon Trotsky's support in his struggle against Stalin, but his call for help went unanswered. Lenin's note of encouragement to Georgian Bolsheviks, dictated on March 6, 1923, turned out to be his last text ever. The next day, he suffered his third stroke, which left him paralyzed.

Under pressure from Lenin and facing a revolt of the republics, Stalin abandoned his idea of autonomization and embraced the Union option, but he drew the line on the question of confederation. At the Twelfth Party Congress, convened in April 1923, he and his supporters successfully crushed the opposition mounted by the Georgians and Ukrainians. Khristian Rakovsky, the Bulgarian-born head of the Ukrainian government, speaking on behalf of the latter, made reference to Lenin's last notes on the nationality question in order to attack the party and government apparatus as agents of great-power chauvinism. He proposed to strip the central government of nine-tenths of its powers, transferring the rest to the republics.

Rakovsky said that solving the nationality question was the key to the success of the socialist revolution. "It is a question of the bond of the revolutionary Russian proletariat with the 60 million non-Russian peasants," he claimed. Stalin was not impressed. He responded that placing "the Great Russian proletariat in a position of inferiority with regard to the formerly oppressed nations is an absurdity. . . . If we lean too far in the direction of the peasant borderlands at the expense of the proletarian region, then a crack may develop in the system of proletarian dictatorship." Stalin and his supporters had won the battle. Rakovsky, the outspoken Ukrainian leader, would soon be removed from Ukraine and sent into honorary exile as Soviet ambassador in London.

The Twelfth Congress adopted a policy of support for local non-Russian cultures in the national republics—a sop for taking away the prerogatives of the republican governments and violating the principles of federalism. The party's position on the cultural front was formulated by Grigorii Zinoviev, who said: "We cannot take the viewpoint of neutrality, the viewpoint that, let us say, in Ukraine or elsewhere two cultures are in conflict, and we shall wait and see what becomes of that. That is not our viewpoint, especially now, when our party is in power. We should play an *active* role in that process, acting in such a way as to make the Azerbaijani peasant see that if a school in his native language appears in his land, then that is thanks to the communists, and thanks particularly to the Russian Communist Party."

At the Twelfth Congress, Stalin also accepted Lenin's view of Russian chauvinism as the main threat to the unity of the country, but he refused to let non-Russian nationalism off the hook. In his concluding remarks, Stalin asserted: "It is only on condition of a struggle on two fronts—against Great Russian chauvinism on the one hand, which is the fundamental danger in our work of construction, and local chauvinism on the other hand—that success can be achieved, for without that two-sided struggle there can be no union of workers and peasants of the Russians and the other nationalities. Otherwise there may be encouragement of local chauvinism, a policy of rewarding local chauvinism that we cannot permit."

Lenin did not attend the Twelfth Congress of his party. He never recovered from the stroke that he suffered in March 1923 and would die in January of the following year. The Second All-Union Congress of Soviets, which convened in Moscow on January 26, 1924, five days after Lenin's death, failed to limit the role of the Union center as he had suggested in December 1922. Instead, it approved the new constitution of the Union and listened to Stalin's oath of loyalty to Lenin and Leninism. "In departing from us, Comrade Lenin enjoined us to strengthen and expand the

Union of Republics," declared Stalin. "We swear to you, Comrade Lenin, that we shall fulfill that commandment of yours with honor!" Lenin's vision of Great Russian chauvinism as the main threat in domestic politics, countered by the affirmative action for non-Russians, would characterize Stalin's nationality policy for the rest of the decade. Stalin was loyal to some of Lenin's ideas but not to others.

Stalin adopted Lenin's model of the Union but adapted it to his needs. His policy of "autonomization" of the republics was now dressed up as a federal union. Even the First All-Union Congress, which had declared the creation of the Soviet Union, was in fact a Russian Congress of Soviets joined by representatives of the soviets of the other republics. Two-thirds of the Chamber of Nationalities in the Soviet parliament consisted of Russian deputies. The change in the façade under Stalin was nowhere more apparent than in the structure of the true backbone of Soviet rule, the Bolshevik Party. It was still called all-Russian and controlled from Moscow, and the republican parties had no more rights than regional party organizations in Russia. The Ukrainian communists had as much autonomy as their counterparts in the Crimea or Bashkiria.

Lenin did not get his way on the issue of confederation, and it remains unclear whether he really wanted that model or simply used it as an argument in his polemics with Stalin. But he won on the issue of the structure of the Union—a victory that would ultimately have even greater consequences for the Russians than for the non-Russians of the former empire. Lenin's victory created a separate republic within the Union for the Russians, endowing them with a territory, institutions, population, and identity distinct from those of the Union as a whole. In the state envisioned by Stalin, the Russians would have continued to share all those features with the empire, now renamed a Union. In Lenin's state, they had no choice but to start acquiring an identity separate from the imperial one. Almost by default, Lenin became the father of the modern Russian nation, while the Soviet Union became its cradle. Lenin's victory did much to fragment the prerevolutionary model of one big Russian nation. The result was a major shift in how Russians perceived themselves and in how others perceived them.

14

NATIONAL COMMUNISM

T HE MEETING WAS ARRANGED IN A RAILWAY STATION RESTAURANT in a Polish town on the Soviet border. A middle-aged man showed an older, gray-bearded man a box of matches that fit the description. The man with the beard was Vasilii Shulgin, the Kyiv-born Russian nationalist who had participated in the dramatic abdication of Nicholas II and then served as an adviser to General Anton Denikin of the Volunteer Army. He had spent the previous few weeks at his estate in Volhynia, which was now part of Poland, getting ready for his clandestine trip to the Soviet Union. The man with the matches was a smuggler who had promised to help Shulgin cross the border.

It was December 1925, and Shulgin was traveling to the USSR to meet with the leadership of a clandestine monarchist organization that had established contacts with Russian émigré circles in Europe. Shulgin crossed the Soviet border in the middle of the night of December 23, 1925. He visited Kyiv, Moscow, and Leningrad, managing to meet with Russian monarchist leaders. He left the Soviet Union on February 6, 1926. Upon his return, Shulgin published a book about his trip, *The Three*

Capitals, which created a sensation and a scandal in Russian émigré circles in the West. Shulgin's visit to the Soviet Union allowed him to assess not only the political climate in the country but also the results of the new nationality policy, known as *korenizatsiia* (literally, "taking root," or indigenization). Shulgin was critical of the Soviet regime but argued that the Bolsheviks were in retreat: the New Economic Policy, a set of measures reinstating elements of the market economy introduced by Lenin after the Civil War, was restoring the country to health and bringing hope of the revival of Russian greatness. Shulgin argued "that Russia has not died; it is not only alive but also brimming with juices."

Although Shulgin was unaware of it, his entire trip to Kyiv, Moscow, and Leningrad had been sponsored and arranged by the Soviet secret police, the GPU. Those who helped him cross the border and conducted negotiations with him on behalf of the bogus monarchist organization were GPU agents. The whole business was a sham created to lure General Petr Wrangel, the last leader of the White movement, to the Soviet Union and arrest him. As Wrangel did not come, the GPU decided to use Shulgin's visit to influence the debate among the anticommunist Russian émigrés in Europe about Soviet Russia, presenting the Bolshevik experiment in a most attractive light. As Shulgin's GPU handlers expected, he left the Soviet Union with the conviction that Russia was in the process of revival, and that the Bolsheviks were inadvertently promoting the rebirth of the Great Russian state. He wrote as much in his book, which was in fact "proofread" by the GPU before it went to print. If Shulgin was duped by his GPU hosts, his assessment of the strengths and weaknesses of the indigenization campaign was accurate enough.

JOSEPH STALIN, THE PEOPLE'S COMMISSAR OF NATIONALITIES AND subsequently general secretary of the party, was the main architect and promoter of the indigenization policy. Stalin's disagreements with Lenin on the structure of the Soviet Union notwithstanding, the two Bolshevik leaders regarded nationalism as an inevitable stage in the development of human society. The sooner one allowed nationalities to flourish, the more quickly they would complete that phase and leave it behind, opening the way to the internationalist society of the future.

The indigenization policy had two main components, one political and social, the other cultural and linguistic. Adopted by the Twelfth Party Congress in April 1923, when Lenin had already left the political scene, the policy was rooted in Lenin's writings on the Ukrainian question, particularly his texts of December 1919, when the Red Army had recaptured Ukraine from the armies of Denikin and the troops of the Ukrainian People's Republic led by Symon Petliura. Back then, Lenin had argued for bringing local cadres into Soviet institutions. Now the party launched an affirmative-action program to staff party and government structures with non-Russians, thereby creating local elites loyal to the regime in faraway Moscow. The cultural component called for the promotion of local languages and cultures, which began with support for education, publishing, and theatrical performances in those languages and ended with the obligatory Ukrainization, Belarusization, and so on of the party and government apparatus, first on the local level and then in the major cities and capitals as well. These measures were intended to emracinate the new Soviet regime in the non-Russian peripheries of the former Russian Empire.

Stalin's reasons for championing the indigenization program were not limited to his belief, held in common with Lenin, that nationalism was an inevitable stage of human development. From the political viewpoint, enlisting local cadres was an obvious way to overcome the hostility that the Bolsheviks had encountered among the non-Russians during the Civil War and mitigate the centralism of the Bolshevik Party structure. Under the terms of the Union treaty, formerly independent states such as Ukraine and Georgia had to give up control of key political functions, including defense and foreign affairs: by way of compensation, they were allowed to increase their indigenous membership in the republican branches of the party and promote their languages in administration, education, and other spheres of public life. Moreover, Stalin needed the support of republican cadres in his struggle for power in Moscow. As the party's leading official in charge of the non-Russian nationalities, he was perfectly placed to develop clients among the republican elites and call on their loyalty as he fought his numerous rivals in the Bolshevik Politburo, such as Leon Trotsky, Lev Kamenev, and Grigorii Zinoviev.

No non-Russian republic was as important in Stalin's political calculations as Ukraine. With Russians "owning" the all-Union communist party, which was called the Russian Communist Party (Bolshevik) until 1925, the Ukrainian communists formed the largest "autonomous" party organization in the country. Until 1923, the head of government in Ukraine had been Trotsky's ally Khristian Rakovsky, who exploited Ukrainian autonomist aspirations to challenge Stalin's position at the center of power. With Rakovsky sidelined at the Twelfth Party Congress in the spring of 1923, and dispatched to London shortly afterward, Stalin worked hard to ensure the loyalty of the Ukrainian Bolsheviks. In April 1925, he put his loyalist Lazar Kaganovich, an ethnic Jew from Ukraine, in charge of the Ukrainian party organization.

The period after the Twelfth Party Congress became known in Ukraine as one of "Ukrainization by decree," meaning that the authorities kept issuing one decree after another, demanding rapid Ukrainization of education, culture, and the government apparatus. But whereas the shift from Russian to Ukrainian in the media and book publishing was rapid, the use of Ukrainian as the working language of administration encountered major obstacles. Deadline followed deadline without the apparatus switching to Ukrainian. The resistance to Ukrainization came from the top ranks of the party, whose membership in 1924 was 45 percent Russian, 33 percent Ukrainian, and 14 percent Jewish.

The second secretary of the Ukrainian Central Committee, Dmytro Lebed, was the author of the theory of the struggle of two cultures. He regarded the Russian language and culture as attributes of the city, and thus of the working class, and the Ukrainian language and culture as attributes of the village. In the conflict of those two cultures, argued Lebed, the communists had to be on the side of the proletariat, not of the petty bourgeoisie and the peasantry. Although Lebed was forced to abandon the public propaganda of his theory before the Twelfth Party Congress adopted the indigenization policy, his views were widespread in the party leadership.

ON HIS VISIT TO KYIV IN DECEMBER 1925, VASILII SHULGIN HAD an opportunity to assess the results of "Ukrainization by decree" at first hand. Signs of the new policy were everywhere. Before the Bolshevik Revolution, the avenue leading to the railway station had been named after

Dmitrii Bibikov, the governor general of Kyiv from 1837 to 1852. It was now called Taras Shevchenko Boulevard to honor the poet who had been arrested in Kyiv during Bibikov's tenure in 1847. On the base of the monument to the Russian count Aleksei Bobrinsky, which had been installed on the boulevard to honor the founder of the sugar industry in the Kyiv region, there was now a pyramid with a sign in Ukrainian celebrating the anniversary of the October Revolution of 1917. The signs on government institutions and shops were also in Ukrainian.

No less disturbing to Shulgin was the fact that his old opponent, the leader of the Ukrainian revolution of 1917, Mykhailo Hrushevsky, was back in Kyiv after years of exile in Central Europe. While Shulgin visited Kyiv incognito, under the name Edward Schmidt, Hrushevsky was living in the open, welcomed by the Bolshevik authorities and holding a position at the Ukrainian Academy of Sciences. Shulgin visited the place in Kyiv where Hrushevsky's house had once stood. It had been burned down by Bolshevik shelling in January 1918. "But that time, too, has passed," wrote Shulgin in his travel log. "And Mr. Mykhailo? He is prospering. He's alive, the old dog. . . . What has fallen to the lot of Mykhailo himself is 'not much,' just the capital' of the republic, which burned down his home, true enough, but only 'by misunderstanding.' That is obvious from the fact that Hrushevsky has made his peace with the USSR, returned to Kyiv, and is now mumbling praise to Soviet rule in the language of black magic. Obviously, for establishing the 'Ukrainian republic.'"

But on his visit to Kyiv Shulgin also encountered strong opposition to the indigenization policy. On his train journey from Kyiv to Moscow, he became a witness and then a participant in a conversation about the merits of Ukrainization. "What do you want? My little girls should know a language that would be of some use to them. Tell me what they're going to do with that language!" remarked a Jewish woman, born in Ukraine but now living in Moscow. Shulgin was glad to hear Russian spoken in the streets of Kyiv, seeing it as a sign of the failure not only of the Ukrainian project but also of Bolshevik rule, which associated itself with it. Indeed, Kyiv continued to speak mainly Russian, notwithstanding the quite impressive efforts of the Bolshevik government to switch city names and signs from Russian to Ukrainian and to introduce Ukrainian into the educational system.

THE LACK OF PROGRESS OF LINGUISTIC UKRAINIZATION IN THE cities, especially among the ethnically Russian or highly Russified working class, was a fundamental concern of Oleksandr Shumsky, a former member of the Borotbist faction of the Ukrainian Socialist Revolutionary Party who became Ukraine's commissar of education in the early 1920s. In 1925, a few months after Stalin appointed Lazar Kaganovich to head the Ukrainian party, Shumsky appealed to Stalin to begin the Ukrainization of the working class and replace Kaganovich with Vlas Chubar, an ethnic Ukrainian who then headed the government of the republic. Shumsky was generally unhappy with the progress of the Ukrainization campaign and demanded that Kaganovich extend it from the party and government apparatus to the working class. Shumsky was appalled by the very same thing that had inspired optimism in Vasilii Shulgin: signs and many newspapers in Kyiv were in Ukrainian, but the population at large spoke Russian.

Stalin formulated his views on the progress of Ukrainization in a letter to the Ukrainian Politburo in April 1926. It was a direct response to Kaganovich's complaints about Shumsky and his criticism of the Ukrainization drive. Stalin threw his support behind Kaganovich, whom he kept as leader of the Ukrainian party, against Shumsky. According to Stalin, Shumsky was guilty of two major errors. He refused to distinguish the Ukrainization of the party and the state apparatus from that of the working class: the first had to proceed as planned, argued Stalin, but the second had to be stopped. "We must not force Russian workers en masse to give up the Russian language and culture," wrote Stalin. Shumsky's second alleged error was his refusal to recognize that, given the weakness of indigenous communist cadres in Ukraine, Ukrainization managed by the intelligentsia was likely to take on "the character of a battle for the alienation of Ukrainian culture and Ukrainian society from all-Union culture and society, the character of a battle against Russian culture and its highest achievement—against Leninism."

Stalin's letter was not an attack on Ukrainization as such, but it insisted that the party needed a certain kind of Ukrainization. The party was to proceed with the policy within the apparatus but avoid alienating the working class. No less important, Ukrainization was to be conducted in a way that would not alienate the Ukrainian public from Russia. To ensure the fulfillment of those tasks, the policy had to be implemented by trusted Bolshevik cadres headed by Stalin's right-hand man in Ukraine, Kaganovich, who was ordered to speed up cultural Ukrainization. In May 1926, the Ukrainian Central Committee approved a number of new decrees on the policy, and Kaganovich took personal responsibility for the success of the Ukrainization drive. In 1927, the rebellious Oleksandr Shumsky was replaced as commissar of education by the old Bolshevik Mykola Skrypnyk, who put all his Bolshevik zeal and conviction into the Ukrainization policy.

As envisioned by party decrees, Ukrainization proceeded on two fronts—the recruitment of local cadres and the linguistic Ukrainization of the existing apparatus. The first trend was reflected in the rise of the portion of ethnic Ukrainians in the party ranks. Between 1925 and 1927, ethnic Ukrainians became a majority in the party, their numbers growing from 37 to 52 percent of the membership. At the same time, the share of ethnic Russians dropped to 30 percent, while the percentage of Jews, the second-largest minority in Ukraine, remained essentially the same, falling from 20 to 18 percent of the membership. The linguistic Ukrainization of the apparatus was led by Kaganovich himself, who delivered his report to the Central Committee for 1927 in Ukrainian.

The percentage of Ukrainian-language newspapers grew from under 40 percent in 1925 to more than 60 percent in 1927, while Ukrainian-language book production increased from 40 to 54 percent. There was growing pressure on party and government bureaucrats to learn Ukrainian as Kaganovich began to deliver on the threat of firing officials who failed to master the language. More than 250 employees lost their jobs owing to the new party line. Cultural Ukrainization made its most impressive strides in the educational sphere, where by the end of the 1920s almost 98 percent of ethnic Ukrainian schoolchildren were being taught in Ukrainian. The Ukrainization drive also affected university teaching—the realm of science and high culture—with the share of Ukrainian-language classes increasing from 33 percent in 1927 to 58 percent in 1929.

An important sphere in which the policy made little headway was the city street. The cities remained largely if not exclusively Russian-speaking, as the proponents of Ukrainization had little influence on the working class.

234 - LOST KINGDOM

This resulted in the gradual Russification of Ukrainian peasants who left their villages to work in the cities. There was also resistance and resentment on the part of Russified Ukrainians, especially ethnic minorities, which were a significant part of the Ukrainian population. Vasilii Shulgin would probably have noticed little difference on the streets of Kyiv if he had been able to visit the city in 1928—the last year of Kaganovich's rule in Ukraine and of the party's all-out drive for Ukrainization.

THE INDIGENIZATION POLICY MEANT DIFFERENT THINGS IN DIF-ferent republics, given the uneven development of cultures in the Russian Empire and varying levels of mobilization of elites and the public at large in support of the policy. If in republics such as Ukraine and Georgia the central authorities had to adjust their policy to accommodate the grow-ing demands of proponents of the local culture and political autonomy, in other places indigenization meant the imposition of cultural policies from above. Moscow got busy creating new ethnic territorial entities, promoting the education of indigenous elites in languages whose written form had yet to be created, and developing literatures that had not yet existed. This pertained especially to ethnic groups in the far north, as well as to some na-tionalities in the North Caucasus and Central Asia. In the western border-lands of the former empire, those who benefited the most from Moscow's nation-building efforts were the Belarusians—an essential component of the imperial-era tripartite Russian nation.

The Bolsheviks proclaimed the creation of the Belarusian Communist Party and the Belarusian Soviet Republic in December 1918, after gaining control of most of Belarus in the wake of the German retreat. The republic lost more than half its territory to Poland as a result of the Treaty of Riga (1921), which was signed by representatives of the Russian Federation on behalf of the rump Soviet Belarus. Although it was now reduced to a nar-row strip of land around the city of Minsk, the Belarusian state was needed by Moscow to counteract possible efforts on the part of the Poles, especially supporters of Józef Piłsudski, the head of the new Polish state, to create Polish protectorates in Ukraine and Belarus. In order to turn the tables on the Poles, the Soviets had to recognize and enhance the existence of a distinct Belarusian nationality—a step that the Soviet leadership, Stalin in particular, was prepared to take despite the protests of its own cadres on the ground, who believed in one big Russian nation, at least when it came to Belarus.

At the Tenth Party Congress, which concluded a few days before the signing of the Riga treaty, Stalin did his best to silence party officials who had doubted the existence of the Belarusian nation by evoking the Ukrainian example and the laws of history. "I have a note saying that we communists are allegedly imposing the Belarusian nationality artificially," Stalin told the delegates. "That is untrue, for there exists a Belarusian nation that has its own language, distinct from Russian; hence Belarusian culture can be raised only in its own language. Such things were heard some five years ago about Ukraine, about the Ukrainian nation. And not long ago it was still being said that the Ukrainian republic and the Ukrainian nation had been thought up by the Germans. Yet it is clear that the Ukrainian nation exists and that the development of its culture is a communist responsibility. One cannot go against history."

The authorities defined Belarusian nationality on the basis of research by ethnographers and linguists and the maps they produced, in particular Yefim Karski's ethnographic map first published in 1917. According to that map, Belarusians on the Soviet side of the border inhabited not only the Minsk region, which was included in Soviet Belarus, but also the areas around Mahilioŭ, Vitsebsk, Homel, and Smolensk, which were parts of the Russian Federation. The Karski map helped the Soviet nation-builders define the new borders of Soviet Belarus, which in Moscow's opinion had to be extended if they were to be treated seriously by the Poles. The first two regions were transferred to the Belarusian republic in 1924, more than doubling its population from 1.5 million to 3.5 million. The Homel region was added in 1926. Smolensk, however, which had been part of the Muscovite tsardom since 1654, stayed in Russia.

In many cases, the transfers were accomplished not only without consulting the local population but even against its wishes. But some inhabitants who spoke Belarusian nevertheless associated themselves with Russia and Russianness in the tradition of the anti-Polish nation-building project of imperial times. Avel Yenukidze, a close ally and relative of Stalin, stated with regard to the transfers: "This is a blow to the local population, and I understand the fear of the Belarusians. Their children understand Russian better than Belarusian and, from the cultural viewpoint, we are sacrificing the interests of the people. . . . But in this case we are guided by the political consideration that we must expand Belarus and draw the attention of foreign countries to her."

When it came to Moscow's foreign-policy considerations, the Soviet Belarusian project was never purely defensive. It also had a strong offensive component with regard to Belarusian lands that had gone to Poland under the Riga treaty. As in the case of Soviet Ukraine, the Bolsheviks wanted to present Soviet Belarus as a beacon of national revival to attract fellow Belarusians on the Polish side of the border. The Belarusization policy was first placed on the party agenda in early 1921, a few months before the signing of the Riga treaty. In January of that year, a group of thirty-two Belarusian communists issued a declaration calling for the unification of the Belarusian lands into one socialist state and demanding the comprehensive Belarusization of the republic's educational and cultural life. At that point, Belarusian, Russian, Polish, and Yiddish were declared official languages of the republic. Belarusian was accorded primacy as the language of the republic's largest nationality, which legitimized the creation and existence of the Soviet Belarusian state.

The Twelfth Party Congress of April 1923 strengthened efforts to promote cultural Belarusization by declaring indigenization as official party policy. A key figure in the Belarusization drive was Usevalad Ihnatoŭski, a former member of the Belarusian Socialist Revolutionary Party, who joined the Bolsheviks in 1919 and became people's commissar of education of Soviet Belarus in 1920. Between 1924 and 1926, he was in charge of the propaganda department of the Belarusian Central Committee, and after 1928 he served as president of the Belarusian Academy of Sciences. Ihnatoŭski's pre-Bolshevik career was not much different from that of his Ukrainian counterpart, Oleksandr Shumsky, who also belonged to the left wing of the Socialist Revolutionary Party and was a leading national communist.

Belarusization, promoted by Ihnatoŭski and his allies among the Belarusian national communists, was similar to Ukrainization in the neighboring republic. Both policies were more successful in bringing local cadres into the institutions of the new regime than in the cultural "conversion" of the Russian-speaking urban population. Between 1922 and 1927, the number of ethnic Belarusians in the Belarusian Communist Party more than tripled. Significant progress was also achieved in the switch to Belarusian and other local languages for purposes of official propaganda, with the main newspaper of the Belarusian Bolsheviks beginning Belarusian-language publication in 1927. Even so, the Belarusian language and culture did not achieve dominance in the print media: of the nine newspapers published in the republic at the time, four were issued in Russian, three in Belarusian, and one each in Polish and Yiddish.

The promoters of indigenization and linguistic Belarusization faced major problems achieving their goals, not only for the working class and the party and government apparatus but also in the educational system. The problem stemmed from the underrepresentation of Belarusians in general—and Belarusian speakers in particular—in the cities. In 1922, Jews constituted 60 percent of the student body in the Belarusian universities, with Belarusians accounting for only 31 percent. Party officials decided to improve the language statistics by expelling students who failed to learn Belarusian and increasing the number of ethnic Belarusians in the student body to roughly 60 percent. This positive discrimination in favor of Belarusians meant negative discrimination against Jews, who constituted between 40 and 60 percent of the Belarusian urban population and had been correspondingly represented in the university system. Forced linguistic Belarusization, coupled with aggressive affirmative action in favor of Belarusian students, many of them with peasant roots, was often viewed negatively by the urban population, a good part of which was highly skeptical of the Belarusization project from the outset.

In the 1920s, as in the revolutionary era, the nationality policy of the central government in the western borderlands of the former empire was defined largely in response to the threat posed by the Polish question. But there was also a major difference: if before 1917 the local population had been mobilized against that threat under the banner of Russian nationalism, the mobilizing force was now that of Ukrainian and Belarusian nationalism. The strategy of the central authorities would further evolve in the late 1920s and early 1930s as local nationalism was pushed aside and partly replaced by a variant of traditional Great Russian nationalism.

IN DECEMBER 1925, IN ONE OF HIS CONVERSATIONS WITH SOVIET opponents of indigenization, Vasilii Shulgin came up with a politically correct and effective way of resisting the policy. "I said that division into small nationalities lay [as an obstacle] on the path to internationalism," recalled Shulgin later. "That the greater the number of people and the greater the territory covered by one language, the easier the transition to internationalism. That although the party had temporarily agreed to the creation of individual republics, each one to speak its own language, that was by no means an ideal situation; hence every true communist should try to restore the dominance of the Russian language in everyday life as the principal language on the whole territory of the USSR."

That argument was shared to a greater or lesser degree by many party officials who opposed indigenization. The nationality issue became a hot potato in inter-party struggles, with Grigorii Zinoviev, a leader of the so-called Left Opposition, attacking Stalin and others for pushing Ukrainization too far. Stalin allowed Ukrainization to proceed apace. There was no change of policy in 1925, or in 1926; nor was there an official reevaluation of the threat posed by great-power chauvinism as compared with local nationalism—the former continued to be regarded as the main threat. But a few years later, the policy began to change, coming to be more in line with Zinoviev's critique of indigenization than with Stalin's defense of it. Ironically, the change began as soon as Stalin got rid of Zinoviev as a political rival. In the fall of 1927, Zinoviev was expelled from the party along with Leon Trotsky, Lev Kamenev, and their supporters on accusations of antiparty activity. In 1928, Kaganovich was recalled from Ukraine. As far as Stalin was concerned, his Ukrainization effort there had already run its course.

Stalin's victory over his opponents in the Politburo meant that in future he would need less support from the national republics and would not have to appease their leaders with new concessions on the nationality question. The GPU was ordered to prepare the first major trial of members of the prerevolutionary intelligentsia, so-called members of the "Change of the Landmarks" movement. These were old, often nationally minded cadres who had used the indigenization drive to engage in cultural and academic activities. Stalin and his new appointees in the republics did their best to create the impression that in the realm of nationality policy they were not following in the footsteps of a recently defeated opposition, but in practice they were putting a brake on indigenization and opening a new front of struggle against local nationalism.

The shift in the power balance within the party leadership due to Stalin's victory over the opposition was only one of the reasons for the change in nationality policy. Another one lay outside the Soviet borders. Whereas Lenin had formulated his policies on the nationality question with an eye to world revolution and the possibility of future European and Asian membership in an international Soviet Union, Stalin had no such illusions by the late 1920s. The conventional wisdom of the day, fully embraced by Stalin, was that the Soviet Union, surrounded by hostile bourgeois powers, could rely only on itself to guarantee its survival.

In 1926, two conservative coups took place on the western borders of the Soviet Union. The first brought an old enemy of the Bolsheviks, Józef Piłsudski, to power in Poland, while the second installed the authoritarian government of Antanas Smetona in Lithuania. Stalin and other party leaders began to talk about the end of peaceful coexistence with the West, causing a war scare that led people to hoard food and consumer goods. Stalin asserted in April 1927 that the major threat to the Soviet regime was the prospect of a new imperialist war. In the following month, the British intelligence services raided ARCOS, a Soviet-run company in London engaged in trade between the two countries. The raid proved what the British had known all along—that the Soviets were spying on them, using the trading company as a cover. The British government broke off its diplomatic relations with the Soviet Union, which had been established less than three years earlier.

War was in the air, but the Red Army commanders reported that the country was not ready for it. The secret police found peasants in the strategic borderlands increasingly dissatisfied with the regime and waiting for the arrival of the Whites, Poles, or Ukrainian nationalists. Given such attitudes among the population, there were fears that the tenth anniversary of the Soviet state, marked in the fall of 1927, might turn out to be its last. The war scare passed, but not without a major impact on Soviet policy. Many scholars associate the war scare of 1926–1927 with the origins of Stalin's authoritarian and eventually dictatorial rule, the beginnings of industrialization and collectivization to modernize the Soviet economy, and changes in relations between the center and the republics. The latter kept their own Communist Party structures and nascent parliaments, called Supreme Soviets, and supported local cultures, but key political, economic, and cultural decisions would now come increasingly from Moscow and Moscow alone. Those decisions would encroach on the autonomy of local elites, which would eventually be integrated into a huge administrative pyramid centered on and ruled from the all-Union center.

Around the same time, the government in Moscow became more cautious with regard to policies that might alienate the Russian majority. It also began to see the cultural and political mobilization of the non-Russian nationalities not as an instrument for destabilizing adjoining states and bringing the world revolution to Central and Western Europe, but as bridgeheads for foreign aggression against the Soviet Union. That threat, real or imagined, became a major factor in the party's rethinking of nationality policy in the Polish borderlands. Support for non-Russian nationalism was curtailed to prevent the West in general, and the Polish leadership in particular, from turning it against the center.

Nowhere was the link between the changed international situation and nationality policy more apparent than in Soviet Belarus, a polity created more in response to international pressures than in response to domestic demands. The war scare culminated in June 1927 with an event directly related to Belarus—the assassination of the Soviet ambassador to Warsaw, Petr Voikov. The assassin was a nineteen-year-old student, Barys Kaverda, who belonged to a pro-Polish Belarusian organization. Ukrainian and Belarusian nationalism in neighboring Poland suddenly appeared to change from an opportunity to a threat to the Soviet Union. Many party officials began to suspect that England was turning border states against the USSR, and that those states, in turn, were exploiting anticommunist Russian, Ukrainian, Belarusian, and Polish organizations to undermine the Soviet state.

In 1928, Moscow sent a member of the Ukrainian leadership, Volodymyr Zatonsky, to inspect the implementation of nationality policy in Belarus. Zatonsky, a "company man" who readily adjusted his views to changing party policy, produced a devastating report. It claimed that leaders of the Belarusian cultural revival in the party ranks were orienting themselves toward the parochial world of the village and allying themselves too closely with non-communist intellectuals, many of them recent émigrés from Poland. Zatonsky's critique of Belarusian nationality policy led to a purge of the Belarusian party apparatus, government, and Academy of Sciences to root out Belarusian nationalism. By the end of 1929, such charges had been used to dismiss the commissar of education, Anton Balitski, and the head of the party press department, Aliaksandr Adamovich. Altogether, close to 10 percent of the party membership was expelled. Many of those individuals would be arrested and given long sentences in a purge that began in December 1930. Among its victims was one of the leading architects of Belarusization, the former party official and then president of the Belarusian Academy of Sciences, Usevalad Ihnatoŭski. Dismissed in 1930, he committed suicide in 1931, foreshadowing the fate of a number of leaders of the Ukrainian indigenization drive, who found themselves under similar attack a few years later.

Ukrainization, which Zatonsky regarded as the model for his critique of practices in Belarus, fared little better in the eyes of Moscow. In the autumn of 1929, as leading figures of the indigenization policy were removed from their positions in Belarus, the GPU attacked prominent Ukrainian academicians and educators with prerevolutionary backgrounds in a highly publicized show trial of alleged nationalists. A total of 474 individuals were accused of belonging to the bogus Union for the Liberation of Ukraine, whose members had allegedly conspired with Piłsudski and leaders of the Ukrainian emigration in the West to start an uprising in Ukraine and separate it from the Soviet Union. Forty-five of the accused, among them the vice president of the Ukrainian Academy of Sciences, Serhii Yefremov, were found guilty and sentenced to forced-labor camps for terms ranging from two to ten years. Mykhailo Hrushevsky, the leader of the Ukrainian revolution, was arrested and exiled in 1931. He would die under suspicious circumstances in Russia in 1934.

In December 1932, in the midst of policy discussions that would lead to the Great Ukrainian Famine a few weeks later and take the lives of close to 4 million victims, Stalin attacked Mykola Skrypnyk, the old Bolshevik who had replaced Oleksandr Shumsky in 1927 as commissar of education, for non-Bolshevik conduct of Ukrainization. Stalin explained peasant resistance to the forced collectivization of agriculture, which the Bolsheviks launched in 1929, and their grain requisitions of 1932 by blaming it on agents of Józef Piłsudski and Ukrainian nationalists in Poland and Ukraine. In the months and years to come, Stalin and his propagandists would claim that Ukrainization had been hijacked by foreign agents and nationalists, who had exploited it against the party, alienating the Ukrainian peasantry from Moscow and endangering the communist project in the countryside instead of helping to implement it.

The Politburo ordered a stop to Ukrainization outside Soviet Ukraine, mainly in the Kuban and Far Eastern regions of the Russian Federation, which had significant Ukrainian populations. That decision led to the closing of newspapers, schools, and teacher-training institutions, and eventually to the Russification of hundreds of thousands of ethnic Ukrainians. In Soviet Ukraine, Stalin installed new leaders of the party and the secret police. He also ended the Ukrainization not only of the proletariat but also of large groups of bureaucrats and engineers working for the ever-increasing number of institutes and enterprises belonging to all-Union ministries. The Ukrainian Famine took place in the midst of a full-scale onslaught by Stalin against the Ukrainian political elite and the Ukrainian language and culture—a well-established link that prompts many in Ukraine today to speak of the Great Famine as a genocide aimed not only at the peasantry but also at the Ukrainian nation as a whole.

The termination of the Ukrainization policy and the purge of the party officials and intellectuals who had led it produced a wave of arrests as well as suicides of major figures on the Ukrainian political and cultural scene. Fearing arrest, Mykola Skrypnyk committed suicide in July 1933. Two months earlier, the writer and poet Mykola Khvyliovy had shot himself. As early as 1926, Stalin had attacked him for calling on Ukrainian writers to turn away from Moscow and orient themselves toward Western Europe. Oleksandr Shumsky, whom Stalin accused of protecting Khvyliovy, was arrested in 1933. He would be murdered on Stalin's orders in 1946 by a group of killers from the secret police who entered his train carriage in the middle of the night and administered poison that made the killing look as if it had been caused by a heart attack.

IN UKRAINE AND BELARUS ALIKE, THE REVERSAL OF INDIGENIZA-tion suspended the development of non-Russian languages and cultures at a moment when increasing numbers of peasants, driven out of the villages by the collectivization campaign, were beginning to migrate to the cities. The cities, in which the Russian language and culture were dominant, turned millions of Ukrainian- and Belarusian-speaking peasants into Russian-speaking workers and intellectuals, even though the cities themselves became predominantly Ukrainian and Belarusian in ethnic composition. In the 1930s, the Russification of the Ukrainian and Belarusian peasantry proceeded at a rate that imperial proponents of a big Russian nation could only have dreamed of.

There was, however, a catch. Linguistic and cultural Russification did not obliterate non-Russian nationality, and millions of new Ukrainian and Belarusian urbanites would be officially classified and treated as such, not as Russians. Their languages and cultures would continue to exist, although clearly subordinate in status. Local non-Russian cadres were still recruited to the party and promoted to positions of responsibility in party and government structures. Affirmative action with regard to local cadres continued into the 1930s. Such policies encouraged ethnic Russians with little or no knowledge of Ukrainian or Belarusian to list their nationality as that of the titular group in their republic of residence. Among those who did so was a young party apparatchik named Leonid Brezhnev. Born to Russian parents in the Ukrainian town of Kamenske, he gave his nationality as Ukrainian. By the time he became head of the Communist Party and the most influential Soviet leader in 1964, his official documents identified him as a Russian. The conflicting legacies of indigenization would reverberate for decades to come.

15

THE RETURN OF RUSSIA

ON JANUARY 30, 1936, THE LEADING SOVIET NEWSPAPER, *Pravda*, published a front-page photo of Joseph Stalin that became one of his most popular images. The smiling dictator was shown embracing a cheerful young girl who had just presented him with a large bouquet of flowers. The photo would be widely reproduced, appearing in numerous Soviet newspapers and journals as well as on posters. A five-meter statue of Stalin with the girl would be installed in a Moscow subway station with the inscription, "Thank you, Comrade Stalin, for our happy childhood." Besides presenting Stalin as the indulgent head of a happy Soviet family, the photo promoted his image as the father of the Soviet peoples.

The girl in the photo was a Buriat, a member of the largest indigenous Siberian nationality. On January 27, 1936, three days before the photograph was published, Stalin, his chief lieutenant and head of the Soviet cabinet, Viacheslav Molotov, and other Soviet leaders had welcomed a delegation from the Buriat-Mongol Autonomous Republic of the Russian Federation in the Kremlin. It was a solemn reception, accompanied by the presentation of gifts to the workers and peasants of the region. Suddenly, in the middle of the proceedings, the six-year-old Gelia Markizova, the daughter of the republic's commissar of agriculture, bored with the speeches of the collective farmers, grabbed two buckets bought in advance by her mother and began walking to the head table. Asked where she was going, she answered, "To Stalin." With the meeting interrupted, Stalin sat Gelia on the table. She put her arm around his neck, and the moment was captured by a Soviet photographer.

The Buriat-Mongolian delegation had been deliberately chosen for the special reception. Although the autonomous republic, which was located near Lake Baikal, had a population of less than half a million people—in a country of over 150 million—it had major strategic importance for the rulers in Moscow. The republic was located on the border with Mongolia and Manchukuo, the puppet Manchurian state controlled by Japan. Soviet-Japanese relations had been marked by numerous border incidents. They had reached a new low in November 1935, as Nazi Germany and Japan signed the Anti-Comintern Pact, a treaty directed against the Soviet Union that derived its name from the Communist International, the Moscow-directed organization of the world communist movement. Bringing the Buriat leadership to Moscow was the Kremlin's way of demonstrating its commitment to the region and ensuring the population's loyalty to the Stalin regime.

The article on the front page of *Pravda* accompanying the photograph was titled "One Family of Peoples." It celebrated the national liberation of the Buriat-Mongols as a consequence of the October Revolution, as well as the economic development of the region allegedly brought by collectivization, and emphasized the Russian role in bringing those benefits to the region. "With the active assistance of the Russian proletariat, Buriat-Mongolia has taken the road of progress and gained every possibility for the further development and growth of its national culture," stated the unsigned article. Approximately half the population of Buriat-Mongolia consisted of ethnic Russians or Eastern Slavs. One-third was made up of Buriats, part of the Mongol ethnic community, who were settled on all sides of the Mongol-Soviet-Manchukuo border. To strengthen the security of the region, the loyalty of both the Russians and the Buriats in the autonomous republic had to be ensured, and the *Pravda* article on the Russo-Buriat alliance sought to assist in achieving that end.

Besides endorsing Russian ties with a key republic, the article praised the Russians as the leading Soviet nation and lashed out against those who called that role into question. "The nation that has given the world such geniuses as Lomonosov, Lobachevsky, Popov, Pushkin, Chernyshevsky, Mendeleev, and such giants of humanity as Lenin and Stalin—a nation that prepared and carried out the October Socialist Revolution under the leadership of the Bolshevik Party—such a nation can be called a 'nation of Oblomovs' only by someone who takes no account of what he is talking about." The reference was to a tradition that had begun with Vladimir Lenin himself, who had referred to negative features of Russian history and national character by associating them with Oblomov, a character in a nineteenth-century novel who became a symbol of laziness and indecisiveness.

Although the *Pravda* attack was not directed against Lenin, it signaled a major shift in the Bolshevik treatment of Russia and Russianness. For the first time in such an authoritative publication, the Russians, especially the prerevolutionary Russians, were presented not as an imperial nation of exploiters but as a nation of major literary and cultural figures. In addition to bringing about the October Revolution, they had given the world such figures as Lenin and Stalin, and the latter, an ethnic Georgian, was now presented as a Russian as well. The Russians stood above the other nations of the Soviet Union, guiding them along the road to the bright communist future. Anyone who dissented from that proposition was now dismissed as a "lover of verbal flourishes poorly versed in Leninism."

THE *PRAVDA* ARTICLE'S PRAISE FOR THE RUSSIANS AS THE LEGITimate leaders of the peoples of the Soviet Union and its defense of the Russian national character had been provoked by growing tensions with Japan and Germany as well as by an intensification in Stalin's struggle with his opponents in the party leadership. But the Soviet leader's reevaluation of the role of the Russian nation in imperial history and in post-1917 socialist construction had been long in the making.

The attack on national cadres in Ukraine, Belarus, and other non-Russian republics that began with the trial of alleged members of the Union for the Liberation of Ukraine in 1930 put an end to the earlier policy presenting Russian great-power chauvinism as the main threat to the regime. The similar "Academy Case" of 1930 in Russia, which featured as its main targets academician Sergei Platonov and Russian historians of the old school who were accused of monarchism and Russian nationalism, involved close to one hundred suspects, as compared to more than four hundred in the case in Ukraine. The Russian defendants were sentenced in camera—that is, in private—while the Ukrainians were put through a highly publicized trial open to the general public. The Soviet propaganda machine was sending a message to society, and that message was loud and clear: non-Russian nationalism constituted the main danger to the regime.

In 1930, Stalin and his group in the Politburo also began taking steps to stop the practice, previously encouraged by the regime, of presenting prerevolutionary Russia in exclusively negative terms. In December of that year, the Stalin-led party secretariat had issued a resolution on the writings of leading Soviet satirist Demian Bedny, who had blamed the Russian peasantry's resistance to collectivization on traditional Russian laziness and backwardness. "False notes expressed in sweeping defamation of 'Russia' and 'things Russian'" were now detected in Bedny's pamphlets. They were deemed to be an attack not on the uncollectivized peasantry but on Russian workers, "the most active and most revolutionary detachment of the global working class." The resolution read: "The attempt to apply the epithets 'lazybones' and 'habitual stove-sitter' cannot fail to be redolent of crude falsehood." In a personal letter to Bedny, Stalin accused him of "libel against our people, discrediting the USSR, discrediting the proletariat of the USSR, discrediting the Russian proletariat."

The change of party policy to present non-Russian nationalism as the principal danger to the USSR was sealed in January 1934 with Stalin's speech to the Seventeenth Party Congress, in which he asserted that "the main danger is represented by the deviation against which people ceased to struggle and that was therefore allowed to develop into a danger to the state." He illustrated his point with a telling example: "In Ukraine, even quite recently, the deviation toward Ukrainian nationalism did not represent the main danger, but when people ceased to struggle against it and allowed it to develop to such an extent that it closed ranks with the interventionists, that deviation became the main danger." There were no concomitant references to Russian chauvinism. The decisions made by Stalin and the party in the months following the congress showed that the party was prepared to rehabilitate some elements of prerevolutionary Russian nationalism.

In July 1934, the Central Committee decided to begin preparing for state celebrations of the centennial of the death of Alexander Pushkin, a poet all but ignored by officialdom during the previous decade. The Bolshevik regime, which had come to power in opposition to the empire of the tsars and built its reputation by attacking the imperial Russian past, now began to regard itself as a continuator of the cultural and state-building traditions of the tsars. In June 1934, history classes, which had been abolished in the 1920s, were reinstated in Soviet schools by special resolution of the Central Committee. A few months earlier, at a special meeting of the Politburo to discuss history textbooks, Stalin had decided on a new course to be called "The History of the USSR," putting special emphasis on Russia's historical mission: "In the past, the Russian people gathered other peoples. It has begun a similar gathering now." Prerevolutionary Russian history was back in favor, as was the concept of the motherland, which was crucial to the formation of Russian nationalism.

The article in *Pravda* that accompanied the publication of the decision to reintroduce history courses was titled "For the Motherland." It declared love for the motherland as one of the main virtues of the Soviet citizen. That rehabilitated notion was paired with another key Stalinist concept, treason. "Whoever raises his hand against the motherland, whoever betrays it must be annihilated," thundered the party's standard-bearing newspaper. This judgment ran counter to the ideas of Karl Marx and Friedrich Engels, the theoreticians of the communist movement, who declared in their founding document, *The Communist Manifesto* (1848): "The working men have no country." The *Pravda* article explained this departure from Marxist dogma by the fact that the founders of Marxism had written before the victory of the Russian Revolution, which changed the situation dramatically and endowed the working class with a fatherland. That line of argument had been introduced by Stalin in 1931, when he stated publicly: "In the past, we did not and could not have a fatherland. But now that we have overthrown capitalism, and power belongs to us, to the people, we have a fatherland and will defend its independence."

Stalin also criticized Engels's ideas directly. In his article "The Foreign Policy of Russian Tsardom" (1890), Engels had characterized the Russian Empire as "the mainstay of European reaction, its last fortified position and its great reserve army at once." Stalin found many of Engels's observations questionable. "That tsarist rule in Russia was a mighty fortress of all-European (as well as Asian) reaction cannot be doubted. But it may be doubted whether it was the last fortress of that reaction," wrote Stalin to the members of the Politburo. Stalin noted what he saw as the "shortcomings" of Engels's article and called it "one-sided"—an unheard-of criticism of a founding father of Marxism in the Soviet Union. He argued against the publication of the Russian translation of the article in *Bol'shevik*, the party's leading theoretical journal, since it might be viewed as reflecting the official line. Stalin's argument won the day, and the article was not published.

STALIN'S REVISIONIST MEASURES INDICATED THE EVOLUTION OF his thinking on nations and nationalism in the wake of Hitler's rise to power in Germany, a country all-important to the Bolsheviks. Through most of 1933, despite Hitler's vitriolic anticommunist rhetoric, Stalin had tried in vain to preserve the close economic and even political ties with Germany that had been established during the previous decade. Hitler was not interested in cooperating with Stalin, as the Soviet leader understood by the end of 1933. But aside from being a foreign threat, the Nazis were an ideological challenge and an example to emulate. Hitler's rabid nationalism, which helped him unite Germany around his leadership, made an impression on the communist leadership of the Soviet Union. What followed was a set of changes in Soviet policies at home and abroad.

Hitler was exalting, consolidating, and mobilizing the German nation. What nation could Stalin mobilize—Russian, Soviet, proletarian? If the answer was "all of the above," then how should its components be related? For some time, there were no clear answers to those questions, and as the months and years passed a difference of opinion emerged between Stalin and his old ally and then nemesis Nikolai Bukharin. Expelled from the party leadership in 1929, Bukharin was allowed to return to the public arena in early 1934 with his appointment as editor in chief of the second most influential Soviet newspaper, *Izvestiia* (News). An internationalist by conviction and an opponent of all nationalism, including Russian, Bukharin toed the party line when in July 1934, in connection with the reintroduction of history into the school curriculum, he praised the notion of the Soviet motherland and Soviet patriotism. Nevertheless, he defined the latter in international terms as "love of work, culture, the historical future of humanity, love of the noblest ideas of the age."

Bukharin was one of the main promoters of the notion of the Soviet people, which for him was devoid of any particular national coloration. Within that paradigm, he felt as comfortable attacking what he saw as the negative features of the Russian national tradition as he did any other tradition in the USSR. For Stalin, that was a problem. In 1929, Stalin had written a major work on the nationality question, protesting claims that the disappearance and merger of nations could take place in one country before the victory of the world revolution. Nations formed before the October Revolution continued to exist after its victory, argued Stalin. Thus he imagined the Soviet people as a family of nations united and led by the Russians. More than once he publicly used "Russian" and "Soviet" as equivalent terms, and as time passed he began to think of the Russians as the quintessential Soviet people. In July 1933, raising a toast at a meeting with writers, he invited them to "drink to the Soviet people, to the most Soviet nation, to the people who carried out the revolution before anyone else." He then added: "Once I said to Lenin that the very best people is the Russian people, the most Soviet nation."

As far as Stalin was concerned, attacking the Russians not just in the Soviet but also in the historical context was coterminous with attacking the Soviet people as a whole. His first public salvo against Bukharin and the long Bolshevik tradition of negative treatment of imperial Russia was fired with the 1936 *Pravda* article celebrating the reception of the Buriat delegation at the Kremlin. The trigger was Bukharin's article in *Izvestiia* praising Lenin on the anniversary of his death and developing Lenin's reference to the Oblomov-like characteristics of prerevolutionary Russians, whom Bukharin called a "nation of Oblomovs." Stalin's reaction in *Pravda* to Bukharin's article left no doubt that party policy had changed. What had been perfectly acceptable for Lenin or Bukharin himself to say in the 1920s and early 1930s was now denounced as a subversion of Leninism.

The agitated Bukharin wrote directly to Stalin, telling him that he was being attacked for no reason. "I well understand that you [the intimate *ty* rather than the formal *vy*] are conducting high policy on a grand scale, preparing the country for victory in warfare as well, and that you want to draw on all that is best, including great national traditions. That is why you were particularly wounded by the 'nation of Oblomovs.' For my part, as I explained, I wanted to emphasize particularly the *national*-liberation role of Bolshevism and the working class." Bukharin understood the motivation for Stalin's turn toward Russian nationalism but did not recognize that in Stalin's mind, the introduction of any new party line required targets for attack, public campaigns unmasking enemies of the regime, and, ultimately, new victims. Stalin was condescending, writing "Big baby" on Bukharin's letter. Bukharin would be accused of antiparty activities a few months later; he was arrested in February 1937, and shot in March 1938. He was executed for allegedly conspiring against the party and the state, being in the employ of foreign powers, and preparing for the dismemberment of the country.

Bukharin was not the only target of the "defend Russian history" campaign unleashed by Stalin in early 1936. Very soon another victim was found in Demian Bedny, the satirist who had already been reprimanded for his criticism of Russian national traditions in 1930. In the fall of 1936, Stalin's close ally Viacheslav Molotov, the head of the Soviet government, had walked out on a performance of the opera *Bogatyri* (Heroes), based on Bedny's libretto. The opera made fun of a key figure of the imperial Russian historical narrative, Prince Vladimir of Kyiv, his retinue, and the baptism of Rus'. In November 1936, the Politburo issued a resolution forbidding any more performances. Bedny's libretto was deemed "an attempt to exalt the robbers of Kyivan Rus' as a positive revolutionary element." It allegedly slandered popular Russian heroes and gave "an anti-historical and mocking depiction of the baptism of Rus', which was in fact a positive milestone in the history of the Russian people, as it promoted the drawing together of the Slavic peoples with peoples of higher culture."

The resolution signaled a dramatic reversal of many of the party's earlier policies, as it not only endorsed imperial Russian symbols but

also praised the advent of Christianity—the main target of the fierce antireligious campaigns launched by the party in the late 1920s and early
1930s—and dismissed the notion of the banditry of pre-Soviet times as
foreshadowing modern revolution. According to a report by the secret
police, the decision to close down performances of the opera met with
general approval from the artistic community. Many Russian artists saw
the decision as rehabilitating Russian history and, indeed, the Russian nation. "The history of the great Russian people may not be distorted," said
an actor. The prominent Soviet playwright Konstantin Trenev is alleged
to have said, "I am extremely pleased by the resolution. I am proud of it
as a Russian. No one may spit in our face." Another playwright, Vsevolod
Vishnevsky, said, "It's a lesson of history: don't touch our people. History
will prove useful, and very soon at that. The opera *Minin [and] Pozharsky:
Salvation from the Interventionists* is now in preparation."

Vishnevsky was referring to a play about two major figures of the
imperial Russian pantheon, Prince Dmitrii Pozharsky and "Citizen"
Kuzma Minin, the "saviors" of Moscow from the Polish occupation in
1612. Heroes of prerevolutionary Russia, celebrated inter alia in a monument erected on Red Square in Moscow in the early nineteenth century,
Pozharsky and Minin had been ridiculed in the 1920s by numerous Bolshevik authors, among them Demian Bedny, who had accused the prince
of corruption. Now the duo was restored to favor, and one of Stalin's
favorite Russian authors, Mikhail Bulgakov, wrote the libretto for the
new opera in the summer of 1936. The opera was never performed, as
Bulgakov was accused of presenting the Polish characters in a positive
light and not showing enough love for the Russian people. True Russian
patriotism was found instead in the imperial opera *A Life for the Tsar*
by Nikolai Glinka. It was performed to great acclaim in February 1939
under the politically correct title *Ivan Susanin*—the name of a Russian
peasant who allegedly saved Tsar Mikhail Romanov by sacrificing his
own life. The opera dealt with the same period of Russian history as Bulgakov's *Minin and Pozharsky*.

It was not just Russian history and its heroes that were back in favor but also the tsars, previously anathematized by Bolshevik propaganda.
They were featured in books and articles as well as in films—by far the
most effective Soviet propaganda instrument of the period. In November

1937, Stalin declared at a reception in honor of his commissar of defense: "The Russian tsars . . . did one good thing—they shook up the huge state all the way to Kamchatka. We received that state as an inheritance. And we Bolsheviks were the first to bind and strengthen that state as one indivisible state, not in the interest of the landowners and capitalists but for the benefit of the workers—all the peoples making up the state." That year, a feature film, *Peter the First*, based on a novel by the former White émigré Aleksei Tolstoy, was released to the Soviet public. The production was sanctioned by Stalin himself.

The following year saw the release of another Soviet blockbuster dedicated to the heroic deeds of Russian rulers of the past. The main character of the film *Aleksandr Nevsky*, produced by the outstanding Soviet director Sergei Eisenstein, was Prince Aleksandr Nevsky, a saint of the Russian Orthodox Church. The film glorified his thirteenth-century war with the Swedes and the Teutonic Knights as a heroic defense of the Russian land. In one line, Nevsky, referring to his Western enemies, says: "Whoever comes to us with a sword shall perish by the sword." The phrase, which became a classic of Soviet propaganda, was never spoken by the real prince but was based on the words of Jesus from the Gospel of Matthew: "For all who take the sword shall perish by the sword." Stalin wanted more, asking his aides to produce a film about another Russian tsar and enemy of the West, Ivan the Terrible. Imperial Russian glory was revived for the sole purpose of mobilizing Russian nationalism in preparation for what Stalin and his circle regarded as an inevitable war with the capitalist West.

In 1939, the Tretiakov Gallery invited Muscovites and visitors to the Soviet capital to view masterpieces of imperial Russian art from its vast collection. It was a major hit with the public, which was happy to feel reconnected with the homeland's imperial past. If that feeling was familiar for older visitors, it was somewhat disturbing to the young people, who had been brought up in an atmosphere of Bolshevik internationalism devoid of attachment to Russian history or identity. "Last night, as I walked home from the exhibit through the center of the city, along Red Square, past the Kremlin, past the old spot where executions took place, past St. Basil's Cathedral, I suddenly felt again a sort of deep kinship with the paintings at the exhibit," wrote the teenage schoolgirl Nina Kosterina in her diary. "I am a Russian. At first this frightened me—were these, perhaps, chauvinistic stirrings within me? No, chauvinism is foreign to me, but at the same time, I am a Russian. As I looked at Antokolsky's magnificent sculptures of Peter the Great and Ivan the Terrible, I was swept with pride: these people were Russians."

THE STALIN REGIME'S LEGITIMIZATION OF ASPECTS OF IMPERIAL Russian politics and culture helped mobilize Russian nationalism in the service of the Soviet state and solidified Russia's status as the leading Soviet nation.

In May 1936, a *Pravda* editorial lauded the patriotism of all Soviet peoples and their contributions to the construction of socialism, placing special emphasis on the Russians. "First among these equals are the Russian people, the Russian workers and the Russian toilers, whose role throughout the whole great proletarian revolution has been exceptionally large, from the first victories to the present day's brilliant period of development," it said. This theme was further developed by the former Soviet censor Boris Volin, then editor in chief of the *Historical Journal*, who published an article titled "The Great Russian People" in the journal *Bol'shevik* (where Stalin had forestalled the publication of Engels's article) in the fall of 1938. "The great Russian people leads the struggle of all the peoples of the Soviet land for the happiness of mankind, for communism," wrote Volin. "The friendship and love of all the peoples of the USSR is growing for the first among equals and the leader among the foremost—the Russian people." From then on, the Russians would be referred to not only as "first among the equals" but also as the "great Russian people."

The official formula used by Soviet propaganda to define relations between the Soviet nations was "The friendship of peoples." But when it came to relations between the regime and the population, officialdom appeared to consider some nations friendlier to the state than others. The newfound trust in the Russians went hand in hand with distrust of other nationalities. Gone were the days when the party had readied itself for a revolutionary war that would bring communism to the rest of Europe and the world. In the years leading up to the outbreak of World War II, Stalin was preparing his country for possible foreign invasion and busy clearing the space behind prospective front lines of potential traitors, the so-called fifth column. Ethnicity, not class, was becoming the criterion whereby true patriots could be distinguished from traitors.

If the Russians were solid citizens, then non-Russians with traditional homelands or significant diasporas outside the Soviet Union were seen as potential traitors and targeted in a number of repressive operations that culminated during the Great Terror of 1937–1938. As Stalin purged the party and state apparatus, targeting real or potential enemies of his rule, millions of people were arrested in the middle of the night and sentenced by "troikas"—panels of three "judges," including a party official, a secret policeman, and a prosecutor. The majority would be sent to the Gulag, a network of concentration camps where prisoners worked in the harsh conditions of Siberia and other remote parts of the USSR to extract gold and iron ore and cut lumber. Sentences ranged from ten to twenty-five years without the possibility of parole. But those who were sent to the Gulag were the lucky ones. At least 600,000 of those arrested and judged by the troikas were summarily executed. The whole society would be terrorized and traumatized. The families of those who were killed or imprisoned, designated as "family members of an enemy of the people," were left to live as second-class citizens. Children who had both parents arrested were sent to foster homes for "reeducation."

First on the list were Soviet citizens of German, Polish, and Japanese or of Far Eastern origin whose loyalty to Moscow, it was thought, might be divided in the event of a crisis between the Soviet state and their brethren abroad. In August and September 1937, Stalin's secret police arrested and sentenced more than 55,000 ethnic Germans, who were accused of being German agents. Close to 42,000 of them were sentenced to death and executed by secret-police squads. Next came the Poles. In the fall of 1937, close to 140,000 Soviet citizens of Polish nationality were sentenced for alleged acts of espionage and anti-Soviet activities, and more than 110,000 of them were shot. Also targeted were Romanians, Bulgarians, Latvians, Finns, Greeks, and members of other nationalities. The repatriates were suspected of being Japanese spies. Altogether, between August 1937 and November 1938, the Soviet regime sentenced more than 335,000 people who had been arrested as part of the "nationality operations." Close to 250,000 of those arrested, or 73 percent, were executed.

The victims of the purge included Ardan Markizov, the commissar of agriculture of the Buriat-Mongolian Autonomous Republic, whose daughter, Gelia, had presented Stalin with flowers in January 1936. Markizov was arrested in November 1937 and accused of belonging to a bogus pan-Mongolian organization that was allegedly seeking to tear the Buriat-Mongol republic away from the USSR. He was shot in June 1938. Gelia's career as a child star (she was routinely invited to school events, and girls all over the Soviet Union had their hair cut in her style) came to an end when she was eight years old. The posters and statues with the image of her embracing Stalin stayed in place, but propaganda now referred to them as a depiction of Stalin and Mamlakat, a Tajik girl who had received the Order of Lenin for her work on a collective farm. Gelia wrote a letter to Stalin declaring her father's innocence. The response came in the form of the arrest of her mother, who had dictated the letter. Both mother and daughter were exiled to Kazakhstan. Two years later, Gelia's thirty-two-year-old mother was dead. According to one version, she committed suicide; according to another, she was assassinated by the secret police to avoid further embarrassment to the authorities—the Markizovs kept Stalin's gifts and portraits of Gelia with Stalin in their Kazakhstan exile.

RUSSIA'S RETURN TO PRIMACY IN THE 1930S CAME AT THE EXpense of many other Soviet nationalities. It was a zero-sum game that began in the wake of the war scare of 1927 with Poland and reached its peak in the months leading up to the outbreak of World War II in September 1939. That period was punctuated by a number of foreign-policy shifts caused, among other things, by Hitler's assumption of power in Germany in early 1933 and the signing of the Anti-Comintern Pact between Germany and Japan in the fall of 1936. Stalin had abandoned the communist dreams of the 1920s about a victorious world revolution and was preparing for a potential defensive war on two fronts, against Germany in the west and Japan in the east. The non-Russian peoples, earlier regarded as vanguard elements of a future revolutionary war, were now perceived as potential turncoats. Ensuring the loyalty of the Russians, the largest Soviet nationality, became crucial in the preparations for war.

The transformation of the Russians from a people guilty of imperial domination to the leading Soviet nation coincided with and was fueled by Stalin's defeat of his opponents in the late 1920s and his rise to supreme power in the course of the 1930s. Accordingly, the revival of traditional notions of fatherland and patriotism went hand in hand with the Stalin regime's emphasis on the paramount importance of the Russian state, and these positions were accompanied by a growing cult of strong rulers involving the rehabilitation of the Russian tsars, most notably Peter I and Ivan the Terrible. Although Russian nationalism often returned to the political scene in the garb of imperial Russia, the new understanding of Russianness was different from the one prevailing before 1917. The Russian nation of the late 1930s no longer included the Little or White Russians, who were now officially recognized as distinct Ukrainian and Belarusian nationalities. This made the Russian nation of the pre–World War II era coterminous in ethnic and territorial terms with the Great Russians of the pre–World War I period. The shock of war would test the new boundaries, the strength of the new nation, and the commitment of its members to the state that had helped to create it.

16

THE GREAT PATRIOTIC WAR

THE CHALLENGE WAS TO FIND THE RIGHT FLAG. THERE WAS NO shortage of red flags or red fabric in the Soviet Union, but getting a red flag with a white circle and a black swastika in the middle was no easy task in the Moscow of 1939. Hitler had gotten rid of the black, red, and yellow tricolor of the Weimar Republic the year he came to power, replacing it with the black, white, and red flag of the new Reich. In 1935, he changed the flag once again, choosing a red field with a swastika in a white circle. Since then, no senior German officials had visited the Soviet Union, and neither the People's Commissariat of International Affairs nor the Kremlin protocol service had appropriate flags available to greet the Nazi foreign minister, Joachim von Ribbentrop, who was coming on a hastily organized visit on August 23, 1939. They finally found the flags they needed at a Moscow movie studio, where they were used to shoot antifascist propaganda films.

As Ribbentrop's plane made a soft landing at the Moscow airport, he was greeted not only with swastika flags but also by a guard of honor and the friendly faces of Soviet officials. In the early hours of August 24, Ribbentrop signed a nonaggression treaty with his Soviet counterpart, Viacheslav Molotov. Photos taken on the occasion show a happy Joseph Stalin, with a portrait of Lenin looking on benevolently. In signing the communist-fascist alliance with Germany, the Soviet Union made an about-face in international politics, breaking off negotiations with Britain and France.

The secret protocol of the Molotov-Ribbentrop Pact envisioned the division of Poland and the rest of Eastern Europe between Hitler and Stalin, effectively launching World War II, which would begin on September 1, 1939, with a German attack on Poland. Stalin believed that by signing the pact he had outmaneuvered the Western powers, postponed a Soviet conflict with Germany, and pushed Hitler toward a war with the West. He also believed that by claiming Moldavia, eastern Poland, and most of the Baltics as his sphere of influence, and, if required, as an occupation zone, he had moved the first Soviet line of defense farther west, improving the country's geostrategic position.

The pact with Nazi Germany meant not only a change of Soviet foreign-policy rhetoric but also a major shift in propaganda efforts at home. The attacks on Hitler and Germany that had until recently been a hallmark of Kremlin propaganda were abandoned, but that was not all. The Molotov-Ribbentrop Pact had a major impact on the Stalin regime's nationality policy. It was not only the alliance with Hitler that had to be justified at home and abroad, but also the impending annexation of territory on the western borders of the USSR. In the 1930s, non-Russian Soviet nationalities with a significant presence outside the Soviet Union had been regarded as liabilities. But as the government's foreign policy switched from one of defense to offense, those nationalities suddenly became an asset, allowing the regime to destabilize neighboring countries and legitimize its forthcoming aggression. It was something of a return to the policy of the 1920s, when the regime had expected a victorious revolutionary march to the West in which the non-Russian nationalities would play a major auxiliary role. The immediate beneficiaries of the foreign-policy shift were the Soviet republics of Ukraine and Belarus.

When the Soviet Union entered World War II in September 1939, it justified its annexation of the Polish-ruled western Ukrainian and Belarusian lands as the liberation of fraternal peoples from oppression and their reunification with their brethren. From then on, Stalin would have to balance the interests of the newly empowered Russian nation with the demands and expectations of the minorities. That balancing act would prove most important in the case of relations between the Russians, Ukrainians, and Belarusians—the East Slavic core of the Soviet Union.

ON SEPTEMBER 17, 1939, THE RED ARMY CROSSED THE POLISH-Soviet border and began its advance into central Poland, which was already under German control. Viacheslav Molotov, who had signed the nonaggression pact with Ribbentrop less than a month earlier, addressed Soviet citizens by radio to explain what many of his compatriots, to say nothing about the rest of the world, saw as an act of naked aggression undertaken in conjunction with the antidemocratic and anticommunist Nazi regime. Molotov's explanation was surprisingly simple: the Red Army had crossed the border to protect fellow Eastern Slavs—the Ukrainians and Belarusians who had settled in the eastern provinces of Poland. "The Soviet government," claimed Molotov, "cannot be expected to take an indifferent attitude to the fate of its blood relatives, Ukrainians and Belarusians residing in Poland who previously found themselves in the position of nations without rights and have now been completely abandoned to the vagaries of fate. The Soviet government regards it as a sacred obligation to extend a helping hand to its brethren Ukrainians and brethren Belarusians residing in Poland."

The formula had been produced by Stalin himself in the course of nocturnal deliberations with the German ambassador in Moscow, Friedrich Werner von der Schulenburg, whom Stalin summoned to his Kremlin office in the early hours of September 17. A week earlier, Molotov had told Schulenburg that the Soviet government was going "to declare that Poland was falling apart and that it was necessary for the Soviet Union, in consequence, to come to the aid of the Ukrainians and the White Russians 'threatened' by Germany." He then added, according to the German report on the meeting: "This argument was to make the intervention of the Soviet Union plausible to the masses and at the same time avoid giving the Soviet Union the appearance of an aggressor." The Germans protested, but Molotov would not budge. "The Soviet government unfortunately saw no possibility of any other motivation," he allegedly told Schulenburg, "since the Soviet Union had thus far not concerned itself about the plight of its minorities in Poland and had to justify abroad, in some way or other, its present intervention."

It fell to Stalin himself to change the Soviet formula, removing from it the reference to the German threat. What remained was a reference to the threat allegedly posed by the disintegration of the Polish state, but the peoples to be saved from it were the same—the Ukrainians and Belarusians. The list of those whom the Soviet Union allegedly wished to rescue was incomplete. Missing were not only the Jews, of whom there were significant numbers in the soon to be "reunited" provinces, but also the Poles: the Soviet-German demarcation line that Molotov and Ribbentrop had drawn in August 1939 left not only ethnically Ukrainian and Belarusian territories, but also parts of the Warsaw and Lublin provinces—which had been settled largely by Poles—on the Soviet side. Stalin clearly did not want to annoy Hitler by mentioning that he was saving Jews, while claiming that he was saving Poles from Poles made no sense whatever. Stalin wanted some nationalities but not others, and the Poles constituted a special challenge that went beyond the legitimacy question.

The USSR had long abandoned its earlier attempts to gain the loyalty of ethnic Ukrainians and Belarusians living in Poland and other neighboring states in order to promote world revolution. With the rise of the German threat, it ceased to regard the members of those nationalities living in the USSR as allies in a future Soviet offensive against the West and began to see them as a potential threat to the USSR in case of a German invasion. The most recent threat of such a scenario had come in March 1939, with the German destruction of Czechoslovakia. In the eastern part of the Czechoslovak state, the government of Transcarpathian Ukraine had declared its independence, and fears ran high in Moscow that Hitler would use that declaration to declare war on the USSR under the banner of reunifying the Ukrainian lands. Hitler decided not to play the Ukrainian card against Stalin and awarded Transcarpathian Ukraine to the Hungarians, who crushed the pro-independence movement there. But Stalin had learned his lesson. He wanted no more Ukrainian or Belarusian enclaves outside the USSR; nor did he want to "share" any ethnic group, the Poles in particular, with his new ally.

In mid-September, Stalin decided to renegotiate the pact and change the dividing line between the German and Soviet spheres in Eastern Europe. He asked Ribbentrop to come back to Moscow. The Nazi foreign minister obliged. A Soviet movie camera captured his arrival in Moscow on September 27. Dressed in a long leather coat, Ribbentrop greeted the Soviet commanders with a Hitler salute. The next day, Ribbentrop and Molotov drew a new line on the map, which Stalin signed in blue and Ribbentrop in red. Under the new arrangement, Stalin traded Polish ethnic territory around Warsaw and Lublin for the Baltic state of Lithuania. For the time being, this meant that the Soviet occupation of Poland would be limited to territories settled largely by Ukrainians and Belarusians. Most of the East Slavic territories, including the city of Lviv, which had briefly been held by the tsarist army in 1914–1915, would now be under Stalin's control—the unexpected realization of a dream of generations of imperial Russian nation-builders.

The new occupiers from the East entered Lviv under the Soviet Ukrainian banner—a change reflected in the name of the Red Army forces engaged in the operation, which were called the Ukrainian Front. In Belarus, similar Red Army units constituted the Belarusian Front. In justifying the Soviet entry into World War II and the annexation of the newly occupied Ukrainian and Belarusian territories, Stalin relied on the rhetoric of the 1920s, which meant a partial return to the policy of national communism and exploitation of the cultural aspects of Ukrainian and Belarusian nationalism. In the fall of 1939, the former provinces of eastern Poland were declared parts of the Ukrainian and Belarusian Soviet Socialist Republics. This was proclaimed a triumph of Soviet nationality policy and a manifestation of the friendship of peoples. The use of the nationality card in the western parts of the newly enlarged republics brought back policies promoting Ukrainian and Belarusian cultural agendas that had first been implemented in the 1920s.

But these were different times. Russian nationalism was now at the core of the new Soviet identity, and the mobilization of other East Slavic nationalisms was conditioned by that new reality. The laws on the incorporation of the former Polish territories into the Ukrainian and Belarusian republics infringed on Russia's status as the only "great nation" in the USSR—the Ukrainians and Belarusians were given that appellation as well. But some great nations were still more equal than others, or even showed a tendency to absorb others. Thus Vladimir Picheta, the president of Minsk University in the 1920s, who was arrested in 1930 on charges of being both a Great Russian chauvinist and a Belarusian nationalist, decided after his release from prison that it was much safer to be accused of chauvinism than nationalism. In a brochure written for mass circulation, he welcomed the annexation of eastern Poland as the reunification of historical Russian lands.

If one can trust the reports of Stalin's secret police, Soviet entry into the war was met with enthusiasm by much of the Soviet population. The younger generation, indoctrinated in Soviet Marxist ideology and exposed to antifascist rhetoric, mistook it for the beginning of a Soviet-German war, the long-awaited struggle between communism and fascism. Many members of the Soviet Russian intelligentsia welcomed it as a reclamation of "ancient Russian lands"—a reprise of the imperial euphoria of the first months of World War I. Finally, many Soviet Ukrainian and Belarusian intellectuals welcomed the war as a reunification of their native land. The management of relations between Stalinist dogma, newly dominant Russian nationalism, and the reasserted Ukrainian and Belarusian nationalism would involve numerous twists and turns of official policy.

As always, the Ukrainians presented the main challenge to the regime in the formulation of the new nationality discourse and, eventually, policy. The rehabilitation of the traditional Ukrainian historical narrative, expressing pride in Ukrainian Cossack history, began a few years before the start of World War II, largely in preparation for the war and, not surprisingly, as part of the rehabilitated Russian imperial narrative. Only those parts of the Ukrainian narrative that fitted the prerevolutionary imperial narrative were selected for inclusion.

The key symbol of the new treatment of the Russian and Ukrainian historical narratives was the seventeenth-century Cossack hetman Bohdan Khmelnytsky, who had been denounced in Soviet literature of the mid-1930s as a "traitor and ardent enemy of the Ukrainian peasantry" and the architect of "union between the Ukrainian and Russian feudal lords." The authorities boarded up the large monument to him in downtown Kyiv whenever communist demonstrations took place and considered tearing it down altogether. But Khmelnytsky was also a major hero of Russian imperial historiography who had brought about the "reunification of Rus." That turned out to be the key factor in the rehabilitation of Khmelnytsky in Soviet historical discourse. Given the prevailing circumstances, the rehabilitation of Khmelnytsky began in Moscow, not in Kyiv, and it was undertaken at the highest level.

In August 1937, Soviet newspapers published an official statement on history textbooks that criticized the outdated approach to the Ukrainian hetman. "The authors do not see any positive role in Khmelnytsky's actions in the seventeenth century, in his struggle against Ukraine's occupation by the Poland of the lords and the Turkey of the sultan," declared *Pravda*. The author of the passage was Stalin himself. He went on to say that the annexation of Ukraine and Georgia to the Russian state was a "lesser evil" as compared with their takeover by other foreign powers. The elements of the traditional Ukrainian and Georgian narratives that glorified their unification with Russia were now restored to favor.

With the change of policy in Moscow, Ukrainian writers embraced the possibility of reasserting at least part of their heritage. The young Ukrainian playwright Oleksandr Korniichuk promptly wrote a play titled *Bohdan Khmelnytsky* in which he lauded the Cossack hetman for his war against Poland. Believers in the old class-based approach to history attacked Korniichuk, but the party leadership in Moscow backed the politically shrewd author. In 1939, the play was performed at the Malyi Theater in Moscow and began its triumphal circuit of theaters throughout the USSR. The film version, produced in 1941, received the highest literary award, the Stalin Prize. Khmelnytsky had become a member of the Soviet pantheon of heroes on a par with Aleksandr Nevsky and Minin and Pozharsky.

Korniichuk's play was among the theater productions brought to Lviv and western Ukraine in the wake of the Soviet annexation of the region. Korniichuk himself served as a plenipotentiary of Soviet Ukrainian culture in the newly occupied territories and played an important role in the Ukrainization of the cultural scene that was formerly not just dominated but monopolized by the Poles. In the fall of 1939, Polish theater and opera productions were swiftly replaced with Ukrainian and Russian ones. The authorities proceeded with the Ukrainization of the press and the educational system. Ethnic Poles were purged from administrative, cultural, and educational institutions. Arrested en masse, many of them were imprisoned or exiled to remote parts of the Soviet Union, including former politicians and police officers and veterans of the military.

Although the local Ukrainian intelligentsia was recruited to help with the de-Polonization and Ukrainization of the region's administration, education, and culture, key positions were reserved for cadres from the east, such as Mykhailo Marchenko, the new president of Lviv University. He was parachuted into his position from the Institute of Ukrainian History in Kyiv, where he had headed the department of the history of feudalism and had been working on a dissertation on the Ukrainian-Polish wars of the second half of the seventeenth century. On Marchenko's watch at Lviv, Polish professors were removed from administrative positions at the university, Ukrainian-language courses were introduced, and the number of ethnic Ukrainian students increased. From 1919 to 1939, the university's official name had been Jan Kazimierz University, in honor of John II Casimir, the king who had fought against Bohdan Khmelnytsky in 1651. Now the name was changed to Ivan Franko National University of Lviv. Franko was a major Ukrainian writer and political activist of the pre–World War I era.

Marchenko was hated by the Polish professors, many of whom lost not only their administrative positions but also their jobs. But it soon turned out that Marchenko himself was under suspicion. He was removed from his position in the spring of 1940 and placed under police surveillance after his return to Kyiv. He was arrested in June 1941 on charges of maintaining ties with the Ukrainian nationalist underground. The rise and fall of Marchenko at the helm of Lviv University coincided with the rise and fall of Ukrainization in the newly annexed territories. Although Moscow made an all-out push for Ukrainization between the fall of 1939 and the spring of 1940, supporting the local Ukrainian cadres and going after the old Polish guard, by summer the policy had changed. The Poles were still persecuted, but some steps were also taken to accommodate them, while the Ukrainians were favored in cultural policy but attacked for real or perceived manifestations of political nationalism. As far as Moscow was concerned, it was a short step from dedicated party

Ukrainizer to Ukrainian nationalist: constant vigilance was required to keep in step with the party line.

One reason for changing nationality policy and broadening the scope of repressions and deportations was the course of the war and Stalin's foreign-policy calculations. The fall of Paris to the Nazis in May 1940 caught Stalin by surprise—he had expected a lengthy conflict on the western front. Now Hitler could turn east and attack the Soviet Union at almost any time. The Soviet dictator, still believing that the farther west he moved his borders, the more security he gained, rushed to claim his part of the booty in accordance with the Molotov-Ribbentrop Pact of 1939. He rapidly occupied the Baltic states and claimed Moldavia and ethnically Ukrainian territories from Romania. He also began a war with Finland, which would not go the way of the Baltic states and mounted strong resistance, bleeding the Red Army and minimizing Soviet territorial gains along the Soviet-Finnish border. But claiming territory was only part of Stalin's calculus: securing it in the face of the coming aggression was another major task.

Whom Hitler could count on if he moved into western Ukraine and Belarus was the question that Stalin and his security team were trying to answer in the month after the fall of Paris. The Poles were still disloyal, but, given German policy in occupied central and western Poland, they were no Germanophiles—the executions of thousands of Polish political, cultural, and intellectual leaders were carried out with little or no secrecy and widely known in Polish circles. There was a different attitude among the Ukrainians, with many of them eagerly awaiting the arrival of the Germans. Old-timers looked back fondly to Austrian rule, which had created opportunities for Ukrainians to assert themselves. Many of the younger western Ukrainians rejected not only Polish but also Soviet rule and joined the Organization of Ukrainian Nationalists. They had high hopes that the Nazis would help them establish an independent Ukrainian state. Along with former members of the Communist Party of Western Ukraine, who were suspected of either Ukrainian nationalism or disloyalty to Stalin, Ukrainian nationalists became the main target of the Soviet occupation authorities.

The nationalist leaders' sympathy toward and collaboration with the Germans (in early 1941 they surreptitiously formed two Special Forces battalions under the auspices of German military intelligence) was reason enough for the Soviets to take action against them. Moreover, their brand of nationalism stressed the complete distinctness of Ukrainians from Russians, which exacerbated ethnic tensions resulting from the Stalin regime's reassertion of Russian nationalism. Few sets of data provide a better understanding of Soviet nationality policy in the annexed territories of Ukraine and Belarus than the figures on Soviet deportations of unreliable political elements from those areas. In February 1940, during the first wave of large-scale deportations, close to 140,000 Poles were shipped from western Ukraine and Belarus to Siberia and Central Asia. They included former government officials and policemen as well as military veterans, along with many members of their families. More deportations would follow, targeting Poles, Jews, and finally, Ukrainians and Belarusians. In May 1941, more than 11,000 Ukrainians would be deported from the former Polish territories to the Soviet interior.

THE NOTION OF *PATRIA*, WHICH IN THE RUSSIAN RENDITION OF motherland (*rodina*) and fatherland (*otechestvo*) was fully rehabilitated in the Soviet Union only in 1934, became the rallying cry of the communist leadership after Hitler, having failed to invade the British Isles in the fall of 1940, turned his armies eastward and attacked his former Soviet ally on June 22, 1941.

On that day, Stalin, too stunned to address the population himself, told his right-hand man, Viacheslav Molotov, whose signature stood next to Ribbentrop's on the pact that Hitler had just violated, to read the text of the appeal edited by Stalin himself. Taken by surprise, the Soviet dictator had nowhere to look for consolation, reassurance, and inspiration but to history. The text of the appeal read by Molotov stated, "Not for the first time, our people must deal with an arrogant enemy attacker. In the past, our people responded to Napoleon's campaign against Russia with a patriotic war, and Napoleon suffered defeat, which led to his downfall. That will also be the fate of the arrogant Hitler, who has proclaimed a new campaign against our country. The Red Army and all our people will again wage a victorious patriotic war for the Motherland, for honor, for freedom." The German-Soviet conflict would eventually become known in the Soviet Union as the "Great Patriotic War of the Soviet People."

A few days after Molotov's speech, two Soviet songwriters—the composer Aleksandr Aleksandrov, who had founded the Red Army Ensemble, and the poet Vasilii Lebedev-Kumach—wrote a song that became an emblem of the war. Titled "The Sacred War," it would lead every Soviet morning radio broadcast from the autumn of 1941 until the end of the war. Beginning with the words "Rise, tremendous country, / Rise to do battle to the death," the song referred to the motherland but not to the party. According to one theory, the lyrics had actually been written not by Lebedev-Kumach but by a provincial schoolteacher, Aleksandr Bode, back in 1916, during World War I. Lebedev-Kumach allegedly replaced a few words, writing "fascist" instead of "Teutonic" and "our great Union" instead of "our Russian native land." The song, which revived themes and tropes of prerevolutionary Russian nationalism, could ignore the party but had to take account of the multiethnic composition of the USSR and rally the patriotism not only of the Russians but also of the other peoples.

That was the theme of Stalin's first public speech of the war, delivered on July 3, 1941. After explaining how right he had been to sign the nonaggression pact with Hitler, he called Hitler and Ribbentrop "monsters and cannibals." The distressed Stalin called his subjects "brothers and sisters," trying to create a family feeling and a sense of spiritual, almost religious brotherhood among the Soviet peoples. According to Stalin, the goal of the German invasion was "to reestablish the rule of the landowners, to reestablish tsarism, to destroy the national culture and national statehood of the Russians, Ukrainians, Belarusians, Lithuanians, Latvians, Estonians, Uzbeks, Tatars, Moldavians, Georgians, Armenians, Azerbaijanis and other free peoples of the Soviet Union, to Germanize them and turn them into slaves of German princes and barons."

The appeal had little immediate impact. German divisions were advancing eastward, crushing the resistance of the Red Army, which was manned largely by peasants who had little sense of loyalty to the regime that had put them through the nightmare of collectivization and, in the case of Ukraine and southern Russia, a devastating famine. The non-Russian inhabitants of the western territories that had been newly annexed and quickly lost by the Soviets tended to see the Germans as liberators (they would soon be proved wrong). In the fall, after retreating from the Baltics and Belarus and losing 600,000 soldiers who had been surrounded near Kyiv, the Red Army was waging war on Russian territory for the very survival of the regime. Almost all the non-Russian provinces of the western USSR were lost.

That must have been one of the reasons why, in his next highly publicized address, delivered on November 7, 1941, Great October Socialist Revolution Day, on Red Square in front of troops leaving for the front lines only a few dozen kilometers from Moscow, Stalin dropped all reference to the non-Russians. For him, the war was now a purely Russian undertaking. "The war that you are waging is a war of liberation, a just war," he declared. "May you be inspired in that war by the manly image of our great ancestors—Aleksandr Nevsky, Dmitrii Donskoi, Kuzma Minin, Dmitrii Pozharsky, Aleksandr Suvorov, and Mikhail Kutuzov! May you be shielded by the victorious banner of the great Lenin!" There was no mention of any non-Russian hero, only glorification of the imperial ones who had often been ridiculed by Soviet propaganda only a few years earlier. Even the reference to Lenin had religious overtones, as the Russian verb *oseniat'* (to shield) often means "to bless" or "to make the sign of the cross." With the regime's back to the wall, Stalin was invoking symbols and gods previously discarded and desecrated.

It looked as if the emphasis on the Russian imperial tradition at the expense of the primacy of Marxist-Leninist ideology was working. The transfer of fresh Soviet divisions from the Far East helped Stalin hold on to Moscow in December 1941 and push the Germans back. In January 1943, in the middle of the furious fighting at Stalingrad, Stalin reintroduced military shoulder patches that had been closely associated with the tsarist regime in Soviet prewar propaganda. A less ideological foreign policy allowed for building bridges with former adversaries, Britain and the United States, which formed with the Soviet Union what the British prime minister, Winston Churchill, called the "Grand Alliance" against Germany.

The Western allies, in particular the United States, helped save the Soviet regime by providing weaponry and equipment through the Lend-Lease program, but Stalin wanted more—a second front in Europe. To gain Western public support, he had to shed the image of a crazed atheistic communist bent on world revolution. In 1943, in preparation for the Teheran summit with the Western leaders, Stalin dissolved the Communist International, which Western public opinion regarded as an institution committed to plotting world revolution and the overthrow of democratic governments around the globe. Stalin also made major concessions to the Russian Orthodox Church, allowing the election of the Moscow patriarch to the throne that had remained vacant since the 1920s, when the Bolsheviks' antireligious campaign had begun. With the Russian Orthodox Church getting a new lease on life, an important element of imperial Russian history and identity began its return to public consciousness.

The ideological and cultural return to imperial values culminated with the elimination of "The Internationale," the song of the international socialist movement of the late nineteenth century, as the national anthem of the Soviet Union. In December 1943, the Politburo approved the lyrics and music of a new anthem written by Aleksandr Aleksandrov, the coauthor of "The Sacred War." Its music closely resembled that of Aleksandrov's other hit, the "Hymn of the Bolshevik Party" (1938). But whereas the party hymn had contained not a word about Russia, the new Soviet hymn had no reference to the party. "Great Rus' has forever conjoined / An indissoluble union of free republics," went the first two lines of the new hymn. Stalin had personally edited and approved the lyrics. The non-Russian republics of the Union would now have to rally around Russia in the struggle against foreign aggression.

DURING THE MOST DIFFICULT FIRST MONTHS AND YEARS OF THE war, when the authorities in Moscow focused on stoking the fires of Russian nationalism, their counterparts in other Soviet republics, especially those occupied by the Germans, were allowed and even encouraged to exploit their own nationalism to the maximum in order to mobilize anti-German resistance behind the front lines and motivate their ethnic brethren in the ranks of the Red Army.

Very soon after Molotov's speech of June 22, 1941, Ukrainian writers discovered their own Great Patriotic War as a source of inspiration. Apparently they did not consider the war against Napoleon to be theirs (Napoleon's army had never entered Ukraine). In a letter addressed to Stalin, leading Ukrainian cultural figures claimed that in the early modern era the Ukrainian Cossacks had waged their own patriotic war against the Poles and Germans. Ukrainian historians and propagandists found their own Aleksandr Nevsky in the person of the thirteenth-century Prince Danylo of Halych. Ironically enough, while Nevsky had fought against the West, Danylo had fought the Mongols with the help of Western allies and even accepted a royal crown from the pope. But such historical details were readily overlooked in the process of emulating the elder Russian brother and contributing to war propaganda.

In Belarus, the most prominent national poet, Yanka Kupala, also turned to history for inspiration. He praised the struggle of "my heroic Belarusian people" under Stalin's leadership against the "cannibal and bloodsucker" Hitler. Kupala called for a jacquerie, or peasant revolt, against the invader: "Partisans, partisans, Belarusian sons! / For bondage, for shackles, slaughter the evil Hitlerites so that they do not revive for eons!" Officials at the Belarusian partisan headquarters in Moscow were eager to exploit all available symbols of Soviet Belarusian nationalism. They gave the name of Kastus Kalinoŭski (Konstanty Kalinowski), who had been conveniently transformed in Soviet Belarusian historiography from a leader of the Polish revolt against Russia in 1863 into a fighter for the Belarusian people, to one of the best-known partisan units active on Belarusian territory. Its core consisted of officers of the secret police who were parachuted into western Belarus in the spring of 1943.

While non-Russian heroes were recognized locally, they found it difficult to gain visibility at the all-Union level and function on a par with their Russian counterparts. In mid-1942, Stalin approved the creation of new military awards for Red Army officers. They were named after Prince Aleksandr Nevsky and two tsarist generals, Aleksandr Suvorov, who had crushed the Polish uprising led by Tadeusz Kościuszko in the late eighteenth century, and Mikhail Kutuzov, who had surrendered Moscow to Napoleon in 1812 but had then driven him out of Russia. All three commanders were ethnic Russians. Among the non-Russians, even Bohdan Khmelnytsky, who was as popular among the soldiers as Aleksandr Nevsky, thanks to the film made about him on the eve of the war, was not given similar recognition. Ukrainian cultural figures felt offended.

The situation began to change only in the fall of 1943, when the Red Army began its offensive in Ukraine and Belarus. Late that summer, the best-known Ukrainian filmmaker, Oleksandr Dovzhenko, appealed to the party boss of Ukraine, Nikita Khrushchev, to establish a high military award honoring Bohdan Khmelnytsky. Khrushchev turned to Stalin, suggesting that such an award would raise morale among Ukrainians in the Red Army and beyond. Khmelnytsky, wrote Khrushchev, was very popular in Ukraine, because he had fought for its liberation and the union of the Russian and Ukrainian peoples. Stalin agreed. In October 1943, Moscow announced the creation of an award designed by Ukrainian artists and featuring Khmelnytsky's name in its Ukrainian rather than its Russian transcription. The *Pravda* editorial that accompanied the publication of the decree stressed that the seventeenth-century hetman had been a great statesman and had understood that the Ukrainian people could survive only in union with the fraternal Russian people.

That was just the beginning. A few days later, Stalin ordered four army groups fighting in Ukraine to be renamed as four Ukrainian Fronts. In the spring of 1944, the name "Belarusian Front" was given to three army groups fighting in Belarus. By that time, Ukraine, Belarus, and other republics had their own commissariats of defense and international relations. After the Teheran Conference with Franklin D. Roosevelt and Winston Churchill in December 1943, where Stalin received a much-desired promise to open a second front in Europe, and preparations were made for the formation of what would become known as the United Nations Organization, the Soviet leader initiated constitutional changes creating an array of formally independent Soviet republics, the object being to claim more seats in the future United Nations. None of the republics had real independence, or even autonomy, in administrative matters, to say nothing of military and international affairs, but Stalin managed to convince the Allies to admit Ukraine and Belarus, along with the Soviet Union (understood as Russia), into the UN General Assembly. The big Russian nation, now with three voices instead of one, had reentered the international arena.

The simultaneous mobilization of Russian and non-Russian nationalism in the effort to defeat Germany created new challenges for the Soviet authorities in Moscow, who had to ensure that non-Russian nationalism did not overshadow Russian nationalism. In November 1943, Georgii Aleksandrov, the head of the propaganda department of the party's Central Committee in Moscow, criticized Ukrainian writers for a letter celebrating the liberation of Kyiv from Nazi occupation. According to Aleksandrov, the letter implied that there were "two leading peoples in the Soviet Union, the Russians and the Ukrainians," although it was "universally accepted that the Russian people was the elder brother in the Soviet Union's family of peoples."

Aleksandrov was among the party officials who supported the decision to deny the Stalin Prize to the *History of the Kazakh SSR*, published in 1943 by a group of Moscow and Kazakh authors led by the prominent Soviet historian Anna Pankratova, on the grounds that it discredited imperial Russia. He wrote: "The book is anti-Russian, as the authors' sympathies are on the side of those revolting against tsarism, and there is no effort to exonerate Russia." Pankratova and her colleagues never received the Stalin Prize.

But finding a balance between the class and national principles, as well as between Russian and non-Russian nationalism within that context, was no easy task. As long as the war was being waged, the patriotism of every Soviet nationality was useful. Thus, while Aleksandrov and like-minded party officials and intellectuals pushed the Russian line, patriots of other peoples were allowed to push back. Ukrainian writers and historians protested the attempts of Russian authors to claim Danylo of Halych as a Russian prince, or to refer to western Ukraine as ancient Rus', or Russian land. Pankratova and her colleagues appealed Aleksandrov's decision to higher party authorities, claiming that they could not rehabilitate the colonial policies of the tsars and that, if there had been no oppression before the revolution, there would have been no revolution either.

The senior Politburo members Georgii Malenkov and Andrei Zhdanov tried to settle the dispute by calling a meeting of historians to discuss the work of Pankratova and her colleagues. It ended with no clear winners, and the party postponed its verdict until the end of the war. In August 1945, a high party organ, the Central Committee of the Communist Party of Kazakhstan, issued a resolution condemning the 1943 history of Kazakhstan and ordering Kazakh historians to revise it. One cannot imagine the Kazakh authorities passing such a resolution without an explicit signal from Moscow.

The Soviet victory against Germany marked the end of the nationality policy originating with the Molotov-Ribbentrop Pact of 1939. The status of the non-Russian nationalities was radically downgraded and Russian dominance reasserted—a policy shift signaled by Stalin himself. In a highly publicized toast that he delivered on May 24, 1945, at the Kremlin banquet in honor of Soviet military commanders, Stalin declared:

> As a representative of our Soviet government, I would like to raise a toast to the health of our Soviet people and, first and foremost, of the Russian people. I drink first and foremost to the health of the Russian people because it is the foremost of all our nations making up the Soviet Union. I raise a toast to the health of the Russian people because in this war and earlier it has merited the title, if you will, of the leading force of our Soviet Union among all the peoples of our country. I raise a toast to the health of the Russian people not only because it is the leading people but also because it has good sense, political good sense in every respect, and endurance.

On the following day, the toast was published in slightly revised form in the main Soviet newspapers. In years to come it would be printed and reprinted more than once, signaling the new turn in the party's nationality policy. Oleksandr Korniichuk, the winner of the Stalin Prize for his play *Bohdan Khmelnytsky*, was made aware of the change even before the toast. In early May 1945, his award-winning play was taken out of production when a pro-Soviet Polish delegation visited Ukraine. Korniichuk, who was then still Stalin's favorite playwright, was appalled. He complained that no one had curtailed performances in Moscow of the much more anti-Polish opera *Ivan Susanin*. Korniichuk got nowhere. His play was now subject to criticism and on its way out, while *Ivan Susanin*, a reworking of the imperial-era *Life for the Tsar*, remained on stage.

The regime was prepared to improve relations with the Poles by curbing Soviet Ukrainian nationalism, but not its much more powerful Russian counterpart. The Great Patriotic War was over, and not every brand of patriotism was now welcome.

17

THE SOVIET PEOPLE

Joseph Stalin died on March 5, 1953. Four days later, as part of the ceremonial farewell to the deceased, his body was placed next to Lenin's in the Red Square mausoleum. He was mourned not just as the head of government but also as the leader of working people throughout the world.

The new leaders of the Soviet Union invited the heads of communist governments of Eastern Europe, China, and North Korea as well as the leaders of the communist parties of Western Europe, including those of Italy, France, Spain, and Britain, to join them atop the mausoleum. Those delivering eulogies included members of Stalin's inner circle and representatives of the Soviet intelligentsia, in particular the composer Dmitrii Shostakovich and the writer and war poet Konstantin Simonov. The leaders of the Soviet republics were nowhere in sight, as they were too insignificant in the Soviet hierarchy. The global spread of communism, not the nationality question in the Soviet Union, was the top agenda item for Stalin's successors. Officially, the Soviet nationality question was considered to have been solved by Stalin himself.

"The solution of one of the most complicated problems in the history of social development, the national question, is associated with the name of Comrade Stalin," declared the new head of the Soviet government, Georgii Malenkov, from the top of the mausoleum. "For the first time in history the supreme theoretician of the national question, Comrade Stalin, made possible the liquidation of age-old national dissension on the scale of a huge multinational state." Malenkov then explained exactly what the solution of the nationality question in the USSR entailed: "Under the leadership of Comrade Stalin our party has managed to overcome the economic and cultural backwardness of previously oppressed peoples, uniting all the nations of the Soviet Union into one fraternal family and forging the friendship of peoples."

Conspicuously, Malenkov failed to mention Russia in his praise of Stalin's achievements on the nationalities front. In fact, the Russocentrism of Soviet nationality policy constituted Stalin's main amendment to Lenin's formula for handling the nationality question in a multiethnic state. Apparently Stalin's successors were not certain what to make of that part of his legacy.

The gap between official rhetoric and the less-than-satisfactory condition of the friendship of peoples in the Soviet Union was revealed soon after the state funeral by the actions of the new regime's security tsar, Lavrentii Beria, by far the most powerful of Stalin's successors. In his speech at the funeral, Beria talked not only about the Soviet people but also about the peoples of the Soviet Union. Shortly thereafter, he took the initiative of stopping the anti-Semitic campaign that treated Jews as aliens and agents of the West. Among those whom he released from imprisonment was Polina Zhemchuzhina, the Jewish wife of the man who was officially the second most powerful official in the land, Viacheslav Molotov. On Stalin's orders, she had spent more than four years in prison while her terrified husband had maintained his position in the Soviet leadership. He had to watch his every step as he helped his boss—and his wife's captor—run the country.

In June 1953, Beria gained approval from the party leadership for measures aiming to end the Russification of the non-Russian republics: the first secretaries of party committees now had to belong to the titular nationality, cadres who did not speak the local languages were to be recalled, and official correspondence was to be conducted in the languages of the republics. It sounded like the beginning of a major reform of Soviet nationality policy, turning away from the Russocentrism of the Stalin years back to the indigenization of the 1920s.

We do not know how far Beria was prepared to go in his revision of Stalin's nationality policy. Before the end of June 1953, he was arrested as the result of a plot engineered by his main rival, Nikita Khrushchev, the former viceroy of Ukraine. By the end of the year, Beria would be shot on trumped-up charges of working for the British. He was also accused of attempts to revive bourgeois nationalist elements in the republics and undermine friendship between the peoples of the USSR and the "great Russian people." It now appeared that Stalinist Russocentrism was again the order of the day. But the story was more complicated than that. Despite the execution of Beria, the plotters did not reverse measures taken on his initiative to check the Russification of the non-Russian republican leadership and party apparatus, or of education and culture. Some of those measures would remain in effect until the last days of the Soviet Union.

THE STRUGGLE BETWEEN STALIN'S HEIRS NOTWITHSTANDING, the dictator's death brought about a general relaxation of the political climate. At the end of the war, Stalin had moved to reestablish party control over ideology and culture, which had been shaken during the conflict, and to restore the primacy of Russia and the Russians in the Soviet hierarchy of nations. The Zhdanov period, named after Stalin's chief ideologue, Andrei Zhdanov, brought official attacks on all manifestations of liberalism or deviations from the party line. Real or imagined manifestations of openness to the West and writings that strayed from party-approved models of classical Russian literature of the imperial era came under fire. Among the victims were not only writers and artists but also the all-powerful head of the propaganda apparatus during the war, Georgii Aleksandrov. Aleksandrov was accused of failing to condemn idealism strongly enough in his *History of Western Philosophy*. The renowned film director Sergei Eisenstein was criticized for depicting Ivan the Terrible as a weak and confused leader in the second part of his film about the Russian tsar, whose first part had been admired by Stalin.

The Zhdanov campaign, which sought to uphold the Russocentric character of official ideology and culture, gained new impetus with the start of the Cold War in 1948. Provoked by Soviet behavior in occupied Eastern Europe, where Stalin established communist regimes, and by the geopolitical contest in Turkey and Iran, the new international conflict pitted Moscow against its former British and American allies. The newly created Jewish state of Israel became one of the battlegrounds in an un-declared war for global influence, as the Soviets tried to turn it into their ally in the Middle East. At the same time, the Kremlin began to look with suspicion on Soviet Jewry, suspected of sympathizing with the West. A central aspect of the new ideological campaign in the USSR was an attack on "rootless cosmopolitanism," a term used as a cover for the persecution of Jews and the promotion of xenophobic and anti-Western tendencies in the interpretation of the Russian cultural tradition and identity.

A return to Russocentrism meant a return to antinationalist campaigns in the non-Russian republics. Starting in 1946, party resolutions were passed to combat alleged nationalist deviations in the republics, including Ukraine and Belarus. Literary history became a target in both republics. In Belarus, the authors of one study were accused of drawing a direct line from the "Polish squires" and "Westernizers and liberals of old" to Soviet Belarusian literature while neglecting historical links between Belarusian and Russian democratic literature and culture. In Ukraine, party ideologues questioned details of literary history and exposed "errors," condemning, for example, the failure to represent the progressive role of the Russian people in the opera *Bohdan Khmelnytsky*. Ukraine's best-known filmmaker, Olek-sandr Dovzhenko, also found himself under attack and was confined to Moscow, with no right to visit Ukraine. In 1951, a campaign was launched against one of Ukraine's best poets, Volodymyr Sosiura, for his patriotic poem "Love Ukraine" (1944). What had been welcomed in wartime was now condemned as a manifestation of Ukrainian nationalism.

Nikita Khrushchev took part in the Stalin-inspired attack on Ukrainian cultural figures during his tenure in Ukraine, which ended in December 1949. But once he was no longer under the dictator's thumb after Sta-lin's death in 1953, he continued the turn away from Stalin's policies. In that regard he was a continuator rather than an opponent of his archrival, Lavrentii Beria. Khrushchev and Beria emerged as contenders for power in the post-Stalin leadership, but, as noted above, Khrushchev soon outmaneuvered Beria and had him shot. Beria was dead before the end of 1953. What Khrushchev offered his supporters in the Politburo who feared Beria's growing power and ability to use the secret police against them was a form of collective leadership. It took Khrushchev a good part of the rest of the decade to rid himself of other potential rivals in the Politburo, ranging from the head of the Soviet government, Georgii Malenkov, to the minister of foreign affairs, Viacheslav Molotov, and the minister of defense and hero of the "Great Patriotic War," Georgii Zhukov.

Khrushchev's years in power became known for a number of ambitious reforms, including decentralization of economic decision-making to the regions, attempts to revive struggling Soviet agriculture by paying salaries to peasants, and an ambitious campaign of building new urban housing. But few of his initiatives attracted more attention than his de-Stalinization campaign, which condemned Stalin's crimes against the government and party elite (but not against the people), released most political prisoners from the Gulag—the state-run system of concentration camps—and launched public debate on economic, social, and cultural development. Khrushchev's relaxation of ideological controls in the late 1950s produced a period in Soviet politics and culture that became known as the Khrushchev Thaw.

The search for a new nationality policy became part of Khrushchev's reformist course, which was closely linked to his broader de-Stalinizing agenda. Khrushchev was originally quite hesitant to act on nationality policy. The nature and limits of his early thinking on the nationalities question are well demonstrated by changes to the Soviet anthem. The reference to Stalin was removed in 1955 and replaced with a reference to the party that had been completely absent from the original lyrics that had been written with Stalin's participation. Thus the collective leadership and wisdom of the party replaced the power of the authoritarian leader, but the rest of the anthem, including the opening reference to the Great Rus' uniting the other Soviet peoples, remained intact.

In January 1954, Khrushchev launched his first major public initiative, a lavish celebration of the tercentenary of Bohdan Khmelnytsky's acceptance of Russian suzerainty. The accompanying ideological campaign illustrated that there were limits to how much the Russian imperial narrative could be combined with the non-Russian national narratives under the banner of Marxist rhetoric and Soviet-style "friendship of peoples." The Pereiaslav Council of 1654, at which the Ukrainian Cossack officers had decided to accept the protectorate of the Muscovite tsar, was now to be officially commemorated, as the *Theses on the Reunification of Ukraine and Russia*, endorsed that year by the Central Committee in Moscow, made clear.

The term "reunification" harked back to the preoccupation of Russian imperial historiography with the "reunification of Rus'." It had made sense in the imperial period, when it was an article of faith that Rus'—or rather, Russia—had been inhabited by one people in Kyivan times, then divided by the Mongols, Lithuanians, and Poles, and then finally reunited in the course of the sixteenth and seventeenth centuries under the auspices of the Muscovite tsars. But Soviet historians claimed that Russians and Ukrainians were separate peoples, not mere branches of the same nation. How they could be reunited was a paradox never explained or resolved by Soviet propagandists. What the term made manifest, however, was that the model of the big Russian nation, first divided by foreign enemies and then reunited by Russian rulers, was again in favor.

The theses on the anniversary of the alleged reunification approved by the Central Committee of the Communist Party in Moscow read: "By linking their destiny forever with the fraternal Russian people, the Ukrainian people freed themselves from foreign subjugation and ensured their national development. On the other hand, the reunion of Ukraine and Russia helped considerably to strengthen the Russian state and enhance its international prestige. The friendship between the working people of Russia and Ukraine grew firmer and stronger in the joint struggle against the common enemies—tsardom, the serf-owning landlords, the capitalists, and foreign invaders."

Thus, an event condemned by Soviet historians as absolutely evil in the 1920s because of its role in strengthening tsarism, and then recast as a lesser evil within the discourse of Russian statism in the 1930s, was now declared wholly positive. By acquiring new territories, the tsars had unwittingly strengthened the ties between the Russian and non-Russian working masses. Soviet propagandists had managed to square the circle: Russian imperialism had finally found a way to use class-based discourse to justify its reappearance in the Soviet Union.

The anniversary celebrations were accompanied by a lavish gift presented by the Moscow leadership on behalf of one fraternal people to another—the transfer of the Crimean Peninsula from the jurisdiction of the Russian Federation to that of the Ukrainian republic. On the symbolic level, the transfer was supposed to manifest the level of trust that now existed between the two nations. In practical terms, it meant that the authorities in Moscow did not take the differences between them too seriously and believed that ethnocultural issues could and should be subordinated to administrative and economic considerations. The Crimea, which had had difficulty recovering economically from the devastation of World War II and the Soviet deportation of the Crimean Tatars in 1944, would benefit from administrative integration with the mainland republic on which it depended for most of its industrial and agricultural resources.

The official celebration of Russo-Ukrainian unity also contained an element of Slavic conspiracy against the non-Slavs. With Moscow refusing to allow the return of the Crimean Tatars to their homeland, Ukraine became implicated along with Russia in the unlawful deportation of and discrimination against an ethnic minority. Moreover, Moscow declared the anniversary a major event not only for Russians and Ukrainians, but also for the other Soviet nationalities. Indeed, the historical outline of Russo-Ukrainian relations presented in the *Theses* was used as a template for representing Russian relations with other Soviet nationalities until the collapse of the Soviet Union.

Ukraine's unofficial status was now elevated to that of second most important Soviet republic. Khrushchev, who had served as de facto viceroy of Ukraine for more than a decade, relied heavily on his Ukrainian clients to gain and then strengthen his position in Moscow as the sole leader of the Soviet Union. After conclusively defeating opposition to his rule in the summer of 1957, he began to bring Ukrainian cadres to Moscow and promote them. The first secretary of the Ukrainian Central Committee, Oleksii Kyrychenko, became the de facto second secretary of the Central Committee in Moscow; his successor in Kyiv, Mykola Pidhorny, was installed as secretary of the Central Committee in Moscow after the ouster of Kyrychenko; and the onetime party leader of the Dnipropetrovsk region, Leonid

Brezhnev, became head of the Soviet parliament. By the early 1960s, the Ukrainian party had become the junior partner of the Russian elite in running the Soviet Empire. Although Beria's norm that the first party secretary of a Union republic was to be a member of the titular nationality remained in place, Moscow sent its own people, invariably Russians or Ukrainians, to keep an eye on the locals.

IN HIS SECRET SPEECH AT THE TWENTIETH PARTY CONGRESS IN February 1956, Khrushchev launched a major campaign to revise the Stalinist legacy in all aspects of public life. Stalin was accused of creating and promoting a cult of personality and persecuting loyal Soviet cadres within the party and the Red Army. His atrocities against national minorities were not mentioned or admitted publicly, but in practice under Khrushchev's leadership the Soviet Union took steps to rehabilitate not only individuals but whole nations "punished" by Stalin during the war. In 1957, Khrushchev restored or formed anew the Kabardino-Balkar, Kalmyk, and Chechen-Ingush autonomous republics within the Russian Federation, allowing the minorities deported by Stalin on charges of collaboration with the Germans to return to their ancestral homelands. The rehabilitation was partial, as neither Germans nor Koreans nor Crimean Tatars were allowed to return, although police control over their settlements in exile was significantly relaxed by the authorities.

Khrushchev and his supporters tried to strike a balance between the legacy of Stalinism and what they called a return to Leninist norms—that is, the policies of the 1920s. One of Khrushchev's initiatives that was deeply rooted in the policies of that period was the antireligious campaign, which he launched in the late 1950s. In the course of World War II, Stalin had ended the open persecution of religious believers while putting religious organizations under strict government control. The main beneficiary of that change was the Russian Orthodox Church, which became an agent of the state in the process of Russifying and Sovietizing the western borderlands. In 1946, Stalin arranged the liquidation of the Ukrainian Catholic (formerly Uniate) Church in Galicia and Belarus by following the Russian imperial model of "reunifying" the Uniates with the Russian Orthodox Church. As in the nineteenth century, Russians, Ukrainians, and Belarusians were united in one Russian church. In official terms, however, the liquidation was carried out under the slogan of reunifying the Ukrainian nation in territorial and cultural terms—most Ukrainians had traditionally been Orthodox.

Khrushchev, who was not above using the Russian Orthodox Church as a tool of international policy, allowed its representatives to join the World Council of Churches and even attend the Second Vatican Council as observers in 1962, but he had little use for it inside the country. Moreover, at a party congress in 1961, he announced the construction of the foundations of communist society as the party's main goal for the next twenty years. With the expected advent of communism, a proletarian paradise on earth, promoted as tantamount to a new official religion, the government was not about to tolerate competition in the realm of faith. Khrushchev promised to show the last religious believer in the USSR on a television screen—a manifestation of secular belief in the power of technological progress to crush belief in the supernatural. As a result of this antireligion drive, the government closed half of all Orthodox parishes in the country. Out of forty-seven Orthodox monasteries, only sixteen remained open. Especially harsh measures were taken against the Protestant groups, Baptists and Pentecostals who refused to succumb to government pressure and continued their activities in the underground.

The antireligion campaign turned out to be a major blow to the religious component of traditional Russian identity, which had been tolerated under late Stalinism. It also had the unintended effect of increasing the importance of the Ukrainian clergy in the Russian Orthodox Church. Although the authorities closed Orthodox churches en masse in the traditionally Orthodox regions of Russia, Ukraine, and Belarus, they were much more careful in western Ukraine, where excessive pressure might well have caused believers to abandon government-controlled Russian Orthodoxy and join the "nationalist" Ukrainian Catholic Church, which maintained an underground existence. Most of the approximately 8,000 parishes of the Russian Orthodox Church that survived Khrushchev's antireligious campaign were located in Ukraine, and the majority of those were in the formerly Uniate regions of the republic.

The Russian Orthodox Church was never as crypto-Uniate or as ethnically Ukrainian as during Khrushchev's years in power. In the eighteenth century, most of the Russian Orthodox had been led by Ukrainian bishops, and now Ukrainians constituted the majority of believers as well. No one seemed to bother about the implications of this new development for nationality policy. After all, few in the government saw any future for the church, or, indeed, for nationalities, in the new communist society that Khrushchev and his entourage were busily promoting.

THE YEAR 1961 MARKED THE HIGH POINT OF KHRUSHCHEV'S political career. His power at the top of the Soviet pyramid seemed unshakable. He had gained sufficient authority to remove Stalin's body from the Red Square mausoleum and change the name of Stalingrad to Volgograd. In April, the Soviet Union sent the world's first astronaut, Yurii Gagarin, into outer space. The Soviets were ahead of the Americans in the space race, and now no one doubted that Soviet missiles could threaten them on earth as well. There were problems with fulfilling immediate economic plans, and droughts were affecting agriculture, but overall economic growth was proceeding at a healthy pace of at least 5 percent per year, and the long-term future looked bright.

Khrushchev used the occasion of the Twenty-Second Party Congress, convened in October, to announce an ambitious program for the transformation of Soviet society. He and his aides had been working on it for several years. There was a stunning promise in its concluding sentence: "The party triumphantly proclaims that the present generation of Soviet people will live under communism!" Khrushchev promised the country and the world that in twenty years, the Soviet government would complete the creation of the material and technical basis for communism and build the foundations of a communist society. According to Marxist dogma, national differences would disappear under communism. In 1929, Stalin had rejected demands for the immediate merger of nationalities, noting that differences between nations were supposed to continue under socialism. But now, with socialism running its course and communism around the corner, there was no reason to maintain distinctions between Soviet nationalities—if anything, their merger should be accelerated.

The new party program fully reflected that new thinking even as it gave assurances about the free development and even flourishing of nations in the USSR. Khrushchev declared from the podium of the party congress: "A new historical community of peoples of various nationalities with common characteristics—the Soviet people—has taken shape in the USSR. They have a common socialist Motherland—the USSR, a common economic base—the socialist economy, a common social class structure, a common worldview—Marxism-Leninism, a common purpose—the building of communism, and many common characteristics in their spiritual outlook and psychology." The concept of a Soviet people was not novel per se—Nikolai Bukharin had championed it in the 1930s, and Stalin himself had often used the term—but now it was expected to supersede nations in a few decades, reducing them to mere nationalities.

Khrushchev had moved away from Stalin's view of the nation as defined mainly by a common language, culture, and territory. State, economy, class, and ideology were the main markers of the new Soviet political nation. Although the party program pledged to defend and develop the languages of the peoples of the USSR, in fact there was no alternative to building the new Soviet people on the foundations of the Russian language and culture. The program reflected that fact by pointing not to the future but to the existing situation: "The process now taking place of voluntary acquisition of the Russian language along with the native language has a positive significance, as it promotes the mutual exchange of experience and the access of every nation and nationality to the cultural achievements of all the other peoples of the USSR and to world culture. The Russian language has in fact become the common language of international exchange and cooperation among all the peoples of the USSR."

There was more than just belief in the attainment of communism and ideological fervor in Khrushchev's embrace of the concept of the Soviet people. Some scholars divide his nationality policies into two periods. The first, which preceded his consolidation of power in Moscow in 1957, was marked by the appeasement of republican elites. During this period, the republican elites received greater administrative and economic freedom than they had possessed under Stalin, with the creation of republican ministries and regional economic councils that reduced central control over economic decision-making. In Ukraine, the second Soviet republic, the share of industrial enterprises under republican control increased from 34 to 97 percent. The republics also were given more freedom to establish their own cultural policies. All of this helped Khrushchev secure the support of republican elites in his struggle for power in Moscow. His former clients in Ukraine and the leaders of other republics saw him as their man at the top of the Soviet hierarchy.

The second, sharply different period came after 1957, with Khrushchev firmly in control in Moscow. It brought purges of republican elites in the republics of Central Asia, the Caucasus, and the Baltics as well as new initiatives aimed at the cultural Russification of the borderlands. The Ukrainian and Belarusian elites escaped the purge but not the impact of the cultural Russification policies initiated by Moscow. In 1958, the Union parliament passed a law removing the provision according to which children of non-Russian families were to be educated in their native language, and allowing parents to choose the language of instruction. With most universities teaching in Russian, and highly paid jobs and careers open to Russian speakers only, the law made the rapid Russification of the Soviet educational system all but inevitable.

Particularly hard hit by the new regulations were the Slavic republics, where the language barrier between the local languages and Russian was easy to cross. The situation in Belarus was especially precarious. While Ukraine got its first native party boss in 1953, Belarus had to wait until 1956 for its first Belarusian-speaking party leader, Kiryl Mazuraŭ (Kirill Mazurov). But Mazuraŭ's proficiency in Belarusian gained him no respect in Moscow. In early 1959, when Khrushchev visited Belarus to mark the fortieth anniversary of the proclamation of the Soviet Belarusian republic, Mazuraŭ delivered his address in Belarusian. Khrushchev, who had no problem understanding another East Slavic language after his years in Ukraine, protested. During a visit to the Belarusian State University, he declared: "The sooner we all speak Russian, the more quickly we shall build communism." Decades later, during the years of Soviet rule, when the university sought a professor capable of teaching Belarusian history in Belarusian, there was no suitable candidate.

No Ukrainian leader was reprimanded for delivering his speeches in Ukrainian—they continued to do so into the 1970s—but the lesson was learned. Whereas in 1958, 60 percent of all books published in Ukraine were in Ukrainian, in 1959 only 53 percent were in that language. The figure continued to decline: by 1960, it was 49 percent, and by 1965 it was 41 percent. The decrease in Ukrainian-language titles meant a concomitant increase in Russian-language ones. In Belarus, the decrease of publications in the native language was even more dramatic. Book titles in Belarusian fell from 85 percent in 1950 to 31 percent in 1965.

The rising number of Russian-language publications reflected the Russification of the educational system. In Ukraine, between 1951 and 1956 the percentage of students in Ukrainian-language schools fell from 81 to 65 percent. During the same period, the share of those studying in Russian increased from 18 to 31 percent. Especially worrisome was the status of Ukrainian-language education in the big cities. In 1959, only 23 percent of students in Kyiv were being taught in Ukrainian, while 73 percent were being taught in Russian. As Russification of the educational system gained speed, more and more students in Russian-language schools refused to take Ukrainian or Belarusian even as a subject. By the end of the 1960s in Minsk, 90 percent of students were taking no Belarusian classes at all.

What differentiated the Ukrainian situation from the Belarusian one was the role played in cultural policy by the former Polish territories annexed to the two republics on the basis of the Molotov-Ribbentrop Pact of 1939 and sanctioned by the Western powers at Yalta in 1945. The Ukrainians in Galicia, Volhynia, and, to a lesser degree, in formerly Romanian Bukovyna and Czechoslovakian Transcarpathia had a highly developed national identity that retarded the pace of Russification there and in other parts of the republic. The integration of the Ukrainian west required major cultural concessions long after the war.

In Belarus, urban dwellers in the western part of the country often manifested even less attachment to the Belarusian language, culture, and history than their counterparts in the east. After all, the east had undergone a brief period of cultural Belarusization in the 1920s, while there had been nothing similar in the Polish-ruled west. In 1959, 23 percent of Belarusians in the cities of western Belarus claimed Russian as their native tongue, as opposed to 4 percent of Ukrainian city dwellers residing in western Ukraine. By 1970, the share of Belarusians claiming Russian as their native tongue in the same localities had increased to 26 percent, while the similar category of Ukrainians had decreased to 3 percent—a consequence of migration to the cities by Ukrainian villagers who refused to give up their language.

A major ideological shift occurred in the Soviet Union with the ouster of Nikita Khrushchev in October 1964 by a group of his former protégés led by Leonid Brezhnev. It was a palace coup carried out by conservative elements in the party and state leadership who believed that Khrushchev's reforms were threatening the stability of the regime. The new rulers put an end to a number of Khrushchev's initiatives, including his decentralization of power and his ideological obsession with communism. Brezhnev announced that Soviet society had developed socialism and would have to be satisfied with that for a while. No new dates for the arrival of communism were announced. But while the new leadership removed the promise that the "current generation of Soviet people would live under communism" from the party program, it did not discard the program itself or its commitment to the idea of one Soviet nation.

By the early 1970s, Brezhnev had made the concept of the Soviet nation the centerpiece of his nationality policy. Official propaganda launched a campaign promoting the Soviet way of life, while the new edition of the *Great Soviet Encyclopedia* included a new definition of the Soviet people. That definition dropped the reference to communism as a common goal helping to create one political nation but left references to Marxist-Leninist ideology and the Russian language intact. It added the category of common citizenship: "The Soviet people have one set of supreme organs of state power and state administration in the USSR, and the same all-Union citizenship has been established for all Soviet people," stated the *Encyclopedia*. "The common language of international communication in the USSR is the Russian language."

Cultural Russification was now official policy. The marginalization of non-Russian languages and their elimination from the educational system began in 1970, when a decree was issued ordering that all graduate theses be written in Russian and approved in Moscow. In 1979, the authorities organized an all-Union conference in Tashkent on ways to improve Russian-language instruction; beginning in 1983, bonuses were paid to teachers of Russian in schools with non-Russian-language instruction. Cultural Russification was being intensified, as the future of the Soviet nation-building project depended on its success.

LEONID BREZHNEV AND HIS IDEALOGUES INHERITED FROM NIKITA Khrushchev and his aides a conflicting legacy in the realm of Soviet nation-building. Khrushchev's de-Stalinization campaign, which resulted in a political, ideological, and cultural "Thaw," brought to the fore a generation of activists who believed in the possibility not of building communism, but of reforming socialism in order to make its politics and culture more pluralistic. That entailed the idea of the flourishing of nations and their cultures as opposed to their merging. It was during the Thaw that readers became acquainted with the writings of Aleksandr Solzhenitsyn, the future spiritual leader of Russian opposition to the regime.

The preservation of historical monuments, including religious ones, and ecological concerns found their way into the works of Russian authors, who often focused on the plight of the Russian village devastated by collectivization. They became known as representatives of a new genre of writing called "village prose." Similar concerns were raised by writers in other republics, including Ukraine and Belarus. All of them were driven by loyalty not to the Soviet land or nation but to their republic's nation and identity. While the party was building one Soviet nation on the basis of the Russian language and culture, the writers organized themselves on the basis of national languages and defined their concerns in ethno-cultural terms.

In Russia, the cultural revival triggered by the Khrushchev Thaw produced two political and cultural camps among writers and artists. The first group, closely associated with the literary journal *Molodaia gvardiia* (The Young Guard), was characterized by a conservative and antiliberal brand of Russian nationalism. Its members decried the fate of the Russian village and culture but also praised the idea of a powerful state and promoted thinly veiled anti-Semitism. Russian liberals, for their part, rallied around their own journals, the most prominent of which was *Novyi mir* (The New World): while publishing "village prose," it maintained an antinationalist stance. The clash of different visions for the development of the Russian culture and nation came to the fore in the late 1960s, with Russian conservatives using their journals to accuse their opponents of promoting the Americanization of Russian culture. Liberals responded with attacks on their opponents for their manifestations of

Russian nationalism, their desire to preserve the conservative traditions of imperial Russia, and their attempts to isolate Russian culture from the rest of the world.

A series of articles published in *Novyi mir* in 1969 attacking the Russian nationalism of *Molodaia gvardiia* forced the party leadership to intervene in the conflict. In the course of 1970, the party bosses dismissed the editors in chief of both journals from their positions. While the removal of the editor of *Molodaia gvardiia* signaled a victory for Aleksandr Yakovlev, the interim head of the party propaganda apparatus, his triumph was short-lived. After he published an article in 1972 attacking manifestations of Russian nationalism in literary and cultural life, Yakovlev was dismissed from his high position in the party's Central Committee and sent to Canada as Soviet ambassador. A decade later, he would be discovered there by a rising star of Soviet politics, Mikhail Gorbachev, who brought him back to Moscow in the mid-1980s. Yakovlev would become one of the architects of Gorbachev's reforms.

In the mid-1970s, however, the party leadership preferred to sacrifice Yakovlev in order to make peace with the rising nationalist trend in the Russian intelligentsia, and, more important, to co-opt the rebels and keep that trend under party control. Those who would not be cowed into submission, such as Aleksandr Solzhenitsyn, the unofficial leader of the Russian nationalist intelligentsia, were sent out of the country (Solzhenitsyn was expelled in 1974). Others—such as the new editor of *Molodaia gvardiia*, Anatolii Ivanov, one of the leading authors of "village prose"—had to accommodate their cultural program to the guidelines imposed on them by the party leadership.

The party would continue its support for the Russification of Soviet political and cultural life, sponsoring multimillion-copy press runs of works by Ivanov and other Russian nationalist writers and supporting their cultural initiatives. One such initiative was the celebration of the six-hundredth anniversary of the Battle of the Kulikovo Field in 1980. Although that battle had ended in defeat for the Mongols, aggressors from the East, it was turned on its head in the Soviet media to inspire anti-Western sentiment in Russian society. The Russification of the borderlands and anti-Westernism were two ideological elements that kept Soviet apparatchiks and Russian nationalist writers together throughout the 1970s and 1980s.

While making peace with moderate Russian nationalism, Moscow strongly attacked non-Russian nationalism in the republics, particularly in Ukraine, where the 1960s had witnessed a revival of national-communist ideas, according to which Russification under the guise of internationalism was a betrayal of Leninist policy, and Ukraine could be both culturally Ukrainian and Soviet without contradiction. Leading figures of the 1920s, including Mykola Skrypnyk, who had committed suicide in 1933 after being accused of nationalist deviations, were rehabilitated in the late 1950s and early 1960s. Major literary and cultural figures of the earlier era, including the poet Pavlo Tychyna and the filmmaker Oleksandr Dovzhenko, became active again, providing inspiration, support, and political cover for a new generation of writers and artists, the *shestydesiatnyky* (generation of the sixties). These included the poets Ivan Drach, Lina Kostenko, and Vasyl Stus, who was later arrested and sent to the Gulag, where he died. This generation of cultural activists emphasized the flourishing, not the merging, of the Soviet nations. Scholars began submitting their analyses of historiographic trends and the current cultural situation to party officials. Their memoranda, which can be characterized to some degree as policy papers, challenged the Russocentric approach to history as represented by the 1954 *Theses on the Reunification of Ukraine and Russia* and protested the Russification of Ukrainian education, culture, and politics as a violation of Leninist nationality policy.

The Ukrainian national revival came to an end in May 1972 with the dismissal of the strong-willed first secretary of the Communist Party of Ukraine, Petro Shelest, who had run the republic for almost a decade. He had not only tolerated but also supported the development of Ukrainian culture and a distinct Ukrainian identity. A national communist by conviction, Shelest had secured a large degree of autonomy, if not independence, from Moscow by supporting Leonid Brezhnev in his struggle against numerous opponents in the Moscow Politburo. Brezhnev paid him back by giving him a free hand in economic and cultural matters. But once Brezhnev marginalized his main rival in the Politburo, the former head of the KGB, Aleksandr Shelepin, Shelest's days were numbered.

Like the Ukrainian party leaders of the 1920s whom Stalin had no longer needed after eliminating his opponents, Shelest became expendable. In both cases, what followed the removal of Ukrainian party leaders was an attack on the revival of Ukrainian culture that had taken place on their watch. After being transferred to Moscow and appointed to the politically insignificant position of deputy head of the Soviet government, Shelest was accused of idealizing Ukrainian Cossackdom and other nationalist deviations. Meanwhile, the KGB was arresting nationally minded intellectuals and purging Ukrainian institutions. Under the party leadership of the Brezhnev loyalist Volodymyr Shcherbytsky, Ukraine was turned into an exemplary Soviet republic. With dissidents confined to the Gulag, there was nothing to stop the triumphal march of Soviet nation-building, which in Ukraine meant the reincarnation in socialist guise of the imperial model of the big Russian nation.

The party official who seemingly needed no instruction in conducting a nationality policy appropriate to Brezhnev's USSR was the leader of Belarus, Petr Masheraŭ (Masherov). Masheraŭ ran the republic for fifteen long years, from 1965 until his death in a car accident in 1980. The rapid economic development of Soviet Belarus, a former backwater of Poland and imperial Russia, on Masheraŭ's watch in the 1960s and 1970s made loyalty to the Soviet regime a basic component of the new Belarusian identity. Masheraŭ was reportedly supported by the Soviet premier, Aleksei Kosygin, and on bad terms with Leonid Brezhnev and his group. But unlike Shelest, Masheraŭ survived in office until his unexpected death. While defending the republic's economic interests, he never embraced the revival of the Belarusian language and culture as a cause. Unlike Shelest, Masheraŭ never spoke in public in the titular language of the republic; nor did he show an interest in the premodern history of his country. A partisan fighter during World War II—he received the highest Soviet award, Hero of the Soviet Union, in 1944, at the age of twenty-six—Masheraŭ was interested in only one kind of history, that of the Great Patriotic War.

Masheraŭ built monuments to heroes and victims of the war, turning the history of partisan resistance to the Nazis into a founding myth of the Soviet Belarusian nation. Unlike the Ukrainians, who looked with pride to the times of Kyivan Rus' and the Cossack Hetmanate, the Belarusians lacked a founding myth of their own and readily accepted the all-Soviet mythology of the Great Patriotic War. Masheraŭ had few problems with the local intelligentsia. One of its most talented representatives, the writer Vasil Bykaŭ, dedicated most of his writing to the experience of World

War II—Masheraŭ's own principal interest and a theme that was used to create a close bond between Belarusian and Soviet identity. While Russia and Ukraine produced nationalist dissidents en masse, Belarus remained loyal and grateful to the regime.

BY THE EARLY 1980S, THE TIME WHEN KHRUSHCHEV HAD PROMised the dawning of communism, it was nowhere in sight. But one of its elements, the formation of a single political nation called the Soviet people, had been making real progress. Nowhere was that clearer than in the expansion of the lingua franca of that nation, the Russian language, formally designated as the language of interethnic communication in the USSR. In 1970, 76 percent of the Soviet population claimed proficiency in Russian. Between 1970 and 1989, the number of non-Russians claiming a good working knowledge of Russian increased from 42 million to 69 million. It was a major success, largely achieved in the East Slavic republics of the Union.

The increase in the number of Russian-speakers was unevenly distributed throughout the USSR. Close to 75 million of the 290 million Soviet citizens did not claim proficiency in Russian, and almost all of them lived outside the East Slavic core of the Union. The central authorities were particularly concerned about Central Asia and the Caucasus, where insufficient working knowledge of Russian hindered the effective integration of recruits into the Soviet army, which was then fighting in Afghanistan. Non-Russians in those regions continued to live within their own ethnic groups, with exogamous marriage the exception rather than the rule. Only the Eastern Slavs and highly urbanized Jews freely intermarried. Most of the non-Russians who claimed fluency in Russian to census takers were Ukrainians, Belarusians, and Jews. Out of 65 million Soviet citizens who claimed proficiency in Russian in 1989, 55 million were Ukrainians and Belarusians.

In the course of the 1970s and 1980s, Russification gathered speed in the East Slavic republics of the Soviet Union. This led not only to a dramatic increase in the use of Russian at work and in educational institutions in the large urban centers (with the notable exception of western Ukraine), but also to a decline of national consciousness among Ukrainians and

Belarusians as measured by identification with a mother tongue rather than Russian for census purposes. The number of ethnic Ukrainians who gave Russian as their mother tongue increased from 6 percent in 1959 to 10 percent in 1979 and 16 percent in 1989. Even more dramatic was the decline in national consciousness in Belarus, where the number of Belarusians giving Russian as their mother tongue increased during the same period from 7 to 16 and, finally, 20 percent. Thus, every fifth Belarusian considered himself Russian, no matter what the nationality recorded on his or her passport.

While the prospect of forging one Soviet nation out of Slavs and non-Slavs was clearly in trouble, the formation of a big Russian nation out of the Eastern Slavs was just as clearly under way. There appeared to be no barrier to the realization of the old dream of the imperial nation-builders—the formation of an all-Russian nation. The only thing their successors needed to complete the project was time, but by the late 1980s they had run out of it.

VI

THE NEW RUSSIA

18

RED FLAG DOWN

THREE SOVIET LEADERS DIED IN THE COURSE OF AS MANY years. Leonid Brezhnev, who ruled the country for eighteen years, passed away in November 1982; his successor, the former head of the KGB, Yurii Andropov, succumbed to illness in February 1984; and Andropov's successor, Konstantin Chernenko, followed suit in March 1985. The old Soviet Union had long run out of new ideas. By the mid-1980s, it had also run out of leaders committed to maintaining old ideological, economic, and social models.

The new Soviet leader, the fifty-four-year-old Mikhail Gorbachev, was eager to try new things. The immediate and most obvious challenge before him was the sorry state of the Soviet economy, which was in free fall. Income growth, which had averaged about 14 percent per year in the 1930s, had slowed to about 10 percent in the 1950s, and dropped to approximately 5 percent in the first half of the 1980s. Those were official figures. The CIA estimated the rate of Soviet income growth between 1980 and 1985 at close to 2 percent, while post-Soviet calculations yielded an even lower figure. Meanwhile, the Soviet population was growing at a much faster rate, breaking the 180 million mark in the early 1950s and reaching 280 million in the mid-1980s. Shortages not only of consumer goods but also of food supplies had become part of everyday life by the time Gorbachev assumed office in March 1985. Something had to be done quickly to fix the economy.

Another set of problems facing the new leader had to do with the loss of legitimacy by the ruling party and its elite. The communists ruled the country not only by means of terror and coercion but also with the promise of a brighter future. That future was called the attainment of communism, which in the popular mind meant an abundance of food and consumer goods. Khrushchev had promised the advent of that paradise in the early 1980s. With no communism in sight and the economy in decline, faith in the coming paradise and its prophets hit bottom. In promising a communist future, the authorities had contrasted the achievements of the socialist economy with those of its capitalist counterpart in the West, claiming that Soviet socialism was destined to outperform capitalism in the interest of the toiling masses. That promise was never fulfilled. If the contrast was still plausible in the 1950s and 1960s—the Soviet gross national product (GDP) more than tripled between 1950 and 1965, while that of the United States only doubled—by the 1970s the Soviet economy was no longer competitive. In 1970, it was about 60 percent as large as the US economy; after that, it declined steadily, and by 1989 it was less than half the size of the American economy.

The late 1970s and early 1980s saw the rise of Cold War rivalry between the two superpowers. By that time, the Soviet Union was bogged down in Afghanistan, where it sent its troops in 1979 to support what promised to be a socialist revolution and stop the advance of the West, while the United States had begun its recovery from the psychological shock of Vietnam and the energy crisis of the 1970s, becoming more aggressive in its rhetoric and actions abroad. Under Ronald Reagan, who moved into the White House in January 1981 and stayed in office for two terms, the United States challenged Soviet behavior not only in Afghanistan but also in Poland. Workers' strikes in that country gave birth to the free trade union Solidarity, which contested Polish communist rule and Soviet political control. Reagan revived the arms race, threatening the Soviet Union with the Strategic

Defense Initiative, a program that came to be known as Star Wars and proposed the weaponizing of outer space. The defensive antimissile system that was to be constructed under the Star Wars plan had the potential to change the world balance of power by making the Soviet missile threat to the United States largely obsolete. Although the technical complexity of the proposal made it a pipe dream, Reagan believed in it, as did the Soviets, who knew that they lacked the resources to match American investment in the next round of the arms race.

Gorbachev had to act quickly to deal with the crises of the economy and political legitimacy at home and the economic, ideological, and military competition abroad, now all but lost by the USSR. On the international scene, he attempted to ease tensions by negotiating and signing a number of arms-reduction treaties with the United States that were supposed to free funds for domestic reform and ensure Western assistance to the struggling Soviet economy. Gorbachev also tried to reduce the economic burden on the USSR and improve its image abroad by withdrawing Soviet troops from Afghanistan, which he did in 1988, and allowing the East European satellites of the Soviet Union to decide their own form of government. That decision resulted in the overthrow of their communist regimes in a sequence of largely peaceful revolutions in the summer and fall of 1989, effectively ending Cold War rivalry in Central and Eastern Europe.

But the greatest changes took place within the Soviet Union, where Gorbachev introduced the policy of *perestroika*, or radical restructuring of Soviet society. He began his offensive against the old system on two fronts, introducing elements of private property and the market in Soviet economic space and opening political space for debate. For Gorbachev and his liberal advisers, the two fronts were interrelated, and victory on one was impossible without victory on the other. As the party's old guard resisted economic change, Gorbachev used political reform to soften up or crush his opponents. The key component of perestroika was the notion of *glasnost*, or openness—a series of measures that lifted restrictions on political debate and made party officials vulnerable to criticism by the media and citizens at large.

The change in the Soviet system of government came in 1989 with the first relatively free elections in the USSR since the Revolution of 1917. In the spring of that year, Soviet citizens elected their representatives to a new legislative body, the Congress of People's Deputies. In the following year, Gorbachev used the Congress to make constitutional changes that ended the Communist Party's monopoly of power and created the post of president of the USSR, which became the highest office in the land, superior to that of general secretary of the party. Gorbachev, elected by the Congress as the first president of the USSR, maintained his post of general secretary but used it to maneuver the party out of power. Party officials were allowed to keep their power in the regions only if they were elected to the local parliaments or soviets. The move not only ended the party's political monopoly but also undermined the power of the center. Local officials would henceforth depend on their electorates more than on their superiors in Moscow.

As the former party bosses and leaders of the new democratic institutions born out of the turmoil of perestroika started listening to their electorates, the Soviet Union began to crumble. Electors in every Union republic, from Estonia to Russia to Uzbekistan, and the autonomous republics within them, wanted a say in running their homelands. All of a sudden, people everywhere began to feel that their polities were being mistreated by the government in Moscow. History, language, culture, and, ultimately, nationalism became effective tools of political mobilization, setting the republics onto different cultural, economic, and political trajectories. The introduction of free elections transformed Soviet society, putting the structure and even the integrity of the multiethnic USSR into question. The change was more dramatic than Gorbachev had bargained for, leading in a few years not only to the collapse of the communist regime but also to the disintegration of the Soviet Union.

FEW SOVIET REPUBLICS PLAYED A MORE IMPORTANT ROLE IN dissolving the Soviet Union than the Russian Federation, and no Soviet nationality later felt more betrayed by the collapse of the Soviet polity than the Russians. In the 1930s, Stalin used to call the Russians the most Soviet nation. In the decades after the war, they definitely assumed that status. In fact, they became something more, turning into the core of the Soviet people that the party wanted to form. They were more than ready to integrate others into that core. By the 1970s, only a small minority of Russians, between 2 and 8 percent, insisted on endogamous marriage. To be sure, most of those who told pollsters that they were willing to marry outside their ethnic group expected marriage to entail the linguistic and cultural Russification of the non-Russian spouse, not the other way around. Brezhnev's policy of promoting the concept of the Soviet people along with the Russian language was bearing fruit. (As late as 1998, seven years after the fall of the Soviet Union, 52 percent of Russian citizens polled showed close affinity to the notion of a Soviet people.)

But the 1970s also brought resistance to Brezhnev's policy in the non-Russian republics. In 1978, when Moscow tried to change the Georgian constitution to remove the reference to Georgian as the official language of the republic, students went into the streets of Tbilisi to protest. Moscow retreated. If the Georgians had a reference to the official status of their language in their basic law, other republics tried to gain similar status for their languages, whether or not it was enshrined in their constitutions. Russians and Russian-speakers in those republics who refused or showed reluctance to learn the local language felt discriminated against.

The situation was reminiscent of the 1920s, when the indigenization policy was implemented as a concession to the non-Russians. But the Russians, whose primacy in the Soviet Union had been unquestioned in the 1920s, were now on the defensive, obliged either to adulterate their Russian identity with the concept of the Soviet people or to start treating the non-Russians as equals rather than underlings. Russian nationalists, feeling under siege in what they considered their own state, began to express dissatisfaction. As the regime turned the Russians into the "most Soviet nation," they had had to give up many elements of their traditional, prerevolutionary identity, which included naïve monarchism and religion. Russian populists of the prerevolutionary era had considered those elements to have been based in and maintained by the village. The recovery and preservation of non-Soviet Russian identity was a cause championed by Aleksandr Solzhenitsyn and a score of Russian authors who wrote "village prose," and whose publications were discussed in the previous chapters.

The Russian nation that was to be defended against the communist regime's Sovietization and the rise of cultural assertiveness in the borderlands was deeply rooted in the prerevolutionary past. The new crop of

Russian nationalist thinkers often defined it in the spirit of Russian imperial nationhood, not limited to ethnic Russians but encompassing Ukrainians and Belarusians as well. Given the spread of the Russian language
in Ukraine and Belarus and the ability of Eastern Slavs to communicate
in Russian irrespective of their native language, this linguistic and cultural model of Russianness resembled the imperial ideal of a big Russian
nation. It found support both in the Russian cultural establishment and
among dissidents.

In officially sanctioned texts, references to the population of Kyivan Rus'
as Russians, or old Russians, were commonplace, while Ukrainian and Belarusian territories were often referred to in historical terms as southern and
western Russian lands. The lack of particular terms in the Russian language
to distinguish between Russians and the Rus'—or Ruthenian—people
eased such reversions to imperial discourse. Many underground texts, such
as Vladimir Osipov's journal *Veche* (referring to a popular assembly of
medieval times), published in the early 1970s in print runs of fifty to one
hundred copies, openly propagated their authors' beliefs in the essential
unity of the Eastern Slavs, whom they simply called Russians.

But the model of a pan-Russian nation, whether of Soviet or prerevolutionary imperial vintage, encountered tough sledding among the intellectual elites of the second-largest East Slavic nation, Ukraine. In Russia,
the dissident movement of the 1970s was divided between liberals, represented by academician Andrei Sakharov, the father of the Soviet hydrogen
bomb turned political dissident, and nationalists, represented by the writer
Aleksandr Solzhenitsyn, a former Gulag prisoner who had made a name for
himself during the Khrushchev Thaw. But in Ukraine the dissidents managed to stay together, combining liberalism and nationalism.

That trend defined the ideological and cultural program of the
Ukrainian Helsinki Group—a human rights monitoring organization inspired by the Helsinki Accords of 1975, which obliged the Soviet Union
to abide by international norms in the sphere of human rights. The group
was formed against the will of the authorities in the fall of 1976, soon
after the creation of a similar group in Moscow. While the members of
the group did not put forward Ukrainian independence as their immediate political goal, they argued for Ukrainian cultural and political equality
with Russia. For members of the Ukrainian Helsinki Group, Moscow was

not just the capital of the Soviet Union but also the embodiment of Russia, and struggle against the USSR was a struggle against Russian dominance. A programmatic document of the group adopted in February 1977 made this clear: "We profoundly respect the culture, spirituality, and ideals of the Russian people, but why should Moscow make decisions for us at international forums (like those in Helsinki and Belgrade) on various problems, commitments, and the like?! Why should Ukraine's cultural, creative, scientific, agricultural, and international problems be defined and planned in the capital of a neighboring (even allied) state?"

Russian nationalists realized that Ukraine was a problem for them. In his *Gulag Archipelago*, the key *samizdat* (self-published and secretly distributed without official authorization) text of the era, Aleksandr Solzhenitsyn lamented the failure of earlier attempts to fuse Russians and Ukrainians without giving up hope that they would stay together. He wrote: "In the Kyivan period we constituted a single people, but since then it has been torn apart, and for centuries our lives, habits, and languages went in different directions." He blamed communism, especially that of the 1930s and 1940s, for the rupture that had caused Ukrainians to strive for independence from Russia. But whatever their differences, Solzhenitsyn, the son of a Russian father and a Ukrainian mother, wanted them to stay together. He wrote:

It will be extraordinarily painful with Ukraine. But one has to be aware of the intensity of their general attitude at present. If the question has not been resolved over the centuries, then it is up to us to show prudence. We are obliged to leave the solution to them—federalists or separatists, whoever comes out on top. It would be foolish and cruel not to yield. And the greater our mildness, forbearance, and sagacity now, the greater the hope of restoring unity in the future. Let them live and try it out for themselves. It will soon become apparent to them that not all problems are to be solved by separation.

THE SCENARIO ENVISIONED BY SOLZHENITSYN IN THE 1960S suddenly became reality in the late 1980s with the proclamation of Gorbachev's perestroika. Solzhenitsyn was able to predict the future because he knew the attitudes of Ukrainian political activists, some of whom he had met in the Gulag. By the late 1980s, the political prisoners, including members of the Ukrainian Helsinki Group, had been released. They were free to engage in political activity and propose solutions to economic, political, and nationality problems to a politically awakened population. Although the first Union republic to declare sovereignty—the supremacy of republican laws over those of the Union—in the fall of 1988 was Estonia, in the East Slavic core of the Union the first to do so in the summer of 1990, amazingly, was not Ukraine or Belarus but the "most Soviet" nation of the USSR, Russia itself. What led the Russians to do so?

The answer should be sought first and foremost in the cracks that emerged in the traditional equation of Russian with Soviet identity as the Russian intellectual elite dissociated itself from the failing project of Soviet communism, refusing to take responsibility for its past, present, or future actions. With the Soviet economy faltering and the party losing legitimacy, the non-Russian nationalities revolted against Moscow, the center of that system, and, by extension, against the Russians, the agents and administrators, if not the owners, of the empire. But the Russians refused to take the blame for the abuses of the Soviet system. Russian writers of the "village prose" school had long considered their own republic, not the non-Russian republics of the Union, to be the main victim of the communist regime. Like everyone else, they could now openly assert their claims against the regime and engage in a victimization contest with their accusers.

"The ill-considered collectivization of the 30s inflicted great losses not only on the peasantry but also on the whole Russian people," asserted the Russian "village prose" writer Vasilii Belov, who ran for a seat in the Soviet parliament in 1989. "According to my information," he continued, "Russians now constitute less than half the country's [population]." In 1989, ethnic Russians accounted for 145 million of the 286 million Soviet citizens. Their share of the Soviet population was indeed in decline—a rapidly modernizing nation could not compete in terms of birth rate with traditionally Islamic Central Asian republics. In Tadzhikistan, for example, the population almost doubled between 1970 and 1989, attaining a total of 4.2 million. The low Russian birth rate was regarded not as a characteristic of modernity and an outcome of urbanization but as a dire warning—indeed, a Russian tragedy.

While the Russian intellectual response to the challenges of the crumbling empire was formulated in Moscow, the popular mobilization of Russians and their Russian-speaking allies began in the imperial provinces. If Moscow intellectuals such as Belov represented a sovereign nation in the making, their counterparts in the republics mobilized Russians and Russian-speakers as agents, representatives, and defenders of the Soviet Empire in the non-Russian provinces. In that regard, they relied for support not on Russian political leaders, but on the all-Union leadership, which was trying to keep the Soviet Union alive by mobilizing Russian nationalism in the peripheries.

In the course of 1989, after declaring the sovereign status of their republics, the Balts (Estonians, Latvians, and Lithuanians) went into the streets en masse to protest Moscow's planned changes to the Soviet constitution. Those changes would have allowed the center to override republican legislation with all-Union laws and unilaterally decide the issue of secession from the Union. In an overwhelming rejection of Soviet sovereignty over their republics, the activists of the Baltic national movements, called national fronts, organized a Baltic Way in August 1989—a human chain linking their capitals, Tallinn, Riga, and Vilnius. The demonstration was organized on the fiftieth anniversary of the Molotov-Ribbentrop Pact, which had led to the Soviet occupation of the Baltic states in World War II.

With the support of local communist party committees, which had everything to lose from the Baltic revolt, Moscow struck back, mobilizing ethnic Russians and Russian-speakers in support of the Union. Feeling threatened by the revival of local languages and cultures, the Russian-speaking population of the region generally supported the International Front in Latvia and the International Movement in Estonia, Moscow-backed political organizations whose task it was to counteract the popular fronts created by the titular nationalities.

Estonia and Latvia were more vulnerable to pressure from the center than Lithuania. Latvia, with a population of 2.6 million, was in the most precarious position: Latvians constituted only 52 percent of the population, followed by Russians with 36 percent, Ukrainians with 4.5 percent, and Belarusians with 3.5 percent. In Estonia, Russians, Ukrainians, and Belarusians made up 35 percent of the population. Most of the Russian and East Slavic inhabitants of the Baltic republics were recent migrants working in industrial enterprises established and run by Moscow after

World War II. If the popular fronts were pushing for the sovereignty and eventual independence of the Baltic republics, the international fronts were pushing back.

In Russia, the first wave of political mobilization came with semi-free elections to the Soviet super-parliament in the spring of 1989 and continued through the elections to the Russian parliament in 1990. Like the dissident movement of the previous decade, this one had two main ideological poles—liberalism and nationalism. The proponents of the latter were conservative in their economic and social agenda, stressing the wrongs done to the Russians by the communist regime, while at the same time demonstrating loyalty to communism and solidarity with movements of the International Front type in the Baltics.

The merger of communism and nationalism in Russia received its institutional embodiment in the creation of the Communist Party of the Russian Federation—a process long opposed and disrupted by Gorbachev, who feared that a separate Russian party would spell the end of Soviet communist unity, and thus of the Union as such. Maintaining the Communist Party of the Soviet Union as a de facto Russian party had been a consistent policy since the times of Lenin, who wanted a union of republics but was quite content with Russian dominance over the party. But the Russian communists now demanded a party of their own so as to be on a par with the communists of Ukraine, Belarus, and other republics. They finally got their way in the summer of 1990. The Russian conservatives were now on a collision course with the Union.

Another aspect of Russian mobilization came into existence not in opposition to the non-Russians but in alliance with them. The leaders of the Russian liberal intelligentsia shared their vision of democratic transformation of their societies with the leaders of the popular fronts and national movements in the Baltics, Ukraine, and some other Soviet republics. In the summer of 1989, they joined forces in the Interregional Group of Deputies at the first semi-democratically elected Soviet super-parliament, the Congress of People's Deputies. The Interregional Group found support in Moscow, Leningrad, and other large industrial cities of Russia and the Soviet Union. The democratically minded deputies all rebelled against the Communist Party's monopoly of power, but their ability to define a positive political agenda was limited, with members from the non-Russian republics putting their ethnonational demands first. Gorbachev and the center, for their part, found support among conservative deputies from the non-Russian republics, especially those of Central Asia.

Democratic Russia, a coalition of liberal deputies of the Interregional Group, contested the Russian parliamentary elections of March 1990 and won 190 seats, or roughly one-fifth of the total. This made the Russian liberals switch the focus of their activities from the all-Union to the Russian parliament. In May 1989, they were able to elect their leader, the fifty-eight-year-old Boris Yeltsin, a former Moscow party boss who had parted ways with Gorbachev over the pace of democratic reforms, to the all-important post of chairman. A party official by background, a maverick by nature, and an autocrat by inclination, Yeltsin embraced the program of the democratic transformation of society. The Russian reformers then decided to press ahead with democratic and market reforms by using their power in the Russian parliament. In June 1990, with two-thirds of the deputies in favor, a resolution was adopted on the sovereignty of the Russian Federation, officially still titled the Russian Soviet Federative Socialist Republic.

The idea appealed to liberals and conservatives alike. Yeltsin told the deputies: "For Russia today, the center is both a cruel exploiter and a miserly benefactor, as well as a favorite with no concern for the future. We must put an end to the injustice of these relations." Yeltsin gave voice to the emerging liberal Russian nationalism movement. The object of its loyalty was not the idea of a "small" ethnically based Russian nation, or of the big Russian nation of imperial times, but a nation to be formed out of the inhabitants of the Russian Federation. Although the Russian Federation was overwhelmingly Russian (82 percent) in ethnic composition, it included numerous autonomous republics and regions that had not become Union republics for a variety of demographic, geographic, or historical reasons. With the sole exception of the former East Prussia, now constituted as the Kaliningrad region of Russia, the Russian Federation was territorially continuous from Leningrad (soon to be renamed St. Petersburg) on the Baltic Sea to Vladivostok on the Pacific. It was a good candidate to form a nation, but in 1990 there were numerous odds against that proposition.

In June 1991, Yeltsin won the race for the newly created office of president of the Russian Federation in competition with candidates supported by his onetime protector and then nemesis, the president of the Soviet Union, Mikhail Gorbachev. Unlike Gorbachev, who had been installed in office in the spring of 1990 by the Soviet parliament, Yeltsin was elected by the voters of Russia. As he took office, Yeltsin pledged his loyalty to the citizens of the Russian Federation, promising to defend the interests of the republic and its peoples.

Yeltsin and his liberal supporters regarded the Russian Federation as an engine for the political and economic reform of the entire Union. But the nationalists who voted for Yeltsin saw Russian institutions as an instrument for enhancing Russian identity, providing support for Russian culture, and cutting financial support for the Union republics, which they claimed were bleeding the Russian economy white. But no one advocated the dissolution of the Soviet Union. In the summer of 1991, by creating an alliance with leaders of other republics, Yeltsin forced the embattled Gorbachev to agree to a reform of the Union that would benefit Russia and other well-to-do republics. The new Union treaty negotiated by Gorbachev, Yeltsin, and Nursultan Nazarbayev of Kazakhstan in July 1991 gave the preponderance of economic and political power to the republican leaders, first and foremost to the leader of Russia.

The deal was supposed to become the law of the land on August 20, 1991. But on the previous day, some of Gorbachev's aides, including the heads of the KGB, police, and army, who knew they would lose their positions in the reshuffle, launched a coup to preserve the Soviet Union in its old form. Gorbachev, who refused to go along, was detained by the plotters at his summer resort in the Crimea. Yeltsin and his advisers were taken by surprise as they relaxed in a government compound outside Moscow after a trip to Kazakhstan. They decided to fight back and mobilize the support of the Muscovites. Naina Yeltsin tried to convince her husband not to go: "Listen, there are tanks there: What is the point of your going? The tanks won't let you through." But Yeltsin would not budge. "I had to say something," he remembered later, "so I gave her my best shot: 'We have a little Russian flag on our car. They won't stop us when they see that.'" Yeltsin made it unharmed to the White House, the Russian parliament building in downtown Moscow. The flag was not an issue for the KGB special forces— they simply had not been ordered to arrest Yeltsin. But the flag was an issue for Yeltsin's supporters.

A few hours after reaching Moscow, when Yeltsin first addressed the people from atop a tank in front of the White House, his aides placed a Russian banner behind him. The plotters' banner was the red flag of the Soviet Union. Those who resisted the plot hoisted the white, blue, and red flag of the Russian republic of 1917. Russia rebelled against its communist empire and won. The coup was defeated a few days later, and the old tricolor flag became the official banner of Russian democracy and the Russian Federation. Yeltsin's victory launched Russia on a new trajectory that would prove to be quite different from the one followed by the other Soviet republics.

The attempted coup of August 1991 threatened to undo all the achievements of Yeltsin and his supporters, but they fought back successfully, raising the Russian banner against that of the Union. Yeltsin's victory changed the situation fundamentally, but at the outset it almost killed the project of a new Russian nation. With Gorbachev betrayed by his own aides and shocked by the ordeal, Yeltsin felt himself to be the real power in Moscow. He began the takeover of the Union center by appointing his own prime minister as head of the all-Union government and forcing Gorbachev to revoke his own decrees appointing new heads of the military, police, and security service: people suggested by Yeltsin were appointed instead. Yeltsin and his supporters no longer needed the vehicle of the Russian Federation and its institutions to promote their liberal reforms, which had been envisioned from the very beginning as an all-Union project.

Yegor Gaidar, an ambitious young economist and future author of Russia's economic reforms who, like many liberally minded Muscovites, had rallied around Yeltsin during the coup, wanted the Russian president to save the Union, now as an extension of Russia. "As it seemed to me at the time, that political basis was the only remaining possibility of saving the USSR," wrote Gaidar later. "Gorbachev immediately resigns his post, transferring it to Yeltsin as president of the Union's largest republic. Yeltsin legitimately subordinates the Union structures to himself and, wielding the then unconditional authority of leader of all the people of Russia, brings about the merger of the two centers of power, whose mutual struggle had been one of the basic causes of the collapse."

It was too late. The other republics, most notably Ukraine, were already going their own ways, fearing a Russian takeover of the center as much as or even more than they feared a successful coup. On August 24, 1991, Ukraine, the Union's second-largest republic, declared its independence from the Union, which, first and foremost, under the circumstances, meant independence from Russia. By the end of the week, almost every Union republic that had not declared its independence earlier followed suit. Yeltsin panicked, threatening Ukraine and Kazakhstan with revision of borders and Russian claims on parts of their territory if they insisted on independence. He also dispatched a high-profile delegation to Ukraine to talk sense to the leaders of the de jure independent state. The attempt failed. Yeltsin's ally Anatolii Sobchak, a member of the delegation, was booed by protesters in Kyiv when he tried to talk about Russo-Ukrainian unity. The Ukrainians did not want to stay with Russia. They did not want the Union. They wanted out.

With the collapse of his plan for a Russian takeover of the Union, Yegor Gaidar no longer thought of saving the USSR. His task became that of saving Russia from an all-Union political and economic collapse by means of rapid economic reform. The Russian Federation once again became the focal point of the Russian liberals' reformist aspirations. By declaring the start of radical economic reform in November 1991 without waiting for the other republics, Yeltsin and Gaidar effectively broke up the previously integral Soviet economic space. As Russia went its own economic way, however, it still hoped to maintain some form of economic union. Yeltsin and his advisers recognized the independence of their former allies in the Baltics against the wishes of the Russians and Russian-speakers in that part of the former Soviet Union. As for the rest of the USSR, they tried to put together a confederation in which Russia would play the key role without picking up the all-Union bill. This proved a fiasco. Gorbachev would not settle for the role of a figurehead in a confederation actually run by Yeltsin, and the other republics, led by Ukraine, had already opted for independence.

On December 1, 1991, more than 90 percent of Ukrainian voters supported independence for their republic. Yeltsin bowed to the inevitable. A week later, at the Belavezha hunting lodge on the Belarusian-Polish border, he met with President Leonid Kravchuk of Ukraine and the speaker of the Belarusian parliament, Stanislaŭ Shushkevich, to dissolve the Gorbachev-led Soviet Union and create what he believed would be the Yeltsin-led Commonwealth of Independent States. The Soviet Union was gone, dissolved by the leaders of the three republics that had once constituted a big Russian nation.

No one could have predicted such an outcome even a few months earlier. Without ever declaring—or, indeed, dreaming of—its own independence, Russia became de facto independent. When the Union music stopped playing, Yeltsin and the Russian liberals were stuck with the skeleton of the Russian Federation, which had yet to be filled with economic, institutional, and ideological content. Then there was the new Commonwealth, which many in Russia regarded as a continuation of the USSR. Caught between the Russian Federation and the Commonwealth, the Russian political and intellectual elites had to figure out their new political identity.

In the 1990s, Yeltsin called on his advisers more than once to come up with a new definition of Russian statehood. It was no easy task. At his first inauguration ceremony as president of the Russian Federation in June 1991, Yeltsin had addressed himself to the citizens of the Russian Federation and promised to defend the rights of its peoples. This was the formula that Gorbachev had used in his inauguration address the previous year: Yeltsin simply replaced the USSR with the Russian Federation. There was no mention of the Russian people or nation in his brief speech. At his second inauguration in 1996, Yeltsin promised faithfully to serve "the people" without elaboration. Not only Yeltsin but also other Russian officials were reluctant to define the population of Russia in national terms. In official pronouncements, the inhabitants of the Russian Federation were rarely referred to as the Russian nation.

Few people were more disappointed by the word "nation" falling into disuse than Valerii Tishkov, the director of the Institute of Ethnology and Anthropology at the Soviet and then Russian Academy of Sciences. In the early 1990s, Tishkov was at the forefront of promoting the idea of a Russian civic nation consisting of citizens of the Russian Federation of all ethnic and cultural groups. He called that nation *rossiiskaia*, the adjectival form of the name of the Russian Empire, as opposed to *russkaia*, the term usually used to define the Russian ethnic group, either in its narrow Great Russian incarnation or its extended East Slavic one.

Tishkov had begun to develop his ideas in 1989, the year of the first semi-free elections to the Soviet super-parliament and the creation of a liberal opposition to the regime in the form of the Interregional Group of Deputies. He saw the *rossiiskaia* nation as united across ethnic and cultural lines by a commitment to common values and institutions, with symbols originating not in the imperial Russian past but in the liberal revolution. Tishkov protested against the use of the term "multiethnic Russian people," considering it not only self-contradictory but also politically dangerous, because it denied political legitimacy to the Russian civic nation, investing it instead in ethnic groups that could claim statehood for themselves as discrete nationalities, as happened in the disintegration of the USSR. Some of Tishkov's views, such as his opposition to ethnically based federalism and his preference for territorial autonomy, harked back to the ideas of the Constitutional Democrats of 1917.

The Russian leadership actively promoted the civic model of Russian identity for the first two years of Russia's independent existence. Tishkov was appointed minister of nationalities, and his ideas served as the basis for the Russian law on citizenship adopted by the parliament in November 1991. In the text of the law, citizens were called *rossiiane* rather than *russkie*, and the acquisition of Russian citizenship did not depend on the ethnicity or language of the applicant. But Tishkov's model of the new Russian identity soon began to encounter serious difficulties. The idea of defining Russian nationhood by civic loyalty to the new political institutions became tarnished in the fall of 1993, when Yeltsin used force to crush nationalist and communist opposition to his rule. On Yeltsin's orders, Russian tanks bombarded the headquarters of the conservative opposition to the president, the Russian White House, which Yeltsin and his supporters had heroically defended against the attempted coup two years earlier, and which Tishkov proposed to treat as one of the symbols of the new Russia. Having defeated his opponents, Yeltsin rewrote the constitution, taking powers away from parliament and moving them to the presidential office. Not only was the symbol of the new Russia compromised, but the idea of democracy had suffered a blow from which it would not fully recover.

There were problems outside of Moscow as well. The ethnically based autonomous units of the Russian Federation were not eager to buy into the *rossiiskaia* civic nation. The Chechens wanted outright independence, while Tatarstan and other autonomous republics wanted more rights. In December 1994, Yeltsin ordered Russian troops into Chechnia to end its de facto independence from Moscow. The Chechens fought back, forcing the Russian army to sue for peace in August 1996. Russian troops left the rebellious republic, postponing a decision on its status until the year 2001. If there were enclaves within the Russian Federation that did not want to be part of it, there were also those outside of Russia that wanted to join it. These included the self-proclaimed Transnistrian republic on the territory of Moldova, as well as Abkhazia and South Ossetia in Georgia.

The Russians faced a problem familiar to other ruling imperial nations: the implosion of the empire had produced a class of disenfranchised citizens who considered themselves either members of the formerly dominant nation or sufficiently compromised by cooperation with it to feel unsafe in the former colonial possessions. Russian citizenship laws allowed such individuals to claim Russian or dual citizenship without moving to Russia, which strengthened the cultural and legal components of Russian identity at the expense of its territorial component. According to some estimates, close to 30 million ethnic Russians and Russian-speakers who associated themselves first and foremost with Russia remained outside the borders of the Russian Federation. Many, especially in the Baltics and in the Russian enclave of the Crimea in Ukraine, were eager to claim Russian citizenship, but that desire brought them into conflict with local citizenship laws, which did not welcome dual citizenship and sometimes even prohibited it. The legal conflict turned the post-Soviet space into a powder keg ready to explode.

19

THE RUSSIAN WORLD

ON DECEMBER 31, 1999, THE AILING BORIS YELTSIN USED THE occasion of his New Year's address to make an unexpected announcement. He was stepping down as president of the Russian Federation. His address and the broadcast that followed left no doubt whom Yeltsin wanted to see as his successor—the forty-eight-year-old prime minister, Vladimir Putin, addressed the public immediately after Yeltsin's unexpected announcement.

Putin was a largely unknown quantity at the time of his first New Year's address to the nation. He had entered high-level politics only a few months earlier, in the summer of 1999, when Yeltsin had unexpectedly appointed him as his prime minister. In that post he had been responsible for the country's economic performance and day-to-day administration. Putin—who had been head of the Federal Security Service, post-Soviet Russia's secret police, in 1998–1999, and earlier in his career had been an intelligence officer—had been chosen by Yeltsin's inner circle as a counterweight to Yeltsin's critics, who were planning to unseat him as president in the coming elections. One of the contenders had been the mayor of Moscow, Yurii Luzhkov, who had actively played the Russian nationalist card against Yeltsin, presenting himself as a defender of Russians abroad during his numerous and highly publicized visits to Sevastopol, whose port was home to the Russian navy base in Ukraine. There he had funded a number of social and cultural projects and opened a branch of Moscow University.

Another contender, Yevgenii Primakov, who had become Yeltsin's prime minister in the wake of Russia's financial meltdown of 1998, had championed the reintegration of the post-Soviet space under Russian political control. During his tenure as head of Russia's foreign intelligence and as foreign minister in 1996–1998, Primakov had turned Russian foreign policy away from its Western orientation, seeing the enhancement of Russia's status in the "near abroad"—the term used in Moscow to describe the former Soviet republics—as a requisite for its revival as a great power. Putin was fast-tracked for the presidency by a group of oligarchs close to Yeltsin who were friendly toward the West. Like one of Putin's backers, the multibillionaire Boris Berezovsky, they considered the Primakov reintegration project too costly and contrary to Russia's economic interests.

Yeltsin had helped create the Russian state, but the nation was still in the making. It was now up to his successors to define its character and establish its borders. In his surprising announcement on the eve of the year 2000, Yeltsin addressed himself to the *rossiiane*, members of the civic Russian nation. His heir, Vladimir Putin, who spoke after him, addressed the audience not only as *rossiiane* but also as compatriots. Whether the reference was to citizens of the Russian Federation or included Russians and Russian-speakers abroad was not entirely clear.

THE PROTECTION OF THE RIGHTS OF RUSSIANS AND RUSSIAN-speakers in the Baltics and the countries making up the Commonwealth of Independent States had become a hot-button issue in Russian politics and a rallying cry uniting the nationalist and conservative opposition to Yeltsin and his government in the fall of 1993. After ordering his army to storm the Russian parliament building, which had been occupied by opposition leaders, and imprisoning them, Yeltsin used his 1994 New Year's address to indicate that his government had not abandoned the Russians in the "near abroad." He referred to them as compatriots—people sharing a common fatherland. But what to do about them was not clear. Yeltsin's government originally pushed for dual citizenship for the "compatriots," but it encountered resistance from newly independent countries, including Ukraine, that did not recognize dual citizenship.

Yeltsin's advisers then came up with the idea of Commonwealth citizenship—an idea proposed back in 1991 but shot down by Ukraine. This model was supposed to combine civic citizenship in the Russian Federation with ethnic and culture-based citizenship for Russians and Russian-speakers abroad. Once again, there were no takers among the post-Soviet republics, but Belarus showed readiness to move in a similar direction. In 1997, Yeltsin and the new Belarusian leader, Aliaksandr Lukashenka, signed a charter on the formation of a state union that envisioned common Russian-Belarusian citizenship. By that time, Belarus had reinstated a Soviet-style flag and Russian as its official language. If not entirely stopping its nationalization project, Belarus was scaling it down. The Russo-Belarusian Union presented one more challenge to the civic model of Russian nationality.

The Russo-Belarusian Union never became a full-fledged reality with common government institutions or citizenship. Negotiations on the union were used to satisfy the post-Soviet nostalgia of a significant part of the Russian public still suffering from the shock of losing a larger state and identity. The Russian leadership refused to act on the idea of East Slavic unity to create one "Russian" state. Like Gorbachev's union of 1991, it would have been incomplete without Ukraine. And Ukraine was moving in a direction opposite to the one chosen by the new government in Minsk. In 1997, when Yeltsin and Lukashenka signed their union charter, the Ukrainians negotiated a cooperation agreement with Russia that put a legal end to their lengthy political divorce. The agreement gave Russia a lease on a navy base in Sevastopol in exchange for recognition of the Ukrainian borders and refusal to support pro-Russian separatists in the Crimea. The notion of an East Slavic union now lacked one of its main pillars.

The Russian leadership stuck to the idea of forming a new Russian nation on the political foundations of the Russian Federation. It was a difficult but not impossible task. In 1997, a poll in which respondents could express more than one preference found that 85 percent of citizens of the

Russian Federation associated themselves with the ethnic Russian nation, 71 percent favored the civic nation, and 54 percent were still closely attached to the notion of the Soviet people. In 1996, Yeltsin appealed to Russian intellectuals, asking for their help in finding a new Russian national idea. Most responded with suggestions for basing the new Russian identity on statehood. But there were other ideas as well. The revived Russian Communist Party, whose popularity presented the main political challenge to the regime, tried to keep the all-Union identity of the Russians alive, reinforced by an attachment to East Slavic unity and the Orthodox religion. Radical nationalists advocated a racially pure Russian nation that would not include non-Russian citizens. More moderate nationalists pushed for an East Slavic identity based on culture that would include ethnic Russians and Russian-speakers outside the borders of the Russian Federation.

In 1996, the historical demographer Vladimir Kabuzan published a study of settlements of Russians and Russian-speakers outside Russia. In his new mental map of Russia as an ethnic and cultural entity, he included eastern and southern Ukraine, northern Kazakhstan, and parts of Estonia and Latvia. Kabuzan wanted those territories either to be attached to Russia or established as autonomous units with special linguistic and cultural rights in their respective states. He also suggested the possible separation from Russia of areas populated largely by non-Russians. It was an argument in favor not only of letting Chechnia go but also of forming a Russian nation-state on cultural grounds. The cultural model of Russian nationhood informed the imagination of many opponents of the government, although few of them were prepared to give up any part of the territory of the Russian Federation. They wanted the extension, if not of its territory, then of its extraterritorial powers to cover people whom they considered members of their nation.

VLADIMIR PUTIN WON THE PRESIDENTIAL ELECTION IN MARCH 2000 and took office in May of that year. His opponents had planned for a June election and were caught off guard by Yeltsin's sudden resignation, which advanced the date. The first sign that the election had resulted in the victory of Yeltsin's man but not necessarily of his ideas came in December 2000, when Putin agreed to adopt the music, and, in part, the lyrics, of the old Soviet national anthem as the new symbol of Russia. During Yeltsin's tenure, the music of a patriotic song by the nineteenth-century composer Mikhail Glinka had been adopted as the national anthem, but Russian political and cultural elites could not agree on the lyrics—a sign of problems in searching for Russia's new identity. Against Yeltsin's publicly expressed wishes, Putin resolved the conundrum by going back to the Soviet anthem.

The eighty-six-year-old poet Sergei Mikhalkov, who had coauthored the lyrics in 1943, was asked to draft a new text. This was his third exercise of that kind, the first two having been performed under Khrushchev in 1956 and then under Brezhnev in 1977. Where there had earlier been mentions of Lenin and Stalin, then of Lenin, the party, and communism, there was now a reference to God. The opening reference to the unshakable union of peoples forged by Russia was replaced with praise of "Russia, our sacred state." What remained unchanged in all the versions of Mikhalkov's anthem was praise of the fatherland. The words "Glory to you, our free fatherland," which had figured in the original version of 1943, were reprised in 2000. The immediately following reference to the "Firm bulwark of the friendship of peoples" was replaced with "Union of fraternal peoples for the ages." The Union was thus restored to favor, along with the brotherhood of its constituent peoples. Whether the reference was to the old Union or the peoples of the Russian Federation was for future generations to decide.

When it came to Russian policy in the post-Soviet space, Putin inherited from Primakov the vision of Russia as a great power whose status depended on its integrationist project. Putin believed in Russia's right to dominate the post-Soviet space as its sphere of influence, but he hoped to achieve such dominance by political and economic means, without turning Russian ethnicity, language, and culture in the "near abroad" into instruments of Russian dominance there. In 1999, the parliament discussed different versions of a law on compatriots abroad extensively, and eventually adopted one of them, but it had minimal impact on foreign policy. Putin's policy on Ukraine and Belarus, which did not differ substantially from his policies on other post-Soviet countries, was formulated in a document titled *Strategy for Russia: Agenda for the President—2000* prepared by Russia's Council for Foreign and Defense Policy.

Its authors, who included both Yeltsin-era Westernizers and Primakov-type realists, argued that relations with the "near abroad" should benefit

Russia economically. Political and economic reintegration of the post-Soviet space should proceed from below, with Russian businesses acquiring partial ownership of the transportation infrastructure and local enterprises in the former Soviet republics in exchange for debts accumulated by those countries for Russian natural gas. This strategy could be implemented on various levels—bilateral, subregional, including only selected post-Soviet republics or most if not all of them. The key was to win the loyalty of the new governments and local elites. Thinking of Russia as a divided nation or mobilizing ethnic Russians or Russian-speakers abroad to achieve integrationist goals seemed counterproductive.

This new orientation became known in the first years of the millennium as Russia's liberal empire project. Its ideological formulation came in 2003 in an article by Anatolii Chubais, one of the architects of Yeltsin's privatization reform and then head of the Russian electrical-power monopoly. Chubais argued that Russia's mission in the new century included the construction of a strong democratic state and the foundations of a capitalist economy, but he did not stop there. "It is my profound conviction that Russia's ideology for the whole foreseeable historical future should be liberal imperialism, and Russia's mission should be the construction of a liberal empire," wrote Chubais. As of 2003, he was busy building that empire from below. A few months earlier, his company had acquired control of an atomic electrical-power station in Armenia, and it was eyeing assets in Ukraine, where it helped finance the construction of two nuclear reactors.

Anatolii Chubais was the mouthpiece of the oligarchs—the new group of large business owners who had emerged out of the economic and political chaos of the post-Soviet transformation by being both more innovative and more ruthless than their competitors. They had gained control of the most lucrative parts of the Russian economy, including the oil and gas industry, in the rigged privatization of the mid-1990s. In return for preference from President Yeltsin, they had used their economic and media resources to help reelect him to office in 1996. They had also helped bring Putin to power in 2000. In return, they demanded Putin's loyalty, which Putin was most reluctant to offer. He would spend a good part of his first term in office trying to establish his monopoly of power and free himself of Yeltsin's entourage. Two of the leading oligarchs, Boris Berezovsky and Vladimir

Gusinsky, had taken refuge in the West. A third, Mikhail Khodorkovsky, was arrested. The rest did not challenge Putin's rule.

Putin won his second term as president in March 2004, taking 71 percent of the popular vote. Things could not have looked better for him. Revived by limited economic reforms in the first years of Putin's presidency and by high oil prices, the Russian economy was doing well, growing at a rate of 7 percent per annum. The economic reintegration of the post-Soviet space was also moving forward. It had begun on the regional level in 2000 with the creation of the Eurasian Economic Community, which was joined by Belarus, Kazakhstan, and a number of Central Asian states. Ukraine refused to join, but in 2003 it signed an agreement with Russia, Belarus, and Kazakhstan on the formation of a Single Economic Space. The agreement was ratified by the Ukrainian parliament in 2004.

The key factor for the success of the liberal empire project was political stability in the region and continuity of policy in the neighboring states. Authoritarian regimes were preferred, since their leaders could be counted on to follow a steady policy course as they became dependent on Russia in economic or security terms. Democracies were hard to handle, because the outcomes of elections could be unpredictable. With the Baltic states joining the North Atlantic Treaty Organization (NATO) and the European Union, Belarus getting an authoritarian ruler in the person of Aliaksandr Lukashenka, and Kazakhstan and the other Central Asian republics solidly in the authoritarian camp, the unpredictability of electoral politics in Ukraine and Georgia presented a major challenge to Russian foreign policy. Especially important was Ukraine, the crown jewel in any integrationist project in the post-Soviet space. In 2004, as in 1991, Ukraine remained the largest post-Soviet country after Russia.

Presidential elections were coming up in Ukraine in the fall of 2004. At stake was the future of post-Soviet integration and ownership of the largest network of pipelines linking Russian and Turkmen natural-gas fields with markets in Eastern and Central Europe. The outgoing Ukrainian president, Leonid Kuchma, had allegedly agreed to sell Russia a stake in his country's gas-pipeline system in order to deal with Ukraine's ballooning debt to Russia's gas monopolist, Gazprom. Kuchma introduced his prime minister, Viktor Yanukovych, to Putin as his successor, who would continue his policies. In the fall of 2004, Putin went to Kyiv in hopes of boosting Yanukovych's ratings in his campaign against the pro-reform and pro-Western candidate Viktor Yushchenko. In the weeks leading up to the election, Yushchenko was poisoned with a strain of dioxin that could not be produced in Ukraine but could be produced in Russia. He survived the attempt, but it hampered his further participation in the campaign.

Fed up with Kuchma's corrupt regime, Ukrainian voters had no intention of electing his and Putin's protégé to the presidential office. According to the exit polls, Yushchenko won the race. But that was not the result announced by the head of the government-controlled electoral commission, who told shocked Ukrainians that victory had gone to Yanukovych. The Orange Revolution, named after Yushchenko's campaign colors, followed immediately. At its forefront were students organized in civic youth groups such as Pora! (It's Time!).

Hundreds of thousands of people went into the streets of Kyiv and did not leave until the government agreed to repeat the presidential election, this time under the strict control of international observers, most of them from the West. As expected, Yushchenko won, and Putin congratulated him on his victory, but few doubted that the Russian president perceived the outcome of the Orange Revolution as a major defeat. Putin blamed the West and its pro-democracy campaign in the post-Soviet space for what had happened in Ukraine. He felt threatened not only by the coming to power of a pro-Western candidate in the largest post-Soviet republic, but also by the example that the democratic movement in Ukraine had now set for opponents of his increasingly authoritarian regime in Russia. The exiled Russian oligarch Boris Berezovsky made no secret of his support for the Orange Revolution.

The Russian elites had to regroup both at home and abroad. At home, Putin mimicked the tactics of the leaders of the Orange Revolution by creating numerous youth organizations that would support his regime. The most notorious of them was Nashi (Ours), established in 2005 by a former official of the Russian presidential administration, Vasilii Yakemenko. For years, Nashi would harass real or imagined opponents of the regime. Abroad, Putin did everything in his power to stop what he regarded as Western encroachment on his turf, the post-Soviet space. Of special concern to the Kremlin was Georgia, where the Rose Revolution of 2003 brought to power the pro-Western Mikheil Saakashvili, and Ukraine, where Yushchenko had no illusions about Moscow's role in supporting his opponent and its plans for his country. He launched a pro-Western policy, trying to get Ukraine admitted to the European Union and NATO.

Putin went on record opposing Ukraine's membership in NATO but declared that Russia had nothing against its membership in the European Union. Nevertheless, he used gas supplies to Ukraine—and, through Ukraine, to member nations of the European Union—as a political weapon to bring Ukraine under his economic control and complicate its relations with the West. Earlier, Russia had forced Turkmenistan, the second-largest producer of gas in the post-Soviet space, to sell its gas through Russia, and had used debts accumulated by other post-Soviet countries for gas supplies from and through Russia to exert political pressure.

In March 2005, soon after Yushchenko's inauguration, Russia raised the price of natural gas supplied to Ukraine. On January 1, 2006, it cut all supplies to Ukraine, claiming that Ukraine was stealing natural gas destined for Europe. Supplies were restored four days later, but a new crisis erupted in January 2009, when supplies were cut off again for twenty days for Ukraine, and thirteen days for European customers, leaving southeastern Europe without natural gas in the depths of winter. Depicting Ukraine as an unreliable partner not only for Russia but also for the European Union, Moscow imposed conditions that eventually made Ukraine pay more than Germany for its natural gas.

EU membership was not in the cards for Ukraine. Gas-supply problems aside, the European Union was still dealing with challenges caused by its large expansion of membership in 2004. But NATO membership, which was backed by the United States, could have become a reality for Ukraine. In April 2008, Putin traveled to the NATO summit in Bucharest to campaign against NATO membership for Ukraine and Georgia. He gained the support of Germany and France, and the decision was postponed until December 2008. Putin decided not to wait. After returning from the NATO summit, he established official relations with the self-proclaimed governments of Abkhazia and South Ossetia, the two regions of Georgia that had rebelled against rule from Tbilisi in 1991 and enjoyed Russian support ever since.

In August 2008, the Russian army invaded Georgia, first taking over the separatist enclave of South Ossetia and then marching on the Georgian capital. Thanks only to Western diplomatic intervention, the fighting was stopped, and Russian troops withdrew from Georgia proper. But the two separatist republics remained under Russian control and were formally recognized by Russia as independent states. For the first time in Russia's post-Soviet history, its army had been used beyond its borders to subdue a rebellious neighbor. The liberal empire was gone: the military empire was about to rise.

In December 2008, NATO refused to provide either Georgia or Ukraine with a NATO membership plan. Barack Obama, who assumed the American presidency in January 2009, pressed the "reset" button in relations with Russia. Putin had lost to pro-democratic forces in Ukraine and Georgia in a contest of ballots but won in a war of bullets, stopping the rebellious republics from evading his embrace in the ranks of NATO. One of the lessons that he learned from the outcome of the Orange Revolution was that dealing with governments in the post-Soviet states was not enough for success. One also had to engage with people on the street. The old ideas of his political opponents about a divided Russian nation and its compatriots abroad came in very handy in that regard and were soon put to use in Putin's new foreign policy.

"Have you read Denikin's diaries?" Vladimir Putin once asked Larisa Kaftan, a Ukrainian-born reporter of Russia's leading newspaper, *Komsomol'skaia pravda* (Komsomol Truth). The reference was to the memoirs of a leader of the Russian White Army of the revolutionary era, General Anton Denikin. "No," responded Kaftan, who promised to read the work. "Be sure to read them," suggested Putin, and then added: "Denikin discusses Great and Little Russia, Ukraine. He writes that no one may meddle in relations between us; that has always been the business of Russia itself." Kaftan did as promised and later published an article that included a selection of quotations from Denikin's writings. The one Putin had in mind read as follows: "No Russia, reactionary or democratic, republican or authoritarian, will ever allow Ukraine to be torn away. The foolish, baseless, and externally aggravated quarrel between Muscovite Rus' and Kyivan Rus' is our internal quarrel, of no concern to anyone else, and it will be decided by ourselves."

The conversation took place on May 24, 2009, when Putin, then prime minister of Russia, was visiting the Donskoi Monastery in Moscow. He laid flowers on the grave of Aleksandr Solzhenitsyn, who had died the previous year, and on the graves of several Russian historical figures and intellectuals who had died in the emigration after 1917 and whose earthly remains had now been reinterred in Russia. Among them was General Denikin. The Orthodox archimandrite Tikhon, who was close to Putin and accompanied him on his visit, explained to the journalists that Putin had personally paid for the tombstones on the graves of Denikin and his wife, as well as on the graves of two émigré intellectuals, the philosopher Ivan Ilin and the writer Ivan Shmelev. Russia was taking back its long-lost children and reconnecting with their ideas.

The Russian president was particularly impressed by the writings of Ivan Ilin, who had emerged during the interwar period as one of the leading ideologues of the White movement. At the start of the Cold War, he had written an article titled "What the Dismemberment of Russia Promises the World," directed against what he considered the Western conspiracy to dismember the Soviet Union. "Russia will not perish as a result of dismemberment," Ilin warned Western governments, "but will begin to repeat the whole course of her history: like a great 'organism,' she will again set about collecting her 'members,' proceeding along the rivers to the seas, to the mountains, to coal, to grain, to oil, to uranium." Putin first cited Ilin in his address to the Russian parliament in 2006, when he laid out his plans for reform of the armed forces.

Putin's interest in the graves of Russian nationalist thinkers and generals developed at a time when he was reconsidering the importance of Russian history and culture in the continuing effort to secure and enhance Russian influence in the post-Soviet space. In June 2007, Putin established a special foundation, the Russian World. Its cofounders were the federal ministries of foreign affairs and education. Putin placed Viacheslav Nikonov, the grandson of Viacheslav Molotov and a historian and political consultant close to the Kremlin, in charge of the foundation as its executive director. The officially declared goal of the foundation was to promote the Russian language and culture abroad.

Putin had first gone on record speaking about the "Russian World" (*Russkii mir*) as a concept in 2001, when he had addressed the First Congress of Compatriots Living Abroad. The Russian World, he said, transcended the borders of the Russian state and ethnicity. Five years later, in December 2006, when he addressed a meeting of Russian artists, writers, and intellectuals in his home town of St. Petersburg, he had more specifics: "The Russian World," said Putin, stressing the linguistic and cultural aspect of his vision, "can and should unite all who cherish the Russian word and Russian culture, wherever they may live, in Russia or beyond its borders." He then exhorted the audience to "use that expression—the Russian World—as often as possible." This was the opening salvo of a long-term ideological and geopolitical campaign that became a key factor in asserting Russian influence abroad.

The term "Russian World" has its origins in the mid-nineteenth century and can be found in the writings of Panteleimon Kulish, who was a member of the Brotherhood of Saints Cyril and Methodius and one of the fathers of the Ukrainophile movement. He used the term to define the population that came out of Kyivan Rus'. With Ukraine more of an intellectual project than a political reality at that point, the term did not threaten the foundations of the Ukrainophile movement per se. But the situation would change. The term would later be used by the Russian Slavophiles, who applied it to the ethnic and cultural community within the borders of the Russian Empire. The Revolution of 1917 made it all but obsolete.

The term was rediscovered in the late 1990s by the Russian political consultant Petr Shchedrovitsky, who was trying to formulate policy for the Russian government toward the "near abroad" in the turmoil of the post-Soviet transformation. Starting in 2007, which the government proclaimed the international year of the Russian language, the concept of the Russian World became an integral part of Russian foreign policy. Its "citizens" were located and supported not only in the post-Soviet space but also in Western countries to which Russians had emigrated after 1991. The promoters of the new concept defined Russian identity not only in ethnic or civic terms but also in terms of culture, and they mobilized support for Russian government policies on the basis of attachment to such figures as Pushkin, Tolstoy, and Dostoevsky.

The concept soon attracted the attention of a key figure in the formulation of Russian national identity in the first post-Soviet years, the former minister of nationality affairs in the Russian Federation, Valerii Tishkov. In one of his publications, Tishkov defined the Russian World as a "trans-state and transcontinental association united by its attachment to a particular state and loyalty to its culture." There was irony in his embrace of a cultural notion of Russian identity after having promoted a civic one in the early 1990s, but Tishkov distinguished between Russia and abroad. Immediately after the collapse of the USSR, he had argued that most ethnic Russians and Russian-speakers outside the Russian Federation would not leave their places of residence or assimilate to the local cultures but would stay where they were, preserving their linguistic and cultural characteristics. "My opinion," he said in retrospect, "was originally voiced in support of the view that Russians did not spend centuries settling the territories of eastern Ukraine, the Crimea, and Northern Kazakhstan in order to narrow the Russian World now by so-called repatriation."

In 2007, Tishkov responded to the new signals coming from the Kremlin by presiding over a number of academic initiatives that considered the status of the Russian language in the post-Soviet space. In the following year he delivered a paper on the preliminary results of work conducted by Russian ethnographers and sociologists. Tishkov saw language as the key marker of membership in the Russian World. He asserted that the Russian language was losing its privileged Soviet-era status in the "near abroad," and that Russia had to take measures to protect that status. Tishkov wanted the Russian language to be given official status equal to that of the local language in the countries of the "near abroad." (In Belarus, where Russian had acquired that status, it maintained its dominance over the local language.)

Tishkov proposed that Russia support demands for such status in Kazakhstan, Ukraine, Latvia, Moldova, and Kyrgyzstan. His other idea was to obtain "personal autonomy," meaning individual linguistic rights, for Russian-speakers, whom he also called compatriots, in their countries of residence. Tishkov also saw the Russian World as a means of achieving Russian foreign-policy objectives. "The Russian World is more than present-day Russia," he argued. "That is how it was, and that is how it should be, and the task of specialists is to help people of Russian culture and language preserve their spiritual origins for themselves and their descendants and, along with that, to strengthen Russian influence and authority."

The Russian government put its resources behind the concept of the Russian World in 2007 by creating the Russian World foundation, whose first mandate was to open Russian World centers abroad with the support of a budget of 1 billion rubles provided by the Russian government. By 2013, there were 90 centers in 41 countries tasked with promoting the Russian language and culture. Among the beneficiaries of foundation grants were Natalia Narochnitskaia's Fund for Historical Perspective, which promotes a Russian nationalist vision of history abroad. Among the foundation's partners is the International Council of Russian Compatriots, created in 2002, which has 140 organizations in 53 countries and has been headed by Vadim Kolesnichenko, a longtime member of the Ukrainian parliament from the city of Sevastopol. Kolesnichenko has personally submitted close to twenty bills to the Ukrainian parliament intended to maintain the dominant position of the Russian language in the Ukrainian economic, social, and cultural spheres, which has not changed since Soviet times.

In 2009, the Russian World as an idea and as an integrationist project acquired a new enthusiast in the person of the newly elected sixty-three-year-old patriarch of the Russian Orthodox Church, Kirill (Gundiaev). He was the main speaker at the third congress of the Russian World foundation, which took place in 2009, the year of his election to the patriarchal throne. Kirill had spent the previous two decades as head of the international department of the Moscow Patriarchate, where he had presided over the church's efforts to stop the disintegration of its structures all over the former Soviet Union and preserve its unity.

The main threat to church unity came from Ukraine, where close to 60 percent of the Moscow Patriarchate's parishes had been located before the Gorbachev era. Kirill was instrumental in stabilizing the church after the loss of thousands of parishes in western Ukraine to the revived Ukrainian Catholic Church in 1989–1990. The rebirth of that church, which had been suppressed by Stalin after World War II but maintained an underground existence, had long encumbered ecumenical dialogue between Moscow and the Vatican, turning an already anti-Western institution—the Russian Orthodox Church—into a bulwark of opposition to the outside world.

The rise of national identities and agendas among the clergy and the Orthodox faithful in the post-Soviet space presented another challenge to the dominance of the Moscow Patriarchate in the region and established the Russian Orthodox Church as a watchdog of all-Russian unity. The

Orthodox Church had never changed its official name or its concept of the Russian nation, which it regarded, as in imperial times, as consisting of the three East Slavic peoples. When it came to the preservation of all-Rus' unity, Ukraine was again the key. In the early 1990s, in his capacity as head of the international department of the church, Kirill had successfully beaten back the efforts of Metropolitan Filaret of Kyiv to create an independent Ukrainian Orthodox Church out of those parishes.

Caught between Moscow and Kyiv, the Ukrainian Orthodox divided, with two-thirds of them recognizing the jurisdiction of Moscow and the rest going their own way. Coupled with the loss of thousands of parishes to the revived Ukrainian Catholic Church, the new split increased already existing anxiety in Moscow about the fate of its heritage in the post-Soviet era. Nevertheless, Kirill managed to keep most of the Ukrainian Orthodox under Moscow's jurisdiction. Moscow lost a significant number of parishes in the Baltics but maintained control over those in Belarus.

At the turn of the twenty-first century, Russia, Ukraine, and Belarus remained the core areas claimed and controlled by the Moscow Patriarchate, just as before the Revolution of 1917. Kirill's new role as a promoter of the Russian World helped put East Slavic unity close to the center of the patriarchate's ideology. The church's contribution to the concept of the Russian World was a rhyming slogan, "Russia, Ukraine, and Belarus / There you have it: holy Rus'." The authorship was ascribed to a Ukrainian cleric who had revived Orthodox religious life in the city of Chernihiv during the German occupation, under which religion had been tolerated to a much greater extent than under the Soviets. Kirill recited the slogan on one of his visits to Kyiv. Although his vision of the Russian World expanded to include Kazakhstan and Moldova, Ukraine remained at the center of his attention. As patriarch, he would often visit Ukraine to celebrate Orthodox holidays and real and imagined ecclesiastical anniversaries.

Vladimir Putin joined Patriarch Kirill on his annual pilgrimage to Kyiv in July 2013, when they came to celebrate the 1,025th anniversary of the baptism of Rus'. It was there that Putin first publicly embraced the idea, previously articulated by the church, that Russians and Ukrainians were one people: "We understand today's realities: we have the Ukrainian people and the Belarusian people and other peoples, and we are respectful of that whole legacy, but at the foundation there lie, unquestionably, our common spiritual values, which make us one people."

In less than two years, the vision of Russians and Ukrainians as one people would lead the Russian president and his army across the Ukrainian border, first into the Crimea and then into eastern Ukraine, creating one of the most acute crises not only in Russo-Ukrainian relations but also in world politics.

20

THE RUSSIAN WAR

On February 23, 2014, widely celebrated in Russia as Defender of the Fatherland Day (the former Red Army Day), television viewers all over the world watched a broadcast of the closing ceremonies of the Sochi Olympics. It was a triumph for Russia in more than one way. The Russians had outdone themselves. Not only had they organized very successful winter games in Sochi, known as the capital of the Russian subtropics, but they had also stunningly improved their medal count, rising from eleventh place at the Vancouver Olympics four years earlier to first place, and doing significantly better than their closest competitors, Norway and Canada.

There was much to celebrate and be proud of, and the ceremonies and performances of Russia's leading choirs, orchestras, and artists manifested that pride to the rest of the world. It began with a children's choir singing the Russian national anthem. Those who did not speak Russian but had visited or watched the Moscow Summer Olympics of 1980 (and the 2014 performance was full of allusions to the Olympic symbols of 1980) could not detect any difference between the Soviet anthem of 1980 and the Russian one of 2014. That was not essential. The message that Vladimir Putin was eager to send to his country and the world was that Russia had returned to great-power status.

The cost of the message, calculated as the Russian state expenditure on the Winter Olympics, was a staggering $52 billion—four times the original budgeted amount and seven times greater than the budget of the Vancouver Olympics in Canada. According to some estimates, half the amount was stolen by government officials and businessmen close to them, and many projects remained unfinished by the time of the Olympics. But Putin, who had personally overseen the construction projects and preparations, was satisfied to have achieved his goal. Like the Soviet Union of 1980, the Russia of 2014 was able to finance and organize a world-class event.

The games generated tremendous goodwill for Russia and its president throughout the world. In the months leading up to the games, Putin had demonstrated his own goodwill by releasing a number of high-profile prisoners of the former Gulag camps. Among them was the business tycoon Mikhail Khodorkovsky, who had spent more than ten years in prison, and the members of the feminist punk-rock band Pussy Riot, who had been jailed the previous year for attempting to perform in Moscow's Cathedral of Christ the Savior. Khodorkovsky had been arrested on charges of tax evasion, and the members of Pussy Riot for hooliganism and inciting religious hatred, but few doubted that their real offense had been that of challenging Putin and his grip on political power.

Many hoped that after the Olympics Putin would build upon the goodwill generated by the games and continue with at least symbolic acts of liberalization. The optimists were wrong. Arrests of opposition leaders, including the anticorruption crusader Aleksei Navalny, who claimed that half the money allocated for the Olympics had been stolen, were resumed. The games had been staged to demonstrate that Russia was strong enough to reenter the international scene not as a partner of the West but on its own terms. What those terms were became clear four days after the Olympics ended, when Russia began its military operation to annex the Crimea—a peninsula transferred from Russia to Ukraine in 1954 and recognized by Russia and the international community since 1991 as an integral part of Ukraine. Putin later admitted that he had personally made the decision to "bring back the Crimea" on the early morning of February 23, the last day of the Sochi Olympics.

The annexation triggered an undeclared Russo-Ukrainian war for southeastern Ukraine, producing the worst crisis in East-West relations since the Cold War. It violated international legal norms and treaties, including the 1994 Budapest memorandum, in which Russia, along with the United States and Britain, had assured Ukraine of the indivisibility of its territory in return for the transfer of its Soviet-era nuclear arsenal (the third largest in the world at the time) to Russia. At the core of the crisis was the question of Russian national identity and relations between Russians and Ukrainians, the two nations that Putin has repeatedly called one people.

WHAT HAPPENED IN THE KREMLIN AND RUSSIA IN THE MONTHS and years leading up to the crisis that can explain Vladimir Putin's agression against Ukraine?

Putin's geostrategic vision of Russia and its role in the post-Soviet space contributed greatly to the origins and conduct of the war. The Russian president wanted Ukraine to join the Eurasian Union, a Russia-led political, economic, and military bloc whose creation he put forward as one of his principal goals in late 2011, when he was preparing to become president of Russia for the third time. This time the situation in Ukraine looked promising. Not only had Putin's old protégé Viktor Yanukovych been elected president in 2010, but the Ukrainian gas debt to Russia had ballooned after Russia stopped supplying gas to Ukraine in January 2009, forcing Prime Minister Yulia Tymoshenko to sign a trade deal with Gazprom that was disadvantageous to Ukraine. The Ukrainian government had refused to follow in the footsteps of Belarus, whose government had agreed, after Russia cut off supplies in 2007, to sell a 50 percent stake in its pipeline infrastructure to Russia (Minsk would lose all control over the pipelines in 2011). Instead, in order to obtain a price deduction for new gas, the government of Viktor Yanukovych extended the Russian lease on the Sevastopol navy base for the next twenty-five years.

The Russian president wanted more: his goal was Ukraine's membership in the Eurasian Union. While in its geostrategic objectives the

Eurasian Union was a successor to Yevgenii Primakov's idea of using the Commonwealth of Independent States to ensure Russia's special role in the "near abroad," its intellectual underpinnings went back to the Eurasianist school of Russian émigrés of the 1920s and 1930s. In post-Soviet Russia it fed off the neo-Eurasianist brand of Russian nationalism developed by Aleksandr Dugin, a political philosopher with strong rightist and even fascist intellectual leanings. Dugin, who was shunned by the political elite of the 1990s, gained the ear of Putin's advisers and, consequently, access to the Russian media in the new millennium. Dugin wanted to build a Eurasian empire on completely new foundations, whereas Putin was trying to reintegrate the old one. Ideology was key for Dugin and secondary for Putin. What was common to their projects, despite their many differences, was the idea of exploiting divisions in Western societies, including those between their liberal cores and far left and far right fringes, in order to position Russia as the beacon of conservative values throughout the world—a country and civilization that would defend traditional European values against their alleged distortion by the decadent liberalism of the postmodern era. That vision of Russia's new role in the world found a close ally in the vision of the Russian World advanced by Orthodox intellectuals.

In Ukraine, Yanukovych had publicly given up on his country's aspirations to join either NATO or the European Union, but the Ukrainian government continued its preparations for signing an association agreement with the EU. Putin's visit to Kyiv in July 2013 and his endorsement of the idea of one Russian nation were part of the strategy to stop that movement. In the following month he added an economic argument to the ideological one, declaring a trade war against some Ukrainian products.

In late November 2013, Yanukovych, pressured by Putin, refused to sign the association agreement with the European Union long promised to his people. This sudden change of course produced mass protests in Kyiv, akin to those that had taken place during the Orange Revolution ten years earlier. After dozens of protesters were killed by police fire on February 20, 2014, parliament rescinded the president's power to use force. As the riot police left the city, Yanukovych and his advisers followed with a fortune in stolen funds—a few weeks earlier Putin had transferred $3 billion to Ukraine as a bribe not to sign the EU agreement. Yanukovych went to the

Crimea and was taken from there to Russia on a Russian naval vessel based in Sevastopol.

With his man in Kyiv forced out of office and a new Ukrainian government professing its commitment to integrating Ukraine into European economic structures, Putin and his advisers decided to partition the country. The plan approved by the Russian president on the last day of the Olympics was put into action in the Crimean capital of Simferopol on February 27, 2014, when a band of heavily armed men with no insignia on their uniforms took control of the Crimean parliament. As the new prime minister of the autonomous republic, they installed a pro-Russian politician who had previously obtained only 4 percent of the popular vote in the Crimea. Backed by Russian military units and mercenaries, the new Crimean government engineered a referendum from which Ukrainian and Western observers were barred.

The results of the referendum that took place on March 16, 2014, were reminiscent of Soviet-era elections: 92 percent of the vote in the Crimea was declared to be in favor of joining Russia. In Sevastopol, 123 percent of the vote was said to be in favor. It was an affront to democracy and common sense. Ethnic Russians constituted a majority on the peninsula, which was overwhelmingly Russian-speaking, but, judging by polls conducted only a month earlier, most of the population preferred to stay in Ukraine. On March 17, 2014, the day after the referendum, the new Crimean authorities declared the peninsula independent of Ukraine. The same day, President Putin signed two documents, one recognizing Crimean independence, the other initiating a treaty between the Russian Federation and the independent state of the Crimea on the annexation of the latter. Contingency plans that included the annexation of the Crimea and the destabilization and possible partition of the rest of Ukraine had been in place at least since the Budapest summit of NATO in 2008, when Putin had told President George W. Bush that Ukraine was not a real country but a conglomerate of regions, and that accession to NATO could produce resistance in eastern and southern Ukraine.

In 2014, however, annexation was triggered not by an expansion of NATO or of the European Union, but by Ukrainian insistence on signing an association agreement with the EU. Putin had clearly been emboldened by his success of 2008, when he had gotten away with the invasion of Georgia and the de facto annexation of part of its territory. The association agreement with the European Union did not come with a promise of EU or NATO membership for Ukraine, but it threatened to derail Putin's plans for the creation of a viable Eurasian Union, which would be incomplete without Ukraine. Hence Putin's resort to drastic measures to stop the Ukrainian drift to the West. Many believed that his actions produced the opposite result, pushing Ukraine toward the West to a degree unthinkable before the Crimean annexation.

MARCH 18, 2014, WAS A COLD AND GLOOMY DAY IN MOSCOW. BUT St. George's Hall in the Large Kremlin Palace, which had been built by Tsar Nicholas I in the mid-nineteenth century, was brightly lit with huge crystal chandeliers and glittering with gold. At the podium the custodians had installed two banners, the tricolor flag of the Russian Federation and the presidential standard decorated with the Russian coat of arms— the double-headed eagle and the image of St. George the Dragon-Slayer defeating the enemies of Russia. The members of the Russian Federation Council (the upper house of the Russian parliament) as well as the deputies of the Russian State Duma (its lower house), government ministers, and representatives of government-controlled civic organizations, were joined by the new leaders of the Crimea, which had recently been occupied by the Russian army.

The members of the Russian political elite and their guests were waiting for the appearance of Vladimir Putin, now in his third term in office and fifteenth year at the helm of the country's power structure—twice as president, twice as prime minister, and now as president once again. They greeted him as he entered, rising to their feet. Putin asked them to take their seats and began his speech. From the Western viewpoint, he had a difficult task ahead of him, that of providing a rationale for the takeover of the Crimea—the first annexation of territory of a sovereign state by a major European power since the end of World War II. Putin did not seem to mind the difficulty of his task. Most of his argument dealt not with legality but with history and culture.

The Russians, he asserted, had been divided against their will by the fall of the Soviet Union. He recalled the Soviet collapse as a time when gross injustice was done to the Russian people: "The big country was gone. It was only when the Crimea ended up as part of a different country that Russia realized that it had not simply been robbed but plundered." He continued:

> I heard residents of the Crimea say that back in 1991 they were handed over like a sack of potatoes. That is hard to disagree with. And what about the Russian state? What about Russia? It humbly accepted the situation. This country was then going through such hard times that, realistically, it was incapable of protecting its interests. But the people could not reconcile themselves to this outrageous historical injustice. All these years, citizens and many public figures came back to this issue, saying that the Crimea is historically Russian land and Sevastopol is a Russian city.

Russia's critics began drawing parallels between Vladimir Putin and Adolf Hitler, noting how both leaders had used the ethnic minority question: Hitler to partition Czechoslovakia and annex Austria in the Anschluss of 1938, Putin to annex the Crimea. The Crimean Anschluss was on everyone's mind. Putin did not avoid historical parallels. Indeed, he said that he counted on Germany understanding his action by drawing a parallel not with the Anschluss but with the unification of East and West Germany in 1989: in both cases, he maintained, partitioned nations were reunited. But his argument about the need to protect ethnic Russians against potential threats harked back to 1938 rather than 1989.

The Russian president claimed that Russian identity was under threat in Ukraine, but he provided no proof of discrimination. He also claimed to be protecting Russians in Ukraine from Western expansion. "With Ukraine, our Western partners have crossed the line, playing the bear and acting irresponsibly and unprofessionally," said Putin. "After all, they were fully aware that there are millions of Russians living in Ukraine and in the Crimea. They must really have lacked political instinct and common sense not to foresee all the consequences of their actions. Russia found itself in a position from which it could not retreat." Thus, Russia had acted to protect Russians beyond its borders against all threats real or imagined, and she was justified in using force and annexing territory if Russians were deemed to be threatened. But it was not only ethnic Russians who needed Russia's protection: it was also Russian-speakers in the "near abroad." "Millions of Russians and Russian-speaking people live in Ukraine and will continue to do so," said Putin. "Russia will always defend their interests using political, diplomatic, and legal means."

In the months leading up to the Russian annexation of the Crimea, Putin repeatedly went on record asserting that Russians and Ukrainians were one and the same people. "We are one people," declared Putin in a TV interview in September 2013.

> And however much nationalists on both sides—there are nationalists both among us and in Ukraine—may be offended by what I have just said, that is the actual fact of the matter. Because we have the same Kyivan baptismal font in the Dnieper; we certainly have common historical roots and common fates; we have a common religion, a common faith; we have a very similar culture, languages, traditions, and mentality. . . . To be sure, we have our own particularities and our own ethnic coloring throughout. By the way, Ukrainian culture, the Ukrainian language, dances, and music—they are wonderful. I, for one, always take delight in that.

Putin's claim that Russians and Ukrainians were one and the same people and his branding of those who believed otherwise as nationalists ran counter to a long Soviet and post-Soviet tradition of treating Russians and Ukrainians as historically and culturally close, but still separate peoples. Putin's statement challenged the foundations not only of Ukrainian national identity but also of modern Russian identity. The affirmation that Russians constituted a distinct people had been the legitimizing foundation of Russia's revolt against the dying Soviet Union in 1991 and of the existence of the Russian Federation ever since.

Putin's thinking on the issue of Russo-Ukrainian unity harks back to the pre–World War I writings of Petr Struve, the Russian Social Democrat turned liberal. "I start with the conviction that there is an all-Russian culture and its organ, the all-Russian language," wrote Struve in 1912. "The term 'Russian,'" he stated in the same article, "is not some kind of abstract 'average' of the three 'terms' (with the prefixes 'great,' 'little,' and 'white') but a living cultural strength, a grand, developing, and growing national force." Struve was not opposed to the development of the Ukrainian language or folk culture, but approved of it only on the local, rural level, where there was no access to or influence on high culture, education, and urban life. In 2014, Putin brought about the reincarnation of Struve's ideas at the highest level of Russian politics.

Following the annexation of the Crimea, Putin's approval numbers went through the roof, from 66 percent in December 2011, as he prepared to return to the president's office for the third time, to 89 percent in June 2015. Government control over the principal media outlets, as well as harassment and silencing of the opposition, were largely responsible for the surge. But there is little doubt that Putin's actions in the Crimea met with the approval of the Russian public. In his speech of March 18, 2014, Putin cited the results of public opinion polls conducted in Russia on the eve of the formal annexation of the Crimea. "Ninety-five percent of the people think that Russia should protect the interests of Russians and members of other ethnic groups living in the Crimea—95 percent of our citizens," asserted Putin. "More than 83 percent think that Russia should do this even if it will complicate our relations with some other countries. A total of 86 percent of our people see the Crimea as still being Russian territory and part of our country's lands."

VLADIMIR PUTIN USED HIS SPEECH ON THE ANNEXATION OF THE Crimea not only to provide historical and ethnocultural justification for his aggression but also to assure Russia, Ukraine, and the world that the Crimea was a special case, and that the Russian Federation would claim no other region of Ukraine. "I want you to hear me, my dear friends," he said, addressing the citizens of the country he had just partitioned. "Do not believe those who want you to fear Russia, shouting that other regions will follow the Crimea. We do not want to divide Ukraine; we do not need that."

In March 2014, Putin believed that he could achieve his goal of keeping Ukraine within the Russian sphere of influence without further annexations of its territory. The shock of losing the Crimea was supposed to win the Ukrainian elites back to Moscow by showing what could happen to other regions of the country as well. Putin's foreign minister, Sergei Lavrov, demanded the federalization of Ukraine, giving veto power to its individual regions over the country's foreign policy. Kyiv refused, and in April 2014 Russian intelligence services began destabilizing the Russian-speaking areas of Ukraine's east and south. An anti-Kyiv propaganda campaign was conducted under the banner of defense of the Russian language and Russian identity against Ukrainian nationalism. The idea of creating a buffer state to be called New Russia, after the name of an imperial province that had once existed in the region, was brought to eastern and southern Ukraine by Russian propagandists. They supplemented references to the Russian imperial past with rhetoric that went back to the Great Patriotic War—the founding historical myth of Putin's regime in Russia. Supporters of the Ukrainian government were portrayed not only as nationalists and agents of the decadent West, but also as fascists.

Fueled by Russian imperial mythology and Soviet nostalgia, the ideological campaign failed to engulf all of the projected New Russia but gained substantial traction in the Donbas region of eastern Ukraine—part of the old Soviet rust belt that bordered on the Russian Federation and had the largest percentage of ethnic Russians anywhere in Ukraine outside the Crimea. Its destabilization became a joint project of the Russian intelligence services and Russian nationalists—an alliance personified by Igor Girkin, *nom de guerre* Strelkov, a retired officer of the Russian intelligence service and an active contributor to Russian nationalist media outlets. Girkin later claimed that it was through his efforts that the conflict in the Donbas had grown violent and turned into a full-blown military confrontation. Indeed, he and his group, who came to the region from the Crimea, were the first to open automatic fire, killing an officer of the Ukrainian security services and provoking a military response from the Ukrainian side.

Girkin and his supporters, who flooded the region in the spring and summer of 2014, brought with them a brand of Russian imperial nationalism that considered not only ethnic Russians but also Russian-speakers of all ethnic backgrounds to be quintessentially Russian. Their views were best formulated by Aleksandr Prokhanov, the editor of the Russian nationalist newspaper *Zavtra* (Tomorrow), which featured Girkin as one of its authors. According to Prokhanov, Russian-speaking citizens of eastern and southern Ukraine were being threatened with genocide and had the right to rebel, while Russia had an obligation to protect them. He saw no future for Russians so defined in a united Ukraine, which could be nothing but an anti-Russian and pro-Western country. The only solution, he maintained, was to partition Ukraine.

These ideas had been brought to Ukraine from Russia in the years leading up to the events of 2014 and had inspired many activists of the "Russian Spring," as Russian nationalists dubbed the insurrection in the Donbas, which was directed and funded from Moscow. Among their exponents was a thirty-year-old historian turned small-time entrepreneur, Pavel Gubarev. As a youth, he had belonged to an ultra-nationalist and, according to some observers, fascist organization called Russian National Unity. In April 2014, at a gathering of a couple of hundred activists, Gubarev was elected "people's governor" of Donetsk, the main city of the Donbas. Neither Gubarev nor Girkin thought of the Donbas as a future independent republic: they envisioned it as part of New Russia, and New Russia in turn as a constituent part of the Russian Federation. Gubarev, in particular, saw the conflict as part of a revolution against the Ukrainian oligarchs, who, like their Russian counterparts, had taken control of the most lucrative sectors of their country's economy, inspiring envy and hatred among the impoverished population of the post Soviet state. In Gubarev's view, the revolt was also part of the larger struggle of the Russian World against the corrupt West. "The Russian church has blessed us for the war that we are waging. It is a war for the Russian World, for New Russia," declared Gubarev in June 2014, addressing members of the Donbas militia at the height of the military conflict in the region.

In the spring of 2014, Russian nationalists, who had often criticized Putin for indecisiveness, threw their support behind him and his policies. Putin, in turn, was glad to make use of their services and sent the most dangerous radicals out of the country, letting them die in the mining towns and on the fields of Ukraine. But the incipient alliance between the government and the radical nationalists under the banners of the Russian World was shaken in the summer of 2014 as the vision of New Russia failed to materialize, and the two self-proclaimed republics of the Donbas region, one centered on the city of Donetsk, the other on the regional center of Luhansk, found themselves on the verge of collapse.

To save the situation, the Russian government increased the flow of mercenaries, volunteers, and arms and ammunition across the Ukrainian border.

It also sent anti-aircraft missile complexes into Ukraine. One of them, called Buk (Beech Tree), and reportedly staffed by Russian servicemen, shot down a Malaysian commercial airplane, flight MH 17, en route from Amsterdam to Kuala Lumpur, killing all 283 passengers, including 80 children and 15 crew members. The Joint Investigation Team, whose members represented Australia, Belgium, Malaysia, the Netherlands, and Ukraine, was able to establish the launch site, type of missile, and route by which the missile complex was brought from Russia to the rebel-held part of Ukraine and returned to the Russian Federation after the plane was shot down.

The covert support provided to the rebels by the Kremlin was insufficient to withstand the pressure of the Ukrainian army. As in the Crimea, a Russian military occupation was required if the "Russian Spring" was to succeed. After some hesitation, the Russian government sent its troops into battle in August and September 2014 to save the rebel enclaves from imminent military defeat. In the first months of 2015, Russian soldiers, allegedly on leave from their units, were again sent into battle to drive Ukrainian forces out of the strategically important railway junction of Debaltseve, which linked key areas of the Donetsk and Luhansk regions. The two rebel republics were saved, but what to do with them was by no means clear. They became a continuing problem not only for Russia's economy and international standing but also for the future of the Russian World project and Russian policy in the "near abroad."

Disillusionment with the Russian World also engulfed the Donetsk and Luhansk republics, which found themselves on the verge of economic collapse and with no prospect of either joining Russia or surviving on their own. In fact, the New Russia project was effectively abandoned by the Kremlin as too costly. True believers, such as Gubarev, were removed from real power in the Donbas, which shifted from Russian nationalists and their local supporters to people who had no clear ideological agenda but were fully loyal to Moscow. Gubarev was lucky to survive an assassination attempt when he tried to challenge a Kremlin appointee as supreme ruler of the republic.

In 2015 alone, three of the most prominent local warlords who had helped raise the revolt the previous year were assassinated for failing to fall into line with the new policy of the Kremlin, which considered the economic burden of maintaining the Donbas too heavy and sought to push the region back into Ukraine as a federal unit with veto power over the country's foreign policy. Gubarev rebranded the old slogan by claiming that the Donbas, to which he referred as New Russia, was a torch that would help bring the rest of Ukraine back to the Russian World. It was a tall order.

The annexation of the Crimea and the war in the Donbas—which had taken almost 10,000 lives by the end of 2016, with at least twice as many wounded, hundreds of thousands left homeless, and millions leaving the conflict zone as refugees—killed any appeal that the Russian World project might have had not only in Ukraine but also in neighboring Belarus. "And if there are any here who consider that the Belarusian land is part of, well, as they say nowadays, 'the Russian World,' and almost of Russia itself, forget it," declared the traditionally pro-Russian president of Belarus, Aliaksandr Lukashenka, in January 2015. "There was no [independent Belarus] previously, but now there is, and that has to be reckoned with. And we will not give our land away to anyone."

The Russian World was now associated not just with Pushkin and the Russian language but with a land grab that had cost thousands of dead and wounded and disrupted millions of lives.

AFTER THE CRIMEAN ANNEXATION AND THE DONBAS DEBACLE, Vladimir Putin continued to speak of Russians and Ukrainians as one and the same people. This rhetoric, however, was rebuked abroad and found less and less support in Russia itself. Between November 2005 and March 2015, the number of Russian citizens who believed that the two peoples were one and the same dropped from 81 to 52 percent. While historically there had been a high level of sympathy between the two peoples, by March 2014, owing to Russian media coverage of the events in Ukraine, most Russians had developed a negative attitude toward Ukrainians.

There was a similar result in Ukraine, where the image of Russia became generally negative by the fall of 2014 as a result of Russian actions in the Crimea and the Donbas. The Donbas conflict also lessened the appetite of average Russians for the use of force abroad. In March 2014, at the peak of the Crimean euphoria, 58 percent were in favor of using force to protect the Russian minorities there, but that share fell to 34 percent one year later. Between 1998 and 2015, the share of Russians who wanted to change the borders of their state by absorbing other territories fell even more precipitously, from 75 percent to 18 percent.

Russia has paid a high price for its invasion of Ukraine in terms of the lives of its citizens who either were sent to eastern Ukraine or volunteered to go there to fight on the side of the rebel republics and never came home. Russia has also spent significant financial and material resources badly needed at home on the war and on support of the flagging Crimean economy, as well as on the devastated separatist republics. Moreover, Moscow has suffered a major blow to its international prestige and has had to deal with the crippling effect of the economic sanctions introduced by the international community since the start of the conflict.

The first wave of sanctions was introduced by the United States on March 17, 2014, the day on which President Putin ordered the preparation of a treaty incorporating the Crimea into the Russian Federation. The sanctions, which originally targeted only individuals in Russia and in the Crimea responsible for the overthrow of the legitimate Ukrainian government and annexation of the peninsula, were extended to include Russian corporations on July 17, 2014, the day on which Malaysian flight MH 17 was shot down. The sanctions were further extended in the days following that incident by a host of countries, including the United States, Canada, Japan, Australia, New Zealand, and members of the European Union. The sanctions have had a profoundly negative effect on the Russian economy, helping to send it into recession: the per-capita GDP fell from $15,553 in 2013 to $9,053 in 2015. Lack of access to international financial markets led to a significant devaluation of the Russian currency and the rise of consumer prices, bringing new hardships to Russian citizens.

There is good reason to regard the Russo-Ukrainian conflict as a milestone not only in Putin's presidency and Russia's relations with the West, but also in the formation of the modern Russian nation. One of the answers it has offered to the eternal Russian question is quite clear: it is not only difficult but impossible to step into the same river twice. The imperial construct of a big Russian nation is gone, and no restoration project can bring it back to life, no matter how much blood and treasure may be expended in the effort to revive a conservative utopia.

EPILOGUE

T HE QUESTION OF WHERE RUSSIA BEGINS AND ENDS, AND WHO
constitutes the Russian people, has preoccupied Russian thinkers for
centuries. The collapse of the Soviet Union in 1991 turned these concerns
into a big "Russian question" that constitutes a world problem: What
should be the relation of the new Russian state to its former imperial possessions—now independent post-Soviet republics—and to the Russian
and Russian-speaking enclaves in those republics?

The current Russo-Ukrainian conflict is only the latest turn of Russian
policy resulting from the Russian elite's thinking about itself and its East
Slavic neighbors as part of the joint historical and cultural space, and ultimately as the same nation. The conflict reprises many of the themes that
had been central to political and cultural relations in the region for the
previous five centuries. These included Russia's great-power status and influence beyond its borders; the continuing relevance of religion, especially
Orthodoxy, in defining Russian identity and conducting Russian policy
abroad; and, last but not least, the importance of language and culture as

tools of state policy in the region. More importantly, the conflict reminded the world that the formation of the modern Russian nation is still far from complete.

The fall of the Soviet Union and Russia's failure to maintain control of the post-Soviet space, either through the Commonwealth of Independent States or through the more flexible project of forming a Russian "liberal empire"—a sphere of influence controlled through economic power and cultural ties—provided the immediate geopolitical context for the Russian leadership's decision to use military force to try to maintain its dominance in the region. But why did the Russians decide to fight in Ukraine against those whom Vladimir Putin himself repeatedly called part of the same people as the Russians?

Ukraine today is at the very center of the new "Russian question." Because of its size, location, and, most importantly, historical and cultural ties to Russia, Ukraine was, is, and probably will remain for some time a key element in the Russian elites' thinking about their own identity and destiny. Is Russia to become a modern nation-state, or will it remain a truncated empire, driven into ever new conflicts by the phantom pains of lost territories and past glories? The rise of Russia as both nation and empire has been closely associated with Ukraine, not only because of Russian historical mythology but also because of its record of territorial expansion into Eastern and Central Europe, and the reformulation of its identity according to concepts first formulated by European thinkers of the early modern era, and explained to the Muscovite elite by the Kyivan literati.

Ukraine and Ukrainians were central to Muscovy/Russia's search for identity from the seventeenth century when Kyivan monks advanced the idea of common "Slavo-Rossian" nationhood, and it remained central during the development of the imperial Russian project by St. Petersburg intellectuals in the eighteenth century, as well as during the imperial struggle against nineteenth-century Polish insurgents for political and cultural influence, and, finally, during the formation of the Soviet Union, with Ukraine as its key element, in the twentieth century. Russian visions of empire, great-power status, and nationhood all hinged on a view of Ukraine as a distinct but integral part of Russia. Many in the Kremlin and beyond have regarded the possibility of Ukraine leaving the Russian sphere of influence as an attack on Russia itself.

Ukraine's departure is destined to spell the end of Moscow's imperial ambitions in the post-Soviet space. "Without Ukraine, Russia ceases to be an empire, but with Ukraine suborned and then subordinated, Russia automatically becomes an empire," wrote Zbigniew Brzezinski in a seminal article in *Foreign Affairs* in 1994, a few years after the Soviet collapse. Brzezinski raised the stakes for the West in the Russo-Ukrainian conflict even higher when he suggested that "Russia can be either an empire or a democracy, but it cannot be both." Around the same time, Edward L. Keenan, a leading Harvard expert in Russian history, suggested that if the Soviet collapse indeed marked the disintegration of the Russian Empire, then it would have to lead to a Russo-Ukrainian war. The outbreak of that war twenty years later made the connection between the Soviet demise and Russian imperial collapse apparent to the world at large.

Ukraine's departure also shatters the imperial model of Russian national identity, in which Ukrainians are still perceived as part of one Russian nation. Post-Soviet Russian identity is probably best imagined as a set of concentric circles. At the center of them is the core of Russian ethnic identity. The first concentric circle surrounding this core deals with Russian political identity based on Russian citizenship. There follows a circle concerning East Slavic identity. The final and outer layer consists of all other participants in Russian culture—the Russian-speakers of the world. The architects of the "Russian World" project, backed by both the Russian state and the Russian Orthodox Church, define Russians as bearers of Russian language and culture, irrespective of ethnic origin or citizenship. The Ukrainians, as the central element of the East Slavic layer outside the Russian core, are instrumental in making post-Soviet Russian identity work as a transnational phenomenon. That identity, imperial in its main features, threatens the stability of the whole East European region, extending from Moldova, where Moscow backs the separatist republic of Transnistria, to Latvia and Estonia, members of the EU and NATO with sizable Russian-speaking populations.

The Crimean annexation and the war in the Donbas brought together Russian statists and Russian nationalists both within and outside the government. It boosted the morale of both groups at a time when nostalgia for former Soviet and East Slavic unity was in decline in Russia and in other post-Soviet states. Although the Russian government was quite successful in mobilizing support among the largely ethnic Russian population of the Crimea, the effect of Russian propaganda in the Russian-speaking—but for the most part ethnically Ukrainian—regions of eastern and southern Ukraine was mixed at best. The pan-Russian idea was brought to Ukraine by armed militias along with authoritarian rule and the concept of a nation monolithic in ethnicity, language, and religion—a proposition that was always a hard sell in the historically multiethnic and multicultural borderlands of Eastern Europe. Thus, Russia succeeded in annexing or destabilizing areas where the majority or plurality of inhabitants considered themselves ethnic Russians, but failed in culturally Russian areas where most of the population associated itself ethnically and politically with Ukraine.

The long-term outcome of the conflict and its impact on nation-building in the region are still unclear, but, contrary to the wishes of its authors, it accelerated the disintegration of one big Russian-dominated historical and cultural space and strengthened the model of ethnic nationhood on both sides of the front line. The Russian government decided to annex only territory with a predominantly ethnic Russian population (the Crimea); the plan of turning the mainly ethnic Ukrainian but Russian-speaking southeastern region of Ukraine into a Russian dependency failed; and Russia refused to consider an annexation scenario for the Donbas, which it had helped to destabilize. Ethnic Russians inhabiting a peninsula not adjoining Russian territory found themselves eligible for annexation in the eyes of the Kremlin, but Russian-speakers immediately across the border were denied that honor.

On the Ukrainian side, Russian aggression mobilized the multiethnic and multicultural Ukrainian political nation, and Russia's annexation of the Crimea, with its predominantly ethnic Russian population, and the loss of a good part of the Donbas, where that population constituted a plurality in the big cities such as Donetsk, dramatically increased the percentage of ethnic Ukrainians in the territorially diminished Ukrainian state. As a result of the conflict, Russia became more ethnically Russian and Ukraine more ethnically Ukrainian. More and more Ukrainians of all ethnic backgrounds tend today to embrace Ukrainian culture as a symbol of their identity.

Will the Russian government and the Russian political and cultural elites accept the "loss" of Ukraine? This is the essence of the "Russian question" in its present form. As recent events have shown, the unresolved Russian question threatens peace and stability in Europe and the world in general. This threat is no less serious than the one posed in the nineteenth and early twentieth centuries by the German question—the idea of uniting all the German lands to forge a mighty German Empire.

Many believe that the outbreak of World War II can be traced back to the failure to resolve the German question by peaceful means, and some find a parallel between Hitler's Germany and Putin's Russia in their use of the nationality card to destabilize and annex neighboring territories. The Russo-Ukrainian conflict has already become the worst international crisis in East-West relations since the end of the Cold War. It remains to be seen whether the annexation of the Crimea and the war in the Donbas are the final episodes in the disintegration of the USSR or a new and terrible stage in the reshaping of European borders and populations.

The answer will depend on the ability and readiness of the Russian elites to accept the post-Soviet political realities and adjust Russia's own identity to the demands of the post-imperial world. The future of the Russian nation and its relations with its neighbors lies not in a return to the lost paradise of the imagined East Slavic unity of the medieval Kyivan state, but in the formation of a modern civic nation within the borders of the Russian Federation. This was the path followed by former imperial metropoles such as Britain, and modern nation-states like Germany, which recognized the independence of English- and German-speaking countries and enclaves beyond their borders. The alternative might be a new Cold War or worse.

ACKNOWLEDGMENTS

THE RUSSO-UKRAINIAN WAR THAT EXPLODED IN 2014 COMPELLED me to write this book. But in many ways, it is a continuation of my earlier project on the history of East Slavic identities, which resulted in the publication of *The Origins of the Slavic Nations* by Cambridge University Press in 2006. For years since the publication of that book, I have been teaching a seminar on "East European Identities: Russia and Ukraine," which helped me continue the inquiry begun in *The Origins* into the nineteenth and twentieth centuries. The Russian annexation of the Crimea and the ongoing war in eastern Ukraine put the current debates about Russian history and identity into the center of my research and writing. Recent events also prompted me to turn what would otherwise have been a purely academic monograph into a work for a larger audience that tackles big questions of immediate political and cultural importance.

While this book has been long in the making, and a good part of it is based either on my earlier works or on research specifically done for this volume, much of my account and analysis relies on excellent work done by others. Many of them have been my friends and colleagues, to whom I owe many intellectual debts.

My understanding of Muscovite history and identities has been informed by the works of Charles J. Halperin, Valerie Kivelson, Nancy Kollman, and Donald Ostrowski. I found the monographs of Zenon E. Kohut and Barbara Skinner very useful in dealing with Russian imperial politics of the eighteenth century. The works of Serhiy Bilenky, Mikhail Dolbilov, Faith Hillis, Alexei Miller, Oleksii Tolochko, and Andrei Zorin helped me grasp the complexities of Russian imperial nationality and religious policies in the western borderlands of the Russian Empire. The writings of David Brandenberger, Terry Martin, Richard Pipes, Ana Procyk, Per Rudling, Roman Szporluk, and Serhy Yekelchyk provided the basis for my understanding of twentieth-century developments.

John LeDonne, Roman Procyk, and Igor Torbakov graciously agreed to read the manuscript and made a number of important corrections and comments. I would also like to thank Richard Wortman for inviting me to speak in his seminar on Russian imperial history at Columbia University, and one of the participants in the seminar, Nathaniel Knight, for sharing with me his archival findings on Osyp Bodiansky and Nikolai Nadezhdin. My colleague Tim Snyder from Yale and Jonathon Wyss from Beehive Mapping generously allowed me to use some of their maps in this book, as did the editors of the Cambridge University and University of Toronto presses. Myroslav Yurkevich did an excellent job of "Englishing" my prose. As always, my wife, Olena, has been the most careful and critical reader of the numerous drafts of this book and helped make it more reader-friendly.

I am grateful to Jill Kneerim for convincing Lara Heimert to add this work to the impressive list of historical writings published by Basic Books. Lara enthusiastically embraced the concept and, with her advice and careful editing, turned the manuscript into the book it is today. I was happy to work once again with the Basic Books team, including Betsy DeJesu, Roger Labrie, Alia Massoud, and Jennifer Thompson. At Basic Books I also had the pleasure of collaborating again with Kathy Streckfus and Collin Tracy. None of the people mentioned above have anything to do with any shortcomings in this book. If there are any, please blame them on the author or, even better, on the complexity of Russian history itself.

NOTES

INTRODUCTION

viii "gatherer and protector": "Tseremoniia Otkrytiia pamiatnika kniaziu Vladimiru," *Prezident Rossii*, November 4, 2016, http://kremlin.ru/events/president/news/53211.

 x "a political principle which holds": Ernest Gellner, *Nations and Nationalism*, 2d ed. (Ithaca, NY, 2009), 1.

 "Britain had an empire": Geoffrey Hosking, "The Freudian Frontier," *Times Literary Supplement*, March 10, 1995, 27.

CHAPTER 1: THE BIRTH OF THE TSARDOM

 5 "Batu placed battering rams": *Ipat'evskaia letopis'* (St. Petersburg, 1908), col. 785.

 "Meanwhile, people ran": Ibid.

 9 "From antiquity you": Serhii Plokhy, *The Origins of the Slavic Nations: Premodern Identities in Russia, Ukraine, and Belarus* (Cambridge, 2006), 137.

11 "The towns and lands": V. T. Pashuto, B. N. Floria, and A. L. Khoroshkevich, *Drevnerusskoe nasledie i istoricheskie sud'by vostochnogo slavianstva* (Moscow, 1982), 172.

13 "Your father, Sire": Mikhail Krom, *Mezh Rus'iu i Litvoi: Pogranichnye zemli v sisteme russko-litovskikh otnoshenii kontsa XV–pervoi treti XVI veka* (Moscow, 2010), 100.

16 "the tsar's name": Mikhail Zazykin, *Tsarskaia vlast' v Rossii* (Moscow, 2004), 57.

CHAPTER 2: THE THIRD ROME

23 "a new Tsar Constantine": Iakov Lur'e, *Ideologicheskaia bor'ba v russkoi piublitsistike* (Leningrad, 1960), 378.

24 "All Christian kingdoms": Pavel Miliukov, *Ocherki po istorii russkoi kul'tury* (Moscow, 1995), 31.

25 "In the place where they held": Makarii (Metropolitan), *Istoriia russkoi tserkvi* (Moscow, 1996), vol. 6, 34.

"For the old Rome fell": Donald Ostrowski, *Muscovy and the Mongols: Cross-Cultural Influences on the Steppe Frontier, 1304–1589* (Cambridge, 2002), 239.

28 "I turn to you": Makarii (Metropolitan), *Istoriia russkoi tserkvi*, vol. 6, 98.

32 "We would wish": Serhii Plokhy, *The Cossacks and Religion in Early Modern Ukraine* (Oxford, 2001), 306.

33 "accept their Roman faith": Ibid., 312.

34 "of the same worship": Ibid., 319.

"The only pious tsar": Makarii (Metropolitan), *Istoriia russkoi tserkvi*, vol. 6, 357.

CHAPTER 3: THE IMPERIAL NATION

39 "Live long-awaited solace": Simeon Polotskii, *Virshi*, eds. V. K. Bylinin and L. U. Zvonareva (Minsk, 1990), 27–33.

41 "After all, you are a Russian": Pavel Miliukov, *Ocherki po istorii russkoi kul'tury* (Moscow, 1995), 53.

"Oh, poor Rus'": Vasilii Kliuchevskii, *Russkaia istoriia* (Moscow, 2013), 184.

43 "Muscovy, that is": Serhii Plokhy, *The Origins of the Slavic Nations: Premodern Identities in Russia, Ukraine, and Belarus* (Cambridge, 2006), 337.

44 "starting from our Dnieper": Ibid., 272.

45 "One must labor": Elena Pogosian, *Petr I—Arkhitektor rossiiskoi istorii* (St. Petersburg, 2001), 226.

49 "Why should we": Vasilli Trediakovskii, *Izdrannye proizvedeniia* (Moscow, 1963), 523.

"The sage Theofan": A. P. Sumarokov, *Izbrannye proizvedeniia* (Moscow, 2015), 27.

"Unevenness of style": Boris Uspenskii, *Izbrannye trudy* (Moscow, 1994), vol. 2, 294.

50 "the majesty of Spanish": Mikhail Lomonosov, *Ob obrazovanii i vospitanii* (Moscow, 2014), 168.

CHAPTER 4: THE ENLIGHTENED EMPRESS

56 "It was clearly apparent": Evgenii Gusliarov, *Ekaterina II v zhizni* (Moscow, 2004), 151.

57 "In the true glory": *Rossiiskoe zakonodatel'stvo X–XIX vekov* (Moscow, 1987), vol. 5, 23.

59 "Little Russia, Livonia, and Finland": Andreas Kappeler, *The Russian Empire: A Multi-Ethnic History* (Harlow, UK, 2001), 107.

61 "Among Your Imperial Majesty's subject peoples": Sergei Solov'ev, *Sochineniia v vosemnadtsati knigakh* (Moscow, 1994), vol. 13, 123.

    "Finding myself": V. Sheremetevskii, "Georgii," in *Rosiiskii biograficheskii slovar'* A. Polovtsova, vol. 4, s.cv.

63 "Her Royal Majesty the All-Russian Empress": "Peterburgskaia konventsiia mezhdu Rossiiei i Prussiei," *Pod stiagom Rossii* (Moscow, 1992), 132.

64 "Her Royal Highness the Imperial Queen": Ibid.

65 "In time, we should obtain Galicia": Vsevolod Solov'ev, *Istoriia padeniia Pol'shi* (Moscow, 2015), 219.

    "to deliver the lands and towns": *Sbornik Russkogo istoricheskogo obshchestva* (St. Petersburg, 1885), vol. 47, 473.

66 "The experience of the past": Ibid.

    "Her Imperial Majesty has restored": K. V. Ratnikov, "Istoricheskie formy otrazheniia pravitel'stvennoi politiki v obshchestvennom soznanii," *Al'manakh sovremennoi nauki i obrazovaniia* (Tambov, 2016), no. 6, 157.

    "Having trampled on the sacred rights": Andrei Zorin, *Kormia dvuglavogo orla: Literatura i gosudarstvennaia ideologiia v Rossii v poslednei treti XVIII– pervoi treti XIX veka* (Moscow, 2001), 155.

67 "during the troubled times of Russia": Barbara Skinner, *The Western Front of the Eastern Church: Uniate and Orthodox Conflict in Eighteenth-Century Poland, Ukraine, Belarus, and Russia* (DeKalb, IL, 2009), 204.

    "the most suitable eradication": Ibid., 203–204.

CHAPTER 5: THE POLISH CHALLENGE

71 "One Pole is a charmer": Norman Davies, *God's Playground: A History of Poland* (Oxford, 2005), vol. 1, 386.

73 "I love your nation": V. I. Picheta, "Pol'skaia konfederatsiia v 1812 godu," in *Otechestvennaia voina i russkoe obshchestvo* (St. Petersburg, 1812), vol. 3, 159.

74 "We are restoring Poland": Ibid., 157.

    "Let Lithuania, Samogitia": Ibid., 159.

75 "In every noble, let him encounter": *Otechestvennaia voina 1812 goda: Sbornik dokumentov i materialov*, eds. Evegneii Tarle and Anatolii Predtechenskii (Moscow, 2015), 30.

76 "We hope . . . that this philoprogenitive": *Polnoe sobranie zakonov Rossiiskoi imperii* (St. Petersburg, 1830), vol. 32, 481–482.

77 "Will they say that she": Nikolai Karamzin, *Polnoe sobranie sochinenii* (Moscow, 1998), vol. 18, 11.

79 "Warsaw is at Your Majesty's feet": Boris Tarasov, *Nikolai I: Rytsar' samoderzhaviia* (Moscow, 2006), 355.

80 "Whose will Volhynia be?": Serhii Plokhy, *The Gates of Europe: A History of Ukraine* (New York, 2015), 153.

82 "How to establish popular education": *Reka vremen (kniga istorii i kul'tury)* (Moscow, 1995), vol. 1, 70.

83 "Why not translate": P. A. Viazemskii, *Estetika i iteraturnaia kritika* (Moscow, 1984), 23.

    "For some time we have been": Aleksandr Pushkin, *Sobranie sochinenii v desiati tomakh* (Moscow, 1959–1962), vol. 7, 267.

    "one and the other": Aleksandr Andreev, *Istoriia gosudarstvennoi vlasti v Rossii* (Moscow, 1999), 160.

84 "God, Sovereign, and Fatherland": *Reka vremen*, vol. 1, 72.

CHAPTER 6: THE BATTLE FOR THE BORDERLANDS

86 "As long as I live": *Russkii biograficheskii slovar'*, vol. 11, part 1, 45.

    "Nicholas, Tsar of Poland": Dmitrii Oleinikov, *Nikolai I* (Moscow, 2012), 254.

88 "Finland, Estland, Livland": *Konstitutsionnye proekty Rossii: 1799–1825* (Munich, 2007), 139.

89 "All illustrious rulers": Aleksei Miller, "Triada grafa Uvarova i natsionalizm," *Istoricheskie zapiski*, no. 11 (2008): 191.

    "belonged to Russia in ancient times": *Konstitutsionnye proekty Rossii*, 156.

91 "The major fact in the history": Stephen Velychenko, *National History as a Cultural Process* (Edmonton, 1992), 98.

93 "precious to all Russia": *Kievskii universitet: Dokumenty i materialy, 1834–1984*, eds. M. Belyi and V. Zamlinskii (Kyiv, 1984), 14.

    "to smooth over as much as possible": Sergei Uvarov, *Gosudarstvennye osnovy* (Moscow, 2014), 51.

97 "Immeasurable Russia": Aleksei Chaplin, "Russkoe imia i russkaia vera Ukrainy," in *Moskva* 10 (2016): 231.

98 "how to turn Uniates": *Zapiski Iosifa mitropolita Litovskogo* (St. Petersburg, 1883), vol. 2, 14–15.

98 "In order to warm the hearts": Ibid., 18.

100 "With Lithuania's detachment": Ibid., 83–84.

"the reconsolidation": Ibid., 91.

CHAPTER 7: THE ADVENT OF UKRAINE

106 "Brothers! A great hour is upon us": A. V. Smirnov, "Stranitsy zhizni i tvorchestva istorika," in Nikolai Kostomarov, *Russkaia istoriia v opisanii ee glavneishikh deiatelei* (Moscow, 2004), 18.

110 "It seems to us": *Taras Shevchenko v krytytsi*, ed. Hryhorii Hrabovych (Kyiv, 2012), vol. 1, 4.

"We would advise him": Ibid., 6.

"For Russian readers": Olga Andriewsky, "The Russian-Ukrainian Discourse and the Failure of the 'Little Russian Solution,' 1782–1917," in *Culture, Nation and Identity: The Ukrainian-Russian Encounter, 1600–1945*, eds. Andreas Kappeler, Zenon E. Kohut, Frank E. Sysyn, and Mark von Hagen (Edmonton, 2003), 191.

111 "The Great Russians live side by side": Ibid.

"The uncovering of a Slavic": *Kyrylo-Mefodiivs'ke tovarystvo: U triokh tomakh*, eds. H. I. Marakhov and V. H. Sarbei (Kyiv, 1990), vol. 1, 62.

112 "The political evil": Ibid., 64.

113 "Ukraine will become": Ibid., 169.

"Along with favorite poems": Ibid., 67.

114 "so that all may know the fate": Ibid., 68.

"Obviously the work": Aleksei Miller, *Ukrainskii vopros v politike vlastei i russkom obshchestvennom mnenii (vtoraia polovina XIX veka)* (St. Petersburg, 2000), 56.

"Harsh measures will make": *Kyrylo-Mefodiivs'ke tovarystvo*, vol. 1, 308.

"Through the minister of popular education": Ibid., 293.

115 "writers should be most careful": Miller, *Ukrainskii vopros*, 58.

"In the south, in Kyiv": Petr Zaionchkovskii, *Kirillo-mefodievskoe obshchestyvo* (Moscow, 1959), 138.

"Shevchenko was sent to the Caucasus": Vissarion Belinskii, *Polnoe sobranie sochinenii* (Moscow, 1956), vol. 12, 441.

116 "Oh, those topknots": Ibid.

"turned out to be": *Kyrylo-Mefodiivs'ke tovarystvo*, vol. 1, 63.

"some kind of murky": Ibid., 294.

"The Little Russians were eventually affected": Alexei Miller, *The Ukrainian Question: The Russian Empire and Nationalism in the Nineteenth Century* (New York, 2003), 60.

117 "I read Konysky": Serhii Plokhy, *The Cossack Myth: History and Nationhood in the Age of Empires* (Cambridge, 2012), 318.

118 "The fact that I love Kyiv": Mikhail Maksimovich, "Otvetnye pis'ma M. P. Pogodinu," *Russkaia beseda* 2 (1857): 85.

"The supposed Little Russians": Mikhail Pogodin, *Drevniia russkaia istoriia do mongol'skogo iga* (Moscow, 1871).

119 "Language—that is the true boundary": Mikhail Pogodin, *Izbrannye trudy* (Moscow, 2010), 341.

120 "he was carried out": Memoir of E. F. Iunge, in *Kievskaia starina* 28, no. 1 (1890): 23.

"No law, no institution": David Saunders, "Mykola Kostomarov (1817–1885) and the Creation of the Ukrainian Ethnic Identity," *Slavonica* 7, no. 1 (2001): 15.

CHAPTER 8: GREAT, LITTLE, AND WHITE

126 "I have always been of the opinion": Quotation supplied by Nathaniel Knight.

128 "Well, and what if": Aleksandr Gertsen, "Rosiia i Pol'sha: Pis'mo vtoroe," *Kolokol*, 1859.

"You have expressed an opinion": Mykola Kostomarov, *Pys'mo do vydavtsia "Kolokola"* (Lviv, 1902), 15.

129 "Besides the Rus' nationality": Nikolai Kostomarov, "Dve russkie narodnosti," *Osnova*, no. 3 (1861): 34.

"If the South Russian nation": Ibid., 78.

132 "Russian or, better, Belarusian": Mikhail Dolbilov, *Russkii krai, chuzhaia vera: Ètnokonfessional'naia politika imperii v Litve i Belorussii pri Aleksandre II* (Moscow, 2010), 199.

133 "strong in numbers, popular education": Ibid., 220.

"The children of the old Krivichians": Ibid., 221.

134 "to restrain all foolish Great Russian passions": Ibid., 212.

"Russia is now saving Belarus": Ibid., 221.

"They write to us": Ibid., 222.

CHAPTER 9: KILLING THE LANGUAGE

137 "That phenomenon is all the more deplorable": Aleksei Miller, *Ukrainskii vopros v politike vlastei i russkom obshchestvennom mnenii (vtoraia polovina XIX veka)* (St. Petersburg, 2000), 241.

138 "In our time, the question": Ibid., 79.

139 "Teaching the Little Russian people": Ibid., 82–83.

140 "Debate continues in the literature": Ibid., 100.

141 "Ukraine has never had its own history": Mikhail Katkov, *Imperskoe slovo* (Moscow, 2002), 146.

"Outrageous and ridiculous sophistry!": Ibid., 144.

144 "You, Messrs. Ukrainophiles": [Nikolai Rigel'man,] "Sovremennoe ukraino-fil'stvo," in *Ukrainskii vopros v russkoi patrioticheskoi mysli*, comp. A. Iu. Minakov (Moscow, 2016), 179, 184.

145 "put a stop to the activity": Miller, *Ukrainskii vopros*, 241.

146 "to support the newspaper *Slovo*": Ibid., 243.

147 "Austria's attention to the Ruthenians": Ibid., 201.

148 "Our Ruthenian people": *Proekt politicheskoi programy dlia Rusi avstriiskoi* (Lviv, 1871), 9–10.

149 "The Ukrainian question, presented": Ibid., 12–13.

CHAPTER 10: THE PEOPLE'S SONG

158 "We working men of St. Petersburg": *Khrestomatiia po istorii SSSR*, ed. Yurii Korablev (Moscow, 1988), 42.

161 "The very credit of our priests": Theodore Weeks, *Nation and State in Late Imperial Russia: Nationalism and Russification on the Western Frontier* (DeKalb, IL, 1996), 180.

162 "had already made": *Zaborona ukraïns'koho slova v Rossiï*, introduction by Mykhailo Hrushevs'kyi (Scranton, PA, 1916), 33, 43.

164 "The Belarusians, too, are following": D. Kotsiubinskii, *Russkii natsionalizm v nachale XX veka: Rozhdenie i gibel' ideologii Vserosiiskogo natsional'nogo soiuza* (Moscow, 2001), 310.

165 "The representatives of the nation": *Primary Sources in Russian History 1801–1917*, ed. John Etty (Corby, UK, 2009), 77.

167 "I am profoundly convinced": Petr Struve, "Obscherusskaia kul'tura i ukrainskii partikuliarizm: Otvet ukraintsu," *Russkaya mysl'*, no. 1 (1912): 66.

168 "We are not guided by aspirations": S. Breiar, "Partiia kadetov i ukrainskii vopros, 1905–1917," in *Issledovaniia po istorii Ukrainy i Belorussii*, vyp. 1 (Moscow, 1995), 89–110.

169 "the good of the motherland lies": *Rossiia, 1900–1917: Dokumenty, materialy, kommentarii*, ed. I. K. Kir'ianov (Perm, Russia, 1991), 130.

170 "The members are local": I. V. Omelianchuk, "Chislennost' Soiuza russkogo naroda v 1907–1914 godakh v pravoberezhnykh ukrainskikh guberni-iakh," in *Belorussiia i Ukraina* (Moscow, 2006), 156.

"sowing enmity": Ibid., 159.

171 "The Black Hundred political organization": *Politburo TsK RKP(b)—VKP(b) i Kommintern, 1919–1943* (Moscow, 2004), 64.

172 "I am a little Russian": Kotsiubinskii, *Russkii natsionalizm*, 303–304.

"The Mazepists are well aware": Ibid., 305.

CHAPTER 11: THE FALL OF THE MONARCHY

176 "A great historical fact": *Petereburgskii listok*, August 19, 1914.

"True to its historical precepts": Viacheslav Shatsillo, *Pervaia mirovaia voina, 1914–1918: Fakty, dokumenty* (Moscow, 2003), 89.

177 "Brothers! . . . The judgment of God is upon us!": M. K. Lemke, *250 dnei v tsarskoi stavke*, ed. L. M. Suris (Moscow, 2015), vol. 1, 31.

179 "I shall establish the Russian language": P. S. Romanov, *Rus'* (Moscow, 2015), vol. 2, 314.

181 "Let the borders that cut": Lemke, *250 dnei v tsarskoi sravke*, 30.

182 "an end to the anti-state system": S. Breiar, "Partiia kadetov i ukrainskii vopros, 1905–1917," in *Issledovaniia po istorii Ukrainy i Belorussii*, vyp. 1 (Moscow, 1995), 89–110.

184 "The farther we traveled": *Perepiska Nikolaia i Aleksandry Romanovykh, 1914–1915 gg.* (Moscow, 1923), 164.

185 "Your Imperial Highness": *Put' moei zhizni: Vospominaniia mitropolita Evlogiia (Georgievskogo)* (Moscow, 1994), 248.

"Let there be one mighty": Sergei Sergeev-Tsenskii, *Preobrazhenie Rossii* (Moscow, 1956), 282.

"For the last time I felt": *Ol'ga Aleksandrovna: Memuary* (Moscow, 2003), 159.

188 "to the whole people": Pavel Miliukov, *Istoriia vtoroi russkoi revoliutsii* (Moscow, 2014), 49.

189 "Recognizing the independence": E. Ketola, "Revoliutsiia 1917 goda i obretenie Finliandiei nezavisimosti: Dva vzgliada na problemu," *Otechestvennaia istoriia* 6 (1993): 29.

CHAPTER 12: THE RUSSIAN REVOLUTION

194 "Broad autonomy for Ukraine": Mykhailo Hrushevskyi, *Na porozi novoi Ukrainy: Statti i dzherel'ni materialy* (New York, 1992), 146.

196 "The Socialist Revolutionaries": Vladimir Lenin, *Polnoe sovranie sochinenii* (Moscow, 1969), vol. 32, 350.

197 "the Ukrainian People's Republic and its right": Ibid., vol. 35, 144.

198 "mercilessly to destroy all officers": Nikolai Azovtsev, *Direktivy komandovaniia frontov Krasnoi armii, 1917–1922* (Moscow, 1971), 45.

"order has been reestablished": Viktor Savchenko, *Avantiuristy Grazhdanskoi voiny* (Moscow, 2000), 53.

201 "If Ukraine remains indifferent": Anna Procyk, *Russian Nationalism and*

Ukraine: The Nationality Policy of the Volunteer Army During the Civil War (Edmonton, 1995), 73.

202 "The former vigor": Ibid., 74.

"off this disoriented group": Anders Rudling, *The Rise and Fall of Belarusian Nationalism, 1906–1931* (Pittsburgh, 2015), 73.

203 "the earliest stages": Ibid., 74.

204 "Today we, the Rada": Nicholas P. Vakar, *Belorussia: The Making of a Nation. A Case Study* (Cambridge, MA, 1956), 103.

205 "The first important question": Rudling, *The Rise and Fall of Belarusian Nationalism*, 90.

CHAPTER 13: LENIN'S VICTORY

215 "Measures should be taken": Vladimir Lenin, *Polnoe sovranie sochinenii* (Moscow, 1969), vol. 39, 335.

"Soviet institutions must have": Ibid.

216 "Among Bolsheviks": Ibid., vol. 40, 45.

"as a party that violates": Ibid., vol. 39, 251.

220 "It is important that we not": Ibid., vol. 45, 212.

221 "Comrade Kamenev": Ibid., vol. 45, 214.

222 "The Georgian who takes": Ibid., vol. 45, 360.

223 "It is a question of the bond": *Dvenadtsatyi s'ezd Rossiiskoi kommunisticheskoi partii* (Moscow, 1923), 529.

"the Great Russian proletariat": Ibid., 596.

224 "We cannot take the viewpoint of neutrality": Ibid., 604.

"It is only on condition of a struggle": Ibid., 598.

"In departing from us, comrade Lenin": *Propagandist*, no. 21 (1939): 22.

CHAPTER 14: NATIONAL COMMUNISM

228 "that Russia has not died": Vasilii Shulgin, *Tri stolitsy: Puteshestvie v krasnuiu Rossiiu* (Moscow, 1991), 417.

231 "But that time, too, has passed": Ibid., 100.

"What do you want?": Ibid., 204.

232 "We must not force": Terry Martin, *The Affirmative Action Empire: Nations and Nationalism in the Soviet Union, 1923–1939* (Ithaca, NY, 2001), 214, 216.

235 "I have a note saying": *Desiatyi s'ezd Rossiiskoi kommunisticheskoi partii* (Moscow, 1921), 213.

"This is a blow": Anders Rudling, *The Rise and Fall of Belarusian Nationalism, 1906–1931* (Pittsburgh, 2015), 140.

238 "I said that division into small": Shulgin, *Tri stolitsy*, 207.

CHAPTER 15: THE RETURN OF RUSSIA

246 "With the active assistance": "Edinaia sem'ia narodov," *Pravda*, January 30, 1936.

247 "The nation that has given the world": Ibid.

248 "The attempt to apply the epithets": *Soviet Culture and Power: A History in Documents, 1917–1953*, eds. Katerina Clark, Evgeny Dobrenko, Andrei Artizov, and Oleg V. Naumov (New Haven, CT, 2007), 69.

"libel against our people": Benedikt Sarnov, *Stalin i pisateli* (Moscow, 2008), 495.

"the main danger is represented": Iosif Stalin, *Stat'i i rechi ob Ukraine* (Moscow, 1936), 223.

249 "In the past, the Russian people": David Brandenberger, *National Bolshevism: Stalinist Mass Culture and the Formation of Modern Russian National Identity, 1931–1956* (Cambridge, MA, 2002), 34.

"Whoever raises his hand": "Za rodinu," *Pravda*, June 9, 1934.

250 "That tsarist rule in Russia": Iosif Stalin, "O stat'e Ėngelsa 'Vneshniaia politika russkogo tsarizma,'" *Bol'shevik*, no. 9 (May 1931): 1–5.

251 "love of work, culture": Aleksandr Vdovin, *Russkie v XX veke: Fakty, sobytiia, liudi* (Moscow, 2004), 78.

"Once I said to Lenin": Ibid., 103.

252 "I well understand": Ibid., 89.

"an attempt to exalt the robbers": Viktor Danilov, *Vlast' i formirovanie istoricheskogo soznaniia sovetskogo obshchestva* (Moscow, 2005), 116.

253 "The history of the great Russian people": *Vlast' i khudozhestvennaia intelligentsia*, eds. Oleg Naumov, Andrei Artizov (Moscow, 1999), 337.

254 "The Russian tsars": Vdovin, *Russkie v XX veke*, 407.

"Last night, as I walked home": Brandenberger, *National Bolshevism*, 106.

255 "First among these equals": Ibid., 43.

"The great Russian people leads": Boris Volin, "Velikii russkii narod," *Bol'shevik* 9 (1938): 34.

CHAPTER 16: THE GREAT PATRIOTIC WAR

261 "The Soviet government": Serhii Plokhy, "The Call of Blood: Government Propaganda and Public Response to the Soviet Entry into World War II," *Cahiers du monde russe* 52, nos. 2–3 (2011): 303–304.

"to declare that Poland": Ibid., 295.

265 "The authors do not see": Serhy Yekelchyk, *Stalin's Empire of Memory: Russian-Ukrainian Relations in the Soviet Historical Imagination* (Toronto, 2004), 15–26.

268 "Not for the first time": "Vystuplenie po radio V. M. Molotva 22 iiunia 1941 g.," *Khrestomatiia po istorii Velikoi Otechestvennoi voiny*, comp. V. E. Lebedinskaia (Moscow, 2015), 37.

269 "to reestablish the rule": Iosif Stalin, *O Velikoi Otechestvennoi voine Sovetskogo naroda* (Moscow, 1948), 13.

270 "The war that you are waging": Ibid., 40.

272 "Partisans, partisans": Ianka Kupala, *Izbrannye proizvedeniia* (Moscow, 1953), vol. 2, 222.

273 "two leading peoples": David Brandenberger, *National Bolshevism: Stalinist Mass Culture and the Formation of Modern Russian National Identity, 1931–1956* (Cambridge, MA, 2002), 158.

274 "The book is anti-Russian": Ibid., 125.

CHAPTER 17: THE SOVIET PEOPLE

278 "The solution of one": "Rech' tovarishcha G. V. Malenkova," *Kommunist*, no. 3 (1953): 12.

282 "By linking their destiny": "Theses on the Three-Hundredth Anniversary of the Reunion of Ukraine and Russia," in *Towards an Intellectual History of Ukraine*, eds. Ralph Lindheim and George S. N. Luckyj (Toronto, 1996), 303–304.

286 "The party triumphantly": *Program of the Communist Party of the Soviet Union* (Moscow, 1962).

287 "A new historical community": *XXII s'ezd KPSS—Steniograficheskii orchet* (Moscow, 1962), vol. 1, 153.

"The process now taking place": *Program of the Communist Party of the Soviet Union.*

288 "The sooner we all speak Russian": Mamasharif Nishanov, *Obnovlenie dukhovnoi zhizni natsii* (Tashkent, 1992), 30.

290 "The Soviet people have one set": S. T. Kaltakhchian, "Sovetskii narod," in *Bol'shaia sovetskaia ėntsiklopediia* (Moscow, 1970), s.v.

CHAPTER 18: RED FLAG DOWN

305 "We profoundly respect": Osyp Zinkevych, *Ukrains'kyi pravozakhysnyi rukh* (Toronto, 1978), 22.

"In the Kyivan period we constituted": Aleksandr Solzhenitsyn, *Arkhipelag Gulag* (Moscow, 2000), books 5–7, 47.

"It will be extraordinarily painful": Ibid., 49.

306 "The ill-considered collectivization": Roman Szporluk, *Russia, Ukraine, and the Breakup of the Soviet Union* (Stanford, CA, 2001), 194.

309 "For Russia today, the center": Serhii Plokhy, *The Last Empire: The Final Days of the Soviet Union* (New York, 2014), 37.

310 "Listen, there are tanks there": Ibid., 95.

311 "As it seemed to me": Iegor Gaidar, *Dni porazhenii—i pobed* (Moscow, 1996), 81.

CHAPTER 19: THE RUSSIAN WORLD

322 "It is my profound conviction": Anatolii Chubais, "Missiia Rossii v XXI veke," *Nezavisimaia gazeta*, October 1, 2003.

326 "Have you read Denikin's diaries?": Larisa Kaftan, "Pochemu Putin liubit Denikina," *Komsomol'skaia pravda*, June 25, 2009.

   "No Russia, reactionary or democratic": Anton Denikin, *Kto spas Sovetskuiu vlast' ot gibeli?* (Moscow, 1991), 10.

327 "Russia will not perish": Ivan Il'in, *Chto sulit miru raschlenenie Rossii?* (Moscow, 1992), 15.

328 "The Russian World": Marlene Laruelle, *The "Russian World": Russia's Soft Power and Geopolitical Imagination* (Washington, DC, 2015), 13.

329 "trans-state and transcontinental association": V. A. Tishkov, "Russkii iazyk i russkoiazychnoe naselenie v stranakh SNG i Baltiki," in *Vestnik Rossiiskoi Akademii nauk* 77, no. 5 (2008): 416.

   "My opinion": Ibid.

   "The Russian World is more than present-day Russia": Ibid.

331 "We understand today's realities": "Pravoslavno-slavianskie tsenoosti—osnova tsivilizatsionnogo vybora Ukrainy," *Prezident Rossii*, July 27, 2013, http://kremlin.ru/events/president/news/18961.

CHAPTER 20: THE RUSSIAN WAR

339 "The big country was gone": "Address of the President of the Russian Federation Vladimir Putin," *Prezident Rossii*, March 18, 2014, http://en.kremlin.ru/events/president/news/20603.

340 "We are one people": Vladimir Putin, interview with Channel One of Russian TV and the Associated Press, *Prezident Rossii*, September 4, 2013, http://kremlin.ru/news/19143.

   "I start with the conviction": Oleh S. Ilnytzkyj, "Modeling Culture in the Empire: Ukrainian Modernism and the Death of the All-Russian Idea," in *Culture, Nation, and Identity: The Ukrainian-Russian Encounter (1600–1945)*, eds. Andreas Kappeler, Zenon E. Kohut, Frank E. Sysyn, and Mark von Hagen (Edmonton, 2003), 308.

341 "Ninety-five percent of the people": "Address of the President of the Russian Federation Vladimir Putin," March 18, 2014.

"I want you to hear me": Ibid.

343 "The Russian church has blessed": "Russkaia tserkov' blagoslovila DNR na voinu," *Vzgliad*, June 12, 2014.

345 "And if there are any here": "Lukashenko: Schitaiushchie, chto Belorussiia—chast' russkogo mira—zabud'te," *Regnum*, January 29, 2015.

EPILOGUE

349 "Without Ukraine, Russia ceases": Zbigniew Brzezinski, "The Premature Partnership," *Foreign Affairs* 73 (March–April 1994): 72.

BIBLIOGRAPHY

INTRODUCTION

Tim Baycroft, *France*, Inventing the Nation (London, 2008); Stefan Berger, *Germany*, Inventing the Nation (London, 2004); Linda Colley, *Britons: Forging the Nation, 1707–1837*, 3d ed. (New Haven, CT, 2009); Ernest Gellner, *Nations and Nationalism*, 2d ed. (Ithaca, NY, 2009); Geoffrey Hosking, "The Freudian Frontier," *Times Literary Supplement*, March 10, 1995; Carsten Humlebaek, *Spain*, Inventing the Nation (London, 2014); Serhii Plokhy, *The Origins of the Slavic Nations: Premodern Identities in Russia, Ukraine, and Belarus* (Cambridge, 2006); Vera Tolz, *Russia*, Inventing the Nation (London, 2001).

CHAPTER 1: THE BIRTH OF THE TSARDOM

Michael Cherniavsky, "Klan or Basileus?: An Aspect of Russia Medieval Political Thought," in idem, ed., *The Structure of Russian History* (New York, 1970), pp. 75–77. Simon Franklin and Jonathan Shepard, *The Emergence of Rus, 750–1200* (London, 1996); I. Gerasimov, S. Glebov, A. Kaplunovski, M. Mogilner, and A. Semyonov, eds., "Novaia imperskaia istoriia Severnoi Evrazii," chapter 5, *Ab Imperio*, no. 3 (2014): 363–407; Charles J. Halperin, *The Tatar Yoke: The Image of the Mongols in Medieval Russia* (Bloomington, IN, 2009); Mykhailo Hrushevsky, *History of*

Ukraine-Rus', vol. 1 (Edmonton, 1997); Janet Martin, *Medieval Russia, 980–1584*, 2d ed. (Cambridge, 2008); Donald Ostrowski, *Muscovy and the Mongols: Cross-Cultural Influences on the Steppe Frontier, 1304–1589* (Cambridge, 2002); V. T. Pashuto, B. N. Floria, and A. L. Khoroshkevich, *Drevnerusskoe nasledie i istoricheskie sud'by vostochnogo slavianstva* (Moscow, 1982); Jaroslaw Pelenski, *The Contest for the Legacy of Kievan Rus'* (Boulder, 1998); Serhii Plokhy, *The Origins of the Slavic Nations: Premodern Identities in Russia, Ukraine, and Belarus* (Cambridge, 2006); Daniel Stone, *The Polish-Lithuanian State, 1386–1795* (Seattle, 2001).

CHAPTER 2: THE THIRD ROME

Michael Cherniavsky, *Tsar and People: Studies in Russian Myths*, 2d ed. (New York, 1969); Chester S. L. Dunning, *A Short History of Russia's First Civil War: The Time of Troubles and the Founding of the Romanov Dynasty* (University Park, PA, 2004); Borys A. Gudziak, *Crisis and Reform: The Kyivan Metropolitanate, the Patriarchate of Constantinople, and the Genesis of the Union of Brest* (Cambridge, MA, 1998); Mykhailo Hrushevsky, *History of Ukraine-Rus'*, vol. 7 (Edmonton, 1999); Tat'iana Oparina, *Ivan Nasedka i polemicheskoe bogoslovie kievskoi mitropolii* (Novosibirsk, 1998); Donald Ostrowski, *Muscovy and the Mongols: Cross-Cultural Influences on the Steppe Frontier, 1304–1589* (Cambridge, 2002); Maureen Perrie, *Pretenders and Popular Monarchism in Early Modern Russia: The False Tsars of the Time of Troubles* (Cambridge, 2002); S. F. Platonov, *The Time of Troubles* (Lawrence, KS, 1970); Serhii Plokhy, *The Cossacks and Religion in Early Modern Ukraine* (Oxford, 2001).

CHAPTER 3: THE IMPERIAL NATION

Liah Greenfeld, *Nationalism: Five Roads to Modernity* (Cambridge, MA, 1992); M. S. Grinberg and B. A. Uspenskii, *Literaturnaia voina Tred'iakovskogo i Sumarokova v 1740-kh—nachale 1750-kh gg.* (Moscow, 2011); Georg B. Michels, *At War with the Church: Religious Dissent in Seventeenth-Century Russia* (Stanford, CA, 2000); Serhii Plokhy, *Ukraine and Russia: Representations of the Past* (Toronto, 2008); Elena Pogosian, *Petr I—arkhitektor russkoi istorii* (St. Petersburg, 2001); Hans Rogger, *National Consciousness in Eighteenth-Century Russia* (Cambridge, MA, 1960); Tatiana Tairova-Yakovleva, "The Role of the Religious Factor and Patriarch Nikon in the Unification of Ukraine and Muscovy," *Acta Polonia Historica* 110 (2014): 5–22; Vera Tolz, *Russia, Inventing the Nation* (New York, 2001); Boris Uspenskii, "Foneticheskaia struktura odnogo stikhotvoreniia Lomonosova (istoriko-filologicheskii ėtiud)," in idem, *Izbrannye trudy*, 2 vols. (Moscow, 1996–1997), 2:207–241; V. V. Vinogradov, *Ocherki po istorii russkogo literaturnogo iazyka* (Moscow, 1982).

CHAPTER 4: THE ENLIGHTENED EMPRESS

John T. Alexander, *Catherine the Great* (New York, 1989); Liah Greenfeld, *Nationalism: Five Roads to Modernity* (Cambridge, MA, 1992); Zenon Kohut, *Russian Centralism and Ukrainian Autonomy: Imperial Absorption of the Hetmanate, 1760s–1830s* (Cambridge, MA, 1989); John LeDonne, *The Grand Strategy of the Russian Empire, 1650–1831* (Oxford, 2003); Jerzy Lukowski, *The Partitions of Poland, 1772, 1793, 1795* (New York, 1999); Robert K. Massie, *Catherine the Great: Portrait of a Woman* (New York, 2011); Barbara Skinner, *The Western Front of the Eastern Church: Uniate and Orthodox Conflict in Eighteenth-Century Poland, Ukraine, Belarus, and Russia* (DeKalb, IL, 2009); Yuri Slezkine, "Naturalists Versus Nations: Eighteenth-Century Scholars Confront Ethnic Diversity," *Representations* 47 (Summer 1994): 170–195; Sergei M. Soloviev, *History of Russia*, vol. 46, *The Rule of Catherine the Great: Turkey and Poland, 1768–1770*, trans. Daniel L. Schlafly Jr. (Gulf Breeze, FL, 1994).

CHAPTER 5: THE POLISH CHALLENGE

Serhiy Bilenky, *Romantic Nationalism in Eastern Europe: Russian, Polish, and Ukrainian Political Imaginations* (Stanford, CA, 2012); John LeDonne, *The Russian Empire and the World, 1700–1917: The Geopolitics of Expansion and Containment* (Oxford, 1996); Dominic Lieven, *Russia against Napoleon: The True Story of the Campaigns of War and Peace* (London, 2009); Alexei Miller, "'Official Nationality'? A Reassessment of Count Sergei Uvarov's Triad in the Context of Nationalism Politics," in idem, *The Romanov Empire and Nationalism: Essays on the Methodology of Historical Research* (New York, 2006), 139–160; idem, "Istoriia poniatiia 'natsiia' v Rossii," *Otechestvennye zapiski* 1 (2012); M. Polievktov, *Nikolai I: Biografiia i obzor tsarstvovaniia* (Moscow, 1918); Piotr S. Wandycz, *The Lands of Partitioned Poland, 1795–1918* (Seattle, 1975); Andrei Zorin, "Zavetnaia triada: Memorandum S. S. Uvarova 1832 goda i vozniknovenie doktriny 'pravoslavie—samoderzhavie—narodnost'," in idem, *Kormia dvuglavogo orla: Literatura i gosudarstvennaia ideologiia v Rossii v poslednei treti XVIII–pervoi treti XIX veka* (Moscow, 2001), 337–370.

CHAPTER 6: THE BATTLE FOR THE BORDERLANDS

Inna Bulkina, "Politika Nikolaia I v Iugo-Zapadnom krae i uchrezhdenie Universiteta Sv. Vladimira," *Trudy po russkoi i slavianskoi filologii: Literaturovedenie* 7 n.s. (Tartu, 1999); Wasyl Lencyk, *The Eastern Catholic Church and Czar Nicholas I* (New York, 1966); Alexei Miller, "'Official Nationality'? A Reassessment of Count Sergei Uvarov's Triad in the Context of Nationalism Politics," in idem, *The Romanov*

Empire and Nationalism: Essays on the Methodology of Historical Research (New York, 2006), 139–160; idem, "Istoriia poniatiia 'natsiia' v Rossii," *Otechestvennye zapiski* 1 (2012), www.strana-oz.ru/2012/1/istoriya-ponyatiya-naciya-v-rossii; Marian Radwan, *Carat wobec Kościoła greckokatolickiego w zaborze rosyjskim, 1796–1839* (Lublin, 2004); Aleksei Tolochko, *Kievskaia Rus' i Malorossiia v XIX veke* (Kyiv, 2012); Stephen Velychenko, *National History as Cultural Process: A Survey of the Interpretations of Ukraine's Past in Polish, Russian, and Ukrainian Historical Writing from the Earliest Times to 1914* (Edmonton, 1992).

CHAPTER 7: THE ADVENT OF UKRAINE

Olga Andriewsky, "The Russian-Ukrainian Discourse and the Failure of the 'Little Russian Solution,' 1782–1917," in *Culture, Nation, and Identity: The Ukrainian-Russian Encounter (1600–1945)*, ed. Andreas Kappeler, Zenon E. Kohut, Frank E. Sysyn, and Mark von Hagen (Edmonton, 2003), 182–214; Alexei Miller, *The Ukrainian Question: The Russian Empire and Nationalism in the Nineteenth Century* (New York, 2003); Orest Pelech, "The History of the St. Cyril and Methodius Brotherhood Reexamined," in *Synopsis: A Collection of Essays in Honour of Zenon E. Kohut*, ed. Serhii Plokhy and Frank Sysyn (Edmonton, 2005), 335–344; Thomas M. Prymak, *Mykola Kostomarov: A Biography* (Toronto, 1996); David Saunders, "Mykola Kostomarov (1817–1885) and the Creation of a Ukrainian Ethnic Identity," *Slavonica* 7, no. 1 (2001): 7–24; Andrei Teslia, "'Slavianskii vopros' v publitsistike M. P. Pogodina, 1830–1850-kh gg.," *Sotsiologischeskoe obozrenie* 13, no. 1 (2014): 117–138; Aleksei (Oleksii) Tolochko, *Kievskaia Rus' i Malorossiia v XIX veke* (Kyiv, 2012); P. A. Zaionchkovskii, *Kirillo-Mefodievskoe obshchestvo (1846–1847)* (Moscow, 1959).

CHAPTER 8: GREAT, LITTLE, AND WHITE

Mikhail Dolbilov, *Russkii krai, chuzhaia vera: Ètnokonfessional'naia politika imperii v Litve i Belorussii pri Aleksandre II* (Moscow, 2010); Aleksandr Dulichenko, *Vvedenie v slavianskuiu filologiiu* (Moscow, 2014); Orlando Figes, *The Crimean War: A History* (New York, 2012); Efim Karskii, *Belorussy*, 3 vols. (Moscow, 1955–1956); Alexei Miller, *The Ukrainian Question: The Russian Empire and Nationalism in the Nineteenth Century* (New York, 2003); V. Petronis, *Constructing Lithuania: Ethnic Mapping in Tsarist Russia, ca. 1800–1914* (Stockholm, 2007); Steven Seegel, *Mapping Europe's Borderlands: Russian Cartography in the Age of Empire* (Chicago, 2012); Darius Staliunas, *Making Russians: Meaning and Practice of Russification in Lithuania and Belarus After 1863* (New York, 2007); P. V. Tereshkovich, *Ètnicheskaia istoriia Belarusi XIX–nachala XX vv. v kontekste Tsentral'no-Vostochnoi Evropy* (Minsk, 2004).

CHAPTER 9: KILLING THE LANGUAGE

Andrii Danylenko, "The Ukrainian Bible and the Valuev Circular of July 18, 1863," *Acta Slavica Iaponica* 28 (2010): 1–21; John-Paul Himka, *Religion and Nationality in Western Ukraine: The Greek Catholic Church and the Ruthenian National Movement in Galicia, 1867–1900* (Montreal, 1999); Johannes Remy, "The Valuev Circular and Censorship of Ukrainian Publications in the Russian Empire (1863–1876): Intention and Practice," *Canadian Slavonic Papers* 49, nos. 1–2 (2007): 87–110; David Saunders, "Mikhail Katkov and Mykola Kostomarov: A Note on Petr A. Valuev's Anti-Ukrainian Edict of 1863," *Harvard Ukrainian Studies* 17, nos. 3–4 (1993): 365–383; idem, "Russia and Ukraine Under Alexander II: The Valuev Edict of 1863," *International History Review* 17, no. 1 (1995): 23–50; idem, "Pan-Slavism in the Ukrainian National Movement from the 1840s to the 1870s," *Journal of Ukrainian Studies* 30, no. 2 (Winter 2005): 27–50; Anna Ve ronika Wendland, *Die Russophilen in Galizien: Ukrainische Konservative zwischen Österreich und Russland, 1848–1915* (Vienna, 2001).

CHAPTER 10: THE PEOPLE'S SONG

Faith Hillis, *Children of Rus': Right-Bank Ukraine and the Invention of a Russian Nation* (Ithaca, NY, 2013); Oleh S. Ilnytzkyj, "Modeling Culture in the Empire: Ukrainian Modernism and the Death of the All-Russian Idea," in *Culture, Nation, and Identity: The Ukrainian-Russian Encounter (1600–1945)*, ed. Andreas Kappeler, Zenon E. Kohut, Frank E. Sysyn, and Mark von Hagen (Edmonton, 2003), 298–324; D. A. Kotsiubinskii, *Russkii natsionalism v nachale XX stoletiia: Rozhdenie i gibel' ideologii Vserosiiskogo natsional'nogo soiuza* (Moscow, 2001); I. V. Omelianchuk, "Chislennost' Soiuza russkogo naroda v 1907–1914 gg. v pravoberezhnykh ukrainskikh guberniiakh," in *Belorussiia i Ukraina: Istoriia i kul'tura. Ezhegodnik 2005/2006* (Moscow, 2008), 145–164; Richard Pipes, "Peter Struve and Ukrainian Nationalism," special issue of *Harvard Ukrainian Studies* 3/4, Part 2, *Eucharisterion: Essays Presented to Omeljan Pritsak on His Sixtieth Birthday by His Colleagues and Students* (1979–80): 675–683; Serhii Plokhy, *Unmaking Imperial Russia: Mykhailo Hrushevsky and the Writing of Ukrainian History* (Toronto, 2005); George Y. Shevelov, *The Ukrainian Language in the First Half of the Twentieth Century (1900–1941): Its State and Status* (Cambridge, MA, 1989); Theodore R. Weeks, *Nation and State in Late Imperial Russia: Nationalism and Russification on the Western Frontier, 1863–1914* (DeKalb, IL, 1996).

CHAPTER 11: THE FALL OF THE MONARCHY

A. Iu. Bakhturina, *Politika Rossiiskoi imperii v Vostochnoi Galitsii v gody Pervoi mirovoi voiny* (Moscow, 2000); Faith Hillis, "Making and Breaking the Russian Empire: The Case of Kiev's Shul'gin Family," in *Imperiale Biographien: Elitekarrieren im Habsburger, Russischen und Osmanischen Vielvölkerreich (1850–1918)*, ed. Malte Rolf and Tim Buchen (Munich, 2015), 178–198; E. Ketola, "Revoliutsiia 1917 goda i obretenie Finliandiei nezavisimosti: Dva vzgliada na problemu," *Otechestvennaia istoriia*, no. 6 (1993); Eric Lohr, *Nationalizing the Russian Empire: The Campaign Against Enemy Aliens During World War I* (Cambridge, MA, 2003); *Otrechenie Nikolaia II: Vospominaniia ochevidtsev* (Moscow, 1990); Alexander Victor Prusin, *Nationalizing a Borderland: War, Ethnicity and Anti-Jewish Violence in East Galicia, 1914–1920* (Tuscaloosa, AL, 2005).

CHAPTER 12: THE RUSSIAN REVOLUTION

Jörg Brechtefeld, *Mitteleuropa and German Politics: 1848 to the Present* (London, 1996); Mykhailo Hrushevs'kyi, *Na porozi novoï Ukraïny: Statti i dzherel'ni materialy* (New York, 1992); Richard Pipes, *The Formation of the Soviet Union: Communism and Nationalism, 1917–1923*, rev. ed. (Cambridge, MA, 1997); Anna Procyk, *Russian Nationalism and Ukraine: The Nationality Policy of the Volunteer Army During the Civil War* (Edmonton, 1995); Per Anders Rudling, *The Rise and Fall of Belarusian Nationalism, 1906–1931* (Pittsburgh, PA, 2015); Timothy Snyder, *The Red Prince: The Secret Lives of a Habsburg Archduke* (New York, 2008); Nicholas P. Vakar, *Belorussia: The Making of a Nation: A Case Study* (Cambridge, MA, 1956).

CHAPTER 13: LENIN'S VICTORY

Francine Hirsch, *Empire of Nations: Ethnographic Knowledge and the Making of the Soviet Union* (Ithaca, NY, 2005); Terry Martin, *The Affirmative Action Empire: Nations and Nationalism in the Soviet Union, 1923–1939* (Ithaca, NY, 2001); idem, "An Affirmative Action Empire: The Soviet Union as the Highest Form of Imperialism," in *A State of Nations: Empire and Nation-Making in the Age of Lenin and Stalin*, ed. Ronald Grigor Sunny and Terry Martin (Oxford, 2001), 67–92; Liliana Riga, *The Bolsheviks and the Russian Empire* (New York, 2012); Vasyl Shakhrai and Serhii Mazlakh, *On the Current Situation in the Ukraine*, ed. Peter J. Potichnyj (Ann Arbor, MI, 1970); Yuri Slezkine, "The USSR as a Communal Apartment, or How a Socialist State Promoted Ethnic Particularism," *Slavic Review* 53, no. 2 (1994): 414–452; Ronald Suny, *The Revenge of the Past: Nationalism, Revolution, and the Collapse of the Soviet Union* (Stanford, CA, 1993); idem, *The Making of the Georgian Nation* (Bloomington, IN, 1994).

CHAPTER 14: NATIONAL COMMUNISM

David Brandenberger, *National Bolshevism: Stalinist Mass Culture and the Formation of Modern Russian National Identity, 1931–1956* (Cambridge, MA, 2002); James E. Mace, *Communism and the Dilemmas of National Liberation: National Communism in Soviet Ukraine, 1918–1933* (Cambridge, MA, 1983); Ronald Grigor Suny and Terry Martin, eds., *A State of Nations: Empire and Nation-Making in the Age of Lenin and Stalin* (Oxford, 2001); Stephen Velychenko, *Painting Imperialism and Nationalism Red: The Ukrainian Marxist Critique of Russian Communist Rule in Ukraine, 1918–1925* (Toronto, 2015).

CHAPTER 15: THE RETURN OF RUSSIA

David Brandenberger, "Stalin's Populism and the Accidental Creation of Russian National Identity," *Nationalities Papers* 38, no. 5 (2010): 723–739; David Brandenberger and Mikhail V. Zelenov, "Stalin's Answer to the National Question: A Case Study on the Editing of the 1938 Short Course," *Slavic Review* 73, no. 4 (2014): 859–880; Viktor B. Dënningkhaus, *V teni "bol'hogo brata": Zapadnye natsional'nye men'shinstva v SSSR, 1937–38 gg.* (Moscow, 2011); Geoffrey A. Hosking, *Rulers and Victims: The Russians in the Soviet Union* (Cambridge, MA: 2006); Donald Ostrowski, "Alexander Nevskii's 'Battle on the Ice': The Creation of a Legend," *Russian History/Histoire russe* 33, nos. 2-3-4 (Summer-Fall-Winter 2006): 309–312; Benedikt Sarnov, *Stalin i pisateli*, vol. 1 (Moscow, 2007).

CHAPTER 16: THE GREAT PATRIOTIC WAR

Olia Hnatiuk, *Vidvaha i strakh* (Kyiv, 2015); Ianka Kupala, *Zbor tvoraŭ*, 7 vols., vol. 7, *Vershy: Pereklady 1918–1942* (Minsk, 1974); Roger Moorhouse, *The Devil's Alliance: Hitler's Pact with Stalin, 1931–1941* (New York, 2014); *Nazi-Soviet Relations, 1939–1941: Documents from the Archives of the German Foreign Office*, ed. Raymond James Sontag and James Stuart Beddie (Washington, DC, 1948); Serhii Plokhy, "The Call of Blood: Government Propaganda and Public Response to the Soviet Entry into World War II," *Cahiers du monde russe* 52, nos. 2–3 (2011): 293–320; Timothy Snyder, *Bloodlands: Europe Between Hitler and Stalin* (New York, 2010); Iosif Stalin, *O Velikoi Otechestvennoi voine Sovetskogo naroda* (Moscow, 1948); Serhy Yekelchyk, *Stalin's Empire of Memory: Russian-Ukrainian Relations in the Soviet Historical Imagination* (Toronto, 2004).

CHAPTER 17: THE SOVIET PEOPLE

Wayne Allensworth, *The Russian Question: Nationalism, Modernization, and Post-Communist Russia* (Lanham, MD, 1998); Aleksandr Baigushev, *Russkaia partiia vnutri KPSS* (Moscow, 2005); Yitzhak M. Brudny, *Reinventing Russia: Russian Nationalism and the Soviet State, 1953–1991* (Cambridge, MA, 2000); Stephen Carter, *Russian Nationalism: Yesterday, Today, Tomorrow* (New York, 1990); Ariel Cohen, *Russian Imperialism: Development and Crisis* (Westport, CT, 1996); Michael Confino, "Solzhenitsyn, the West, and the New Russian Nationalism," *Journal of Contemporary History* 26, nos. 3–4 (1991): 611–636; Simon Cosgrove, *Russian Nationalism and the Politics of Soviet Literature: The Case of Nash Sovremennik 1981–1991* (New York, 2004); Nathaniel Davies, *A Long Road to Church: A Contemporary History of Russian Orthodoxy*, 2d ed. (Boulder, 2003); John Dunlop, *The Faces of Contemporary Russian Nationalism* (Princeton, NJ, 1983); Ivan Dzyuba, *Internationalism or Russification? A Study in the Soviet Nationalities Problem*, ed. M. Davies, 2d ed. (London, 1970); Kuchkar Khanazarov, *Reshenie natsional'no-iazykovoi problemy v SSSR* (Moscow, 1982); David Marples, *Belarus: A Denationalised Nation* (Amsterdam, 1999); Tatstsiana Mikulich, *Mova i ėtnichnaia samasviadomasts'* (Minsk, 1996); Nikolai Mitrokhin, *Russkaia partiia: Dvizhenie russkikh natsionalistov v SSSR, 1953–1985* (Moscow, 2003); Roman Solchanyk, "Politics and the National Question in the Post-Shelest Period," in *Ukraine After Shelest*, ed. Bohdan Krawchenko (Edmonton, 1983), 1–29; Roman Szporluk, *Russia, Ukraine, and the Breakup of the Soviet Union* (Stanford, CA, 2001); Vladislav Zubok, *Zhivago's Children: The Last Russian Intelligentsia* (Cambridge, MA, 2011).

CHAPTER 18: RED FLAG DOWN

Mark R. Beissinger, *Nationalist Mobilization and the Collapse of the Soviet State* (Cambridge, 2002); George W. Breslauer and Catherine Dale, "Boris Yel'tsin and the Invention of a Russian Nation-State, *Post-Soviet Affairs* 13, no. 4 (1997): 303–332; Timothy Colton, *Yeltsin: A Life* (New York, 2008); E. N. Danilova, "Izmeneniia v sotsial'nykh identifikatsiiakh rossiian," *Sotsiologicheskii zhurnal*, nos. 3–4 (2000); Mark Harrison, "Soviet Economic Growth Since 1928: The Alternative Statistics of G. I. Khanin," *Europe-Asia Studies* 45, no. 1 (1993): 141–167; David D. Laitin, *Identity in Formation: The Russian-Speaking Populations in the New Abroad* (Ithaca, NY, 1998); Marlene Laruelle, *In the Name of the Nation: Nationalism and Politics in Contemporary Russia* (New York, 2009); Marlene Laruelle, ed., *Russian Nationalism and the National Reassertion of Russia* (New York, 2009); Emil' Pain, "Imperskii natsionalizm (Vozniknovenie, evoliutsiia i politicheskie perspektivy v Rosii)," *Obshchestvennye nauki i sovremennost'*, no. 2 (2015): 54–71; Petr Panov, "Nation-Building in Post-Soviet Russia: What Kind of Nationalism Is Produced by the Kremlin?" *Journal of Eurasian Studies* 1, no. 1 (2010): 85–94; Serhii Plokhy, *The Last Empire: The Final Days of the Soviet Union* (New York, 2014); Peter Rutland, "The Presence of Absence: Ethnicity Policy in Russia," in Julia Newton and

William Tompson, eds., *Ideas and Leadership in Post-Soviet Russia* (New York, 2010), 116–136; Valery Tishkov, *Ethnicity, Nationalism and Conflict in and after the Soviet Union: The Mind Aflame* (London, 1996); Edward W. Walker, *Dissolution: Sovereignty and the Breakup of the Soviet Union* (Lanham, MD, 2003).

CHAPTER 19: THE RUSSIAN WORLD

Ronald D. Asmus, *A Little War That Shook the World: Georgia, Russia and the Future of the West* (New York, 2010); E. N. Danilova, "Izmeneniia v sotsial'nykh identifikatsiiakh rossiian," *Sotsiologicheskii zhurnal*, nos. 3–4 (2000); M. Golovanova and V. Shergin, *Gosudarstvennye simvoly Rossii* (Moscow, 2003); Vladimir Kabuzan, *Russkie v mire: Dinamika chislennosti i rasseleniia (1719–1989). Formirovanie etnicheskikh i politicheskikh granits russkogo naroda* (St. Petersburg, 1996); Pål Kolstø and Helge Blakkisrud, eds., *The New Russian Nationalism: Imperialism, Ethnicity and Authoritarianism, 2000–2015* (Edinburgh, 2016); Mara Kozelsky, "Religion and the Crisis in Ukraine," *International Journal for the Study of the Christian Church* 14, no. 3 (2014): 219–241; Marlene Laruelle, ed., *Eurasianism and the European Far Right: Reshaping the Europe—Russia Relationship* (Lanham, MD, 2015); Marlene Laruelle, *The "Russian World": Russia's Soft Power and Geopolitical Imagination* (Washington, DC, 2015); Aleksei Miller, ed., *Nasledie imperii i budushchee Rossii* (Moscow, 2008); Anastasia Nesvetailova, "Russia and Belarus: The Quest for the Union; or Who Will Pay for Belarus's Path to Recovery?" in *Contemporary Belarus: Between Democracy and Dictatorship*, ed. Elena A. Korosteleva, Colin W. Lawson, and Rosalind J. Marsh (London, 2003), 152–164; Emil' Pain and Sergei Prostakov, "Mnogolikii russkii natsionalizm: Ideino-politicheskie raznovidnosti (2010–2014)," *Polis*, no. 4 (2014): 96–113; Hrihoriy Perepilitsa, "Belarusian-Russian Integration and Its Impact on the Security of Ukraine," in *Belarus at the Crossroads*, ed. Sherman W. Garnett and Robert Legvold (Washington, DC, 1999), 81-1-3; Igor Torbakov, "Emulating Global Big Brother: The Ideology of American Empire and Its Influence on Russia's Framing of Its Policies in the Post-Soviet Eurasia," *Turkish Review of Eurasian Studies*, no. 3 (2003): 41–72; Andrei P. Tsygankov, *Russia's Foreign Policy: Change and Continuity in National Identity* (Lanham, MD, 2006); Andrew Wilson, *Ukraine's Orange Revolution* (New Haven, CT, 2006).

CHAPTER 20: THE RUSSIAN WAR

Paul Goble, "Russian Support for Putin's View that Russians and Ukrainians Are 'One People' Falling, Polls Show," *Window on Eurasia*, June 26, 2015; Paul Roderick Gregory, "Deconstructing Putin's Approval Ratings: One Thousand Casualties for Every Point," *Forbes*, June 8, 2015; Steven Lee Myers, *The New Tsar: The Rise and Reign of Vladimir Putin* (New York, 2015); Roland Oliphant and Tom

Parfitt, "Vladimir Putin Praises Russian Patriotism and Claims: Ukrainians and Russians Are One," *Telegraph*, March 18, 2015; "Rossiisko-ukrainskie otnosheniia v zerkale obshchestvenngo mneniia: sentiabr' 2015," Levada-Tsentr, May 10, 2015, www.levada.ru/old/05-10-2015/rossiisko-ukrainskie-otnosheniya-v-zerkale -obshchestvennogo-mneniya-sentyabr-2015; Yuri Teper, "Official Russian Identity Discourse in Light of the Annexation of Crimea: National or Imperial," *Post-Soviet Affairs* 32, no. 4 (2016): 378–396; Igor Torbakov, "A Parting of Ways? The Kremlin Leadership and Russia's New-Generation National Thinkers," *Demokratizatsiya: The Journal of Post-Soviet Democratization* 23, no. 4 (Fall 2015): 427–457; idem, "Ukraine and Russia: Entangled Histories, Contested Identities, and a War of Narratives," in *Revolution and War in Contemporary Ukraine: The Challenge of Change*, ed. Olga Bertlsen (Stuttgart, 2016), 89–120; Andreas Umland, "Eurasian Union vs. Fascist Eurasia," *New Eastern Europe*, November 19, 2015; Andrew Wilson, *Ukraine Crisis: What It Means for the West* (New Haven, CT, 2014), 118–143.

INDEX

SERHII PLOKHY is the Mykhailo Hrushevsky Professor of Ukrainian History at Harvard and the director of the university's Ukrainian Research Institute. The prize-winning author of many books, including *The Last Empire*, *The Gates of Europe*, and *The Man with the Poison Gun*, Plokhy lives in Arlington, Massachusetts.